THE WORLD IN A CITY

THE WORKING CLASS IN AMERICAN HISTORY

Editorial Advisors
James R. Barrett, Julie Greene, William P. Jones,
Alice Kessler-Harris, and Nelson Lichtenstein

A list of books in the series appears at the end of this book.

THE WORLD IN A CITY

MULTIETHNIC RADICALISM IN EARLY TWENTIETH-CENTURY LOS ANGELES

DAVID M. STRUTHERS

UNIVERSITY OF ILLINOIS PRESS
Urbana, Chicago, and Springfield

© 2019 by the Board of Trustees
of the University of Illinois
All rights reserved
1 2 3 4 5 C P 5 4 3 2 1
♾ This book is printed on acid-free paper.

Library of Congress Cataloging-in-Publication Data
Names: Struthers, David M., author.
Title: The world in a city : multiethnic radicalism in early
    twentieth-century Los Angeles / David M. Struthers.
Description: Urbana : University of Illinois Press, 2019.
    | Series: Working class in American history | Includes
    bibliographical references and index.
Identifiers: LCCN 2018051851| ISBN 9780252042478
    (hardback) | ISBN 9780252084256 (paperback)
Subjects: LCSH: Labor movement—California—Los
    Angeles—History—20th century. | Radicalism—
    California—Los Angeles—History—20th century.
    | Intercultural communication—California—Los
    Angeles—History—20th century. | Race relations—
    California—Los Angeles—History—20th century. |
    BISAC: SOCIAL SCIENCE / Ethnic Studies / General.
    | SOCIAL SCIENCE / Social Classes. | HISTORY /
    United States / State & Local / West (AK, CA, CO, HI,
    ID, MT, NV, UT, WY).
Classification: LCC HD8085.L73 S77 2019 | DDC
    331.8809794/9409041—dc23
    LC record available at https://lccn.loc.gov/2018051851

E-book ISBN 978-0-252-05131-9

To Freya with hope for a better world.

CONTENTS

	Acknowledgments	ix
	Introduction	1
1	Economic Development, Immigration, and the "Labors of Expropriation"	17
2	Creating Connections through Radical Practices	35
3	Solidarity and the Legacy of Exclusion	65
4	Internationalism and Its Limits	81
5	Organizing Mobile Workers	106
6	The Baja Raids	127
7	A Culture of Affinity	157
8	The Contours of Repression	184
	Conclusion: Regeneration, Decline, and Reordering the Left	209
	Notes	229
	Bibliography	259
	Index	277

ACKNOWLEDGMENTS

Over the years in the United States and Denmark that it took to bring this book into the world I've incurred personal and scholarly debts. The community of scholars I get to see every other year at the European Social Science History Conference (and more often through mediated connections) is truly remarkable and has helped me develop my ideas. They include Bert Altena, Constance Bantman, Raymond Craib, Tom Goyens, Steven Hirsch, Ruth Kinna, Geoffroy de Laforcade, Carl Levy, Kirwin Shaffer, and Lucien van der Walt. Barry Pateman was incredibly helpful in my early research. Devra Weber helped put me on the path to becoming a historian and has continued to support me in this endeavor ever since. It is not a short journey. Peter Cole and Kenyon Zimmer were ideal co-editors on a different project that helped refine my thinking about the global and internationalism. Kenyon Zimmer deserves special note for generously sharing sources and suggestions since we were graduate students in Pittsburgh. Christina Heatherton also shared important files from Leavenworth Penitentiary. Michele Presutto kindly shared his detailed research on Italian participation in the Baja raids. Kirwin Shaffer read the entire manuscript and provided suggestions and encouragement at a particularly important juncture. Cathryn Halverson also gave me important feedback on a few early chapter drafts. Martyn Bone, Nanna Hansen, and Christa Vogelius have all lent support, assistance, and friendship in Copenhagen. Laurie Matheson welcomed me to University of Illinois Press, and then James Engelhardt brought my book through the review process with encouragement, responsiveness, and insightful criticism. The anonymous re-

Acknowledgments

viewers proved incredibly knowledgeable and committed to this project. Their extensive feedback was invaluable, went well beyond the call, and earned my sincere gratitude.

I thank my parents, also, for always believing in me, even when they probably shouldn't have, and Irina for her patience and support.

THE WORLD IN A CITY

INTRODUCTION

While Pedro Coria made his way in "tramp" fashion in empty freight cars on an organizing trip in 1913, his journey came to an abrupt end outside of San Luis Obispo, California, when a train severed his left foot. He endured two painful surgeries and convalescence, while his comrades took up a collection for an artificial limb through the pages of *Regeneración*, the newspaper of the anarchist Partido Liberal Mexicano (PLM).[1] Losing a foot did not seem to slow Coria down. On the morning of September 28, 1917, he slept in after arriving back home in Los Angeles the day prior from yet another organizing trip, this time to Northern California's Shasta County for the Industrial Workers of the World (IWW), a revolutionary syndicalist union. As luck would have it, that morning United States federal agents orchestrated a coordinated series of raids across the country against the IWW. While walking toward the IWW office on North Main Street in central Los Angeles, unaware of the morning's events, Coria ran into a group of fellow workers on the street. They told him that officers ransacked their office, arrested several members, and were now searching for him.[2] Coria went into hiding before escaping to Mexico, where he continued agitating and organizing.

Pedro Coria maintained lifelong connections to the IWW and anarchist movement. In 1946 he penned a letter of greeting to the twenty-fifth IWW convention from Morelia, Michoacán, which read in part: "Some day [we] will do away with the boundary lines made by the exploiting class for their own benefit, until then [we] will never forget."[3] Coria went on to recall his friendships and his personal

Introduction

connections to some of the most difficult events in early-twentieth-century labor and radical history.

Friendships and the efforts of grassroots organizers like Coria created a broad community of solidarity that held the IWW and PLM together, two of the most active radical organizations in Los Angeles and throughout the region into Mexico. Affinities and solidarities energized the radical movement in Los Angeles and the networks—regional and transnational—cultivated by migrants and organizers. Participants forged alliances to advance antinational and international class-based revolutionary goals, and these social connections, coupled with their ideals, sustained activism and engendered some of the broadest examples of multiracial cooperation in U.S. history. Radical organizing gave form to a culture of affinity that spanned formal activism, personal friendships, and space in Los Angeles and connected far-reaching global solidarities during the early twentieth century. Connecting the seemingly disconnected yet myriad moments of struggle brings new understanding to Los Angeles, one of the most diverse cities on the planet.

In 1946, the same year Pedro Coria penned his letter to the IWW convention, Carey McWilliams set the agenda for studying Los Angeles when he argued that the city was a "racial and cultural rectangle: White, Negro, Mexican, and Oriental."[4] Since then historians have excavated the history of Los Angeles's diverse residents, class structure, and urban and suburban development.[5] This scholarship documented the global significance of Los Angeles, the city's central role in the histories of Mexican Americans and Mexican immigration, Japanese Americans, and the western African American experience.[6]

Recently, Scott Kurashige looked back to McWilliams by examining "triangular" race relations between African Americans, Japanese Americans, and whites in early-twentieth-century Los Angeles.[7] Works by Shana Bernstein and Mark Wild also took multiracial Los Angeles as their subject by studying forms of interracial interaction from the street to formal community-based civil rights organizing.[8] One significant contribution of these books is that they began the process of piecing together the complex mosaic of interracial relationships between nonwhites without losing focus on racial and class hierarchies. Kurashige wrote of his effort as taking up what he saw as "the primary challenge to comparative ethnic studies scholarship ready to move from documenting the oppression and resistance of minorities to locating the emergence of a nonwhite majority."[9] In the early twentieth century, nonwhite majorities formed in many neighborhoods, worksites, and radical organizing spaces, prefiguring contemporary multiracial community formations.

Community formation in Los Angeles occurred through staggering population growth and economic development throughout the early twentieth century, a period of mass migration that challenged existing constructions of race, ethnicity, and nation throughout the Americas. Los Angeles's position as a confluence of immigration streams across the Atlantic and Pacific during this era of increasing global ties funneled racially and ethnically diverse migrants to the region. Residents interacted at work and on their neighborhood street corners, in shops, bars, pool halls, and meeting spaces. Similarly diverse mobile workers then extended the reach of Los Angeles's urban community. Migratory workers created social connections at the varied sites of their laborers, along the path of their travels, and in communities often hundreds of miles away from jobsites as they moved through the networks they, and workers like them, built for commodities. Racial diversity and mobility opened possibilities for labor and radical organizing.

In *The Practice of Diaspora*, Brent Hayes Edwards situated Paris as the key to the rise of black internationalism in the 1920s: "Paris is crucial because it allowed boundary crossing, conversations, and collaborations that were available nowhere else to the same degree."[10] The multiracial composition, residency, and work patterns in Los Angeles and the region during the early twentieth century created similar boundary crossing space as Paris did for blacks in the 1920s.[11] For instance, Matt Garcia argued in *A World of Its Own*, his study of the citrus-growing valleys east of Los Angeles, that Mexican American women workers in the early twentieth century formed "temporary protest movements out of their common experiences." Even more significant, he identified a "cultural affinity within non-white sectors and single-sexed workforces" around which people sought to better their lives.[12] Gerald Horne observed in his study of African Americans and the Mexican Revolution, *Black and Brown*, that the "cause of [racial] equality was adopted mostly by Euro-Americans on the margins of society, such as socialists and anarchists." McWilliams himself wrote of a communist-led meeting for agricultural workers of twelve nationalities in the 1930s in which the speakers were translated into Armenian, Russian, and Spanish.[13] These scholars documented moments when people formed solidarities that came close to representing their racially diverse communities.

A broad spectrum of leftist thought circulated in this period, available for people to adapt and incorporate into their organizing and for them to make their own.[14] Los Angeles's political Left consisted of a constellation of ideologies oriented toward ameliorating social and class-based concerns. Anarchism, syndicalism, socialism, and "bread and butter" trade unionism comprised the most consolidated ideological currents, but people, organizations, parties, and movements brought them to life. Radical outlooks, like that of anarchists and syndicalists, rejected voting and most other forms of formal political participation in favor of seeking a more fundamental reorganization of society than the American Federation of Labor (AFL) or Socialist Party. Collectively the Left pushed their concerns to the front and center of Los Angeles's politics through labor, electoral, and revolutionary organizing. The extreme pushback by conservative forces in business and government further indicate the importance of these voices in this crucial period of Los Angeles's development.

As people did the untidy work of organizing, drawing from their understanding of the world around them, they turned their ideals into movements through collaboration and scission. At the most basic level anarchists sought a stateless world organized according to free association and mutual aid; they diverged among themselves, however, over their views of organizing tactics, cooperation with unions, and insurgency. Further, local conditions shaped the outlook of participants across this global movement. Kenyon Zimmer described anarchists in the late nineteenth century and early twentieth century as "a movement *in* movement. It was also a movement *of* movements, worldwide in scale but composed of overlapping groups and networks loosely demarcated by characteristics such as location, language, and nationality."[15] In Los Angeles anarchists grouped themselves according to language and ethnicity, with Mexican, Italian, and Jewish organizations being the largest. The PLM occupied the regional center of a globally significant node in the anarchist movement. Solidarity among anarchists bound the anarchist movement across its contours and textures.[16]

The Preamble to the IWW Constitution began directly—"The working class and the employing class have nothing in common"—and the syndicalism expressed therein positioned industrial unions, direct action, and the general strike as the tools to achieve revolutionary change. It differed from socialists and later Communists by privileging worker power and the labor movement over political action to achieve revolutionary change. The IWW's founding convention in 1905 bought together a range of voices on the left, including unionists, socialists, and anarchists, a grouping that created friction and splits over the next few years. The IWW spread its message in Los Angeles, the borderlands, and Mexico through traveling organizers, street speaking, and song to become a leading voice for unskilled multiracial workers. Many anarchists were active in the IWW in and near Los Angeles, especially in Spanish-language organizing. In Mexican and indigenous radical circuits, IWW and PLM organizing was often indistinguishable.

With wider appeal than anarchism or the IWW, proponents of socialism included the Socialist Party, Socialist Labor Party, and independent socialist organizers. Socialists saw the need for both political participation, like running for office and voting, and labor-based struggle to combat capitalist ills. The last of these major groupings represented in Los Angeles was the craft unionism of the AFL, which sought to organize skilled workers according to their trade. Many of Los Angeles's AFL leaders held membership in the Socialist Party and brought a wide-ranging vision to trade-union organizing from their participation in late-nineteenth-century labor and reform movements. In this period the AFL in Los

Angeles frequently ventured into politics, rarely adhering to the notion of "pure and simple" trade unionism.

Anarchism, syndicalism, socialism, and trade unionism advanced starkly divergent positions on political participation, organizing tactics, and the state. Further disagreements arose over whom to include, usually along lines of race and gender, that did not necessarily find justification in these ideological perspectives. In Los Angeles, though, many organizers maintained multiple formal affiliations that influenced groups advancing different visions of working-class struggle. Individual workers also affiliated with different groups over time—less an indication of ideological drift than seizing opportunity in a shifting organizing landscape. As organizers and workers moved between group affiliations, the organizations themselves supported each other to a surprising degree given their differences. After the Russian Revolution in 1917 the subsequent growth of Communist Parties through the 1920s added another ideological and organizational force that reconfigured global political alignment. Alliances in Los Angeles changed as well.

Immigration, mobile work patterns, and the process of community formation combined in Los Angeles and the region to create a cosmopolitan environment in which discussions about the strength of international solidarity opened real actionable choices. Racial and ethnic diversity along with the breadth of national origin of the region's workers presented organizers the opportunity to put internationalism to use locally in their movements. For example, in 1909 the Socialist Party held an "international meeting" to bring together the English, German, Mexican/Spanish, Russian, and Hungarian language/national branches in their own organization in Los Angeles.[17] The IWW routinely issued calls for international and interracial solidarity. In 1910 D. Bond exhorted in the *Industrial Worker*, "Workingmen of all countries, unite."[18] Enrique Flores Magón articulated his position in terms similar to that of many other anarchists in a speech in 1916: "The world is our country and all men are our countrymen. It is true that, by birth, we are Mexicans, but our minds are not so narrow, our vision not so pitifully small as to regard as aliens or enemies those who have been born under other skies."[19] When socialists, the IWW, and anarchists generated novel forms of multilingual interracial organizing in Los Angeles and the region, they did so by rearticulating internationalist and antistatist streams of thought to create a local internationalism rooted in place. Across ideology leftists most commonly drew from internationalism to find common ground, while they used race to draw distinctions between people.

Cooperation and solidarity generated through local internationalism took many forms: joining a union, organization, or association; donating money; protesting; cooking meals; buying guns; sheltering fugitives; subscribing to a newspaper; striking; not scabbing; or even giving a supportive greeting on the street. The intentional coalition-building practices of the IWW and the PLM, in particular, combined with the tactics that arose out of necessity by mobile laborers to create a layered, multiracial, radical community of significant geographic breadth that repeatedly surged and withdrew through subsequent moments of struggle. Participants changed over time—though with some continuity—as area residents created connections and forged solidarities in new and changing circumstances.

Different forms of interracial organizing brought distinct challenges. White-led efforts to organize nonwhite workers drew upon different power relationships and histories than when nonwhite workers organized with other nonwhite workers. This book documents an intersectional process in which non-Anglos instigated the broadest and most successful moments of interracial organizing. It also shows that racially exclusionary organizing by whites could at times be more flexible and situationally dependent than most scholars have allowed. For example, white socialists in Los Angeles made a significant break with the AFL's racist exclusion when they attempted to open the trade union to Japanese and Mexican membership in 1903. All the same, Japanese and Mexican laborers faced different decisions, such as whether or not to join the AFL, knowing its racist history and practices. Would these same workers see common cause with African American, Chinese, or Sikh workers? What about immigrants from Europe? In a few years would they find more sympathy with the PLM's revolutionary program for Mexico or IWW organizing?

The broadest moments of interracial cooperation lasted but briefly and came in the absence of the hierarchical organizational structures of the AFL and Socialist Party. Stronger power structures focused institutional power to enforce racism. Interracial affinities developed their broadest form in places influenced by IWW and PLM organizing that lacked the organizational structures to enforce racist exclusion, such as along the bank of the Los Angeles River, in jungle camps and temporary worksites, or in Baja California. The racial composition of the people participating in struggles in these locations came close to reflecting the cosmopolitan population of the region. Even if whites in these spaces held deeply racist beliefs, which many certainly did, they had less power to act upon these beliefs; all the while, the structural manifestations of race still organized society and the economy.

Interracial organizing in a settler colonial society and the racism it entailed, of course, produced contested and uneven results. Racial composition, land use, hiring practices, pay, imprisonment—indeed, nearly every aspect of life in Los Angeles reflected this genocidal history. Even so, the history explored in this book illustrates a thread of working-class culture that creatively sought new solidarities in opposition to racism and capitalism—what I call a culture of affinity—among workers often with the most precarious existences. The influence of the IWW

Introduction

and the PLM gave form to this culture of affinity that spanned formal labor or revolutionary organizing, local grassroots labor struggles, personal friendships, space, and circumstances of proximity among racially diverse residents of Los Angeles, the region, and out through far-reaching global solidarities during the early twentieth century. The episodic character of these multiracial formations necessitates a novel theoretical underpinning. Anarchist theory provides guidance for understanding these interactions. Tracing the nearly constantly reforming instances of interracial organizing and racist retrenchment through the anarchist notion of affinity moves interracial solidarity—rather than an ideological current, organization, or group of people defined by race or nation—into the role of protagonist; its opponents were racism and nationalism. I now turn to exploring this idea in more detail.

Affinity, Anarchism, and Anarchist History

The anarchist and syndicalist movements in the early twentieth century—and by extension their interaction with socialists and trade unions—cannot be understood through Marxist or liberal frames, which Richard Day noted "share a belief that there can be no 'freedom' without the state form (Leviathan or dictatorship of the proletariat), and therefore also share a commitment to political (state-based) rather than social (community-based) modes of social change . . . [a] paradoxical belief that state domination is necessary to achieve 'freedom,'" a condition he termed the "hegemony of hegemony."[20] Using the well-worn Marxist-influenced conceptualizations common in historical writing would have us evaluate a social and political culture through a statist lens that many of the actors in this book actively opposed. Rather, turning to anarchism for theoretical guidance affords the opportunity to understand the subjects on their own terms.

Anarchist theory and practice, specifically the anarchist notion of affinity, have the ability to inform studies of interracial organizing, solidarities, and, more broadly, connections throughout society. This is not as radical a departure as it might first seem. Anarchism and syndicalism influenced many scholars in social science's theoretical canon, yet this strand of thought remains underdeveloped and its origin is often missed. In what follows I briefly reconstruct this intellectual tradition.

Affinity

Many of the libertarian elements present within Marxism can be traced to the influence of anarchism and syndicalism. The writings of Georg Lukács, for instance, showed a "radically anti-statist tendency" before his movement toward Bolshevism in the early 1920s. Lukács referred to the state as "organized tuberculosis" in his notes on Dostoevsky from 1914–15.[21] Clear anarchist and syndicalist influences are also apparent in Walter Benjamin's work. He formulated a critique of the bourgeois and functionalist university in his 1914 lecture "The Life of Students" by noting an opposition between a community of learning and the state. Benjamin appealed to a "Tolstoyan spirit" that formed "in the mind of the most deeply committed anarchists or in Christian monastic orders." Each penned before the Russian Revolution, these ideas connect back to figures such as Gustav Landauer, Émile Pouget, Georges Sorel, and Leo Tolstoy.[22]

Antonio Gramsci's writing is another strand. Gramsci was immersed in a site of struggle steeped in anarchist traditions, and his political formulations reflected this. Carl Levy argued that in *Prison Notebooks* Gramsci's "notion of subversivism, spontaneity and the peculiar weakness of the pre-fascist left in Italy revolved around the effects of the anarchists and syndicalists on Italian political culture."[23] Without acknowledging it, this line of thought extended the anarchist influenced threads in Gramsci's writing to document cultural forms of resistance and the temporary alliances forged by people through it.

James C. Scott contributed to this thinking through his conceptualization of "infrapolitics" in which he drew a metaphor to the electromagnetic spectrum to describe resistance beyond what is visible to the naked eye. Robin D. G. Kelley incorporated this idea in his studies of African American resistance. Both read a form of politics in people's actions that took place in locations away from traditional political spheres of action. These anarchist-inflected threads of social theory serve to enrich the extensive canon of anarchist writing and provide a point of departure for using affinity in historical writing.[24]

James C. Scott, in *The Art of Not Being Governed: An Anarchist History of Upland Southeast Asia*, made the most notable attempt to use anarchism to inform a work of history. In it he argued that "the huge literature on state-making, contemporary and historic, pays virtually no attention to its obverse: the history of deliberate and reactive statelessness. This is the history of those who got away, and state-making cannot be understood apart from it. This is also what makes this an anarchist history."[25] Scott identified a remarkably mutable form of politics in a space of unconsolidated power. Such changes, however, create problems for historians who rely on records and a bounded area of study: "One challenge for a non-state-centric history of mainland Southeast Asia consists in specifying the conditions for the aggregation and disaggregation of its elementary units." He resolved this dilemma by drawing an analogy to the "fluidity of the molecules," using the natural world to give form to his analysis of the much less tidy social terrain of human interaction in a stateless society.[26]

Disambiguating human life from states and analyzing each as interlocutors is an important step toward writing about spaces with and without functional states; indeed, much transnational history takes this as its aim. Yet, despite the fact that Scott wrote about the other side of state and national formation, his work is not "anarchist history." His movement toward writing anarchist history comes from the attention he pays to shifting alliance formations, a form of politics that echoes the intentional free associations of self-defined anarchists, not that it occurred in a nonstate space. But rather than developing an anarchist analysis of a stateless society, Scott's reference to molecules governed by natural laws borrows more from Max Weber's loose use of affinity than anarchism without clearly articulating either.

Max Weber imported the term "elective affinity" (*Wahlverwandtschaften*) into his work from Johann Wolfgang von Goethe's 1809 novel *Elective Affinities*. Weber used it alongside "affinity" (*Affinität*) and affinities of meaning (*Sinnaffinitäten*) yet never offered a singular definition in his published works.[27] Subsequent scholars argued that Weber used elective affinity "to express the fact that two sets of social facts or mentalities are related to each other or gravitate to each other—even though no direct and simple causality between the two can be established."[28] "Gravitate" alludes to an ill-defined "natural" force structuring action beyond individual decision-making, a clear parallel to James Scott's use of molecules. Benedict Anderson used similar language when he described anarchist ideology itself as a "gravitational force" in *Under Three Flags: Anarchism and the Anti-Colonial Imagination*.[29] Anarchist history, however, demands more clarity than taking nonstate societies as subject or substituting Weberian influenced understandings of society for Marxist paradigms. Returning to anarchist thought provides a way forward.

Anarchism

Anarchists spanning the movement's broad tradition developed the concept of affinity most fully. The values most commonly expressed by anarchists in early-twentieth-century Los Angeles consolidated around opposition to the state, capitalism, and land monopoly. The extreme extent of land monopoly in Mexico and California resonated particularly strongly in the region; it was fitting that the PLM gave new life to the anarchist call for "*Tierra y Libertad*" (Land and Liberty). Anarchists sought to replace these hierarchical systems of violence with forms of voluntary association, exchange, and land distribution. Peter Kropotkin placed free association at the center of his anarchism: "It [anarchism] seeks the most complete development of individuality combined with the highest development of voluntary association in all its aspects, in all possible degrees, for all imaginable aims; ever changing, ever modified associations which carry in themselves the elements of their durability and constantly assume new forms, which answer best to the multiple aspirations of all."[30]

Introduction

Within the anarchist movement, the tactic of organizing according to free association cannot be separated from the desire for revolutionary change. This stance led to the reluctance of many anarchists to articulate clear revolutionary programs as a deliberate political choice. William C. Owen outlined this position, one often reformulated and repeated:

> It is urged that we Anarchists have no plans; that we do not set out in detail how the society of the future is to be run. This is true. We are not inclined to waste our breath in guesses about things we cannot know. We are not in the business of putting humanity in irons. We are trying to get humanity to shake off its irons. We have no co-operative commonwealth, cut and dried, to impose on the generations yet unborn. We are living men and women, concerned with the living present, and we recognise that the future will be as the men and women of the future make it, which in its turn will depend on themselves and the conditions in which they find themselves. If we bequeath to them freedom they will be able to conduct their lives freely, as the changed and improved conditions, brought about by the growth of human intelligence and the added mastery of Nature that will spring from such intelligence, may dictate.[31]

Anthropologist David Graeber recently drew from similar notions when he characterized anarchism as tending "to be an ethical discourse about revolutionary practice."[32] While, Jesse Cohn noted, "anarchists generally think of their aspirations in terms of 'revolution,' the journey—'walk[ing] toward anarchy,' as Errico Malatesta (1853–1932) put it—is at least as important as the goal."[33] Organizing forms are crucial to this journey.

French anarchist Sébastien Faure offered a general definition of affinity—a concept developed through thinking about free association—in his 1934 anarchist encyclopedia: "analogie, conformité, point de contact, ressemblance, rapport, liaison"—analogy, conformity, point of contact, resemblance, relationship, connection. However, he noted that affinity has a "special meaning" among anarchists: "It expresses the tendency which leads men to get closer to one another, to group themselves by similarity of tastes, character, and ideas." His gendered definition distinguished between voluntary associations of anarchists and associations between "millionaires and penniless, rulers and ruled," "forced" by nationalism and militarism. On the particular anarchist practice of forming voluntary associations Faure wrote:

> It is said that anarchists group themselves by affinity. That is correct and there is no doubt that this method of grouping is at once the most normal, the strongest, and the most in keeping with the anarchist spirit ... since it does not undermine the aspirations, character, and liberty of the individual. ... In the

anarchist society we want to build, we conceive of an extraordinary flowering of affinity groups. They will form or dissolve with events—whose course is always capricious—and only by the will—which is always independent—of the interested parties.[34]

Faure emphasized the intentionality of anarchist affinities in movement-building activities, which would then extend throughout society, fluctuating and reforming as the need arose. Intentionality set it apart from the forces "pushing" relationships between structure, cultural forms, and individual action in Weberian uses of affinity. In practice, affinity groups of autonomous individuals joining together for common cause as an intentional method of organization in the anarchist tradition dates to late-nineteenth-century Spain.[35]

Peter Kropotkin took a more expansive view of anarchist practices in his writing than Faure expressed in his definition of affinity. Ruth Kinna argued that Kropotkin distinguished "anarchist principles from anarchist politics" which allowed him to "broaden the field of anarchism to all forms of action and to a wide range of intellectual spheres."[36] The process of translating—literally and figuratively—theory, strategy, and narratives of struggle into consolidated ideologies and organizations was and remains a messy process. Clear tension exists in attributing the ideological label of an organization to all of its members; people may have joined a political party, union, group, or association out of family and community obligation, even narrow or expedient self-interest. It is also crucial to bring focus upon the many people loosely connected to organizations or unaffiliated workers participating in a moment of struggle before slipping away—at least from historical documentation—which makes ideological claims all the more slippery.

However, ephemeral solidarities during a moment of struggle, mutual aid among individuals or organizations, and informal cultural organizing are forms of anarchistic practice even if those involved did not self-identify as anarchists. Rebecca Solnit provided an important guiding step in extending anarchist thought to use as a tool to understand broader social interaction. In *A Paradise Built in Hell* she synthesized disaster sociology and joined it with the key anarchist concept of "mutual aid" to argue that when faced with crisis, people—more often than not—creatively find ways to support one another. She illustrated this point with examples from the San Francisco earthquake in 1906 through New Orleans after Hurricane Katrina in 2005.[37]

From this understanding of anarchist theory and practice, I draw a flexible approach to social interaction, community formation, and organizing that provides a scaffolding for examining individuals and their connections in dialog with formal organizations and states. I use affinity to describe intentional organizing along lines of free association—a form of organizing most often employed by anarchists and syndicalists—that extended to informal ephemeral solidarities at the edges of dedicated activism and away from it. Affinity gives form to the myriad individual cooperative actions that shaped the social practices of resistance often too unstructured or episodic for historians to capture. This approach maintains focus on the continuity of affinity-based organizing practices while tracing changing solidarities, associations, and organizations that formed and dissolved through struggle, repression, and factionalism. A history that fails to look beyond an organizational or statist focus will lose sight of the persistence and commonalities between disparate moments of organizing that produced broad interracial solidarities. These distinctly anarchist uses of affinity have the most to offer historians.

Anarchist History

Several historians have documented examples of temporary alliances upsetting powerful hierarchies, including entrenched race-based forms. This scholarship buttresses the development of a self-consciously anarchist historiography. Ira Berlin, in *Many Thousands Gone*, noted the existence of a "sawbuck equality" between slave and owner in the "lowcountry" of South Carolina and Florida during the "charter generations" in the late seventeenth and early eighteenth centuries:

> Slaveholders generally labored alongside a mixed workforce that was composed of Native-American and African-American slaves, Native-American and European-American servants, and occasionally European-American wage workers. Although slaveholders maintained an unshakable commitment to racial servitude and yearned for the prerogatives of Barbadian grandees, the demands of the primitive, labor-scarce South Carolina economy frequently placed master and slave face-to-face on opposite sides of a sawbuck, where shared labor reduced—if it did not dissolve—the differences of status and color. Such direct, egalitarian confrontations and the polyglot character of the laboring population mitigated the force of chattel slavery and provided Atlantics creoles with leverage to fend off the harshest features of racial domination during the initial period of settlement.[38]

Peter Linebaugh and Marcus Rediker noted in *The Many-Headed Hydra* the multiethnic mobs common on the seaports of the revolutionary Atlantic. Docks, taverns, as well as the lower deck "were places where English, Irish, African, Native American, and West Indian persons could meet and explore their common interests."[39] The most immediate common interest lay in fighting against impressment for which "multiracial mobs helped to win numerous victories."[40]

Similarly, Nyklas Frykman argued for the significance of "lower deck" rebellions such as the one on the Royal Navy ship *Hermione* in 1797. The lower deck increased bonds between sailors "from two, perhaps three continents and over a dozen countries. They counted Irish republican shoemakers amongst them, British, Danish, Dutch, French, Canadian and even Swiss seamen, free blacks from the West Indies and possibly Africa, citizens of the young United States, clerks from England, and peasants from Norway." Frykman concluded that the men involved "moved through and simultaneously helped constitute the vast network of itinerant biographies and shared experiences that ultimately, in its totality, formed the revolutionary Atlantic."[41]

The historiography of the formation of the United Mine Workers (UMWA) assessed why African Americans and whites held "mutual loyalties" in Joe W. Trotter's formulation in eastern coal camps in early twentieth century.[42] Interpretations varied: necessity for workers, a push from companies, and altruism. In the western U.S., with its different racial composition, Philip Mellinger argued that racial inclusion of Chinese and Japanese workers in the UMWA "was the result of nonideological pragmatism in a special situation."[43] The number of distinct local examples of racial barriers breaking down, however, is better understood through the common themes of proximity and the relative power held by racial groups in relationship to other workers, management, and the state—all themes that should come forward when writing anarchist history. With the concept of affinity and these books as points of reference for examining flexible forms of association in relation to race, power, and states, I now return to the history of Los Angeles with anarchist tools for analysis.

Los Angeles and a Culture of Affinity

Los Angeles's population grew dramatically from around one hundred thousand in 1900 to more than one million in 1930. These domestic and international migrants created a foundation for the city's future economic expansion. Workers constructed the infrastructure necessary for future industrial expansion in the city while often migrating out of the city to labor in California's capitalist agriculture industry. This constituted the structural foundation for continued regional mobility and the terrain in which cosmopolitan working-class residents organized their lives. In the city people made homes and communities with ethnic, racial, and national-origin concentration points, but Los Angeles's non-Anglo community centers lay in easy walking distance from each other. In these diverse neighborhoods radicals created spaces of affinity and resistance for their ideas to flourish. Radicals also geographically extended their local community building through publishing efforts based in Los Angeles. Print media spread ideas, but, even more important, communities formed through radical newspapers that reached across the globe. The mobility of people and print helped create a global radical community of solidarity.

The first two attempts to form interracial trade unions in the region came in 1903. The Japanese Mexican Labor Association in Oxnard and the Unión Federal Mexicana in Los Angeles harnessed the organizing energy of workers. Anglo socialists in the trade union movement also supported each union, and this brought about a chance to reckon with the anti-Chinese legacy of the late-nineteenth-century labor movement. The successes, however fleeting, and failures of these two pioneering interracial unions set the tone for future interracial labor organizing. In the years that followed, the growth of Los Angeles's Socialist Party provided an umbrella for even more racially diverse local organizing. However, despite the formation of impressive coalitions, structural criticisms of immigration and outright racism divided socialists and hampered the effectiveness of efforts to organize across race, ethnicity, and nationality. After 1905 early organizing by the Partido Liberal Mexicano and the Industrial Workers of the World gave stronger voice to interracial organizing among Los Angeles's multiracial working class.

Trade unions across California viewed increasing immigration with more fear than opportunity as the first decade of the twentieth century wore on, which led to the California State Federation of Labor launching the United Laborers organizing campaign in 1909. The growth of the IWW also spurred on this decision as a defensive measure. AFL organizers sought to unite urban and rural multiracial unskilled laborers, except Asians, along lines similar to the Japanese Mexican Labor Association and the Unión Federal Mexicana. In the end this union met a similar fate as its predecessors, evidence of continued racism in the AFL and the structural difficulties of bringing California's mobile workers into a craft union structure.

Simultaneous to the United Laborers campaign, the PLM launched its military assault in Baja California in 1911 at the beginning of the Mexican Revolution. While ultimately unsuccessful in military or political terms, the Baja raids were significant for the United States and Mexico. They illustrated the ability of radicals to organize an interracial and international group into a functional military force. Further, the participation of a significant minority of veterans of imperial wars exposed the contradiction of empire as these men pointed guns at the Mexican state for the cause of liberty. Global solidarity for the military campaign in Baja California prefigured international organizing during the Spanish Civil War and produced one of the most tangible examples of interracial cooperation examined.

From 1912 until American entry into World War I in 1917, Los Angeles became a global center for the anarchist and syndicalist Spanish-language press. The city also continued to be fertile ground for radical organizing after the Baja raids and Socialist Party candidate Job Harriman's unsuccessful mayoral bid in 1911. The most important forms of interracial politics continued to develop away from formal organizations, and these years brought violent conflict between workers and the state in Wheatland, California, the Los Angeles plaza, and in Arizona. The connections and diverse coalitions formed in this period had broad reach through radical networks.

American entry in World War I brought with it an unprecedented era of state repression upon radicals, though with uneven results. The large number of arrests, trials, and prison terms forced the radical movement to devote its limited resources to support imprisoned comrades. Meanwhile, Mexico became a vital place of retreat and continued organizing for many radicals and draft resisters during the war. A number of U.S.-based radicals connected to those in Mexico through Los Angeles. After the wartime setbacks, the anarchist movement regenerated itself in the early postwar years and proved resilient in the 1920s. As the decade wore on, existing movements faced the growing influence of Communism. Los Angeles changed on a structural level as well. A hardening of racialized work and residency patterns in Los Angeles worked against interracial organizing, but this form of struggle was not forgotten. It moved to places like Boyle Heights and continued among farm laborers.

This book, then, is a history of the constantly reforming solidarities in a multiracial city during a period of remarkable economic development and population growth. Organizers like Pedro Coria embodied the many layers of the radical movement from on-the-ground organizing at dispersed points of production to creating the mediated connections necessary to draw together people spread across the region through print. The many dedicated organizers who traveled through the U.S. West and crossed the U.S.-Mexico border to form unions, participate in the Mexican Revolution, and evade state repression shaped the transnational culture of affinity. Radical organizing practices complemented the solidarities that arose out of necessity by mobile laborers struggling through precarious existences to create novel forms of interracial cooperation. The radical practices that germinated in Los Angeles and then traveled out into global radical movements produced some of the broadest examples of multiracial cooperation in U.S. history.

CHAPTER 1

ECONOMIC DEVELOPMENT, IMMIGRATION, AND THE "LABORS OF EXPROPRIATION"

Aurelio Vincente Azuara left his native Spain in 1907 at age twenty-two for Mexico before relocating to the United States in 1912 through El Paso, Texas. Unable to find work in the border town, he joined a construction and piling crew for the Santa Fe Railroad near San Bernardino, California, through a labor contractor. He earned $1.50 per day for up to twelve hours of work. Typifying the power of construction companies and railroads over workers in rural areas, his employer forced him to return 75¢ for each day's room and board. He quit after a short time and remembered being "given a slip of paper telling me that I could go to San Bernardino to the road master's office to get my pay." He walked the eighteen miles back to San Bernardino. Once in town he waited for three days to collect $5, upon which he reflected, "I don't suppose that the road master realized that I could not live on hopes waiting."

From there Vincente Azuara made his way sixty miles west to Los Angeles. He recalled: "I worked around in the suburbs of the city and I [have] been able to find work in a construction camp. They were paving some kind of highway, that were [sic] going from Los Angeles to San Fernando." His foreman fired him after a few months because he had too many workers for the job. Vincente Azuara stayed in Los Angeles, where he "was able to wander around the city" finding work. He remembered that "you have to walk all around the town to put a couple of days work sometimes, in some construction building or in paving the street or working on the Edison Company and the gas, on the pipe line." Vincente Azuara remembered railcars of Mexican workers arriving in Los Angeles, supposedly to work on the tracks, but contractors brought more workers than needed for any given project. He stated simply that these people supplied "the agricultural need" for cheap labor. Eventually he signed on to work in the Alaska canning industry through another labor contractor. He worked one season processing salmon before returning to Los Angeles through San Francisco. Vincente Azuara joined the Industrial Workers of the World in California in the fall of 1913.[1]

The rural economy in California developed in advance of Los Angeles's economy, where urban economic growth, especially in the manufacturing sector, occurred slowly until the 1920s. This condition combined with the seasonal nature of agricultural work to produce a set of labor patterns typified by urban–rural and rural–rural movement. The rural economy relied on a similar labor pool as the urban economy, and workers moved through the region, often facilitated by labor contractors. Labor diverse in kind and location typified much of rural and urban employment. Two Anglo AFL leaders in the state understood that, from agricultural labor and canning to the "cutting of timber or logging, building of railways and canals, doing the thousand and one kinds of work now usually designated as 'unskilled,' means going from place to place, it means going where the work is being done."[2]

Writing about the rise of capitalism in the Atlantic world during the seventeenth and eighteenth centuries, Peter Linebaugh and Marcus Rediker argued that historians have failed to properly conceptualize or appreciate the labor required to create capitalist infrastructure: "Expropriation itself, for example, is treated as a given: the field is *there* before the plowing starts; the city is *there* before the laborer begins the working day. Likewise for long-distance trade: the port is *there* before the ship sets sail from it; the plantation is *there* before the slave cultivates the land." They characterized this work as the "labors of expropriation" and this type of infrastructure development occupied many regional laborers.[3] In settler colonial societies it is also crucial to recognize the connected process of indigenous removal.

California had been inhabited by around 150,000 Native Americans in 1846, four years before its accession to statehood. This population plummeted to thirty thousand in 1870. The next census in 1880 counted only 16,277 Native Americans. A combination of causes brought about this catastrophe: "Diseases, dislocation, and starvation were important causes of these many deaths. However, abduction, de jure and de facto unfree labor, mass death in forced confinement on reservations, homicides, battles, and massacres also took thousands of lives and hindered reproduction."[4] Scholars use terms like "erasure," "elimination," and "eliminatory options" to describe the force of this process. In Los Angeles, incarceration was one of many eliminatory options, and the penal infrastructure created for indigenous people seamlessly transitioned to caging multiracial itinerate workers with fluctuating employment that predominated by the late nineteenth century.[5]

Across the state multiracial immigrant workers completed the necessary labor for capitalist economic growth and then worked for wages in the new industries made possible through their labor in these spaces of indigenous removal. They worked first to change the environment and create infrastructure to suit the needs of capital and then they transitioned to laboring within this new terrain. To create the rural economy, workers moved earth, often with hand tools, to control water, erecting dams, levees, and aqueducts. They cleared fields, built roads, and even slaughtered thousands of rabbits for capitalist development.[6] For urban growth in Los Angeles, workers constructed the harbor, installed gas and water pipelines, and strung electric lines. They also created transportation infrastructure. Roads, local passenger rail, and long-distance connections provided the foundation for commercial expansion in Los Angeles and the region.

During this ongoing process laborers commonly moved between jobs that resulted from earlier work, such as in the fields of an industrial agricultural harvest and new infrastructure projects. Taken together, economic development and regional work patterns reflected the uneven geographical development of capitalism in the U.S. Southwest and Mexico during the late nineteenth and early twentieth centuries. As workers built the structural foundation for capitalist development, the labor processes of economic expansion brought Aurelio Vincente Azuara and hundreds of thousands of other workers from around the world into a vibrant cosmopolitan milieu.

Economic Development

As the United States expanded its national boundaries through military conquest and enforced its racialized vision as a settler society during the nineteenth century, it opened land to new forms of economic activity. Corporate actors focused on resource extraction, and transportation drove economic development in this space of American conquest. Additionally, many corporations spanned the Canadian and Mexican national borders through their investments, ownership, and labor recruiting. Cross-border business practices helped shape the United States, Mexico, and Canada into a coherent transnational space for capitalists during the late nineteenth century. Companies such as Anaconda Copper in Montana, Weyerhaeuser timber in the Pacific Northwest, Claus Spreckels's Western Beet Sugar Company in California and Hawaii, Miller & Lux in California, Oregon, and Nevada, the Canadian Pacific Railway Company, the Southern Pacific Railroad, and Phelps Dodge's cross-border mining interests in Arizona and Sonora,

Mexico, led the way in developing a set of modern business practices to maximize profit in the region. These corporations made large-scale land acquisitions, then organized and transported laborers from across the region to mitigate environmental risks and create value from their holdings.[7]

Western business practices were well established decades before the large-scale expansion of Los Angeles's urban economy and economic development in California fit within regional trends. California's admission to the union marked the end of Mexican California and signaled the beginning of the end for the dominant status of Californios. The overproduction of cattle in the waning days of the gold rush contributed to a financial crisis in 1860 and eventually to a sweeping land transfer from the Californio elite to Anglo investors. The consolidation of land ownership across California continued in the 1870s, exemplified most clearly over the Tehachapi Mountains from Los Angeles in the San Joaquin Valley, where the Miller & Lux company gained control of more than four hundred thousand acres by mid-decade. A report in 1872 listed one hundred individuals holding title to nearly 5.5 million acres of land statewide. The prominent free thinker Henry George lived in California during these years, and the monopoly of land ownership became the focal point of his ideas of freedom and justice. George's proposed solution for a single tax on land attracted influential supporters across the country for decades to come.[8]

Much of this land needed improvement before its full profit potential could be reached. The fertile soil of California's Central Valley lacked only water, for the most part, and the new corporate owners moved to irrigate their holdings. Miller & Lux invested in the San Joaquin and King's River Canal & Irrigation Company to gain the most value from its land. The new partners engaged in an ambitious project to "restructure the San Joaquin's waterscape," which, in turn, opened an era of "corporate irrigation to the Far West." As Miller & Lux continued to expand its landholdings, it became clear that "water rights and irrigation systems would ultimately determine who could profit from the valley's natural wealth."[9] The corporate consolidation of land and extensive irrigation projects structured the trend toward intensive monoculture. A wheat boom in the 1870s pushed this profit strategy into near ubiquity. Wheat farming concentrated in the Central Valley and in the San Joaquin Valley, where wheat and alfalfa rose to 96 percent of total agricultural production in 1879.[10]

Water continued to be a key ingredient for profit into the twentieth century, and workers continued to expand irrigation systems to sustain agricultural growth. By 1902 California boasted approximately two million irrigated acres of farmland, and in 1903 the federal government recognized the citrus-belt town of Ontario as the "standard of American Irrigation Colonies."[11] In the intervening years between 1910 and 1920, the acreage of irrigated farmland in California rose from 2.6

million acres to roughly four million acres. By the end of the 1920s, agribusiness organizations made up 2.1 percent of California farms, but the value created on their land totaled 29 percent of crop value in the state.[12]

Throughout the U.S. West, Mexico, and Canada workers constructed a transportation network to accommodate expanding commodity production. From 1880 to 1920 workers laid close to thirty thousand miles of rails as the total length of track in the Southwest grew from 7,436 miles to roughly thirty-six thousand miles. The Southern Pacific Railroad became the leading corporate actor behind rail expansion in the Southwest as well as the largest landowner, employer, and most valued company in the region. As the Southern Pacific consolidated its position in the United States, Mexican president Porfirio Díaz encouraged foreign investment in Mexico. The period of Díaz's rule is referred to as the *Porfiriato*. By 1911 American corporations, led by Southern Pacific, had invested more than six hundred million dollars in Mexican rail projects. From 1876 to 1910 the length of track in Mexico increased from 412 miles to more than twelve thousand miles. The Canadian Pacific Railroad attained similar route mileage by 1918 when it reached just under thirteen thousand miles. Capital investment created corporate ties, and the resulting infrastructure facilitated the transportation of commodities and people in the United States, Mexico, and Canada.[13]

Early economic growth in Los Angeles reflected the broader processes underway in the regional economy. After the period of land transfer from Californios to Anglos in the 1850s and 1860s, fledgling business interests led a voter-approved effort to subsidize the extension of the Southern Pacific Railroad into the city in the 1870s. The city reaped immediate economic benefits from the completion of the line and secured its place as the dominant regional city. However, the arrival of the railroad also brought the Southern Pacific into Los Angeles as a political force. The city's small population and small-city bureaucracy could not counter the political and economic power of the rail titan. The railroad's interests did not align with those of the city's business community, and it levied high shipping rates to and from Los Angeles, which hampered economic development.[14]

Undeterred by the influence of the Southern Pacific, investors flush with eastern funds continued to seek opportunities in the city. Their free-flowing capital created an environment ripe for real-estate speculation and financed the expansion of commercial ranches and farms near to the city. Land use intensified near Los Angeles's urban core, but development continued to lag. In 1890 core businesses such as flour mills and slaughterhouses added value by processing goods produced outside of the city for the local consumer market.[15]

In the mid-1890s a cohort of similarly minded business elites led by Harrison Gray Otis, the publisher of the *Los Angeles Times*, formed a coalition focused on Los Angeles's economic development. The Los Angeles–based group opposed the Southern Pacific, which it viewed as absent and uninterested in developing a diverse economy in the city. These two factions of "private-sector elites" faced off over the direction of economic development in Los Angeles for the next fifteen years.[16] The first major battle between these competing interests occurred over the construction of a harbor in Los Angeles. The lack of a natural harbor had limited Los Angeles's economic reach. The Southern Pacific, under the direction of Henry Huntington, bought land in Santa Monica and threw its weight behind a proposal to build a harbor in that city. If successful, this would have afforded it a monopoly from rail to sea transport. The Otis-led coalition countered by forming the Free Harbor League with the goal of building a municipally owned harbor thirty miles south in San Pedro.[17]

The Free Harbor League had a powerful congressional ally in Senator Harry White, who also served as Otis's personal attorney. White tipped the scale against the Southern Pacific, and Congress allocated $350,000 in 1896 to finance the harbor's initial construction. The Army Corps of Engineers broke ground in 1899, marking the beginning of a new period of development in Los Angeles. The project required an additional $6 million federal investment before the initial phase opened in 1912. In total, including federal money and local bond measures, public investment in the harbor reached forty million dollars by 1930.[18]

The harbor battle marked an epochal change in Los Angeles's politics and growth. With the power of the Southern Pacific checked, business elites organized what political scientist Steven P. Erie characterized as a "state-centered growth machine," which "featured semi-autonomous public bureaucracies and large-scale infrastructure projects as the centerpiece of a more public growth strategy."[19] From around 1895 to 1920, publicly financed infrastructure development drove economic growth in Los Angeles. The civic leaders who worked so hard to create and protect the open shop in Los Angeles used the full weight of city, state, and federal government to organize a foundation for capitalist enterprise. Business power in the city consolidated in the Merchants and Manufacturers Association (M&M), founded in 1896.

Although the harbor eventually facilitated Los Angeles's role as a major player in the global economy, the creation of a modern water and power system more immediately sustained urban growth. The lack of water in Los Angeles limited its population, as local supplies could only support the needs of about three hundred thousand people. Otis and his group initiated a multiyear effort in 1897 to municipalize the Southern Pacific–aligned Los Angeles City Water Company. Their campaign succeeded in 1902 when the city bought out the private system with two million dollars generated by a voter-approved municipal bond. The trend continued in 1907 when the Los Angeles Chamber of Commerce supported a bond measure to help finance the construction of the Los Angeles Aqueduct.

Indicative of the strength of the regional rural economy, the business organization wanted a portion of the water allocated for commercial farming. Los Angeles voters passed this twenty-three-million-dollar measure. Between 1910 and 1932 Los Angeles voters passed another $28.9 million in municipal bonds to finance urban infrastructure expansion.[20]

With rail connections, a harbor, and a modern water and power system, Los Angeles sat poised for an economic boom, but it came slowly. In 1905—the median year between census counts, when the population grew from one hundred thousand to more than three hundred thousand—only 6,876 workers labored in manufacturing occupations. Almost two-thirds worked in the metal or lumber trades, industries geared toward regional consumption. The more than two decades of intensive infrastructure construction eventually paid dividends in the 1920s in the form of an emerging manufacturing sector. The discovery of oil further diversified the local economy during this crucial decade in Los Angeles's economic history.[21]

The Goodyear Tire and Rubber Company became the first eastern corporation to make a major investment in the Los Angeles Basin when it opened a plant in Vernon in 1919. The ease of importing rubber from Indonesia through the port particularly attracted Goodyear. A clear pattern followed with the development of many new factories outside of Los Angeles's city limits: "Locally owned, labor intensive manufactures like apparel, food-processing and furniture tended to be concentrated in the city's original industrial district east of Alameda, between North Broadway and Ninth Street. More capital-intensive branch plants of major corporations, including the West's largest concentration of auto and tire factories, were located southeast of Downtown."[22] Lower taxes in Los Angeles County pulled corporations away from the urban core, but the extensive infrastructure development over the roughly thirty years prior opened the possibility for municipal competition. As industrial development in and near to the urban core created an economic counterweight to rural industries, the location of these new factories pushed along the suburbanization of the city.

The discovery of oil in 1921 further diversified the local economy and, crucially, increased exports. Between 1922 and 1924 annual oil exports through the port rose from twenty-one million to nearly 140 million barrels. In the early 1920s the port of Los Angeles saw few commodities besides oil leaving and northwestern lumber arriving to frame suburban homes around the now-booming metropolis. In 1915 the total commerce of the port measured 2,091,000 net tons. This expanded to 28,213,000 net tons by 1930. The value of goods shipped abroad between 1915 and 1930 rose from $748,000 to $161,000,000. By 1932 Los Angeles surpassed all West Coast ports and all ports nationwide, except New York and Philadelphia, in the quantity of goods shipped.[23]

CHAPTER 1

Immigration and the Labor Process of Economic Growth

In the 1870s and 1880s white immigrants from the East and Midwest set in motion the most important period of population growth in the history of Los Angeles, which continued through the 1930s. As the city's population grew sixfold between 1890 and 1910—from fifty thousand to 319,000—the new arrivals "whitened" Los Angeles's population as the number of native-born whites reached 76 percent. In 1920 the city's population reached 577,000 and nearly doubled again by 1930, to 1,238,000. However, historian Mark Wild argued that this "invasion of middle-class white Protestants concealed smaller but substantial migrant streams that would eventually outstrip Anglo migration rates."[24] In 1900 nearly a quarter of the city's approximately one hundred thousand residents were nonwhite or foreign born. By 1930 the proportion of these groups reached nearly thirty percent. In the context of the scale of population growth in Los Angeles, this increase represented hundreds of thousands of people who created enduring communities in the city. Population in Los Angeles County grew at similar rates. In 1900 it was 170,298; by 1930 it reached 2,208,492.[25]

Los Angeles's position within several overlapping migration networks facilitated the scale and diversity of immigration. The city's location on the Pacific Coast connected it to Chinese, Japanese, South Asian, and Filipino migrations (in that rough chronological order). Extended rail networks and proximity to Mexico enabled the city's role in cross-border movements, especially during the vast rural restructuring in Mexico under Porfirio Díaz and later during the revolution. Europeans emigrated to Los Angeles, most notably from Italy and eastern Europe, and connected the city to Atlantic migration streams. Additionally, African Americans relocated within national borders. Smaller numbers of migrants arrived from South America, Armenia, and Syria, among other places. Put together, these migrants created a vibrant cosmopolitanism in Los Angeles that period census data had only begun to capture.[26]

The racial and ethnic diversity typifying Los Angeles reached out into the surrounding region. Immediately east of Los Angeles in the citrus valleys, "Chinese, Sikh, Japanese, Mexican, Filipino, and white workers" completed the various tasks of citrus of production.[27] In the summer of 1913 workers of twenty-seven different nationalities descended upon one farm in Wheatland, California, just north of Sacramento, to harvest hops. "Syrian, Mexican, Spanish from the Hawaiian sugar plantations, Japanese, Lithuanian, Italian, Greek, Polish, Hindu, Cuban, Porto Rican [sic], and Swedish" workers constituted the largest groups.[28] The next summer, the farm, in response to a locally organized labor boycott, imported around one thousand Spanish families from Hawaii to labor in the fields.[29] This

24

TABLE 1. Population of Los Angeles City and County by Race, 1890–1930

Year	Whites		Negroes		Japanese		Chinese		Mexicans	
	County	City	County	City	County	City	County	City	County	City
1890	95,033	47,205	6,421	1,258	36	26	4,424	1,871	1,293	498
1900	163,975	98,082	2,841	2,131	204	150	3,209	2,111	1,613	817
1910	483,478	305,307	9,424	5,101	8,461	4,238	2,602	1,954	11,793	5,632
1920	894,507	546,864	18,738	15,579	19,911	11,618	2,591	2,062	33,644	21,598
1930	1,949,882	1,073,584	46,425	38,894	35,390	21,081	3,572	3,009	167,024	97,116

Source: Adapted from Natalia Molina, *Fit to Be Citizens? Public Health and Race in Los Angeles, 1879–1939* (Berkeley: University of California Press, 2006), 7.

Note: Between 1890 and 1920 Mexicans were counted as white for the census purposes. In 1890 census takers counted "Negro, Chinese, Japanese, and Indian in one category." See Molina, *Fit to Be Citizens?* 7.

cosmopolitanism also extended through the U.S.-Mexico borderlands. In Bisbee, Arizona, workers came from "Slovenia, Croatia, Montenegro, Bosnia, and especially Serbia. All were part of the Austro-Hungarian Empire, so that many were simply called 'Austrians'"—a reminder of the multiethnic and multilingual states from which some migrants departed. Armenians, Albanians, Finns, Germans, Greeks, Irish, Jews, Spaniards, Welsh, and many others also lived and worked in Bisbee along with Mexicans and Anglos.[30]

Several factors converged to create an environment in which regional business interests could both help create and then draw upon such a diverse labor pool. Technologies such as steamships, railroads, telegraphs, and telephones "annihilated" space by transporting workers and goods and facilitated near-instantaneous communication across vast distances like never before.[31] The direct solicitation and transportation of workers by corporations and labor contractors then pulled people across nations, borders, and oceans. Labor contractors profited from the expanses of sparsely occupied space in the western United States and northern Mexico through their ability to "traverse those spaces and regulate the geographic mobility of workers."[32]

Historian Gunther Peck argued that corporations thrived through their

> remarkable dexterity in mobilizing men thousands of miles across space for particular corporate purposes. Transatlantic steamship companies in the nineteenth century had long been quickening the time it took for passengers to cross the ocean, contributing to that era's "annihilation of space." But it was corporations in the North American West and the padrones who did their bidding that best learned to organize immigrant labor markets at sites of labor demand, creating truly disposable work forces that could be mobilized from remote corners of the earth to equally remote industrial islands at the drop of a hat, whether to lay railroad ties, harvest beets, break a strike, or load low-grade copper ore onto trains.[33]

Corporations and labor contractors were not free to select workers as they chose. Apart from "push" factors nearly as diverse as the immigrants themselves, U.S. immigration policy, with its racist and gendered notions of the qualities of people, strongly influenced who migrated and how they did it. Race and gender also greatly affected migrants' life course, occupation, and prospects for success after arrival. The cosmopolitan makeup of Los Angeles and the surrounding region often strengthened racialized employment patterns and practices and created racialized experiences through the labor processes of economic growth.

Chinese workers constituted the most important source of cheap labor during California's early statehood after attempts to exploit Native American labor failed. Though an even stronger trend in the northern part of the state, Chinese labored in Southern California as well. After a violent and virulent anti-Chinese movement in the 1870s, the U.S. Congress passed the Chinese Exclusion Act in 1882, which both redefined American society and invented a new role for the government as "gatekeeper." Historian Erika Lee argued that "exclusion laws marginalized and constrained generations of Chinese immigrants and the Chinese community in America," but immigration continued through various methods, most often through Mexico and Canada.[34] As Chinese exclusion gradually limited free access to Chinese laborers, Japanese and Mexican laborers, as well as many others, filled this need and completed the manual tasks required by the regional economy. The race of workers changed over time, but the demand for poorly remunerated, backbreaking labor only increased, and this racialized set of labor practices flowed toward the early twentieth century.

Japanese immigration increased toward the beginning of the twentieth century, and Japanese workers became the second "yellow peril" to many whites. Most early Japanese immigrants found employment as agricultural laborers. Richard Steven Street found that "when the first handful of Japanese immigrants made their way to Fresno in 1890, they were turned away by hostile white men. But the following year, about thirty settled into a ten-block-long neighborhood of brick buildings near Chinatown." The number of Japanese working the Fresno raisin-grape harvest grew from around one thousand in 1897 to five thousand in 1902. Of these workers only around half lived locally. Japanese from "as far away as Los Angeles, Sacramento, and San Francisco" supplemented local residents. The growth in their numbers increased the strong position of Japanese labor contractors and regional labor competition. In Fresno in 1900, Japanese contractors moved to "divide up the vineyards into districts and push aside Greek, Armenian, Portuguese, and Chinese field hands."[35] Japanese workers negotiated the ever-present problem of seasonal employment faced by all of the region's workers by "picking the fall and winter citrus crop in Tulare County, traveling to Salinas and Oxnard to thin and harvest sugar beets during the spring and early summer, and filling in the winter with odd jobs and domestic work [so that] they quickly achieved relatively stable year-round employment."[36]

Los Angeles's Japanese population grew significantly after 1900, when it numbered around 150. The 1906 San Francisco earthquake pushed many Japanese south to the city. After the 1907 "Gentleman's Agreement" limited the numbers of new immigrants directly from Japan, migration from the Hawaiian Islands continued. Los Angeles's Japanese community reached roughly ten thousand in 1910, with a similar number living in the county. By 1920 Los Angeles was home to the largest Japanese community in North America. Their population reached twenty-one thousand in 1930. Little Tokyo on East First Street grew into a community center.[37]

Mexican immigration to Los Angeles and the Southwest grew from workers recruited to lay track in the expansion of the region's railroad network. Many early Mexican communities formed near these worksites in the 1890s. As time progressed, Mexicans became the largest group of workers in the region's agricultural economy, which provided its own draw. Los Angeles's Mexican population grew quickly as Mexican workers provided the core labor needed for the city's development. In total, an estimated one million to 1.5 million Mexicans immigrated to the United States between 1890 and 1929. The Mexican population in the city reached around five thousand in 1910; by 1920 it stood at 33,644. This growth turned Los Angeles into one of the largest Mexican urban centers in either country. The 1920s brought even stronger growth of Mexican communities in Los Angeles and the Southwest. Urban areas throughout Mexico also grew, pushed by the rural restructuring underway in the aftermath of the most violent phase of the Mexican Revolution. These events directly connected Los Angeles's growth to Mexico City's during this decade. In 1930, ninety-seven thousand Mexicans lived in Los Angeles.[38] In the region surrounding Los Angeles, the Mexican population grew at a similar pace and scale. For instance, in the citrus areas east of downtown, 150,000 to two hundred thousand Mexicans lived, worked, and formed enduring communities in the 1920s.[39]

The Italians who migrated to California before the gold rush established a small community base for the increased immigration around the turn of the century. In 1900 about two thousand Italians lived in Los Angeles. This number reached ten thousand in 1917 and grew further after the establishment of steamship service between Naples and New Orleans, which conveniently connected to Southern Pacific's rail line to California. The Italian population increased statewide and reached 63,601 in 1910. Italians in Los Angeles found their place in a range of urban occupations, from laborers to small-business owners and bankers. With relatively high skill levels and financial resources compared with those of other immigrant groups, they experienced higher rates of social mobility. Early migrants found opportunity in farming and construction and expanded into small business ownership. The strong institutional foundation of Los Angeles's Italian community in the form of businesses and community organizations allowed for the financing of Italian Hall, built in 1907 at the corner of Macy and Main Streets. Outside the city, Italians labored in the fields and worked as ranch hands. For instance, in 1900, Italians made up Miller & Lux's "largest and most segmented group of workers."[40]

African American migration rates to Los Angeles remained steady from around 1890. African Americans arrived in the city during the Great Migration during World War I, but migration rates never reached the same level as midwestern cities experienced: the increased cost and length of the journey compared with settlement in the Midwest's urban areas moderated total numbers. Further, African Americans who made the trip strongly self-selected, and most came from the urban South. One recent history found that "when compared to major destinations of the Great Migration, Black Los Angeles had an overrepresentation of those who were well educated and from urban areas, primarily New Orleans, Atlanta, and multiple cities in Texas."[41] The city's African American population grew from just over two thousand in 1900 to close to forty thousand in 1930. Yet African Americans never constituted the city's most numerous nonwhite group, a sign of Los Angeles's racial diversity.

African Americans in the city took their places in the economy largely beside other nonwhite workers and new immigrants. Some labored for the Pacific Electric Railway Company's integrated track-laying crews, others worked in the service sector. During World War I some gained a foothold in the burgeoning industrial economy as ironworkers at the Los Angeles Foundry. A survey of African American employment found that from 1900 to 1920, 20 percent of African American men worked as laborers on construction sites. Of other classifiable categories, 15 percent worked as porters, 5 percent to 10 percent as janitors, 5 percent as waiters, and 5 percent to 10 percent as servants. African American employment in skilled construction trades reached a high point of 13 percent in 1910, but this fell to 5 percent during the next decade. In general, African Americans in Los Angeles maintained a living standard slightly above other nonwhite groups.[42]

African Americans in Los Angeles engaged in regional migration patterns to a far lesser extent than other nonwhite groups. This is partially attributable to the urban background of many of the city's African Americans and their strong representation in the urban service sector. Though fewer African Americans engaged in continued rural–urban migration, some did. For example, Pettis Perry, born into a sharecropping family in 1887 in Alabama, left the South in 1917 and continued to move through forty-five states in the next fifteen years. He worked in a "Muskegon auto plant, a Chicago packinghouse, and an Alaskan cannery before gravitating to California." Eventually he "spent winters in Los Angeles and the rest of the year following the agricultural harvest northward from the Imperial Valley to Sacramento."[43]

Convict labor also contributed to the development of Los Angeles. During the seasonal slack winter months of the agricultural industry many laborers—especially white men—descended on Los Angeles. In the 1880s the city began a "war on tramps," and increased arrests produced overcrowding that then fueled the expansion of Los Angeles County Jail's capacity. In the early twentieth century, "when Mexican immigrants were emerging as the city's main source of casual labor, white male inmates on the chain gang clanged through the streets supplementing the similarly unskilled work of Mexicans in the construction of modern Los Angeles."[44]

CHAPTER 1

The significance of the uneven economic development in the city and region lay in the demands it placed on workers. Race, ethnicity, class, and gender influenced how migrants, upon their arrival, engaged the economy and were to participate in labor organizing and politics. However, broad commonalities existed across difference in both the type of work and the continued movement between urban and rural labor. Shifts in the composition of this mobile class of labor occurred throughout the early twentieth century. Segregated labor crews existed but not uniformly, varying by region and type of work, and were usually aided by labor contractors. Japanese crews, for instance, dominated the Fresno raisin-grape harvest. Oxnard's sugar-beet fields employed a roughly even mix of Japanese and Mexican workers. Labor contractors enjoyed particularly strong influence in both areas.

The early-twentieth-century influx of workers pushed the trend toward integrated crews, but race influenced employment and pay. For example, in 1908 the Southern Pacific paid a daily wage of $1.60 to Greek workers, $1.45 to Japanese workers, and $1.25 to Mexican workers. These work crews reflected the changing racial composition of California's working class. In 1909 Mexican workers made up nearly 20 percent of railroad workers in the U.S. West. This number grew to approximately 60 percent at the end of the 1920s. Through this same period, "the percentage of Anglo Americans remained very much the same, 31.3; Asians, Greeks, and Italians disappeared from the tracks partly because of immigration restrictions, partly because they switched to urban jobs, and partly because railroad bosses liked Mexicans better."[45] Differences in pay and varying racial composition of jobsites created the terrain for labor and radical organizing.

Community and Space

Multiracial working-class neighborhoods were the norm in Los Angeles's central districts during the early twentieth century. Regional labor practices, residential proximity, and commerce patterns combined to make interracial interaction daily and routine for most residents. As the city's population increased, working-class whites, Mexicans, Italians, African Americans, Japanese, and other residents constructed physical locations that functioned as community centers or concentration points, yet all lay within easy walking distance of each other within the central neighborhoods. The plaza, the historic city center, functioned as a community space for Mexicans, Italians, and other members of the racially diverse working class. Chinatown lay just east into the 1930s, Little Tokyo a few blocks south of the plaza. African American small businesses concentrated a few blocks farther south along Central Avenue. To the east, Boyle Heights grew into an important Jewish and Mexican neighborhood. Racially mixed neighborhoods in close proximity set the stage for a significant amount of interracial interaction in day-to-day life that broadened residents' experiences.[46]

Around the plaza, ethnic Mexicans, Italians, other European immigrants, and working-class whites shared physical space on the street and in the theaters and pool halls, which many businesses actively encouraged to increase their customer base. For example, the Hidalgo Theatre printed advertising posters in both Spanish and Italian. William McEuen, a University of Southern California graduate student researching the area in 1914, noted, "These institutions are a gathering place for idle men and the ones along North Main Street, especially between the Plaza and the Post Office, are largely frequented by Mexicans." Neighborhood pool halls served as social centers, and they usually featured cigar stands, a barber, and a soda fountain. As vital as these places of commerce and community were to working-class residents, they often fueled the anxieties of middle-class Anglos. McEuen moralized: "The air is filled with tobacco smoke, vile and obscene talk is prevalent, in short the whole atmosphere and influence of these places is unwholesome and destructive."[47]

Shared commerce and advertising also brought people, especially Mexicans and Italians, into proximity for the more banal tasks of banking and grocery shopping. A number of Spanish-language newspapers carried advertisements for Italian-owned businesses, some in Spanish and others in Italian. *El Mosquito* ran several adverts for Italian businesses in central Los Angeles, including the Farmers and Merchants National Bank and the International Savings and Exchange Bank. The paper also carried Italian-language advertisements for the Farmacia Italiana, E. Castellano's liquor store, and an Italian grocery, fruit, and tobacco store on North Main Street.[48] This trend continued into the next decade in the newspaper *El Correo Mexicano*, which pronounced itself an "organ dedicated exclusively to the defense of the Mexican community." The motto did not prevent the fusion of Mexican and Italian commerce from finding a place in its pages. The Farmacia Italiana owned by Carlos Scovazzo that advertised in *El Mosquito* eight years earlier had changed its name to the Farmacia Italo-Mexicana by 1914 and advertised in *El Correo Mexicano*. A similar advert for the Farmacia Italiana dell' Aquila y Botica Mexicana, owned by Leonardo Aquilino, showed this fusion as well. Linguistic similarities between Spanish and Italian and prospects of business growth connected Italian and Mexican communities more directly than others.[49]

Racism, business interests, and consumer preferences created even broader forms of shared commerce in cosmopolitan Los Angeles. Japanese produce stands served a broad clientele, including suburban whites, but white racism pushed many other Japanese small-business owners toward serving the diverse non-Anglo population. The Japanese merchants who owned establishments popular with Mexicans and Italians near the plaza proved "very keen and adroit in stimulating business. They are courteous and attentive at all times; a man is welcome to come in and sit without playing if he wishes to do so."[50] S. Ishimitsu, the owner of Tienda Japonesa on East First Street, sought to stir up business in the pages of *El Correo Mexicano* by promising to "treat Mexicans well in our store." With white racism limiting his expansion, Ishimitsu looked to Los Angeles's non-Anglos to sell his stock of "Vinos y Licores."[51] Consumers, though, balanced their openness with a desire for a commercial link to their places of origin or connection. The La Tienda Mexicana provided just that for Mexicans by stocking "las hojas para tamales, las bellotas de Nogales, Sonora, la carne seca de la Baja California, el queso fresco de Mocorito, y tomates de los Mochis, Estado de Sinaloa, Mexico."[52]

Japanese business owners also looked to the African American community for customers. As Scott Kurashige noted, "certain categories of Issei professionals shunned by whites actively courted black patronage. Japanese physicians and dentists, for instance, regularly advertised in the *California Eagle*," an African American newspaper published in Los Angeles.[53] Additionally, white professionals with radical sympathies often served a broad clientele as a matter of political principle. The Military Intelligence Division in Los Angeles believed that Dr. Edna Jerne "associated with all the leading inner circle radicals of this section," had a "large practice among Russians and Mexicans and the radicals of every kind" during World War I.[54] In the next decade, the Communist Party relied on the sympathies of a Japanese doctor who maintained offices at the Pico House to treat members injured during demonstrations.[55]

While Mexican, Italian, and Japanese commerce remained flexible within existing constraints, racism most strongly affected African American–owned businesses, forcing them to sell primarily within their community. "Black business development," according to Kurashige, "was heavily contingent on the segregated African American consumer market."[56] However, the multiracial reality of the city and region tended to diffuse the harshest racial hostility from being directed at any one group—the Chinese exclusion movement and then Japanese exclusion movement notwithstanding. Both manifested in less virulent forms in Los Angeles than elsewhere in the state. Fluid residential and employment patterns, especially among new immigrants and nonwhites, created an equally fluid environment for typical outlets of racism. For example, Josh Sides argued that "before World War II, most African Americans in Los Angeles lived among and interacted with Mexicans, Japanese, Italians, Jews, and the city's small Chinese population. This arrangement, coupled with the vast size and low population density of the city, mitigated the harshest social and psychological effects of racial segregation by diffusing the racial animosity usually reserved exclusively for blacks in other cities."[57] Another historian of the city, Douglas Flamming, found that "African Americans who grew up along South Central Avenue before World

War II almost always described their neighborhood as multiethnic."[58] The "Harlem Renaissance" writer Arna Bontemps, for example, learned to speak Spanish while growing up in Watts.[59]

As multiracial neighborhoods in central Los Angeles grew and, in many ways, flourished despite difficult living and working conditions, many Anglos moved farther away from the city center as they acquired the means. Streetcars and then automobiles piloted along the rails and roads constructed by the diverse working class helped facilitate movement away from the urban core. Suburban industrial development and residential construction provided the draw. This restructuring of Los Angeles along lines of race and class became stronger after 1910 when, as Mark Wild pointed out, "the city's booming economy fueled a rapid suburban expansion of Anglos, who began to abandon older neighborhoods for newer, more distant districts. The vacuum drew Angelenos of other backgrounds into the older areas, thereby expanding the dimensions of central Los Angeles."[60] As central Los Angeles grew, white suburbs exploded in population. South Gate was just one area among many that "solidified its identity as a community of white working-class families."[61] Another suburban community, Leimert Park, "was a symbol of white privilege during the interwar era—a time when racial animus accumulated and patterns of racial oppression consolidated in Los Angeles."[62] By the 1920s these changes produced multiple political effects. In South Gate property ownership "became the linchpin on workers' class interests as defined in the community. In this way, working-class interests and identity, divorced from workplace concerns, were forged in the neighborhood. It was an identity that hinged on the workers' status as suburbanites. And this status, as we bring it full circle, hinged on race and housing."[63]

Several historians have noted that racial divisions hardened through Los Angeles's population, industrial, and suburban growth during the 1920s. Devra Weber argued that "institutionalized racism, segregation, and economic hardship reinforced the bonds among Mexican workers and underscored their alienation from Anglo society."[64] William Deverell concurred, finding that in Montebello in the 1920s, Anglos, Mexicans, and Japanese "didn't socialize, they didn't interact, and they didn't share much except by accidents of time and space."[65] Similarly, Douglas Flamming wrote that in the 1920s, middle-class African American, Mexican American, and Japanese American leaders in Los Angeles saw their struggles as against the city's Anglos. "All three minority groups" according to Flamming, "acted independently, focusing on their own relationship with the dominant white group."[66] Mike Davis argued in *City of Quartz* that as the twentieth century progressed, the privatization of space, suburbanization, and securitization of Los Angeles turned the city into "Fortress L.A." He counterposed this outcome to Frederick Law Olmstead's conception of "public landscapes and parks as social

CHAPTER 1

safety-valves, mixing classes and ethnicities in common (bourgeois) recreations and enjoyments." Instead, there was a "new class war . . . at the level of the built environment."[67] The outcome that Davis and the others described had yet to be realized during the early twentieth century. Before the 1920s, when industrialization and suburbanization pushed forward with new force in Los Angeles, the organization of space in the city and residential patterns facilitated interracial interaction. Leftist organizing helped incorporate these interactions into their movements. Interracial organizing continued in the 1920s and 1930s, but it faced stronger structural constraints than in prior decades.

■ ■ ■

Migration to Southern California and regional economic development created a cosmopolitan milieu of highly mobile workers. Many working-class migrants shared Aurelia Vincente Azuara's experience of looking for work and seeking some form of stability in their lives. Race, gender, and skill level influenced the outcome. Community formation in Los Angeles reflected the rapid economic development, population growth, and migratory patterns underway during the first thirty years of the twentieth century as people came together in neighborhood streets, shops, bars, pool halls, meeting spaces, and job sites. These conditions brought people into direct contact on the job and in communities, which created shared experiences.

Regional economic development increased connections between urban and rural areas through commodity and capital flows as infrastructure work increased production and facilitated the movement of goods and money. Roads and rails also facilitated the movement of workers. As these workers traveled through the networks they built for commodities, they created their own social connections at the sites of their labor, along the path of their travels, and independent of their work at locations often hundreds of miles away. They formed communities as dispersed, flexible, and mobile as their lives. The mobile working class extended the reach of Los Angeles's diverse urban community through layers of interconnected social ties that reached throughout the U.S. West and Mexico and into the broader world. People also came together, drawn by radical political ideals, which traveled along the economic and migration networks into and out of Los Angeles. Contests over racism, internationalism, and anarchist notions of community apart from states played out in this diverse and dynamic terrain. Radicals did not reverse the forces restructuring Los Angeles, but their organizing provided important outlets for interracial interaction and cooperation.

CHAPTER 2

CREATING CONNECTIONS THROUGH RADICAL PRACTICES

Shortly after Lizzie and Thomas A. Bell, along with their children, visited Eleanor Fitzgerald and her companion, Alexander Berkman, in San Francisco in 1916, Berkman's newspaper, *The Blast*, ran into difficulties with postal authorities for publishing birth-control information. The Bells' daughter Marion recalled the solution they devised to continue distributing the newspaper: "When we got back to Arizona they had trouble mailing *The Blast* from San Francisco, so they sent them to us. We kids went around on bicycles mailing batches in different post boxes. The papers went to Argentina and many other places. I remember thinking how they were being sent all over the world."[1] Newspapers were the most important connecting thread in the regional and global radical movement, surpassing organizations and political parties in their ability to elicit common cause, yet newspapers could not survive without deep interpersonal social ties. Labor and radical organizing—in person and through print—created interwoven personal, organizational, and ideological connections. The multilingual radical press then extended the reach of the local movement, beyond individual experience and knowledge, through a vibrant global print culture.

Personal, organizational, and print connections comprised the Los Angeles Left and its linkages to the global movement. These connections were rooted within the broader community-development process in Los Angeles, yet the strands of the Left created different organizational forms and engaged in different spatial practices, which, in turn, influenced whether groups drew strength from racial diversity or practiced exclusionary forms of solidarity. The crucial community-building function of the radical press then extended the reach of Los Angeles's radical community still further. Radicals clearly and intentionally nurtured an imagined political community in their periodicals.[2] With equal intention and drive they labored to bring their community-building efforts off the printed page. Radical practices combined with the processes of community formation in Los Angeles and the region to create a radical community of significant racial, linguistic, and geographic breadth.

Radical Movements, Radical Communities, and Radical Space

Interracial and multilingual interaction occurred in Los Angeles as a part of daily routine. The spatial manifestations of race and class in the city produced the physical proximity that made this so, a condition that also held true in rural areas. Regular interaction broadened the experiences of individuals and provided a base of shared cultural knowledge but also led to interracial conflict. Among leftists, the cosmopolitan environment turned discussions about international solidarity into choices of action by individuals and local movements. Ideological distinctions along various stopping points of the Left, from trade unionism to anarchism, influenced the formality of organizations, the rigidity of internal hierarchies within organizations, and their spatial practices. Understandings of internationalism and racial distinction combined with organizational form to structure participation within leftist movements in Los Angeles.

Margaret Kuhn, in her study of turn-of-the-century Italy, characterized *case del popolo* (houses of the people) as "spaces of resistance" that brought people together into a shared space within a political culture with a similar ideologically broad range of voices on the left as found in Los Angeles. Kuhn argued that "social spaces rather than shared [political] languages linked coalitions together." Membership in an organization was not required to enter for a free class or to play a game. The radical space inside the walls of a *casa del popolo* "provided informal opportunities to encounter new ideas, recognize commonalities, debate tactics, and maybe then engage in political activity."[3]

The spaces created by leftist organizations in Los Angeles, such as union halls, socialist reading rooms, or anarchist libraries, fit many of these characterizations and proved a vital coalition-building mechanism. However, in this section I am building a broader understanding of radical space. Rather than it being constrained to movement-controlled structures, the myriad locations that facilitated interracial interaction in Los Angeles and out along the paths traveled by mobile workers deserve to be understood as radical space because they facilitated similar practices: from street corners, pool halls, and bars in the city to freight-train boxcars, jungle camps, and sleeping quarters on rural job sites. This was the spatial terrain of the culture of affinity.

In 1875 typographical workers became the first organized trade workers in Los Angeles. Building-trade workers followed suit in the 1880s, and the city's trade unions joined the American Federation of Labor in 1894. During these formative decades of the Los Angeles labor movement influential organizers such as Lemuel Biddle, John Murray Jr., Arthur Vinette, and Fred Wheeler participated in many of the labor and reform movements that sprouted up in the late nineteenth century: Knights of Labor, People's Party, Coxey's Army, and the Bellamy Nationalist movement. These men all held membership in the Socialist Party in the early twentieth century.

This had two primary consequences for trade-union organizing in Los Angeles. First, local AFL leaders drew from this background during the early twentieth century to push Los Angeles labor into electoral politics and broader city reform efforts with the Anti-Citizens' League, Public Ownership Party, and the Union Labor Party.[4] Second, in contrast to the national AFL leadership, which wore the badge of white male supremacy with honor by using the language of a "white man's wage," Lemuel Biddle, Fred Wheeler, and John Murray Jr. understood their local interracial organizing through the lens of socialist internationalism.[5] However, the city's AFL certainly still traded in racist currency. For instance, in 1911 Los Angeles's AFL newspaper *Citizen* proudly remembered that Vinette had taken a "radical and active part in the campaign" to exclude Chinese immigrants from the United States.[6] Murray spoke in support of barring Japanese immigration in 1907. Internationalism clearly had limits for these men when it came to considering immigrant laborers in Los Angeles, which will be discussed in more detail later.

Trade-union organizing in Los Angeles concentrated on occupations with white male workers, relatively stable work locations, and regular employment. The AFL in Los Angeles achieved its greatest success in the building and construction trades, service sector, and manufacturing. In 1911 the Los Angeles Central Labor Council (CLC) represented ninety-one locals with a membership of fifteen thousand.[7] The organized trades waged a grinding, mostly losing war against the Merchants & Manufacturers Association's open-shop philosophy from the early 1900s through the 1920s before they reaped the labor-friendly benefits of the National Industrial Recovery Act in 1933.[8]

The structured, formal bureaucracies of local trade unions evidenced their internal hierarchies, while union halls and offices marked their institutional presence and financial strength. In 1910 the Labor Temple on Maple Avenue opened after a nearly decade-long fundraising campaign spearheaded by the CLC. That year no other building in central Los Angeles stood taller than the $180,000 building financed through the sale of public shares.[9] This financial model and the AFL's representative organization opened this space beyond private spaces for use by white working-class Los Angeles, but the building also projected the racial and gendered hierarchies of the craft union. Additionally, private businesses such as the Maple Bar and Cafe on East Fifth Street in central Los Angeles directly appealed to union members, overwhelmingly white, for their customer base. Another, the Labor Temple Cigar Stand, claimed to be the "only stand in town where ALL the goods bear the Union Label."[10] Union-owned and union-friendly spaces provided locations for working-class whites to come together in formal and informal ways, which at once increased the strength of Los Angeles labor and reinforced the craft union's racial and gendered hierarchies.

In contrast to the AFL, the Socialist Party, the IWW, and anarchists placed significant intellectual importance on the ideals of internationalism or the abolition of states. Indeed, global working-class solidarity rested at the heart of most leftist thought. Internationalism, however, did not operate as a universal and unifying line of thought across the Left. Not surprisingly, these ideals produced uneven results in movements. Materialist-influenced debates over the historical development paths capable of achieving revolutionary change often reproduced racist understandings of colonized people and affected those workers many white leftists excluded from their international solidarity. A less-frequently explored limitation of internationalism is also important. Most articulations of socialist and then Communist internationalism reified the nation and consolidated national territory as the operating unit of solidarity. In the United States, socialists commonly followed similar logic to draw distinctions between nonwhite immigrants in the United States and nationally organized socialist parties around the world—a result being that many white socialists on the West Coast refused to see Asian immigrants living in their communities within the same rubric of internationalism as socialist movements in Asia: the former a threat, the latter a cause to be celebrated.[11]

In 1902 the Socialist Party in Los Angeles had two hundred members in ten local branches.[12] The primary units of party organization consisted of local community-based branches distinct from jobsites. Socialist Party politics in Los Angeles split between a gradualist electoral outlook seen most clearly in the English-speaking groups and a strong community focus in the immigrant, non-Anglophone locals where citizenship and the ability to vote was rare and immediate living and working conditions more dire. Socialist Party locals supplemented community and political formation by creating intentional communities of solidarity that grew into important institutions rooted in Los Angeles's neighborhoods. Prominent socialists included Frances Nacke Noel, chair of Women's Trade Union League, as well as Job Harriman, John Kenneth Turner, Ethyl Duffy Turner, Elizabeth Darling Trowbridge, Lázaro Gutiérrez de Lara, and Rafael Carmona.

The Mexican Branch of the Socialist Party formed in early 1907 behind the efforts of Carmona and Gutiérrez de Lara. Its membership grew substantially when Los Angeles's Mexican Cigarmakers' Union joined en masse, raising its membership to around one hundred. Gutiérrez de Lara, a veteran organizer by the time he moved to Los Angeles, had participated in the 1892 student movement in Mexico City. He lived in Cananea between 1903 and 1906 before fleeing to the United States to avoid the consequences of his participation in the September 1906 Cananea mining strike, one of the opening acts of the Mexican Revolution. His personal connection to the Flores Magón brothers went back to 1895 in Mexico City. Now settled in Los Angeles, he was a member of the Partido Liberal Mexicano. At this time the PLM had anarchist, socialist, and even politically moderate members and supporters. Eventually his socialism, mixed with interpersonal conflict, led to his parting ways with the PLM. However, Gutiérrez de Lara's socialist organizing in Los Angeles brought one of the first signs of the blending of Mexican labor organizing in the United States with organizing for revolution in Mexico.[13]

When Italians formed a socialist local in 1909, they held their meetings at the Mexican Branch headquarters at 702 San Fernando Street. A month later the Italian socialists joined the Mexican Branch. The Mexican group stood as the only language/ethnic socialist branch not formed by European immigrants or Anglos in Los Angeles. In 1908 and 1909 many other immigrant communities in Los Angeles reached sufficient numbers to consolidate around institutions, and Socialist Party locals reflected this in their activity and expansion. Most organized along linguistic, ethnic, racial, and national lines at this time. In 1909 Los Angeles's Socialist Party had German, Hungarian, Lithuanian, Mexican, and Russian branches in addition to English-language branches. Hungarians also formed a chapter of the Socialist Labor Party in 1909.[14]

A group of Young Jewish Socialists chartered in December 1908, establishing Branch No. 248 of the Arbayter Ring (Workmen's Circle), "a secular and nonpartisan socialist mutual aid society founded in 1892."[15] *Common Sense* noted that the Jewish body "receives also Gentiles in its fold, drawing no lines of creed in its progressive missionary work of education of the young people." Two German groups, the Socialist Singing Society and the German Workers' Sick and Death Benefit Society, complemented the German Branch of the Socialist Party. The Jewish group and the German Branch of the Socialist Party both held their meetings at 814 South Main Street. The Socialist Singing Society held its weekly meetings on the third floor of Turner Hall on South Main Street, and the German Workers' Sick and Death Benefit Society did its part "in the work of mutual aid and nation-wide socialist practical solidarity."[16] This locally rooted form of organizing drew people who tended to have relatively stable work and residential patterns.

The Socialist Party's enactment of internationalism reflected its organizational practice of creating locals along racial, ethnic, national, and linguistic lines, with the singular exception of Mexicans and Italians. When the Socialist Party practiced internationalism in Los Angeles, it held joint rallies and protests that brought together its separate organizational units and members of the community. For example, in 1909 Russian socialists organized a night of entertainment at which "16 German socialist singers, a number of Mexican, Hungarian, and English comrades gathered . . . got together Russians and Americans of the neighborhood, and gave them all a fine entertainment of German, Hungarian, and Russian singing and recitation."[17] This is but one example of grassroots community formation encouraged and facilitated by the Socialist Party that grew out of cosmopolitan Los Angeles.

The Socialist Party had fewer financial resources than the AFL, which limited its physical institutional presence. In 1894 Lemuel Biddle managed the Socialist Co-Operative Store just north of the plaza on North Main Street. The shop moved a mile north to Buena Vista Street to expand into selling coal, wood, and blacksmithing services until it closed a few years later. In the early twentieth century the Socialist Reading Room stood as one of the few locations controlled by the party, and it provided space for members to gather and hold small meetings. This space also reflected the more inclusive racial and ethnic membership base of the Socialist Party compared with that of the AFL. Mexican party members routinely found refuge in this space, even though their inclusion within the party could collide with the party's racial order.[18]

The General Assembly of the Socialist Party met at the Elk's Hall on South Spring Street.[19] Socialists brought new symbolic meanings into these private spaces even as their owners maintained control over their use. The owners certainly had profit motives for renting out their halls to all comers, but it also indicated Los Angeles's relatively open political culture in the years before World War I. This changed dramatically during the war and after as the range of acceptable political debate substantially narrowed.

Socialist Party membership in Los Angeles reached a high point of around eight thousand in 1911—the same year that women won the right to vote in California—before it entered into an electoral alliance with the CLC-affiliated Union Labor Political Club. Combined membership stood at twenty-six thousand members. This coalition helped Job Harriman earn 51,796 votes against the winning 85,739 received by the incumbent mayor George Alexander in Harriman's unsuccessful bid for mayor on the Socialist Party ticket in 1911.[20] The election generated as much hope in the run up to polling day as it did disappointment among socialists in the result.

After the electoral defeat, Harriman spearheaded the foundation of the Llano del Rio colony north of Los Angeles in the Antelope Valley. Llano failed dramatically to represent the diversity of Los Angeles. Mostly whites had the means and inclination to purchase into the commune. Efforts at Llano drew socialist resources away from the city in mid-decade, a significant shift away from earlier electoral efforts. This period also witnessed the decline of multilingual socialist organizing in Los Angeles's central districts with the net effect of marginalizing socialists from Los Angeles politics. However, socialists did manage to continue some outreach through the *Western Comrade* newspaper between 1913 and 1918. When Llano del Rio faced a financial crisis in 1917, its remaining members relocated to Louisiana after buying a parcel of cheap land from a lumber company. The Newllano colony survived until 1939, but the move completed the process of socialist retreat as a political force in Los Angeles.[21]

Los Angeles residents drew from two primary strands of radical thought: the syndicalism of the IWW and the array of strategies found in anarchism. In Los Angeles members of the IWW and self-identified anarchists cooperated particularly closely, especially in Spanish-language organizing. IWW members, anarchists, and their sympathizers forged a shared organizing tradition that gave the broadest voice to the region's diverse mobile working class, extended mutual solidarities outward through the global movement, and remained flexible in their organizational form. The IWW and anarchists envisioned political and social organization that softened national distinctions between racially diverse workers in the region. For example, the IWW newspaper the *Industrial Worker* carried an article that read: "The workingman is a citizen of the world. He has no country. He has nothing to feel patriotic over. He recognized no flag except the red flag, which to him is a symbol for revolt, that the battle is on the between the working class and the capitalist class for the possession of the earth and the fullness thereof." The article ended by connecting back to male laborers on the West Coast: "His happy home most often consists of a roll of blankets."[22]

Although many women organized for the IWW, including Laura Payne Emerson in San Diego, the international ideals of the IWW were often inseparable from a hypermasculinity joined with class militancy into a "virile syndicalism."[23] This was especially true in the western United States. At the same time, Emerson, an important figure on the Left, organized laborers in San Diego in 1910, participated in the San Diego free-speech fight, and published the syndicalist newspaper *International* in 1915. She also wrote the lyrics to the song "Industrial Workers of the World." Her leadership position in the San Diego IWW indicates not an exception but rather the ready acceptance of people organizing among a gender-skewed unskilled labor force.[24]

The first IWW local in Los Angeles formed shortly after the foundation of the national organization in 1905, but initially membership grew slowly. Two interrelated strands of traveling organizing led to the regional growth of the IWW. First, indigenous and Mexican organizers such as Fernando Palomares and Fernando Velarde, deeply involved with the revolutionary PLM, expanded the ranks of the syndicalist union while working across the border to push Mexico along the path to revolution. Second, IWW members like Frank Little and other multiethnic and multilingual white organizers spread the word among regional laborers, miners, and agricultural workers. All regional organizing went forward with extremely limited financial support and was mostly independent from the national-level IWW.

Frank Little is often mistakenly identified as Native American or various percentages thereof: "Half Indian, half whiteman, All I.W.W."[25] Before proceeding, a correction to this myth is long overdue. Some of Frank Little's relatives expressed the belief that Little's mother, Almira Hays Little, had limited Native American ancestry, possibly Cherokee, in correspondence with historians. There is no family recollection about this ancestor, though relatives believed that shame prevented Almira from registering as a tribal member. There are grounds to doubt even this limited claim of Little's Native heritage entirely as many Anglo-Americans invented these connections after the genocide. Little's father was an Anglo doctor. His family did not provide him any meaningful personal relationship to the Native American experience or traditions. Any connection to Native American culture that Little felt would have come from growing up in Oklahoma, where he moved with his family as a youth. The family came to Oklahoma as white settlers, where they lived illegally for over four years in Indian Territory, before the federal government opened the so-called Unassigned Lands to white appropriation in 1889. Although the family was not Quaker, he attended a Quaker school with Anglo and Native American children and shared childhood friendships with Native Americans. Little went on to attend the Oklahoma Agricultural and Mechanical College but did not graduate. He joined the WFM in Arizona in 1900.[26] Little himself bears the initial responsibility for these ancestral claims as fellow Wobblie Ralph Chaplin remembered: "Frank Little boasted of being a half-breed."[27] IWW lore also referenced Native Americans in pamphlets and poetry and looked to Native Americans in their mythmaking. Frank Little certainly found his place among iterant and multiracial miners and laborers in the western United States, and Franklin Rosemont characterized him as being "widely regarded by fellow Wobs as the union's single greatest organizer."[28] This is far greater testament to his character and organizing zeal than his race.

In 1906 Fernando Velarde and Rosendo Dorame added a Spanish-speaking branch to Phoenix IWW Local 272. The Phoenix local was one of the first in the region outside of California, and it soon had a majority of Mexican members. That same year the Gran Liga Mexicana de Empleados de los Ferrocarrileros (Great League of Mexican Railway Employees) and Arizona-based anarchist IWW member Albert Ryan corresponded. By 1907, IWW locals had formed in San Diego (Local 245), in the inland citrus town of Redlands (Local 419), the

Imperial Valley town of Holtville (Local 437), and the Arizona copper town of Globe (Local 100). These locations illustrate the IWW's appeal across different industries, from agriculture to infrastructure projects to mining.[29]

In Los Angeles, conversations in a corner bookstore on 7th and Broadway frequented by Wobblies brought members into the new organization before the IWW established an independent institutional footprint. By September 1905, IWW Pioneer Local 68 leased a headquarters at East Sixth Street and Maple Avenue in central Los Angeles. A cigar stand and a free reading room on East Sixth Street emerged in 1906 as the visible institutional signs of the IWW in Los Angeles. But in 1909, Los Angeles Local 12 stood as the sole local in the city, an aftereffect of factional infighting across the nation. Renewed organizing in 1910 grew the number of locals to three, representing metal and mining, building, and public-service workers. In 1910 IWW Locals 1, 12, 18, and 63 shared an office at 243 East Second Street in central Los Angeles, and Local 245 had an office at 212 Fourth Street in San Pedro. Most Los Angeles locals were "recruiting" or "mixed" locals not attached to a particular industry or employer. Membership numbers for the Los Angeles area locals are difficult to determine, but formal membership statewide reached around five hundred in 1910.[30]

Multilingual (especially Spanish-language) IWW organizing in Los Angeles, San Diego, the inland valleys, and Arizona increased these numbers until World War I–era repression at federal, state, and local levels greatly curtailed the freedom to organize. In 1913 the Los Angeles IWW headquarters had moved a block away from the plaza at 429 North Los Angeles Street. Beyond providing office space, it functioned as a meeting hall and a place of refuge after the Christmas Riot on the plaza that year. Los Angeles's Spanish-language IWW newspaper *El Rebelde*, published by Local 602, had its offices at 114 South Spring Street in Central Los Angeles in 1917. When the *New Unionist*—the important IWW English newspaper after World War I–era repression—moved to Los Angeles in 1927, it listed a post office box and not a physical address. Local membership, the group's ability to organization street-level actions, and its institutional presence had declined.[31]

The IWW in Los Angeles, at its most consolidated, operated as a multilingual local movement loosely connected to the national IWW bureaucracy. The IWW was an active and extraordinarily vocal minority on the Left in Los Angeles and the region, and its significance reached well beyond its dues-paying members into broader regional working-class culture. The influence of the IWW in the region is, to a large degree, attributable to its fluid organizing structure, spatial practices, and cultural forms. Informal influence produced a limited historical record, but there are traces. For example, after the bloody confrontation on the Durst farm in Wheatland, California, in 1913, Carlton Parker found that hundreds knew about the IWW in a "rough way. . . . and could also sing some of its songs."[32]

The IWW purposely used well-known hymns—but substituted the songs' lyrics with their own verses.[33]

Anarchists formed clubs, publishing efforts, and reading groups, in addition to working within other organizations. Mexicans, Jews, Italians, and Anglos formed the primary nodes of Los Angeles's anarchist movement, most often with considerable overlap and cooperation between them. The Partido Liberal Mexicano occupied the center of these ethnic groupings in Los Angeles from 1907 to the mid-teens. The most visible anarchist agitation in the region, apart from the PLM's revolutionary planning, focused on creating institutional spaces for their ideals to flourish.

The PLM's influence rose and fell through its building an ideologically broad support structure in the United States, conflict over tactics, personality clashes, repeated imprisonment of its leaders, and the changing revolutionary landscape in Mexico. A close group surrounding Ricardo Flores Magón formed the anarchist core of the party. Through correspondence, its newspaper *Regeneración*, and clandestine revolutionary planning, the PLM connected Los Angeles's anarchist movement to local groups operating throughout Mexico, to the Italian anarchist movement, especially Il Gruppo Diritto all'Esistenza (The Right to an Existence Group) in Paterson, New Jersey, and out into the global anarchist movement. PLM traveling organizers often blended revolutionary and labor concerns with considerable crossover with the IWW, which increased its grassroots community base.

Other prominent anarchists who lived in Los Angeles for significant periods included Tom Bell, Vittorio Cravello, Stephanus Fabijanović, Blanca and Juan Francisco Moncaleano, William C. Owen, Alfred Sanftleben, and Joseph Spivak. The PLM and these individuals turned Los Angeles into a global center of anarchist thought and print. When anarchists participated in workplace organizing, they did so through other vehicles such as the IWW, and some even held AFL membership cards. Always a significant numerical minority of the Left in Los Angeles, anarchists punched above their weight as far as their visibility was concerned. They also managed a remarkable institutional presence.

Before the Baja raids in 1911, the Partido Liberal Mexicano made full use of the office of *Regeneración* at Fourth and Towne, where "they had the whole building and some of them slept and ate there."[34] An additional space for Mexican radical culture was Rómulo Carmona's Librería-Mexicana "La Aurora" north of Chavez Ravine on 664 San Fernando Street. Carmona had previously owned a bookstore in El Paso where he first met Ricardo Flores Magón.[35] Many organizations made their meeting halls available to anarchists. Large groups primarily met indoors at Italian Hall and the AFL also occasionally allowed anarchists to use the Labor Temple. Additionally, anarchists conducted large gatherings in privately owned spaces such as Burbank Hall and Simpson's Auditorium.

In 1913 Mexican and Italian anarchists joined together to open the International Workers' Home with a Modern School at the corner of Yale and Alpine. The large building served as an anarchist community center and accommodated the meetings of a number of radical groups. They managed it by anarchist principles; occupants remained autonomous with none obliged to pay rent. The center housed a doctor, a barber, and many classes, including language instruction in Italian, English, Spanish, French, and Esperanto. The building also served as a recreational and social center, providing space for dances and socializing.[36] Women especially made use of this kind of radical space. For example, Jennifer Guglielmo found that Italian immigrant anarchist women in New Jersey "turned most often to strategies of mutual aid, collective direct action, and to the multiethnic, radical subculture that took shape within their urban working-class communities."[37] Movement-controlled social space was the ideal place for radical culture to flourish.

Anarchists also created community space in their neighborhoods. Mateo Street, south of downtown near the river, remained an intersection between residential housing and industrial production until consumed by expanding industry in the mid-1950s. A strong Mexican and Italian community formed in the neighborhood that included a number of anarchists and the local anarchist club "Luca Continua."[38] The regeneration of radical Los Angeles in the wake of World War I–era repression reflected the changes in residency patterns in the city. In 1924, the Mexican anarchist group El Grupo Anarquista "Obreros Libres" formed in the Belvedere Park neighborhood in East Los Angeles. In 1926 the Libertarian Group—founded as a Jewish group but then broadened—established the Libertarian Center on 2824½ Brooklyn Avenue (Cesar Chavez Avenue today) in Boyle Heights with club rooms and a library. In 1928 it moved a few blocks away to 420 North Soto as a lasting institutional space for anarchism. It had a meeting hall, a library, and additional rooms under one roof. In 1936 Mexican anarchists published the newspaper *El Luchador* in Boyle Heights with the support of the Libertarian Group.[39]

Institution building by leftists formed the backbone of organizing and publishing. Dedicated participants completed the tedious work of raising funds, signing leases, and otherwise maintaining the core framework for worker-led organizations to function. The space in which the threads of the Left, from trade unions to anarchists, operated in Los Angeles was remarkably constrained and interwoven with the focal points of multiracial Los Angeles's community centers. One could easily walk from one office to the next, to a meeting hall, and then home. The same area also encompassed African American, Japanese, and Chinese commercial districts, which all brought life to the central districts, with Mexican and Italian commerce more dispersed. The extensive local light-rail system connected radicals and facilitated movement as it did for the rest of the population.

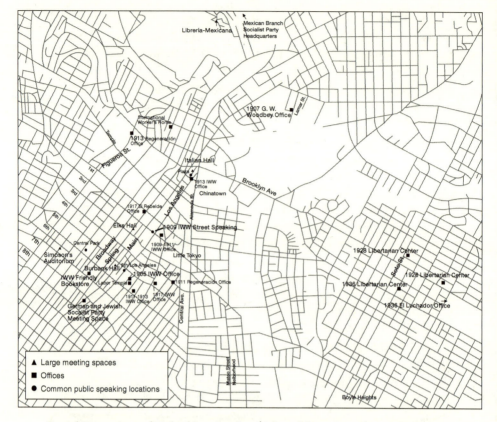

Spatial Dimensions of Radical Los Angeles. (Adapted from City of Los Angeles GIS basemap: https://data.lacity.org/A-Livable-and-Sustainable-City/Street-Centerline/7j4e-nn4z/data)

Syndicalists and anarchists also drove efforts to create community through appropriating spaces intended for other purposes, in addition to formal institution building. Wherever people came together and affinities blossomed, however briefly, they created a form of radical community that turned their surroundings into radical space. This was the terrain of the culture of affinity. Street speaking regularly gave it form.

The plaza, a place about which William C. Owen noted "from time immemorial, ... had been the people's Open Forum," was the spatial center of radical working-class Los Angeles.[40] Although city officials and police contested this with policy and truncheon, Los Angeles's long-standing "political culture of street speaking" developed on the plaza, which gave voice to a broad range of ideas.[41]

Creating Connections through Radical Practices

Police often confronted radicals on the plaza, as was the case when police arrested Lucy Eldine Gonzalez Parsons, the widow of Haymarket martyr Albert Parsons, for selling copies of the Haymarket speeches without a permit in 1913.[42] More frequently, street speaking brought people together in participatory form. Without amplification an unpopular speaker could easily be shouted down or drowned out by another speaker. In 1909 a Los Angeles Wobblie celebrated successful IWW street speaking on the corner of 2nd and Los Angeles Streets by saying that their "only trouble is putting their lungs against the Jesus screamers." A group of African American "religious freaks" spoke on the same corner, "and believe me," the Wobblie said, "not one of the them came to this balmy sunny climate for lung trouble."[43] The bar to entry was also very low; one simply had to walk by, stop, and listen or speak. The radical community thrived in this space and embedded in these participatory practices.

Street speaking in Los Angeles centered on the plaza and Central Park, later renamed Pershing Square. People also found other outlets. In its early years the IWW and its socialist sympathizers held outdoor meetings on an empty lot on the corner of Fifth and Los Angeles Streets in central Los Angeles. In the active summer of 1906 the IWW local held regular meetings at the lot, and the African American socialist preacher Reverend George Washington Woodbey spoke there on a number of occasions.[44] Sun Yat Sen visited Los Angeles several times. In 1905 he spoke in a building on Apablasa Street in Chinatown.[45] After the Christmas riot the *Los Angeles Times* noted another location where workers immersed themselves in radical ideas: "The tamale wagons, the troughs at which the idlers absorb the new ideas of unrest and revolt sown with such recklessness by the I.W.W. and anarchist 'orators' may be kept from the district entirely hereafter, if not by police order."[46]

Another example of radical spatial practices in the city came in 1914 when an army of unemployed workers descended upon Los Angeles in the spring and encamped on the banks of the Los Angeles River. These men washed their dishes and clothes in the river water, slept along the shore, and then walked the short distance from the river to attend rallies around the plaza.[47] They appropriated and then used urban space in a fundamentally different way than intended or condoned by city planners and authorities, creating an equally different urban experience for themselves than that of most city residents. Across Los Angeles, radicals and sympathizers used both public space and underdeveloped private space, in the case of the empty lot on 5th and Los Angeles, to articulate their challenges and build community.

Outside of Los Angeles, Wobblie and anarchist ideals took form in railcars, jungle camps, and other places of independence and refuge. People made the most of capitalist inefficiency by hitching rides in empty freight-train cars to traverse the U.S. West and Mexico. Members of the IWW monopolized the rails on some routes, with only those holding membership cards or sympathies permitted to pass in this enforced radical space. One Anglo Wobblie recalled: "Riding a freight car was miserable, but it was the only way a migratory worker could go from job to job or seek a job in the harvest. The Wobblies used physical force to unload riders who didn't have a red card. Then the railroaders got so they would unload riders who didn't have a red card too. A lot of men took out a card just to ride the trains."[48] However miserable it could be, the appropriate knowledge made this mode of transportation remarkably efficient. A train caught outside of Bakersfield took two and a half hours to Fresno. To get to Oakland from Bakersfield, one needed to get the evening train and switch in Tracy in the middle of the night to arrive by morning. Traveling through the borderlands proved almost as efficient. Traveling from Yuma, Arizona, to Los Angeles took a very manageable twelve hours.[49]

Mexican and indigenous organizers affiliated with the PLM and IWW shared this form of movement. Ethel Duffy Turner wrote of Fernando Palomares: "He was a worker and sometimes vagrant. . . . He rode the rails. He found that American tramps did not discriminate against Mexicans, but that they were all brothers." When PLM member Blas Lara traveled to Mexico from California he rejected an offer of money by saying, "I've got plenty of money. I'm going to ride on 'my trains.' Won't be giving a cent to the Southern Pacific Railroad."[50] Furthermore, people often walked at least part of the way from one location to the next. This forced a corporal interaction with the landscape they traversed, further connecting them to the process of movement.[51]

The travel patterns of radicals broadened the scope of their organizing and encouraged the formation of regional, national, and international affinities. Claudio Lomnitz wrote that the lives of the PLM leaders combined a "precariousness of existence and vast freedom of movement, with agitators such as Blas Lara, Fernando Palomares, Enrique Flores Magón, Práxedis Guerrero, Tomás and Manuel Sarabia, and practically every other leader that one can name or think of moving between, say, agricultural work in the Imperial Valley, construction, work for utilities companies, in lumber mills, mines, on railroads, and more. The combination of precariousness and mobility made for a peculiar kind of sociability, oriented toward establishing relations of support and solidarity between strangers, based on anything from ethnic identification, to politics, to simple 'sympathy.'"[52] A culture of affinity.

The ability of people to move through the region with relative ease improved their utility as workers, and it allowed them to move rapidly to a location of worker struggle, which bolstered support structures across the expanse of the U.S. West and Mexico. For instance, IWW free-speech fights depended on far-flung

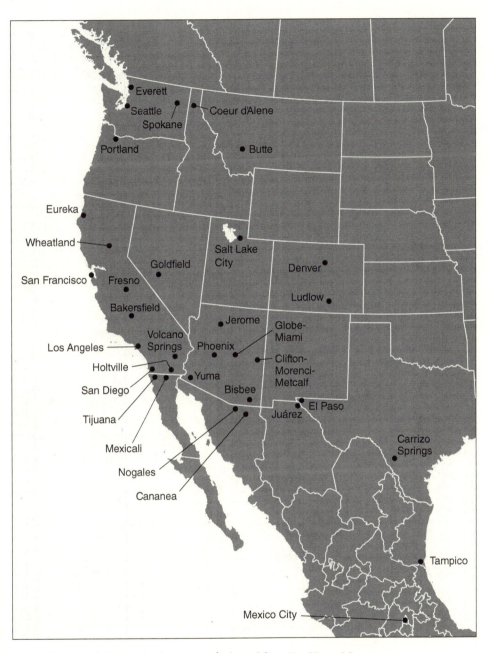

The Radical Geographic Imaginary. (Adapted from FreeVectorMaps.com http://freevectormaps.com)

sympathizers' converging on a single location. When people traversed the region, the social connections they created and the paths they traveled formed a radical geography that did not mirror the productive landscape. This created geographic imaginaries, experiences, and spaces for community formation outside the gaze of the state.

A map of the region that denotes places of major labor and radical struggles looks different from more traditional representations of cities or ecological features. This brings out the different distribution of the productive landscape in the early twentieth century compared with those realities today. The map also illustrates the range of radical spatial practices of workers in the U.S. West and Mexico by reflecting the geographical understandings or the mental mappings of radicals. Los Angeles functioned as a regional and global hub in the radical movement as workers, goods, and ideas moved through the city. The city's importance increased still further as its role in the production of radical print culture expanded.

Community Formation and Print Culture

The immigrant and radical press grew out of and extended the community formation process in Los Angeles and the region. Locally published newspapers facilitated connections from Los Angeles into the region and around the world. A broad range of newspapers originated in Los Angeles apart from the mainstream English-language dailies in the early twentieth century. The non-English immigrant press and radical newspapers varied in their publication language and content, but they had much in common. Both types of newspapers, regardless of their political orientation, connected geographically dispersed linguistic groups through the printed page. The content of the immigrant press turned these papers into cultural and political focal points by keeping readers informed of local events and events in their countries of origin in their native language. The immigrant press was the ideal tool for the consolidation of communities of readers along language and national-origin affiliations yet disconnected from national boundaries.

A sampling of the non-English press in Los Angeles around 1917 provides a window into the linguistic and cultural diversity of the city's print culture. *L'Italo Americano* was a leading voice for the Italian community. Alfred Haij published *California Veckoblad*, "the only weekly Swedish paper in Southern California," at 101½ South Broadway. The Croatian-language paper, *Dalmacja*, which federal authorities found devoted much "attention to petty quarrels between people that speak the language in which it is published," moved to an office at 114 South Spring Street in Los Angeles from San Francisco in 1917. The Greek-language paper *Eche*, edited by C. Marghetis at 232 East Fourth Street, billed itself as "the

Greek newspaper of the Western States and the only one in Southern California." This paper circulated roughly seven hundred issues per week around 1917. All of these newspaper offices were located within a few blocks of each other in central Los Angeles.[53]

Los Angeles's French-language community had two newspapers. A. L. Tourmoux and Theo Gyger published *Le Courrier Francais*.[54] *L'Union Nouvelle*, established in 1879, maintained an office at 140 North Spring Street with a weekly circulation of 1,250 issues around 1917. San Diego's *Deutsche Zeitung* referred to itself as "the only German newspaper on the Southern Pacific Coast."[55] Reflecting the political diversity of Los Angeles's Mexicans, *El Heraldo de México*, an important community-focused conservative newspaper published in the city, sustained a weekly circulation of thirty-seven hundred issues on a subscription base located largely in the local area. The paper had an office at 342 North Main Street in property owned by the paper's publishers Cesar Marburg (a German immigrant to Mexico) and Juan de Heras. The Russian-language *Velikij Okean* (*Pacific Ocean*) also ran for a short time starting in 1910.[56]

The radical press worked in much the same way by helping to facilitate the formation of communities around sets of political ideals and sympathies as the immigrant non-English press supported linguistic and national community in

TABLE 2. Important Labor and Radical Periodicals Published in or near Los Angeles

Title	Publication Years	Orientation
Citizen	1900–1980s	Labor (AFL)
El Correo Mexicano	1912–1920s	Community
Common Sense	1909–1911	Socialist
California Social-Democrat	1911–1916	Socialist
Fuerza Consciente	1912–1914	Anarchist
Huelga General	1913–1914	IWW
Libertad y Trabajo	1908	IWW
Los Angeles Socialist	1901–1909	Socialist
El Luchador	1935–1936	Anarchist
El Mosquito	1905–1907	PLM
New Unionist	1927–1931	IWW
People's Paper	1899–1911	Socialist
Pluma Roja	1913–1915	Anarchist
El Rebelde	1915–1917	IWW
Regeneración	1910–1918	PLM
Revolución	1907	PLM
Roman Forum	1932–1934, 1942–1947	Anarchist/Free thought
Western Comrade	1913–1918	Socialist
Wooden Shoe	1913	IWW

CHAPTER 2

Los Angeles. However, the particular set of practices involved in financing, distributing, producing content for, and consuming the radical press increased its community-building function and strengthened the connections of Los Angeles with the global radical community. Connections were particularly strong in Spanish-language networks.

In 1913 *Regeneración, Pluma Roja, Fuerza Consciente,* and *Huelga General* all rolled off presses in Los Angeles. The simultaneous publication of these four newspapers indicates Los Angeles's position as a world center of Spanish-language radicalism. It also meant that local organizations invested a substantial amount of energy printing newspapers for consumption outside of the city; local subscribers could not sustain four Spanish-language anarchist or syndicalist newspapers. This was part of a process in which ideas and financial resources flowed into Los Angeles, germinated, and then traveled back out on the page.

Financing the Radical Press

The financial realities of publishing a newspaper included generating the funds to purchase or lease a printing press, buy ink, paper, and postage, possibly rent an office, and support financially a limited staff of maybe a few people. Financing for leftist newspapers published in Los Angeles came from a variety of sources that radiated outward from the city, including individuals, clubs, local businesses, and national-level organizations. The newspapers that managed to achieve some sort of financial sustainability and longevity did so on a strong local support base that organized fundraising gatherings and generated advertising revenue to supplement paid subscriptions.

The AFL-affiliated *Citizen* maintained stable finances for decades through the support of individual subscribers and the CLC. The paper also ran a large number of advertisements for local business that often claimed sympathy with labor. In 1910, annual subscriptions cost one dollar; a single issue was five cents. The paper's politics also contributed to its financial success as it focused on bread-and-butter issues and mostly excluded nonwhite workers. White laborers in local unions had more money to support it than did the subscribers to the radical newspapers published in Los Angeles.

Regeneración, the print organ of the PLM, was the most important and widely circulated anarchist newspaper published in Los Angeles. Subscribers to *Regeneración* varied considerably over its life—from perhaps more than twenty thousand as a high to several thousand as a low—and reflected the PLM's public embracing of anarchism in 1911, repeated arrests of its leaders, and the course of the Mexican Revolution. In 1910 annual subscriptions in the United States cost two dollars; bundle orders cost three dollars for one hundred copies, twelve dollars fifty cents for five hundred copies, and twenty dollars for one thousand copies. Individual

52

copies cost five cents. The price of an annual subscription in Mexico rose to five dollars. *Regeneración* also benefited from advertisements from sympathetic businesses such as "El Progreso Restaurant," a barber, and a doctor in 1911. Publishers of anarchist publications offered bundle orders for purchase to allow supporters to carry through their communities, selling the paper and spreading the word. The price for an annual subscription to *Regeneración* dropped to one dollar in 1915 while individual issues remained steady at five cents. In 1916 the group made subscriptions voluntary but recommended readers pay five cents per individual copy. These changes came during a period of declining subscriptions and, more important, its declining ability to act as a political force outside the printed page.[57]

The IWW-affiliated *Huelga General* received limited financial support of the national body, but it still faced great financial difficulty. A supplement to *Huelga General* from March 1914 announced that it would not continue because of "insufficient support on the part of the workers." The editors noted that the lack of funds forced them to "suspend the paper till we can raise more funds."[58] Approximately one thousand people subscribed to the newspaper, a rather limited number for IWW newspapers at the time. *Huelga General*'s successor *El Rebelde* found more success, although its subscription base reached only around two thousand. Annual subscriptions to the paper cost fifty cents, with single issues of the four-page weekly at five cents in 1915. In addition to working to increase its subscription base, *El Rebelde* specifically encouraged its readers to buy issue bundles for redistribution. Twenty-five copies of an issue cost fifty cents in 1915 but climbed to seventy-five cents the next year. If Wobblies then sold copies for the cover price of five cents, their sales would have generated fifty to seventy-five cents per twenty-five-issue bundle, money that could either be returned to the paper in the form of a donation or used for local organizing efforts.[59]

Fundraisers and donations supplemented *El Rebelde*'s coffers. For instance, local Wobblie John Troy organized a raffle for the paper. In 1916 Pedro Coria, Felix Cedeño, Vincente Carrillo, and Mr. Engleback made a cross-county tour publicizing *El Rebelde* and hosting fundraising parties in San Francisco, Philadelphia, and at the Modern School in Los Angeles. In March 1917 a committee organized another local fundraiser dance at Los Angeles's Burbank Hall. Fundraising activities always supplemented paid subscriptions in financing the paper.[60]

An additional form of financing for radical newspapers came in the form of monetary donations. Many publications published the names and amounts of the donations they received. For example, in *Regeneración* this information ran in a recurring section of the paper intermittently referred to as "Los Solidarios." This section included both a roundup of references to the Mexican cause in the radical press and the amount of money raised from various appeals. An additional "Administración" column listed the names of individual donations, which could be as modest as ten cents. Collectively, donations linked the paper to other centers of anarchism, most notably in Ybor City, Florida; Paterson, New Jersey; and cities in South America and Europe.[61]

The financial expressions of solidarity that helped enable publication of anarchist newspapers strengthened interpersonal connections within the radical community. Radicals invested in their shared cause by donating money to support the collective action they envisioned, one of the most critical ways in which they participated in a global movement. Kirwin Shaffer asserted that "anarchojournalism provided a space for average people to have a voice," but, just as important, he said, "it should be noted that not everyone could voice with their pen; sometimes the money they sent to the newspaper's editors spoke just as loudly for them."[62] Even a small amount of money created both a tangible link and a feeling of connection between the giver and receiver. Money, together with this emotive union, the content of newspapers, and personal correspondence, strengthened the perception of community in the anarchist movement beyond resting at the level of the "imagined." Newspapers themselves also supported other groups and publishing projects around the world through direct financial contributions.

Distributing the Radical Press

The United States Postal Service maintained the distribution infrastructure of the only financially viable way for anarchist newspapers to reach individual subscribers outside of their place of publication. Newspaper editors had to apply for a second-class mail permit from the Postal Service to access reduced periodical rates. Papers that were granted the permit carried a column similar to this one from *Regeneración*: "Entered as second-class matter September 12, 1910, at the post office at Los Angeles, California, under the Act of March 3, 1879."[63] Postal Service distribution provided an avenue of repression as the Comstock Law empowered postal inspectors to prohibit "obscene" material from passing through the mail. Relying on the USPS also created bureaucratic mechanizations of control. In 1906 postal authorities rejected *Regeneración*'s mailing permit because, they argued, over half of its circulation went to Mexico.[64] These methods of governmental oversight became one avenue for the federal government's repression of radical periodicals before World War I.

The origins of the Postal Service in the nineteenth century increase the significance of this form of repression. David Henkin argued that "from its creation, the U.S. Post Office was committed principally to facilitating the wide circulation of political news, allowing an informed citizenry to live far from the metropolitan centers of government while remaining active in its affairs. Individual letter-writers, typically merchants, were depended upon to absorb the costs of this political commitment by subsidizing an extremely low rate on newspapers."[65] This policy changed over the century, and as individual letter writing increased, "postal reformers envisioned a mail system in which the state simply encouraged and regulated high volumes of unspecified exchange between customers" rather than using "their monopoly over postal transmission to facilitate and legitimate particular types of political speech."[66] The passing of the Comstock Law in 1873 shifted the role of government in regulating private communication and political speech.

A broad circulation was not just politically desirable for radicals, it was a financial necessity. Surviving subscription lists and circulation information for *Regeneración* allow for a close examination of its distribution. In 1906, perhaps fifteen thousand copies a week rolled off the press. Seventeen thousand issues circulated when William C. Owen assumed the editing duties of the English page in 1911. In a deportation hearing in 1920 Enrique Flores Magón stated that circulation reached twenty-two thousand, but he did not give a year for that number. Table 3 is based on a *Regeneración* subscription list from November 22, 1915, seized by authorities and entered into evidence against Ricardo and Enrique Flores Magón in their 1916 trial for sending obscene materials through the mail. In 1915, the staff printed 3,986 copies of the paper and had 2,619 people on the subscription list. The PLM's grassroots organizational structure had withered by this time, and its leaders faced repeated periods of incarceration in the United States. Its influence in Mexico also decreased substantially. The geographic distribution should be representative of years with higher circulation.[67]

Table 3 shows readers concentrated in Texas and California, and it reveals the paper's strong distribution in Mexico after the Baja raids, in a later period of the revolution. The difference between the number of subscribers and the number of newspapers printed is due to the shipment of bundles for secondary distribution and locals sales. Large bundle orders for onward local distribution in the United States usually moved through couriers, not the postal service. Issues were also sold locally on the streets, from periodical carts, and in bookstores. Qualitatively,

TABLE 3. *Regeneración* Distribution by Leading Destination (Subscribers and Papers), November 22, 1915

	Subscribers		Papers	
Total distribution	2,619	(100%)	3,986	(100%)
Texas	1,052	(40.1%)	1,672	(41.9%)
California	451	(17.2%)	534	(13.3%)
Mexico	74	(2.8%)	500	(12.5%)
Cuba	136	(5.2%)	198	(4.9%)
Arizona	168	(6.4%)	172	(4.3%)
Subtotal of leading destinations	1,881	(71.7%)	3,076	(77.2%)

Source: Sandos, *Rebellion in the Borderlands*, 59.

CHAPTER 2

Tom Bell recalled the crucial role that print media played in organizing across distance during this period. He wrote, "Rural Mexicans were reached, most of them by *Regeneración*.[68]

In addition to individual subscribers and bundle orders, the editorial staffs of other newspapers received copies of *Regeneración*, which further extended the paper's reach. This was most often part of formal news exchanges between papers that worked to expand the coverage of all the papers involved. The socialist *California Social Democrat*, IWW-affiliated *El Rebelde*, in addition to the *Daily Tribune Reporter* and *Pacific Press*, received copies of *Regeneración* in this fashion. The Russian-language *Velikij Okean* and *Chung Sai Yat Po*, a Chinese-language paper in San Francisco, also participated in the exchange. Moreover, the Pacific News Agency in San Diego, *American Economist*, the *Seattle Herald*, and the *Seattle Star* subscribed. The Los Angeles Public Library and Columbia University's library in New York both received weekly issues of *Regeneración*, and San Diego's Carnegie Free Library subscribed to the *Industrial Worker* in 1909. One individual, Gabriel Renteria, even received his copy while incarcerated in the Los Angeles County Jail.[69]

As newspapers created and extended communities of solidarity through subscriptions and distribution, they, in turn, relied on the community they nurtured in difficult times, such as when authorities made sending papers through the mail difficult. This could be as simple as subscribers continuing to offer financial contributions, as was the case after postal authorities revoked second-class mailing privileges for Alexander Berkman's paper *The Blast*. Charlotte Anita Whitney wrote to Alexander Berkman in May 1916: "I saw in a recent copy of 'Regeneracion' that your paper has been suppressed. I am always anxious to see just what does excite the ire of the gentlemen that sit in the seats of the mighty in Washington so I am enclosing ten cents for copies of your paper. I am also sending the hope that soon we may emerge out of darkness with freedom of speech and of press."[70]

Support came in other crucial forms. Tom Bell wrote about how his family helped distribute *The Blast*, produced in San Francisco: "When the Blast was refused the mails . . . it was my children who when the bundle of papers was sent by express to us in Phoenix, Arizona, kept mailing them two or three at a time so as not to attract attention to them."[71] At the same time, Walter Sheridan, secretary of the IWW branch in the Imperial Valley town of Brawley, supported the paper by buying a "bundle order" of *The Blast* directly from Alexander Berkman.[72]

Apart from mailing copies to subscribers, most newspapers relied on additional forms of distribution. In Los Angeles, Rómulo Carmona's bookstore, Librería-Mexicana, was an important local distribution point for radical periodicals and other printed material. A contemporary sociologist observed: "There is one im-

56

portant Mexican bookstore. . . . Here books, papers and magazines of all kinds are sold. Cheap fiction of the very crudest type predominates in the stock of books but dictionaries, works of science and religion are also included in the assortment. This store carries rather a complete collection of the important magazines and papers published in Mexico and those published in Spanish in the United States with a few foreign Spanish papers."[73] Carmona sourced books in Spain from "Francisco Sempere publishing house in Valencia and the 'La Escuela Moderna' in Barcelona" in addition to "Spanish-language publishers in San Antonio, St. Louis, and elsewhere in the United States."[74]

Vendors also distributed newspapers through periodical carts. On a normal day, between three and five set up shop "along North Main Street between the Post Office and the Plaza." The operators of the carts paid a small licensing fee and earned a low wage of between "$1.00 to $2.00." The carts' "stock in trade [consists] of Spanish and Mexican papers, magazines and books. The papers range from 'El Imparcial,' the Los Angeles Times of Mexico City, to 'Regeneración,' the most radical paper published in Los Angeles."[75]

Residents of Los Angeles broadened the scope of this print culture through their subscriptions to papers printed elsewhere, which created direct financial connections between Los Angeles and the various places of publication. Many newspapers published in Mexico traveled through the mail to the city. At mid-decade, the paper *Tribuna Roja* emerged as an important anarchist organ for both countries. Grupo Germinal, connected to the Casa del Obrero Mundial (International House of Labor) in Tampico, published the paper. The first issue appeared in the winter of 1915, but Mexican authorities under Venustiano Carranza suppressed it around September 1916 when they arrested the leaders of the House of Labor. Another issue surfaced as part of a new series in August 1917. The locations on its subscription list read like a map of Spanish-language radicalism in the United States: Metcalf, Morenci, Globe, and Superior in Arizona; Ybor City, Tampa, and West Tampa in Florida; a page of names living in Texas; and Brawley, Holtville, San Francisco, Redding, and Los Angeles in California.[76]

Spanish-language anarchist newspapers circulated throughout the Americas. Another newspaper that made its way north from Mexico was *Evolución Obrera,* published in Toluca. The paper expressed solidarity with workers to the north, and one issue included "an objectionable article on Thomas Mooney, who is declared to have been murdered in the United States." American postal inspectors noted further that the "references made to the American Government are particularly obnoxious, and this item should be confiscated."[77] Moving the other direction, New York's *Cultura Obrera* achieved broad circulation among Spanish-speaking anarchists. The Military Intelligence Division noted in 1918 that "bundles containing from twenty-five to fifty copies of 'Cultura Obrera'—400 West Street,

CHAPTER 2

New York, have been distributed lately through the mining centers of Mexico." Other newspapers circulating included the anarchist organs *El Hombre*, published in Montevideo, Uruguay, and *La Capital* from Rosario, Argentina. Another, *El Diario*, published in Asunción, Paraguay, attracted attention in 1918 for writing about the labor conditions in England. Not only was the anarchist press circulated broadly, the events in which anarchists participated made worldwide news in major dailies. For instance, a full account of the San Diego IWW free-speech fight in 1912 ran in the *Evening News* in Sydney, Australia.[78]

Reporting the News and Spreading the Word

Radicals worked diligently to increase the usefulness of their newspapers through the content that they published. Anarchists, Wobblies, and socialists used their newspapers explicitly as propaganda tools to spread their ideas and as organizational instruments to elicit action. Several radical papers published in the region were multilingual to reach the broadest possible audience. For example, while Ludovico Caminita, the former editor of Italian-language anarchist newspaper *L'Era Nuova* (Paterson, New Jersey), resided in Los Angeles, he put his journalism skills to work at *Regeneración*. Through his efforts, *Regeneración* added an Italian-language section and eventually a separate Italian edition. The Italian column ran from July 1911 to April 1912, which made the paper trilingual—Spanish, English, and Italian—during this period. The Italian-language edition ran for a shorter period, from July 15, 1911, to at least October 28, 1911.

Cogito, Ergo Sum, a short-lived four-page weekly anarchist newspaper published in San Francisco dedicated one full page each to French, Spanish, and Italian, while it ran an article in each language on the front page. In its first issue in September 1908, a number of writers welcomed the publication of the paper, including the prominent Spanish anarchist based on the East Coast, Jaime Vidal. He translated the title of the paper, *I think; therefore, I am*, into Spanish, *Pienso, Luego Soy*, and saw the paper as a vehicle to "express our desires in one language, but to save time it will be printed in three languages."[79] Writers also appealed to transnational linguistic similarities. For instance, in New York's *Cultura Proletaria*, Jaime Vidal wrote to "all Spanish speaking people in the United States," rejecting nationality to appeal to the Spanish language as the common link in "California, Texas, Florida, etc."[80]

Multilingual papers expanded their reach into diverse linguistic communities at the same time that monolingual papers relied on linguistically talented contributors to translate news for publication. In Los Angeles Alfred Sanftleben, a Swiss-born immigrant who "speaks and writes four languages and reads seven," remained a key figure in the Los Angeles Left into the 1930s, while editing a column variously titled "foreign notes" in many socialist and anarchist papers.[81] The

Alfred Sanftleben, 1947. (University of Michigan Library Digital Collections)

column offered a roundup of world labor events that he gleaned from reading an impressive range of international papers. Sanftleben first introduced the PLM to English-speaking socialists as the Mexican "rebels" in November 1906 in *Common Sense*. He wrote about the group in relation to striking textile workers in Orizaba, Veracruz.[82] Sanftleben supported the PLM during its early years in Los Angeles and eventually became the first editor of the English page of *Regeneración* when its publication resumed in 1910. Before 1910, the socialist paper *Common Sense* relied on Sanftleben's language skills to extend its coverage.

CHAPTER 2

Sanftleben individually expanded internationalism on the printed page in Los Angeles. He also added another layer to the practice of internationalism through the friendships and correspondence he maintained with many prominent European anarchists, including Max Baginski, Gustav Landauer, Max Nettlau, and Rudolf Rocker. Sanftleben connected Los Angeles to the movement abroad in a direct personal manner, which he then mediated to the readership of the periodicals to which he contributed.

Newspapers occasionally published reports from foreign correspondents, as was the case when *Common Sense* printed an article titled "a German Comrade Writes from Mexico," which informed readers of a strike by Mexican textile workers in Puebla and Orizaba in October 1907.[83] *Common Sense* published translated articles, on one occasion from the "oldest democratic newspaper in the German language published in Southern California," *Sued Kalifornische Post*, which commented on the socialist free speech fight in 1908: "Viewed from an impartial standpoint these arrests are an injustice comparable to the police administration of countries with an absolutist government."[84]

Anarchists accessed the popular press on occasion as well as drew insights from works published by authors who were not anarchists. This grew from an interest in understanding the world that reached beyond politics in the traditional sense. An example is the travel writing of Harry Alverson Franck, which William C. Owen compared to Peter Kropotkin's *Autobiography of a Revolutionist*. The *Atlantic Monthly* serialized the important piece by the Russian thinker, giving it a wide readership in between his two visits to the United States in 1897 and 1901. Owen reflected on the quality of this work as "its charm and value lay in the comments on individual and social life in the numerous countries visited by Kropotkin." He wrote of Franck's writings in the same regard: "I have found of late a treasure-house in 'A Vagabond Tramp [*sic*] Around the World,' by Harry A. Franck, with its life sketches of workers and of the treatment meted out by the authorities to the penniless and outcast."[85]

The radical press most certainly also sought to elicit action. Before the PLM organized raids into Baja California in the winter of 1910–11, The English-language socialist weekly *People's Paper* openly solicited arms for the planned revolt. Later, people displaced by the Mexican Revolution wrote to *Regeneración* trying to track down relatives. Additionally, scholars of Italian anarchists have argued that some papers also contained "coded messages" for certain knowledgeable readers. The IWW used its West Coast print organ the *Industrial Worker* to give advanced notice of the Fresno free-speech fight and to warn fellow workers to avoid traveling to regions with poor job conditions.[86]

Consuming the Radical Press

Readership and community expanded yet again through consuming the radical press. A well-documented example of institutionalized group readership occurred in Ybor City's cigar industry. *Lectores* reading aloud to the cigar workers on the job "symbolized the independence, distinctiveness, and artisan character of cigar work."[87] In Barcelona anarchists formed reading clubs away from workplaces.[88] Similar practices occurred informally among friends and comrades in public and private spaces. People commonly read periodicals aloud in many communities, if not at work, then at local clubs and especially radical libraries. Enrique Flores Magón told an immigration inspector that "you may multiply" the circulation of *Regeneración* "by 20's because many papers go from hand to hand and are read in groups."[89] Teodocio Nerauchi, an IWW organizer, told his Bureau of Investigation interrogator upon his arrest that *Cultura Obrera* was "being passed around at the Spanish Cafes, and that the three copies found on his person (inside his shirt) were thus handed to him."[90] Edward Fulton provided another example of this practice when writing to his comrade William C. Owen in 1928: "I get a Japanese anarchist paper, published in Tokio. It comes as an exchange. A Japanese 'Chop Suey' man tells me what it says. So you see our party is world wide."[91]

People supplemented the individual- and movement-level international connections created on the page by sharing their experiences from travels abroad. For instance, on a Sunday night in February 1909, an audience packed Los Angeles's Mammoth Hall to listen to a local laborite named Jack Wood recount his service in the British Army in both Ireland and India. While he emphasized the exoticism of faraway lands, especially in India, he also criticized Western and British imperialism: "Alexander the Great wanted India three centuries before Christ. And the Dutch wanted it, and the Portuguese, and the French! Why? Because India is a valuable country and rich. England wanted it and got it. And the Hindoos haven't got it. And that's the cause of troubles past and present."[92] Likewise, people living abroad traveled through Los Angles sharing their experiences in the movement. In March 1907 James Rosen, a socialist from Buenos Aires, stopped in town and gave area residents "interesting details on the labor conditions in several South American Republics." The editors of *Common Sense* thought it "refreshing and encouraging to meet earnest, faithful workers like him, men who literally devote their lives to the cause wherever they go."[93] Lectures such as this satisfied people's interest in understanding the world. They also provided the leftist movement in Los Angeles broadly and those in the audience specifically with personal connections to places they read about.

CHAPTER 2

The Global Anarchist Press

Connections within the Spanish-language anarchist movement in Los Angeles, the Southwest, Mexico, Cuba, and then elsewhere in the Americas drew these locations together into the "Trans-Mexican Network."[94] This was part of a broader set of "overlapping networks of anarchists" predominately among Spanish- and Italian-language speakers: Transatlantic, East Coast of North America, greater Caribbean, U.S.-Mexico, Pacific Coast of South America, Andean, and Río de la Plata.[95] Newspapers, among the other vital social and monetary community support structures, held these networks together. Additionally, anarchist newspapers in other languages consumed in Los Angeles intertwined the city in Pacific and Atlantic radical networks. The synergy of these connections turned Los Angeles into a radical hub of global significance. Newspapers produced by the IWW functioned similarly, as the vital "instrument in the propagation of its ideas and strategies across cultures was a decentralized but well-connected press that emerged in small and large cities throughout Latin America and which was linked in a variety of ways to its predecessors in the United States and Australia. The press itself was transnational in its orientation, nearly always promoting class solidarity above national identity and crossing borders either in the hands of Wobblies on ships or even relocating in exile."[96] Anarchist and IWW newspapers are the visible artifacts remaining from these networks, and they provide an important window onto the strength and interconnections of the global movement.

In 1926 while living in Berlin, the anarchist scribe Diego Abad de Santillan took stock of the global movement for the Buenos Aires anarchist newspaper *La Protesta*. The *Road to Freedom* carried an extensive discussion of his article for its English language readers. Abad de Santillan turned to the most visible sign of the anarchist movement: newspapers. He looked to an 1894 list of anarchist periodicals, compiled by Alfred Sanftleben before he moved to Los Angeles, published in Berlin's *Der Sozialist*. The 1894 list organized papers by language and noted: "German 10, Holland Dutch 2, English 5, Yiddish 1, Italian 13, Spanish 11, Czechoslovak 5, Polish 1, Portuguese 2."[97]

In the thirty years after the publication of the list the world order changed substantially: "fascism in Italy, military dictatorship in Spain, bolshevism in Russia, police dictatorship in Brazil, and the disasters of the world war." Despite this, Abad de Santillan found that the number of anarchist newspapers in print had increased in 1925: "16 in Italian, 10 in French, 42 in Spanish, 8 in German, 2 in English, 3 in Portuguese, 3 in Yiddish, 1 in Polish, 4 in Scandinavian languages, 6 in Holland Dutch, 2 in Japanese, 3 in Russian, 4 in Chinese." The total grew from sixty-three anarchist newspapers in regular circulation in 1894 to 104 in 1925. In Latin America the count grew from nine to thirty-four. Abad de Santillan described a more difficult situation in the United States. Jewish groups continued to make progress, "as the *Freie Arbeiter Stimme* of New York gets support from an infinite number of groups in the United States, Canada, South America, Russia, France, England and elsewhere." They fared far better than other groups in the country: "The Anglo-saxon countries remained stationary, if not to say that they actually retrogressed. The United States reported 9 organs in 1894, and 9 are published today, almost all of them in Spanish, Italian, Russian, and but one in English, the *Road to Freedom*."[98] This arc of time caught both the ascendant and descendant sides of a curve in the number of English-language anarchist publications in the United States. However, examining circulation figures rather than the number of newspapers alters Abad de Santillan's conclusion.

The circulation of anarchist newspapers published in the United States grew steadily from approximately twenty-thousand in the 1880s to nearly 120,000 in 1910. These numbers declined drastically as the "collapse of anarchism's German-speaking wing" followed by state repression in the World War I years. The number of subscriptions reached a low point in 1920 of around twenty thousand before recovering slightly, maintaining numbers between twenty thousand and forty thousand until 1940.[99] Subscribers spread their attention over a list of titles across the range of languages spoken by early-twentieth-century immigrants. Abad de Santillan correctly identified the weakness of the English-language anarchist press in the mid-1920s, but the steady circulation of anarchist newspapers evidenced the continued viability of the anarchist movement after World War I repression.

As a point of comparison, the *New York Times* circulated 175,000 issues in 1910, making the combined circulation figures of anarchist newspapers during the year of their high point in the United States roughly two-thirds of the country's most important daily.[100] When considered collectively, anarchist newspapers constituted a mass media. The comparison also illustrates the limited reach of any single mainstream periodical in this period, and anarchist newspapers fit within a remarkably diverse print milieu in the United States. Most cities had multiple morning and evening newspapers competing for eyes, money, and influence.

Another factor contributed to the arc of anarchist newspaper circulation. The cost of paper rose dramatically during World War I and remained high into the 1920s. Newsprint in New York City cost thirty-six dollars a ton in 1900. The same quantity cost forty-one dollars in 1915 and nearly eighty dollars in 1918. It reached its peak price of $112 in 1920 and then cost between seventy and eighty dollars for most of the decade. Anecdotally, prices could be higher in the U.S. West. Michael Stamm argued that "many newspapers around the country feared that they would be unable to stay in business because of the increased cost of newsprint."[101] The additional weight of political repression increased this challenge for anarchists.

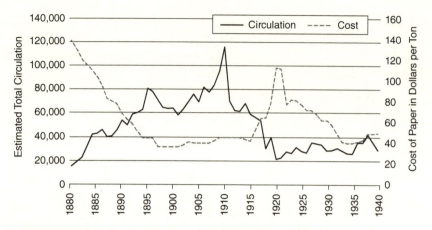

Anarchist periodical circulation and paper cost comparison. (Sources: Michael Stamm, "The Space for News," *Media History* 21, 1:55–73; Kenyon Zimmer, *Immigrants against the State* [University of Illinois Press, 2015], 6.)

They faced continued high prices for paper in the 1920s as they tried to rebuild their movement after wartime legal disruption.

■ ■ ■

The consistent feature throughout the varied content and outlooks of radical newspapers was that they included content relevant across space. Publishers balanced local news with theory and interpretation along different scales of analysis. Kirwin Shaffer found that Caribbean "radicals framed an anarchist interpretation of their realities that was consistent across national borders."[102] This conclusion applies to newspapers produced and consumed in Los Angeles as well. The broad transnational appeal of anarchist newspapers connected the movement through physical copy, financially through subscriptions and donations, and intellectually through the content. The movement practices involved in financing, distributing, producing content, and consuming anarchist newspapers contributed to the strength of transnational anarchism during this period.

Anarchists invested many thousands of hours of labor and a significant amount of their limited financial resources in newspapers. Their commitment to the press layered on local, on-the-ground organizing. The creation of movement-controlled space and radicals meeting, protesting, and picnicking together as families formed the support structure for deep interpersonal connections on the Left. In Los Angeles, solidarity often spanned the breadth of the movement from trade unions to anarchism despite ideological differences. Political outlooks, coalitions, and actions varied over time, but the interplay of the creation of radical space, local organizing, and mediated connections helped generate the region's culture of affinity.

CHAPTER 3

SOLIDARITY AND THE LEGACY OF EXCLUSION

Anti-Asian violence and agitation, growing from the temporally overlapping erasure of indigenous people, functioned as an organizing principle of Anglo society on the West Coast from the first wave of Chinese immigration during California's gold rush, continued through peak periods of Japanese and South Asian immigration in the late nineteenth century and early twentieth century, and led to Japanese internment during World War II. Los Angeles residents perpetrated fewer acts of violence against Asians than elsewhere in the state, though this was only a matter of degree. In 1871 a white mob looted Chinatown and murdered around nineteen people during the Chinese Massacre. The city did not experience a recurrence of pogroms and other violence in the 1880s and 1890s like the outbursts elsewhere in the West. Los Angeles's relatively small Chinese community and slow population growth in the late nineteenth century limited violence, certainly more so than the outlook of its residents. As Japanese immigration increased toward the turn of the new century, the racial order in Los Angeles and the region carried forward the effects of anti-Asian violence through economic development and an influx of new residents.[1]

Anti-Asian organizing played an even more central role in California's white labor movement than it did in broader statewide politics and society. Organized labor stoked race hatred toward Chinese and other Asians to unite white workers, a well-documented process in which whites viewed class in racial terms.[2] The racist origin of California's labor movement in the 1880s cast a long shadow over organizing in the state. In 1893 the Los Angeles Trades and Labor Council led a grassroots anti-Chinese campaign to boycott anyone doing business with

CHAPTER 3

the city's Chinese residents and to insist on the enforcement of the Geary Act. They found a sympathetic figure in Judge Erskine Ross, who went against official orders coming from Washington to not enforce the act, and soon "labor unions and anti-Chinese citizens' committees were sweeping across the Southland with impunity."[3] This campaign ended a month and a half later after the judge ordered more than one hundred Chinese deported without the budgetary allocations to pay the expenses.

The centrality of now decades of anti-Chinese agitation by the white labor movement in California made interracial organizing in Oxnard, California, all the more important. The outlook of white trade union organizers in early-twentieth-century Los Angeles included this tradition of racism and selective solidarity, but also of leftist movements broader than "pure and simple" trade unionism.[4] As racial diversity increased in Los Angeles, three Anglo socialists—Lemuel Biddle, Fred Wheeler, and John Murray Jr.—drew on their understandings of internationalism while holding positions in Los Angeles's Council of Labor (COL) to publicize and assist organizing efforts by Japanese and Mexican laborers.

The COL's first action toward opening their union to the city's racially diverse workforce came in 1902 during an organizing campaign aimed at Mexican laborers in the city. Biddle and Murray worked together in this effort, which resulted in the formation of the AFL-chartered Federal Labor Union number 9614. As a federal union, it was not attached to a jobsite or single trade, an important consideration given the fluidity of the work life of most laborers. Murray joined the union along with a number of other Anglo socialists, and its members elected him to represent the new union on the labor council. The council president, James Gray, initially objected, but after Murray gained the support of Fred Wheeler, his appointment stood. On May 1, 1902, Biddle and Murray gave a well-attended speech, titled "May Day and the Trades Unions," at a celebration of the workers' holiday. The Socialist Party also nominated the pair for its local election ticket in 1902.[5] The union lasted only briefly, even with support from the COL, when most of its members joined the seasonal outflow of workers from the city to the fields. From the surviving sources it is difficult to gauge the support or participation this drive had among the Mexican laborers it sought to organize.

In January 1903 the California State Federation of Labor (CSFL) elected Wheeler to the newly created position of statewide organizer. The AFL national body supported this move when it voted at its 1903 convention in New Orleans to send an organizer to California for two months, despite resistance from some unions, including the shoemakers' union in Los Angeles. Fellow socialist Biddle aided Wheeler in this new position even though the state labor body did not pay him. Murray retained his seat on the labor council from the year prior. In spring 1903, Mexican organizers Alefo Fernandez and A. Nieto joined Biddle

66

and Wheeler. As the four strategized and laid the groundwork for a second union drive of Mexican laborers in Los Angeles, events in Oxnard grabbed headlines.[6]

The Japanese Mexican Farm Association

The city of Oxnard is about sixty miles west of Los Angeles in Ventura County. Quality soil and coastal moisture made it an ideal location for agriculture. Soon after the United States Congress levied a duty on sugar imports in 1897, the town's namesake Henry Oxnard opened a sugar-beet processing factory. Nearby farmers quickly shifted their cultivation priorities, and demand for agricultural workers grew rapidly to accommodate the labor-intensive sugar-beet crop. Mexican and Chinese workers initially filled these jobs, but Japanese overtook Chinese, a long-term effect of the Chinese Exclusion Act in 1882 that limited the availability of Chinese labor. As new workers arrived, they fit into a town with an established racial and spatial order.

Residential segregation undergirded by the proletarianization of non-Anglos divided Oxnard into racialized social worlds, with Anglos predominating in the west side and non-Anglos—Japanese, Chinese, and Mexican—carving out their own existence in the east side, each with identifiable neighborhoods. While racism limited opportunities for nonwhite residents, this spatial arrangement produced locations free from the surveillance of Anglos and resulted in a rich yet often rowdy social life. Newly immigrated single men predominated among Japanese, while many Mexicans were born in California and lived with their families. Japanese and Mexican field hands worked on segregated work crews yet shared work experiences and interacted in the community. The ready availability of jobs minimized competition. Japanese and Mexican field hands also migrated throughout the state and region as work and crops dictated.[7]

A third group of actors, labor contractors and recruiters, occupied a central position in this economy alongside workers and farmers by funneling human power to the fields. Often desperate for labor at crucial times in the growing cycle, farmers turned to Mexican, Japanese, or Chinese contractors for labor, which allowed the contractors considerable power in the beet-sugar business. A local socialist newspaper published a vivid description of the position of workers in relation to the contractors and owners:

> A person in a small office, furnished with a revolving chair and desk, undertakes to furnish laborers to the farmers. Beet Farmer says "I want a hundred men, for which I will pay $2.00 per day." "All right" says Easy Chair, and he goes to the boss Jap and says "Beet Farmer wants 100 men at $1.75 per day." "All right" says Boss Jap and he goes to the toilers and tells them that Beet Farmer wants

help and he will pay $1.50 a day and they can come to his store each Saturday night and get their money. And he does not forget to tell them that he keeps all kinds of supplies, and that he gets jobs for men who trade with him. At the end of one week Beet Farmer pays Easy Chair $1200; Easy Chair pays Boss Jap $1050, and Boss Jap pays the laborers $900.[8]

In this system, the position of contractors, who were usually the same race as the workers that they hired, created a layer of *intra*racial class conflict as the workers in Oxnard formed an *inter*racial union.

Many farmers viewed Japanese labor contractors, *Keiyaku-nin*, as a particular threat to their financial success given their ability to drive up pay rates. In 1902 wealthy Oxnard whites joined forces to reorganize the labor contracting system in Oxnard in their favor by forming the Western Agricultural Contracting Company (WACC). The WACC consolidated its position by requiring all the Japanese and Mexican labor contractors to subcontract through its representatives. The company retained the practice of relying on contractors of the same race and with the language ability to communicate with work crews. Inosuke Inose represented the WACC's Japanese interests; Albert Espinosa represented its Mexican interests. After an aggressive campaign in the 1902 season that saw WACC recruiters traveling through California to round up laborers, the organization eventually controlled 90 percent of sugar-beet contracts in Oxnard. In the winter offseason, local Japanese contractors used their time to organize a response for the next season.[9]

When the workers returned to the fields for the second season under the new contracting system in spring 1903, they faced a WACC wage cut. This created a two-tiered conflict in Oxnard: agricultural laborers wanted higher wages; the labor contractors pushed aside by the formation of the WACC sought to regain the position they had lost. Contractors and laborers formed the Japanese Mexican Labor Association (JMLA) in 1903 to combat the WACC wage cut by returning to the previous year's daily wage structure and inserting the union into the contracting process. The JMLA wanted to make tangible improvements in member's lives as they sought to negotiate labor contracts directly with the farmers. Institutionalizing the union in place of the prior contracting system would have dramatically altered the existing hierarchy, but the independent labor contractors in the JMLA complicated internal matters for the union.[10]

Japanese and Mexican workers showed their mutual solidarity by forming a single union, but for practical reasons the membership divided itself by nationality and language in two coequal branches. This continued the established nationality-based contracting system. Murray and Wheeler, both in Oxnard during the union's formation, probably helped more with bureaucratic formalities than organizing workers given their limited language ability. The members elected

Y. Yamaguchi and J. M. Lizarras as the secretaries of the Japanese and Mexican branches, respectively. Both men were labor contractors pushed out of work by the WACC. In the local socialist press, Lizarras expressed the union's desire to "keep the regular prices." John Murray wrote, "The figure in the case—and dollar and cents figures crop out in all the differences between capital and labor—are as follows: The old price for thinning beets per acre had been from five dollars up, but the company contractors forced the price down to four and a half and even four and a quarter." He contended that this price fell well below a "living wage."[11]

Recruiting workers into the new union took place in the fields and on the streets. Members held street meetings to rally workers to the cause, arguing for the potential power that the laborers could wield if they were well organized. Authorities arrested Yamaguchi for disturbing the peace at one outdoor gathering. After his release on five hundred dollars' bond, a jury acquitted him at trial. Organizers also carried the union message to the point of production. Two Japanese men, K. Obata and K. Yoshinari, found themselves on the wrong side of the law after they traveled to a farm to organize workers. They managed to recruit thirty Japanese men to the JMLA before the owner had them arrested for trespassing. A jury acquitted both because the landowner did not formally ask them to leave the property before their arrest—a sign of the rule of law and relatively open organizing terrain up until this point in time. In fact, it seems that many of Oxnard's Anglo residents supported the union. The *Ventura Free Press* wrote, "The union has the sympathy of the greater part of the residents of Oxnard and especially of the merchants who are willing to see the trade of hundreds of employees who work in the beet fields."[12]

The blossoming union showed its strength with a mass rally on March 6 where members wore buttons with the JMLA's initials over a rising sun and clasped hands. After a successful organizing campaign and with the WACC unwilling to negotiate, the union weighed its options, drawing on their knowledge of the sugar-beet crop. The most time-sensitive period of the growing cycle came after the newly planted seeds sprouted and needed to be thinned. The JMLA had grown to around eight hundred members, and they attempted to use this strength to negotiate with the WACC. The JMLA came to consensus over their demands in executive committee meetings that used English to bridge deeper discussions in Japanese and Spanish. The union asked Murray and Wheeler to represent them in a well-attended yet unsuccessful meeting with growers and the WACC, which refused to budge. This meeting also brought forward conflict between competing contractors within the JMLA, but without an agreement with the growers, this mattered little. After the unproductive meeting the union moved forward with plans to strike. Choosing this time for a work stoppage put the fledgling union in a position of great power if it could prevent the importation of strikebreakers, but this is what the WACC and farmers set out to do.[13]

On March 23 Charles Arnold, a notoriously anti-union beet farmer who had been deputized as a constable, parked his wagon on the street in front of the company-owned lodging house, attempted to load his wagon with nonunion laborers brought to town, and escort them to the fields. A large crowd of local onlookers and JMLA members stood about to gawk and to challenge this antagonistic act when "the last non-union man to get into the wagon carried a shot gun and as he passed a big Mexican the latter took the gun away from him." A volley of gunshots from the boardinghouse upon the union men crowded in the street below immediately followed. Some JMLA members or supporters who had brought guns along as well returned fire and injured two of the strikebreakers.[14]

The violence took the life of one union member; four other members, two Japanese and two Mexican, were seriously wounded. Perfecto Ogaz received the first bullet in his neck. Manuel Ramirez was shot in the leg, while another bullet ripped through Louis Vasquez's abdomen. S. Adachi's nose was "shot nearly off," and Suito took a bullet in his arm. Both Vasquez and Ogaz's wounds required the men be hospitalized. Vasquez succumbed to his wounds, from a bullet that pierced his bladder, at the county hospital three days later, turning the nineteen-year-old into California's first martyr to interracial unionization.[15]

On March 25 representatives of the farmers, the American Beet Sugar Company's factory manager, and the WACC's president came to the JMLA's headquarters to meet with union representatives J. Espinoza, J. M. Lizarras, Kōzaburō ("Joe") Baba, and Y. Yamguchi, an acknowledgment of the union's power. Members filled the small room to capacity, this being the first meeting since the bloodshed. The WACC offered to relinquish two thousand acres of its contracted land if the JMLA would allow nonunion men to work the remainder of the land it controlled. The union declined the offer, stating that it wanted to negotiate directly with the farmers. Murray, speaking at the end of the meeting, "intimated that they [the farmers] ought to be thankful that the union was not striking for a rise in wages."[16] On the morning of March 26 representatives of the farmers held council once more with the JMLA secretaries, this time at the processing plant. The union restated its demand to return to a wage of between five and six dollars per acre of thinned beets, but landowners remained reticent.[17]

The JMLA turned the inquest over Vasquez's death into a major rallying point for its cause. Justice of the Peace W. H. Harris planned to hold the meeting in his own office. When it became apparent that this space could not accommodate the crowd, the union offered to rent out Pioneer Hall to allow its supporters to attend. In the end the judge held the inquest in Ventura with merely an hour's notice given before the train carrying the officials departed. At the hearing many witnesses identified Arnold as having fired the initial shots, but the district attorney refused to charge him, as the inquest was only formally tasked with Vasquez's death. The coroner eventually released Vasquez's body to the union in "such a decayed condition that immediate burial was necessary, thereby attempting to prevent the public demonstration of a big funeral."[18] If, indeed, this was the tactic of authorities, it failed on all accounts. Several hundred Japanese and Mexican workers marched in procession "led by a drum and fife and standard bearers," while a large paper lotus flower lay on the hearse as an offering from his Japanese brothers. After services at the Catholic Church in El Rio, they laid him to rest in its cemetery.[19]

The union created a remarkably well-formed grassroots infrastructure to sustain its organizing: "They had a well-trained corps of officers—secretaries, interpreters, captains of squads, messengers, and most complete system of information. A map of the valley hung on the wall, with the location of the different camps of beet thinners plainly marked."[20] The union also stepped into the void of law and order after the bloodshed by forming a vigilance committee of union men to patrol their neighborhoods in town. The *Los Angeles Times* wrote of this turn of events with horror: "Last night the town was patrolled by armed Orientals ... passers by were startled at having oriental faces stuck out at them from dark corners." The paper continued with the following provocation, nearly an exhortation to race war: "Citizens are wondering how long the peace officers will permit the loud-mouthed agitators and the foreign unionists with guns to run the town. Indignation among the people is running high at the outrages allowed. Wonder is expressed that some of the 'nosing' Japs have not been shot in their tracks. They are liable to be if they stop more citizens."[21]

The mutual hostility continued when the president of the WACC, George Herz, told the *Los Angeles Times* that he remained "more determined than ever to establish its right to hire men, conduct its business in its own way, and keep faith with farmers." Further, he "intimated that the company will have men when the time comes, but as to the rumors that it had on the road a consignment of Huns, Italians or negroes, he had nothing to say. It is pretty certain if the first two races were imported that they would not right away make common cause with a horde of Orientals." As the WACC organized the importation of strikebreakers, the regional movement of workers continued. The Utah Sugar Company transported one hundred Japanese workers from Oxnard north to Ogden "on account of the scarcity of white labor for that work in Utah."[22]

Forced by the progression of beet growth that season, the JMLA won an uneasy victory on March 30 by making their labor unavailable when the crops required it. The WACC turned over five thousand acres' worth of contracts, keeping only eighteen-hundred acres.[23] The *People's Paper* celebrated this victory:

> Farmer after farmer who had previously sworn that "no union should dictate to him" came up meekly to the headquarters and took out a crew of union men with a great big flapping notice nailed to the tail board of his wagon that these were "Union Men." One old granger began to kick when it came to posting up the notice: "I ain't going to be made fun of boys, you can't stick that paper on my wagon." Off the wagon the boys all tumbled, throwing their blankets to the sidewalk at the same time, and the old gentleman immediately caved in. "Stick it up boys—paper the old cart from pole to tail board—but jump on again and lets get out to them beets." The boys put up their sign and once again loaded their blankets back on the belabeled farm wagon.[24]

But the landowners continued to challenge the union after this concession by attempting to import nonunion labor. On April 2 a labor recruiter traveled to Los Angeles to drum up strikebreakers. He rounded up 160 of them only to find out, just before they boarded the train, that one hundred had unionized themselves. A few weeks later owners attempted this same tactic again. This time they shipped seventy-three men, Japanese and Mexican, out to Oxnard from Los Angeles. The armed guards of the employers met them at the station. Union members came as well and persuaded the men to join the union. All seventy-three men left their wagons, walked to the union headquarters, and enrolled.[25]

The next union-breaking effort came when the manager of the family-owned Patterson Ranch in Oxnard, Mr. Roup, tried for himself to gather workers in Los Angeles to undermine the JMLA's control of labor. He gathered "42 negroes and Mexicans" and had them locked in their rail car for the trip to Oxnard, but when the train pulled into the Oxnard station, the men on board tossed their blankets out the windows and climbed out themselves. More drama followed: "The conversion of the last train load of 'strike breakers' was quite a sensational affair, the boys loading up their new converts in wagons and parading them through town with much cheering and applause, while the company's guards sneaked away from the station without a single victim in tow."[26]

Oxnard's small local Chinese population also caught the organizing spirit. On Wednesday, April 1, 1903, the first Chinese union of the AFL submitted an application to the COL. It left no other record and probably failed to move past this stage of organizing. John Murray speculated that it would be granted, as the COL had recently approved the organization of Asians but "of course putting itself on record as at all times being opposed to the admittance of Asiatic laborers to the United States."[27]

Two of Los Angeles's local Anglo-led carpenter unions, 332 and 426, sent money to Oxnard in support. The *Los Angeles Times* chided the president of the COL, Jim Gray, affiliated with the carpenters, and the rest of the COL for endorsing the Oxnard riot at a meeting—a meeting at which the union body resolved to unionize unskilled workers in Los Angeles of all races, even Asians.[28] However, the council made clear that the best interest of white labor motivated its newfound inclusion when it proclaimed: "We do declare our belief that the most effective method of protecting the American working man and his standard of living is by universal organization of wage workers regardless of race or nationality."[29] For his part, Murray observed (or, more accurately, hoped) that "the 'Riot at Oxnard' has made its mark upon the history of the International labor movement, and proved that workers of the world *will* unite."[30] Murray extended this line of thought when he wrote "the Japanese have proven themselves to be apt students of the international working-class movement that believes in a common ownership of the means of production and distribution. Their leaders in California—I speak of those whom I have met and talked with—one and all regard Socialism to be the logical conclusion of the trades union movement." Murray also celebrated broader organizing by Japanese and Mexicans in California under their "own volition."[31] There is little evidence to doubt the sincerity of Murray's high-minded and lofty rhetoric about the JMLA in frequent articles for Santa Barbara's socialist newspaper *People's Paper* and later in "A Foretaste of the Orient," published in the *International Socialist Review*. All the same, Murray's and other socialists' nationalism and desire to protect white workers during Socialist Party discussions over Japanese exclusion in 1907 shine through their use of internationalism, as we will see in chapter 4. Clearly, "unity" of the working class was a tiered relationship on the West Coast for many Anglos, and their vision differed from that of the region's multiracial working class. By April tension in Oxnard subsided just as organizing in Los Angeles took off anew.

La Unión Federal Mexicana

Two days after the bloody March day in Oxnard, the *Los Angeles Times* expressed concern that as the city developed economically, it would not be able to escape the social problems it associated with manufacturing growth. The paper claimed that the city avoided unrest like Oxnard's or in that which arose in the coal regions of Pennsylvania because it had "just begun to emerge from the pastoral state." It supported this reasoning with the belief that the city did not employ a "large number of ignorant foreigners" in a robust manufacturing sector. Though the *Times* doubted that as Los Angeles "grows in importance as a manufacturing city, [it] can remain free from the twin evils which unfortunately attach to manufacturing on a large scale, namely, smoke and strikes."[32] The dust had hardly settled from the violence in Oxnard when one-half of this prediction came true.

Alefo Fernandez and A. Nieto formed the Unión Federal Mexicana (UFM) with Lemuel Biddle in March, while Murray and Wheeler organized in Oxnard. Biddle had a longer-term connection to this organizing reaching back to the failed effort the year prior, and it seems likely that he played a more direct role assisting Fernandez and Nieto in actual organizing than Murray and Wheeler did in Oxnard. However, there is no indication that Biddle spoke Spanish, limiting even his best intentions. When Wheeler returned from Oxnard, he joined the work underway. Biddle, Murray, and Wheeler, all founding members of the Los Angeles's Socialist Party, viewed their efforts in the same context as their support for the JMLA in Oxnard, within a worldwide working-class movement. In an interview about Socialist Party support for track workers, Wheeler "waved his hand expressively to a motto on the wall of the County Council of Labor—to that shibboleth of International Socialism. 'Workingmen of all Countries Unite,' and said, 'It's coming.'"[33] Through the leadership of these men the Socialist Party supported this organizing, as did the COL in Los Angeles.[34] Later, Murray claimed that San Francisco's Mayor Schmitz and Samuel Gompers himself approved of "this new regiment to the army of organized labor."[35] The UFM's struggle combined support from these Anglo institutions while the intense community-based labor in this organizing campaign came from Mexicans in Los Angeles.

The commitment of the Mexican community organizing became clear on April 24, 1903, when about eight hundred members of the Unión Federal Mexicana walked off their construction jobs laying the rails for Henry Huntington's streetcars downtown. They demanded union recognition and a wage increase to $1.25 for a ten-hour day. Police quickly sided against the workers and introduced some strikers to their clubs, arresting others. Many workers in Los Angeles felt the connection to Oxnard as vividly as the city's leading evening paper had a few months before. John Murray claimed that through their heavy-handed tactics, the police risked turning this into another "Oxnard Riot."[36]

The Monday after the laborers walked off the job, evidence of their broad-based support in the Mexican community became apparent. That day the well-traveled and enigmatic Teresa Urrea, popularly known as La Santa de Cabora, revered as a saint and healer by many Mexicans, led a large "crowd of Mexican women" in a march down the railroad tracks in support of the striking workers.[37] These women roused local passions enough to gather fifty new members into the union. The march led to the COL's meeting hall and filled it to standing-room-only capacity. An enthusiastic bilingual meeting conducted in Spanish and English followed. However, in the assessment of English-language socialist press, their inability to gather the support of "some hundred or two negroes, Italians, Scandinavians and Japanese who were in no labor organization and were, in many cases, unable to understand Spanish or English"—the two primary languages of the union—prevented them reaching their full potential that day.[38]

The Unión Federal Mexicana and the COL cultivated support in the Mexican community, especially from women, through personal and family networks. An example of these often-undocumented efforts is visible in a communiqué addressed "To the Wives of the Union." It read in part:

> This circular has as its only object to call attention to the fact of the worst enemy of the union and Mexican workingmen. M. Hamburger, proprietor of an establishment called "People's Store," situated on North Spring street. If he and his comrades, Otis of The Times and Huntington of the street railway company, should have us under their control, not only ourselves, but our families, would be obliged to eat dog meat.
>
> Every good member and loving patriot of Mexican independence who has the conviction that the union deserves better treatment than its slaves should never go into the Hamburger store. If you do otherwise you will offend our compatriots. Make up your mind not to spend any money at Hamburger because he is one of the worst enemies of the union and independent and patriotic Mexicans.[39]

With this the union opened a second front in a contest previously limited to the control of their labor power. They now sought to influence the labor struggle by controlling their spending power, however limited. The COL organized the boycott of A. Hamburger and Sons' People's Store because of the owner's connection to the anti-union *Los Angeles Times*. Hamburger had established an anti-union association of local businessmen with Otis and advertised heavily in the *Times*. The COL sought to incorporate Los Angeles's Mexican population into its effort by encouraging them to join in the boycott.[40]

The names of the two Mexican men who signed the flyer went unrecorded in the *Los Angeles Times*. Rather, the newspaper directed its anger at Biddle, calling him a "cowardly white agitator" and accusing him of hiding "behind the names of two of his Mexican Dupes." "The dodge bears the stamp of the 'Los Angeles Council, American Federation of Labor,' which shows that the bosses have placed the body of white union labor on an equal footing as 'brothers' with the cholos."[41]

At the start of the strike the union claimed eight hundred members. This number swelled to fourteen hundred by April 28, and they needed support. Biddle appealed to the Anglo readers of the *People's Paper* for assistance for those out of work throughout the strike. He stated that eight hundred members initially out on strike left twenty-five hundred people in need, including dependents.[42] His statement provides further evidence of the attention the organizers placed on the community-based effort. If the union hoped that workers' families would observe a boycott on behalf of laborers' larger interests, families had to be included in the COL's support structure. The Unión Federal Mexicana continued to receive support from socialists, and the *Los Angeles Socialist* printed an appeal on behalf of the union in Spanish.[43] Encouraged by the progress, Murray optimistically observed that "throughout all this trouble the Mexican unionist has shown himself to be the equal of any trades unionist in the land, and the greatest of all victories has already been won in Los Angeles, namely unity."[44] Within a trade-union framework, however, Murray's "unity" meant organized Mexicans laboring in a lower-tier occupation and being paid less than whites in the so-called skilled trades.

Through this wave of agitation, Huntington's company delayed, attempting to wait out the track laborers. The *Times* noted on April 30 that "several days ago a helper's union made demand for $2.25 a day, an advance of 25 cents a day, but it was stipulated that an answer could be made on or before May 1."[45] The company undoubtedly trusted its ability to replace the workers, preventing the need to negotiate with the union.

Huntington's company also sought to break the strike by importing Mexican workers from El Paso, the border crossing for many of the Mexicans already in Los Angeles. Unión Federal Mexicana organizers used their knowledge of and connections along the path of labor migration to communicate the situation with the incoming workers. A. M. Nieto told a reporter for the *Record*, "We have sent word to Mexico" through family members to not come to work as strikebreakers in Los Angeles.[46] Through these means the union prompted potential strikebreakers bound for Los Angeles to exit their trains in Yuma, Arizona, and Volcano Springs, California (Mundo today). The company then turned to African American and Japanese workers to replace the Mexican strikers.[47]

The UFM responded by turning their attention toward organizing Japanese workers. The union in Los Angeles recognized the cultural and linguistic challenge of their Mexican membership organizing Japanese workers, so it arranged with the JMLA in Oxnard to send several of its Japanese members to Los Angeles to lend their organizing assistance. The Oxnard sugar-beet workers also sent monetary assistance to their fellow workers in Los Angeles.[48] The *Los Angeles Times* took note of the new effort to include Japanese workers: "Not content with causing a strike among the ignorant peon laborers and thereby jeopardizing the lives of peaceable citizens, the walking delegate is tainting the minds of the electric-railway's Japanese employees. The plan is to organize a 'Japanese Federal Union.'"[49] The connections between Oxnard and Los Angeles came full circle. Anglo organizers from Los Angeles assisted the Oxnard struggle. Indeed, they significantly contributed to the strength of the organization in that city. Just as surely, the JMLA helped the organizing drive in Los Angeles when it returned the favor by sending some of its Japanese members to Los Angeles to lend a hand in organizing with their cultural entrée and language skills.

There is no mention in the historical record of the UFM attempting to organize African American workers. It seems not to have occurred, which surely weakened the union. The one sign of an opening in this direction of organizing came when the socialist press celebrated that a number of African Americans jumped out of their train car in Oxnard and refused to cross the JMLA picket line. When the socialist *People's Paper* covered this event, it made note of the men's race while praising their solidarity. Japanese workers shared the position with Mexicans as the major source of unskilled labor in Los Angeles at this time, which tended to deflect some of the harshest manifestations of racism toward African Americans. During UFM organizing, the socialist press tended to view African Americans as part of a cosmopolitan but unorganized horde that had not yet seen the power of unionization.[50] Salvation, theoretically, was available to all if they joined the just cause of labor, while the allocation of organizing resources evidenced the racial priorities of trade-union and socialist organizing. Given African Americans' strong representation in the semi-skilled service sector and the racism excluding them from many skilled trades, it is certainly also clear that many would not have seen Los Angeles trade unions as path for personal or community betterment.[51]

For a week the Unión Federal Mexicana succeeded in keeping most of its affiliated workers off the job through its strong community support structure. The next turn of events came on April 29 when white streetcar operators were to join the striking track workers. The organizers of the strike hoped to tie up traffic by having drivers leave their streetcars in place throughout the city as they walked off the job. The first driver abandoned his car at Spring and Fifth Streets, but by all accounts the strike fizzled quite magnificently when only twelve out of seven hundred operators participated. Still, the COL rallied behind the effort, and during a meeting that day in support of the drivers "a motion carried to adjourn" so those gathered could "give a physical demonstration of sympathy." Eighty-five attendees then marched down Fifth Street, with, according to the *Los Angeles Times*, "'Czar' Jim Gray, Socialist Editor Murray, Agitator Biddle and other notorious ones in the ranks." They walked along the tracks, encouraging riders and workers to exit the railcars. The group then marched to the city's maintenance barn and tried to get men out of the cars until the police arrived. An additional twenty linemen quit in the "western part of the city," far from enough workers to make the job action effective. The failure also took the wind from the sails of the striking track workers in the UFM.[52]

In response to the unrest the *Los Angeles Times* issued a similar exhortation to class warfare as it had made to race war in Oxnard two months prior: "The union agitators active in this trouble, local and foreign, should be ordered out of the city by the police as any other dangerous criminals would be. If that course would not reach them the public should rise up and drive them out, and I predict that if they keep up their distardly [*sic*] work the latter action will be taken." The article attributed this statement to a "prominent citizen," but the paper clearly endorsed the sentiment. The *Times* also labeled Biddle and others in the COL as "Peon Seducers," claiming that they needlessly aroused the foreign workers.[53]

Failure and Hope in Oxnard and Los Angeles

As the thinning season drew to completion in Oxnard in April the JMLA appeared to have imposed its will upon the farmers. The union successfully defended its position from strikebreakers, ended the domination of the WACC, and restored its members' original wages. It is less clear how far the union inserted itself as the negotiator of labor contracts in place of the Japanese and Mexican contractors independent of the WACC.[54] The JMLA entered into contracts during the spring of 1903, but it was unable to do so again during the next season. One reason for their difficulty in turning their organizing skills and enthusiasm into a sustainable union is directly attributable to the AFL and Samuel Gompers. The JMLA filed for official charter with the national body of the AFL in April. Samuel Gompers accepted the Mexican branch but not the Japanese branch in a letter to the union on May 13. Gompers overruled local labor consensus, as the JMLA had the support of Los Angeles's COL.[55]

Gompers was not a distant bureaucrat when he made this decision. He had visited Los Angeles as recently as the previous summer to tour the region and to meet with the city's labor council. On this visit his traveling companions preceded his arrival by a few days, and a brass band warmly received them at the train station.[56] The organizing efforts of the JMLA, especially given the local AFL support, offered the AFL an opportunity to reexamine its racist policies. Yet Gompers once again made it clear that Asians had no place within the house of labor. He attributed his decision to his desire to abide by immigration laws that barred entry to Chinese and "propositions for the extension of the exclusion laws to the Japanese."[57]

Upon receiving Gompers's letter the Mexican branch of the JMLA declined to sell out the Japanese workers with whom they had bled: "Better go to hell with your family than to heaven by yourself," a speaker at a public gathering declared.[58] The *Los Angeles Times* speculated that Gompers's refusal to recognize the union would mean its end. This certainly contributed, but the withdrawal of the Japanese labor contractors pushed aside by the formation of the WACC made this result even more certain. Another perennial regional organizing problem also contributed. After the local growing season ended many workers left Oxnard for other parts of California or farther afield in search of employment, which made maintaining a lasting institutional union presence exceptionally difficult. Still others traveled for more personal reasons. The secretary of the Japanese section, Y. Yamaguchi, returned to Japan to tend to the affairs of his ailing father that spring, but before leaving California he promised to correspond with the *People's Paper* about the state of the labor movement in Japan.[59]

In June, John Murray reflected on the impact of the Gompers's rejection of the JMLA and the failure of the UFM in Los Angeles. Murray attributed the failure of the UFM to "our inability to promise the Japanese, who were at work on the road, admission into the A. F. of L." He went on to place the blame squarely at the feet of Samuel Gompers:

> How could we ask them [the Japanese] to come out with their Mexican co-workers when no recognition of their organization and a denial of their rights as wage-workers would be all their reward? It was at the risk of broken heads and starvation that the Mexican Federal Labor Union of Los Angeles was formed—for the police used their clubs on the men who dared to lay down their tools—and in such warfare to raise race prejudice is unpardonably folly, a folly for which President Gompers must soon answer to the unions of southern California who are unanimous in demanding recognition for their brother wage-workers, the Japanese.[60]

The rejection of the JMLA's charter by the AFL and of the failure of the UFM by its inability to include Japanese workers and others to its cause marked a serious setback for proponents of interracial unionization under the AFL in the region. In September 1903 the JMLA joined the Labor Day parade in Santa Barbara, one of its last recorded actions.[61]

In 1904 the COL once again attempted to organize within the UFM organization, marking the third year in a row of its organizing with Mexicans in the city. The COL printed a circular in Spanish and distributed it, in the words of the *Los Angeles Times*, "among the swarthy-skinned laborers." It read in part:

> Back in the month of March of the past year there was initiated in this city a movement which evidence among all Mexicans a judicious and reasonable tendency to go forward. Naturally, this conduct awakened sympathy among the Americans who worked to help us, who expended not only their applause to moralize our spirits, but more than once contributed their funds to remedy our necessities. The struggle was new to us, and being strangers in the exercise of this class of activity the idea which first shone like the sun began to decline in public opinion. Many causes contributed toward determining a disastrous end, which concluded our prestige as a social element. We were accused of

incivilities, ignorance, and scant culture: as if judgment were passed upon an entire nation for the crimes of one malefactor, or the ravings of one fool. . . . We are grateful to announce that we have in our power a new opportunity which gives us the right to belong to the American Federation of Labor. There are no differences among us over faiths we respect all beliefs, religious as well as political; the end which we seek is very high, for it deals with patriotism.[62]

The appeal struck a conciliatory tone by addressing the prior year's failure and stayed firmly within the AFL's ideological terrain by appealing to American patriotism. The effort of the COL notwithstanding, failure over the previous two years reached into 1904 when the union could only muster fifty workers to go out on strike, a far cry from more than a thousand in 1903, and the strike quickly fizzled.[63] This marked the last significant attempt by the COL to organize with nonwhite, unskilled, migrant workers in the city until the California State Federation of Labor launched the United Laborers campaign in 1910.

■ ■ ■

The demand for labor by California's agricultural industry and urban development in Los Angeles presented new problems and the potential for novel solutions. Capitalist agriculture conditioned the seasonal migration of many laborers now with increasing numbers working on urban infrastructure in Los Angeles. Nonwhite immigrants filled the majority of unskilled labor positions. Racism and the urban-trade focus of the AFL limited the solidarity of most trade-union members. However, local grassroots organizing in Oxnard and COL-supported organizing in Los Angeles presented the white labor movement with the opportunity to move past decades of racist organizing across the state. The result was mixed. In Oxnard, the remarkable dexterity that Japanese and Mexican organizers, contractors, and laborers showed in their union, along with the vital public support of the Anglo socialists, gave rise to a brief victory that faded against the racism of the national AFL and structural difficulties imposed by the seasonal character of agriculture. In Los Angeles the ready availability of laborers and difficulty of interracial and multilingual organizing contributed to defeat, though the power of Huntington and the city's other powerful business leaders ruled the day. The legacy of both unions reached beyond their lack of lasting success. These episodes of interracial labor organizing set the stage for multiracial organizing efforts in and around Los Angeles in the years that followed. They illustrated possibilities that increasingly found more welcome outlets in the Socialist Party and with Industrial Workers of the World, and among anarchists.

CHAPTER 4

INTERNATIONALISM AND ITS LIMITS

An hour before Emma Goldman took the stage of Los Angeles's Burbank Hall in May 1907 for the first of four lectures in the city, an enthusiastic crowd filled the building's seven hundred seats despite the refusal of the *Los Angeles Times* to print a paid advertisement for the event. The occasion marked Goldman's return to the "Sunny City" after last visiting in 1898, and she remembered it fondly: "If I have accomplished nothing more than to rekindle the enthusiasm of our long-lost brother, W. C. Owen, my work at Los Angeles has been amply rewarded." She continued with high praise for the English immigrant anarchist, "Few of our young readers and comrades are familiar with that name, but those of us who remember such intellectual towers as Dyer D. Lum and John Edelman will recollect W. C. Owen as one of the ablest and ardent workers in the movement at that period." Goldman's visit prompted anarchists in Los Angeles to organize the Social Science Club to "form a nucleus for further educational work" with the support of "fifty-five charter members."[1] That July, Goldman traveled with Max Baginski to the International Anarchist Conference in Amsterdam, where she shared her thoughts on the state of the anarchist movement in the United States gathered during her recent cross-country speaking tour. She reported to her comrades that "anarchist agitation in the United States is being carried on in almost all the various languages spoken in this country, including Japanese, Armenian, etc."[2]

Locally, in Los Angeles, the disparate pieces of an interracial and multilingual community of solidarity came together in 1907. In March the African American preacher and socialist orator George Washington Woodbey established an office

CHAPTER 4

for "the next two or three months" across the Los Angeles River from the plaza on Lamar Street.[3] The Pozzo Construction Company erected Italian Hall, a new center for the local Italian community that also hosted radical speakers, a block from the plaza on North Macy and Main Streets the same year.[4] Ricardo Flores Magón and Enrique Flores Magón contributed to the breadth of the radical community when they surfaced publicly in 1907. The brothers had surreptitiously arrived in Los Angeles in autumn 1906 after a continent-stretching journey attempting to escape agents of the Mexican president Porfirio Díaz.[5]

The racial diversity of workers who lived or passed through Los Angeles increased as the city's population expanded. The city's political left unevenly reflected these demographic trends. Organizing by Mexicans, African Americans, Japanese, and other non-Anglos pushed their diverse agendas, while many white-led organizations also learned how to draw upon this racial diversity in locally rooted organizing practices to forge new alliances and create more inclusive movements. However, the racism and nationalism of whites continued to draw lines of exclusion. Consistent with California's past, whites directed their most vehement racism against the increasingly diverse Asian population: Chinese, Japanese, and South Asian. Internationalist ideals reached their limit unevenly across ideology, individuals, and organization, but their limit was race. Leftists who raised their voices to challenge racism through strident appeals to internationalism moderated this trend and created space for institutional multiracial organizing in Los Angeles.

As George Fredrickson noted, the word "racism" was adopted in the 1930s to "describe the theories on which the Nazis based their persecution of the Jews." He built a contextual understanding of racism more specific than its being "merely an attitude or set of beliefs," holding that racism "also expresses itself in the practices, institutions, and structures that a sense of deep difference justifies or validates." Fredrickson continued, "Racism, therefore, is more than theorizing about human differences or thinking badly of a group over which one has no control. It either directly sustains or proposes to establish *a racial order*."[6] The extension and then denial of AFL institutional resources based on race discussed in chapter 3 reflected the maintenance of a Anglo-dominated racial order within the labor movement. While most people, leftists included, held deeply racialized understandings of people, radicals tended to focus on the relative organizability of people according to race, which often led to positive conclusions drawn from the labor militancy of Japanese, Mexicans, and Italians. Local forms of internationalism gave rise to interracial solidarities in Los Angeles in an environment of continually lurking racism on the left, which draw out the racial understandings of Anglos and their manifestation in maintaining or refuting the Anglo-dominated racial order. The events examined document challenges to and the continuation of race-based decisions within leftist movements. The challengers sought to reconfigure the racial order in the United States and around the world through internationalism; others reached more limited conclusions with their use of an internationalism mired in race and nation.

The Growth of the Institutional Left in Los Angeles

In June 1905, discontented trade unionists, socialists, syndicalists, and anarchists—some native born, many not—convened in a steamy convention hall in Chicago to forge an alternate path to the American Federation of Labor. Weeks before the convention, Los Angeles's Emancipation Club, an independent socialist group in Los Angeles, held a series of Sunday morning meetings in its clubhouse on South Figueroa Street to decide its future. The issue before the members was whether to affiliate with the Socialist Party, the Socialist Labor Party, or the "new industrial union, about to be formed in Chicago."[7] No one from Los Angeles attended the founding convention of the Industrial Workers of the World, but the local community received updates from the convention floor by Bertha Wilkins in the socialist newspaper *Common Sense*. She detailed the sentiment of the first days in Chicago: "One could not but feel that it was a convention big with meaning. . . . [T]his feeling of distrust against the American Federation of Labor found expression in a long but able arraignment written and read to the convention by Secretary Trautman."[8] The union that emerged in Chicago threatened AFL hegemony as the voice of labor in the United States and grew into an important outlet for working-class radicalism around the world.

Those in favor of joining the IWW in Los Angeles won the day, and on July 12, 1905, the Emancipation Club "disorganized and immediately after adjournment called a meeting of those present to order and proceeded to organize a branch local of the Industrial Workers of the World." The following Sunday it held a meeting on the corner of Second and Figueroa, inviting "all Revolutionary Socialists who are proletarians" to organize an application to charter the local with the national IWW.[9] By September, IWW Pioneer Local No. 68 established a headquarters on the corner of East Sixth Street and Maple Avenue in central Los Angeles and inserted a radical new voice into working-class politics in Los Angeles.[10] Claude Riddle, president of IWW Local No. 12, detailed the differences between the new organization and the AFL in an appeal to *Common Sense*'s readership in October 1905. He emphasized three points. First, the IWW sought to "unite the entire working class." Second, the IWW had an end goal of creating an "industrial republic" to concentrate workers' power. Third, the IWW would refuse to make contracts, the sacred tenet of the AFL.[11]

Anglos predominated in these early days of the IWW in Los Angeles, and their organizing efforts remained limited to propaganda rather than the job and street actions that made the union's name a few years later. Affiliated members spread the word in print and on street corners. It spread further still through the region's informal interpersonal radical information networks. Mortimer Downing, a member of an anarchist club in Los Angeles when the IWW local chartered, first learned about IWW organizing in Los Angeles through a conversation on a train when a comrade told him about a bookstore on Seventh and Broadway frequented by Wobblies, and Downing joined the union shortly afterward. By the summer of 1906 an IWW cigar stand and a free reading room on East Sixth Street did their part to spread the gospel of industrial unionism in Los Angeles. The union also took to the streets to expand its base. In the summer of 1906 members held regular street meetings on the corner of Fifth and Los Angeles in central Los Angeles. Regardless of the initial debate within the Emancipation Club, interorganizational cooperation continued to be commonplace in the city like when the IWW local organized a May Day gathering in 1906 with the Socialist Party and the Socialist Labor Party.[12]

Mexicans would soon take a leading role in the IWW in Los Angeles and the Southwest. However, around 1905 and 1906 the primary Mexican organizational presence in Los Angeles centered on other intuitions. Founded in 1905 with Modesto Díaz as its president, the Club Liberal Justicia joined La Unión Fraternal Mexicana as the two most prominent Mexican organizations in Los Angeles. La Unión Fraternal Mexicana met regularly on Saturday nights and often cooperated with the Club Liberal Justicia. For instance, the two groups hosted a joint Cinco de Mayo party in Los Angeles in 1906. Mexicans in Vernon organized an even larger celebration that year than the joint party in Los Angeles, with a free barbecue. Also in 1906, representatives of the Club Liberal Justicia traveled to San Gabriel to serve as the guests of honor at a dance.[13] These functions served the vital role of strengthening the social ties upon which community and radical politics rested. Mexican organizing increased community strength in a difficult environment for labor organizing at jobsites.

In addition to hosting and participating in community functions, the Club Liberal Justicia published the Spanish-language newspaper *El Mosquito*, which first went to press in November 1905. F. H. Arismendez directed operations at the paper and balanced its content between using it as forum for organizing against Mexican president Porfirio Díaz and covering matters of concern to Mexican workers in Los Angeles, indicative of the transnational concerns of Mexicans in Los Angeles. Further, *El Mosquito* facilitated interracial, interethnic, and multilingual cooperation as it remained at the center of Los Angeles's Mexican community.

All of the articles printed in *El Mosquito* were in Spanish, but roughly half of the advertisements in the surviving issues appeared in Italian. The revenue generated through the advertisements of Italian-owned businesses meant that

Los Angeles's Italian community significantly contributed to funding the paper. The businesses varied from banks and pharmacies to liquor stores and grocery stores. The construction contractor John Genella advertised his services and his membership in Fil di Fer, an Italian benevolent society, in the paper. The Atlantic Grocery offered a discount to members of Fil di Fer, which suggests that local Italians read the newspaper as well.[14] From the pages of *El Mosquito* the interconnectedness of Los Angeles's Mexican and Italian communities appeared unlabored and preexisting in 1906.

The Anglo-dominated labor organization, renamed the Los Angeles Central Labor Council in 1904, recognized the importance of *El Mosquito* among Spanish-language readers in Los Angeles. When the AFL in Los Angeles ventured beyond "pure and simple" trade unionism into politics, it turned to the paper. In 1906 the CLC elected Unión Federal Mexicana organizer Lemuel Biddle to its presidency. Biddle's first major initiative was an attempt to gain labor a place in city governance through the Public Ownership Party. The labor council appealed to "Mexicanos y Españoles" living in Los Angeles through the pages of *El Mosquito* to vote for the party in local elections. Eduardo Gomez served as the point man for the council's efforts to reach out to Spanish speakers, and *El Mosquito* printed the Public Ownership Party's preamble in Spanish.[15] Seeking electoral support was a markedly different form of multiracial and multilingual organizing than organizing unions on jobsites. This effort did not bring new people into the AFL as members, yet it indicated the continuation of the Los Angeles trade union's broader vision of inclusion when compared to the national AFL. It also illustrated the CLC's attention to their electoral prospects in a racially diverse city even though Mexicans and Italians naturalized at very low rates, so few were eligible voters.[16]

The formation of the Mexican branch of the Socialist Party marked the first time a nonwhite group created an institutional home in a white-led leftist organization in Los Angeles. The Mexican branch chartered in 1907 and grew into a major forum for Mexican working-class organizing in Los Angeles. Lead organizers Rafael Carmona, a Spaniard, and Lázaro Gutiérrez de Lara, recently arrived from Mexico, contributed greatly to its success, and their enthusiasm gathered new members. They spoke Sunday afternoons on the plaza and taught a socialist night school for Mexicans and Spaniards in the Socialist Party reading room.[17] The socialist newspaper *Common Sense* credited the men with the growth of the branch and complimented Gutiérrez de Lara for his "fast improving in the use of the English language."[18] Anselmo Figueroa also actively participated in it. The leaders of the Club Liberal Justicia and the Mexican Branch of the Socialist Party, less Rafael Carmona, all assumed various roles in the Partido Liberal Mexicano as it regathered in Los Angeles in 1907. In southern California and Arizona grassroots organization-blending agitation by Mexicans associated with the PLM, IWW, and Socialist Party moved forward between 1906 and 1907.[19] All the while Anglo acceptance of Mexicans on equal terms remained elusive.

In keeping with its mission to educate as well as organize, in 1906 the socialist paper *Common Sense* ran a series of articles on political economy "to lay bare the fallacies taught in a textbook on political economy now in wide use in American schools." Lesson 21, on "our peon population," began in the language of turn-of-the-century social science by asserting that one does not have to travel to the packinghouses of Chicago to find the "inhumanity and essential criminality of the profit system. In fact we do not need to leave Los Angeles." The author compared Mexican contract laborers from Michoacán, "where most of this class for labor has been secured," imported to work on the tracks of both the steam and local electric railroad companies to the more common vision of industrial exploitation in Chicago. The analysis noted the structural position of Mexican laborers in the regional economy and presented them as victims of American capitalism like workers in a packinghouse. But their sympathetic treatment struck a distinctly racist tone when the author argued, "The American laborer hated him for lowering the American standard of wages and living to a Mexican standard."[20]

In the minds of the article's white socialist readership this surely conjured the more restrained structural critiques of Chinese immigration, but the difference rested in the authors' attributing their perceived deficiencies of Mexican workers to the ills of capitalism. They were not determined by race. This left open the possibility that through education and organizing these "problems" could be overcome, and many white socialists created the space for this change to occur within their own organization. Mexicans and other nonwhites could achieve a salvation of sorts in the eyes of Anglo socialists through the adoption of socialist ideals.

Attaining this salvation remained elusive as Mexican organizing continued to brush against the persistent racism of the Anglo-led Socialist Party. Editors of *Common Sense* had indeed once chided their readers, "We feel rather ashamed for the 'white' Irish-Dutch-Anglo-Saxon combination of 'superior' beings that can't show up at business meetings" to complement the Mexican Branch's strong participation.[21] *Common Sense* also wrote about the "Cholo Lawyer," referencing Lázaro Gutiérrez de Lara, addressing a crowd of twenty-three in the socialist reading room.[22] This derogatory reference to the well-educated Gutiérrez de Lara resonated differently from the comment about "'superior' beings." When the paper referred to Gutiérrez de Lara, it often took pains to emphasize his education as a way to distinguish him from Mexican laborers, downplaying his race through his education. Even as the socialists enthusiastically welcomed the Mexican Branch into their organization, this acceptance was not on equal terms. Similarly, a few years later Emma Goldman's anarchist magazine *Mother Earth* referenced Gutiérrez de Lara as "a cultured Mexican."[23] What many white leftists viewed as the ignorance of peon laborers often took on clear racial meanings, but most people in the anarchist, syndicalist, and socialist movements allowed for a greater degree of flexibility than that found in the broader society. In this case, through education and participation in the Socialist Party, Mexicans could overcome negative categorizations. Perhaps.

Although the Socialist Party had very few African American members and did not have an African American section like the Mexican Branch, George Washington Woodbey found an outwardly welcome home in the Socialist Party and gained a remarkable public voice in Los Angeles and San Diego. In spring 1907, *Common Sense* credited Woodbey for African American workers in Los Angeles "beginning to sit up and take notice."[24] Woodbey also participated in a broad conversation over leftist tactics. After Emma Goldman visited in 1907 he criticized her lecture on direct action at a public gathering at the lot at 5th and Los Angeles Streets. In this speech he laid out his vision of struggle as distinct from Goldman's. The preacher argued for a combination of "direct and political action," setting his brand of socialism apart from her anarchism.[25]

Woodbey supported his position by arguing that Abraham Lincoln's election resulted in the end of slavery, and that Civil War "only opened the way for political action in connection with the constitutional amendments and reconstruction." This position did not grow from any sort of provincialism on the part of Woodbey. He showed his worldly knowledge with further examples of leftist political action: craft-union men belonged to the Socialist Party in Germany and "the advice to refrain from violence and use caution must have come from the unions themselves who thought it wise to wait and get possession of the guns by political action." He also spoke out against anti-immigration sentiment within the Socialist Party and in the country at large. But in the end Woodbey's emphasis on electoral politics wedded his proposed direction of struggle to citizens of the United States with voting rights, a similar focus as the Anglo-dominated Socialist Party.[26]

Woodbey engaged national politics in the same period that he critiqued Emma Goldman. He gave two speeches in response to Senator Benjamin "Pitchfork" Tillman of South Carolina. He spoke both in Burbank Hall and out of doors, again at Fifth and Los Angeles Streets. Woodbey argued that the senator erred in his belligerent racism because he "ignores the economic phase of the question. The labor question is at the bottom of the race question.... The negro is an exploited workingman first and a negro afterwards." Woodbey continued his line of reasoning by holding that "the negro, once despised as a chattel slave, is now despised as a wage slave along with the white, yellow and brown wage slaves." He went on to say that "the black capitalist is no better than the white capitalist," which asked African Americans to question putting racial solidarity over class solidarity and what would constitute racial uplift.[27] He shared his insistence on valorizing class-based organizing, believing that race was secondary to class exploitation with the vast majority of the Left when they considered race at all. Woodbey's views on race and class, in turn, reinforced this view for many white socialists in Los Angeles.

Other African American organizing through these years also created space for community organizing. The Los Angeles Sunday Forum, formed by the First African Methodist Episcopal Church in 1903, afforded African Americans free space to speak their minds. It met in Odd Fellows Hall on Eighth Street. Even though the forum did not have a radical political affiliation, a historian of African American Los Angeles wrote that "even sympathetic observers pointed out, some black Angelenos expended a bit too much hot air at those afternoon meetings."[28] Just as surely, these meetings laid part of the groundwork for African American community organizing then and in the coming years.

A Change in Tone? Arguments over Japanese Exclusion

The "Gentlemen's Agreement" between the United States and Japan limiting Japanese immigration made 1907 a watershed year for racial politics. This increased the importance of the growing institutional presence of multiracial leftist organizations in Los Angeles shaped by socialist internationalism. Many whites looked to internationalism, one of many alternatives to nationalism, to see racial difference in their own community through the principle of international solidarity. Yet the internationalism of most socialists also strengthened the nation as the operating entity of international solidarity. Combined, this terrain continued to be fertile ground for racism and nationalism among socialists.

Public interest in the winter of 1907 toward Japanese immigration increased pending the "Gentleman's Agreement," and the Socialist Party in California agreed to hold a referendum of its members to determine socialists' support. This generated an extended public debate within the party and showed in striking terms the interplay between the international ideal, nation-based thinking, and the racism of many white socialists. The January 12, 1907, issue of *Common Sense* ran as its masthead an excerpt of August Bebel's address to the jury in his 1872 trial: "The capitalist does not ask if the workingman whom he exploits speaks German or Swedish, English or French, or if he has a white, or black or yellow skin. Against this 'international' exploitation of the workingman there is only one remedy: 'The international fraternization of the exploited.'"[29] This quote framed two articles on Japanese immigration.

Cloudesley Johns, a prominent Los Angeles socialist, believed it "necessary for the triumph of the world movement for the emancipation of the working class that there should be international class solidarity. . . . That is an assertion, and no Socialist will deny its truth." Johns continued a line of reasoning shared by many socialists that acknowledged the high ideal of internationalism but compromised as a local expedient. He argued that aside from a shared class, workers have "modes of conduct and thought which create friction between the different blood." He supported his argument by connecting Japanese immigrants on the West Coast to the American Civil War, noting that "several million men of an alien race, which previously had existed in the condition of domestic animals, were made the political equals of their late masters." He then treated the "race" question as being on equal terms as the opposition of the capitalist and worker, finding that "almost every effective step in the direction of a solution has been through the cultivating of the feeling of independence in the blacks, tending to make them withdraw from close contact with the whites." He attributed this factor as being causal in what he viewed as the slow growth of socialism in the South. He based his final analysis on the simple thought that there were "only so many 'good' jobs offered the workers; the number is less than the number of white workers on the Coast. Ergo, each Jap that secures a 'good' job here deprives a worker of our own race of such a job." He never questioned the assumption that race should constitute a worker's first line of solidarity and warned that with unchecked Japanese immigration California would have a "race" problem like that of the South.[30]

Kasper Bauer responded to Johns with a strident "Defense of Internationalism." He claimed that the state convention holding the referendum "destroyed, in the minds of many of our younger comrades, a goodly portion of their sense of the fitness of things." He pointed to an earlier moment of globalization than his own to explain Asian immigration: "When European capitalism broke down Oriental seclusion and established the world-market, it followed the law of its existence: it compelled not only the mingling of commodities but of men also." Further, he argued, "It would be futile for anyone to make a 'race problem' out of the capitalist necessity to exploit foreign markets, just as it is fundamentally wrong to construe our civil war into an attempt to solve a race problem." He concluded with a challenge to his comrades, asking them: "Are we going to help to develop the instinct and run it deeper and deeper into the mire of race, and finally national prejudice, or are we going to stand firmly by Socialist truths and do our duty in developing the intelligence of the worker?"[31] Bauer separated race and nation through internationalism while criticizing socialists' anti-immigration positions as joining race to nation. He argued against racist nationalism and restrictive immigration policies as a protective measure for the white working class on the West Coast. He saw the alternative as socialist internationalism.

The debate continued, and one of the newly formed Social Science Club's first public discussions also addressed Japanese exclusion. *Common Sense* reported that the "exclusionists were in hopeless minority" but they "had able defenders" in John Murray and John Kenneth Turner.[32] It is important to remember that Murray was a tireless supporter of the Japanese Mexican Labor Association in Oxnard, and he and Turner would soon become the most active Anglo socialist supporters of the Partido Liberal Mexicano. Both men supported the PLM, before siding with Francisco Madero in 1911, and continued involvement in the Mexican cause generally for years thereafter. Turner went as far as gathering arms for the Baja rebellion in 1910 and early 1911. What at first glance seems like a contradiction on the part of Turner evidences his view of the relative racial positioning of Mexicans against Japanese. In the case of Murray, bettering the condition of "American" workers remained his first priority, of which his conceptualization did not include Asians. Perhaps Murray viewed curtailing Japanese immigration as necessary to reduce "surplus" labor and increase the bargaining power of workers already on the West Coast. Tellingly, however, not once did the group debate the question of European immigration.

Craft labor in Los Angeles continued to rely on Asian laborers as its "indispensable enemy." Los Angeles's union weekly, the *Citizen*, held that "American manhood requires American ideals. Reduce the common man to the level of the Chinaman or Japanese, and teach him to be content with their standards of living, and the debasement of American manhood must follow."[33] With their racism well established, the extent to which the *Citizen* justified its anti-immigration positions is striking. Once, the paper compared its own opposition to Japanese immigration to a "certain episode" in Japan's imperial expansion when "Japanese manufacturers imported cheap Chinese coolly labor under contract." The paper reported that the "Japanese workers promptly protested," which resulted in the expulsion of the Chinese workers.[34]

However, the *Citizen* enthusiastically reported that Rafael Carmona spoke on "behalf of the Mexican laborers and for the Mexican workingmen's paper [*Regeneración*] published in Los Angeles." It held that "Mr. Carmona is a very enthusiastic and persistent worker and is having good success. He is well educated and also knows how the Mexicans live and what they need."[35] Further evidence of the divergent views toward African Americans, Japanese, and Mexicans in the Los Angeles AFL.

Many socialists and anarchists wrote against anti-Asian agitation within their movement and in society as a whole. The San Francisco–based paper the *Emancipator* described its politics: "This Paper has no right to call itself an organ of 'The Industrial Workers of the World,' but it stands as an advocate of industrial unionism."[36] For all intents and purposes, though, it was an anarchist newspaper and regularly carried articles by prominent anarchists, including Ludovico Caminita, an Italian in Paterson, New Jersey, during its short life between 1906 and 1907. Caminita later moved to Los Angeles to organize with the PLM in 1910 and 1911. In May 1907 the *Emancipator* ran an article showing the potential of interracial support: "We Denounce the Mexican Czarism" as it condemned the rule of Porfirio Díaz and declared, "The cause of the victims of the Dictator of Mexico is our cause."[37] While it dedicated a large part of this four-page issue to Mexico, it also reprinted a translation from the Japanese socialist paper *Kakumei* (*Revolution*) from Berkeley.

The editor of the *Emancipator* expressed his pleasure in printing the article as a way to show "our sentiments of fraternity to our Japanese brothers." In the article, Kiichi Kaneko, a Japanese socialist who immigrated in 1899 and assisted his wife Josephine Conger-Kaneko in editing the *Socialist Women*, considered the relationship between white socialists and Japanese immigrants.[38] He recalled, "Some time ago I was asked by a Japanese friend in Tokio to express what I think of the American Socialist's attitude toward the Japanese situation in San Francisco." Kaneko continued, "I am not, of course, to represent here the Japanese people and their interests at large. The reason is that I, as an individual, gave up my old country a long time ago, and I do not care any longer to be a subject of any particular nation. In other words, I am a plain Socialist." After presenting an internationalist ideal as the highest goal of socialism, he critiqued his white comrades for not living up to it: "So far as I know, not a single Socialist paper in this country spoke out plainly on this Japanese question without showing race prejudice." Further, he declared: "Their socialism is American socialism, and not scientific socialism. It is national socialism, but not international socialism."[39] Kaneko clearly articulated the limitation of internationalism tied to nations with racial orders among whites on the West Coast.

In the article, he also responded to criticism of excessive Japanese patriotism by white socialists, arguing that "Japanese are more radical, more revolutionary, and less patriotic than are American comrades," evidenced by a letter of solidarity that Japanese socialists sent to their Russian comrades during the height of the Russo-Japanese War. Kiichi Kaneko concluded his article with hope that "all American Socialists will give up 'America' just as I did 'Japan,' and come to real, international, scientific socialism, and shake hands with all people of all climates without any prejudice and distinction." The editor of the *Emancipator* then added his thoughts on the subject. He railed against the Japanese and Korean Exclusion League, calling its leaders "thugs, crooks and grafters" before ending with the following declaration: "Before the socialists of the world, without distinction of races, colors or nationalities, we affirm that the International Solidarity among the workers and thinkers of the world is the 'sine qua non' of Socialism."[40]

In Southern California around the same time, the *People's Paper* celebrated that translations of "many of the leading Socialist books" circulated in Japan. Further, it praised Uta Imai and her fellow socialists for their work "attacking the old customs that make slaves of women." Uta Imai edited the journal *Woman of the Twentieth Century* and spoke and wrote English "admirably." American newspapers often published her articles.[41] Similarly, *Common Sense* actively promoted the newspaper *Kakumei.* The paper had one English page with the "other pages mimeographed in Japanese because the capitalist Japanese printing plants refused to print the paper." After several "Japanese mass meetings" held in the Bay Area, Los Angeles's socialist weekly encouraged its readers to support the Japanese paper.[42]

As socialists in Los Angeles debated Japanese exclusion and the broader direction of internationalism in their movement, the *People's Paper* reported that a white mob drove "Hindus" from Bellingham, Washington, after which not "a solitary Hindu" remained. The newspaper sterilely reported that these refugees—who by modern euphemism were the victims of "ethnic cleansing"—simply "sought new locations." Of those who fled their homes in terror "about forty arrived in Seattle.... A large party left for Los Angeles and other southern cities and others sought protection in British Columbia." India, being a British colony, entitled the refugees to British consular protection in the United States; however, Bernard Pelly, the British vice consul in Seattle, did not extend this support. The report continued that he "has not yet been officially notified of hostilities toward these British subjects demonstrated at Bellingham. He states today that he did not intend even to inquire into the affair unless formal complaint is lodged with him."[43] The next year, in January 1908, in Live Oak, a small town north of Sacramento, residents reenacted the Washington scene when "a mob marched to a camp of Hindu workers, burned it to the ground, beat and terrorized a hundred or more Hindus in the camp, drove them out of the community, and, in doing so, robbed them of about $2,500."[44] The choices made by movements had real consequences even if Los Angeles did not witness similar acts of violence locally.

The Partido Liberal Mexicano

Los Angeles's Club Liberal Justicia was a part of a network of political clubs in the Southwest and Mexico affiliated with the Partido Liberal Mexicano. Some *club liberales* or liberal clubs created an above-ground presence while others, especially in Mexico, remained clandestine. This form of organizing built upon the *mutualista* tradition in Mexico and increased after Porfirio Díaz outlawed unions. The Club Liberal Justicia served as a conduit for the expansion of the PLM's support base in Los Angeles before the arrival of its leadership. Ricardo Flores Magón, the PLM's leading public figure, was born in 1874 in the state of Oaxaca two years before the revolution of Textepec ushered Porfirio Díaz into the Mexican presidency. Ricardo and his brothers, Enrique and Jesús, entered the political world at young ages. On the occasion of Díaz's third reelection in 1892, the three participated in student demonstrations in May of that year. The government effectively suppressed this movement and forced Ricardo, who emerged as a leader, briefly into hiding. Ricardo soon turned his attention to journalism, learning to set type and gaining editorial skills. He then found his own voice when he established the newspaper *Regeneración* with Lisenciado Antonio Horcasitas and Ricardo's older brother, Jesús, in Mexico City in 1900. They poured their collective energy into the newspaper, and it became the main forum for their political agitation. It only took five months before police arrested Ricardo for his writing; the paper closed in 1901.[45]

Facing the repressive apparatus of the Porfiriato, which in 1903 prohibited the circulation of any periodical containing his writing, Ricardo fled to the United States with his younger brother, Enrique, after being released from another stint in prison for his political activities. They arrived in Laredo, Texas, in January 1904. The two moved first to San Antonio and then to St. Louis, Missouri, prompted by an incident when "a ruffian sent by Díaz, entered my domicile, and would have stabbed me in the back had it not been for the quick intervention of my brother, Enrique."[46] St. Louis provided them a brief respite from persecution. They revived *Regeneración* with a now fairly solidified group of comrades that had joined them in the city. At this point the leaders, or Junta Organizadora, of the PLM gathered in St. Louis included Ricardo Flores Magón, Enrique Flores Magón, Juan Sarabia, Antonio Villarreal, Librado Rivera, and Manuel Sarabia.[47]

The PLM fit well into St. Louis's cosmopolitan working-class districts. Much to the dismay of the Anglo press, Chinese, Polish, Irish, German, Turkish, Italian, Spanish, Honduran, Venezuelan, Brazilian, and Argentinean revolutionaries made their home in the midwestern city. In St. Louis, Ricardo and the others met the Spanish immigrant anarchist Florencio Bazora. Bazora actively supported the group by gathering donations and selling copies of *Regeneración* in St. Louis. He also participated in the founding convention of the IWW in Chicago, although little is known about his life. Bazora continued to support the PLM from St. Louis after the group relocated to Los Angeles through fundraising and donations until at least 1914.[48]

The political trajectory of the PLM informed their coalition building and tactics. PLM organizers, members, and supporters lived in a dynamic world, and their political beliefs, methods, and alliances proved flexible. From the time Ricardo and Enrique Flores Magón fled Mexico in 1904 until the Baja raids in 1911 they endeavored to create the broadest possible coalition in the United States against the regime of Porfirio Díaz. Simultaneously, they inspired and organized with *club liberales* in Mexico and near the border in the United States. The individual political leanings of its leadership based in the United States varied from anarchist to socialist, but they all proved willing to reach out to labor and even political liberals for support.

While in St. Louis in 1906 the group wrote and published the clearest exposition of their political ambitions up to that point. The "Programa y Manifesta" held true to the party's name and consisted of liberal reforms of the state including, checks on the power of clergy, land reform, and worker's rights. This document positioned the PLM to the left but still within the broader liberal reform movement in Mexico that included others such as Francisco Madero. The PLM's political openness helped it to build a broad support base in the United States and Mexico before the Mexican Revolution began in 1910. Ideological and personal differences within the PLM and among its supporters mattered less when they were insurgents organizing against Porfirio Díaz being persecuted by Mexican and United States authorities than they would after the outbreak of the Mexican Revolution and the ascendency of Francisco Madero in 1911. These events ripped open internal splits along preexisting cracks among the leadership and out through the solidarity network that the PLM had worked so hard to gather. At this point, however, the survival of the PLM as an organization and the very lives of its leaders won the day.[49]

St. Louis did not long provide the safe haven the PLM so desperately sought. The Furlong Secret Service Company, which worked for the Mexican government with the full support of the American authorities, harassed the junta. Ricardo remembered being called to the postmaster's office in St. Louis to report on the finances of *Regeneración*, a necessity to qualify for a second-class mail permit, when he saw a detective waiting. He recalled, "This same detective led the officers who arrested me."[50] Police arrested Ricardo with his brother Enrique and Juan Sarabia. The three remained in jail for three months as the Mexican government requested their deportation.

U.S. authorities eventually released the men on bail in January 1906. Fearing death in Mexico if deported, Ricardo jumped bail and fled north to Toronto in March. He then traveled to Montreal, Quebec, the day before Canadian police "called on [his] abandoned domicile" in Toronto after Díaz's agents located him. The effort to arrest Magón did not stop the revolutionary undercurrent generated by the movement, as participants kept power in the network diffuse. While he was in Canada, his "Mexican comrades in Mexico were planning an uprising." This was the PLM's first attempt at armed revolt, and it came a few months after the suppression of striking miners in Cananea in June 1906. In September Ricardo traveled to El Paso to join the revolt, but authorities discovered his presence on the border and police raided the junta's office in October. Ricardo and Modesto Díaz escaped aboard an empty Santa Fe boxcar. Less fortunate, Antonio Villarreal and Juan Sarabia were arrested. The uprising never got off the ground, but police captured a subscription list to *Regeneración* Sarabia was carrying and rounded up two hundred supporters in northern Mexico over the next few months. Ricardo then lived underground with a twenty-five-thousand-dollar reward advertised for his capture; he noted, "Hundreds of thousands of leaflets bearing my picture and a description of my personal features were circulated throughout the Southwest."[51]

In November 1906 Ricardo and Modesto Díaz climbed out of a railcar in Los Angeles and initially found shelter in the bookstore owner Rómulo Carmona's house near the plaza. From this point until World War I–era repression, Ricardo and the junta of the PLM maintained Los Angeles as their base of operations through their all-too-frequent stints in prison.[52]

Race, Chinese, and the PLM

When PLM leaders finished writing down their vision for change in Mexico in 1906, they ended up with a fifty-two-point *Programa y Manifesta*. The document reflected the organizational position of the PLM at the time; even though its members were anarchists and socialists, they outlined a reformist agenda for Mexico. The *Programa* included two planks, fifteen and sixteen, under the heading *Extranjeros* (Foreigners). These two planks did not receive special emphasis among a host of constitutional and land-reform measures put forth by the PLM at the height of its liberal public presentation. Plank 15 read: "Prescription that by the sole fact of acquiring landed property foreigners lose their former nationality and become Mexican citizens."[53] In the extended *Exposición* published at the same time, the PLM justified its stance as follows: "It is unnecessary to declare in the program that under equal conditions preference has to be given to the Mexican over the foreigner, because that is already consigned in our constitution. As an efficacious means to avoid foreign preponderance and to guarantee the integrity of our territory, nothing seems to be more convenient than the naturalization as Mexican citizens of such foreigners as acquire landed property."[54] This plank had a degree of progressiveness, providing citizenship and legal participation in Mexican society to immigrants who purchased land, but it still maintained a strong focus on Mexico as a nation, seeking to limit the potential of foreign influence and outside loyalty.

Plank 16 of their program sought simply to "Prohibit Chinese Immigration." They also justified this position in the *Exposición*: "The prohibition of Chinese immigration is before all a measure of protection for the workingmen of other nationalities, and principally of Mexico. The Chinaman, generally disposed to work at the lowest wages, submissive, small in aspirations, is a great obstacle for the prosperity of the other workingmen. His competency is lamentable and must be avoided in Mexico. Generally speaking, the Chinese immigration to Mexico does not produce the least bit of benefit."[55] The PLM framed its opposition to

CHAPTER 4

Chinese immigration in terms of economic protectionism while simultaneously positioning Chinese immigrants at the bottom of a racial and national hierarchy.

Taken together, these two planks aimed directly at two interconnected processes in Porfirian Mexico that distinguish the anti-Chinese position of the PLM, which fit within broader Mexican *antichinismo*, from the dominant strains of anti-Chinese hostility in the United States. Immigrant numbers in Mexico grew through the late nineteenth century, facilitated in part by open immigration laws. The Porfirian administration saw immigration as a way to "undermine indigenous resistance" and to feed its national colonization project.[56] Chinese immigrants became the primary human face of these policies as *"motores de sangre"* (engines of blood).[57] Jason Chang argued that "the Porfirian administration introduced Chinese men as racialized instruments of policy in order to expand and deepen the power of the state through the expansion of infrastructure projects."[58] By the outbreak of the revolution in 1910, Mexicans indelibly associated Chinese with "Porfirian national colonization and assumed to involve support for its underlying ideologies of Indian racism and widespread dispossession."[59]

The PLM's *Programa y Manifesta* reflected these broader processes and sought to combat the long history of land dispossession of Mexicans and of foreign, largely U.S.–based, investment-driven economic development under Porfirio Díaz.[60] Taking aim at foreign land ownership and immigration was taking aim at the Porfiriato. Through its existence, the PLM most consistently advanced the belief that access to land provided the foundation for a world changed in their vision: *Tierra y Libertad*. This core PLM belief, often connected to indigenous resistance, varied from that of other anarchists who were more focused on urban and industrial workers. These differences contributed to the discord among anarchists after the failure of the Baja raids in 1911. The *Programa* shared in the broader sweep of *antichinismo* in Mexico, which created a different premise for the PLM's anti-Chinese position from that of whites on the West Coast of the United States.

Little is known of the internal debate surrounding the formulation of the PLM's platform, but fragments of dissent remain in the historical record. The Club Liberal Justicia in Los Angeles published the *Programa y Manifesta* in *El Mosquito* in August 1906 but did not reprint it in full. Most significantly it skipped over the plank seeking to end Chinese immigration. The group did not provide an explanation to its readers for the omission. The following year *Common Sense* published an English translation of the *Programa*, including the anti-Chinese plank.[61]

The internal dynamics regarding planks 15 and 16 took an interesting turn when the PLM managed to begin publishing *Regeneración* again in 1910.[62] The first new issue (November 26, 1910) reprinted the *Programa* in Spanish without the anti-Chinese plank. A translation on *Regeneración's* English page, edited by

Alfred Sanftleben, included the anti-Chinese plank. A month later an English translation of the longer explanative document, the *Exposición*, ran over three issues and again included the anti-Chinese plank.[63] *Regeneración* did not print an explanation for the discrepancy, but its inclusion in English certainly made the Mexican rebels more palatable to Anglo socialists and trade unionists by giving them another shared enemy, Chinese. The English page also reflected Alfred Sanftleben's editorial hand more so than the that of the junta.

The different content in Spanish and English is also a window into the PLM's complicated position trying to organize for revolution in Mexico and also to appeal for support in the United States. The PLM reached out to a broad range of Americans, from craft labor to anarchists, which shaped much of its public rhetoric. For the PLM leaders who looked to socialism for guidance, such as Antonio Villarreal, Lázaro Gutiérrez de Lara, and Juan and Manuel Sarabia, their thinking on both planks probably connected to their view of Mexico as backward economically and needing to progress along a fixed industrial development path.[64] After splitting with the socialist members during the outbreak of the Mexican Revolution and the Baja raids, those who remained in the PLM publicly identified as anarchists and their commitment to internationalism and antistatism grew stronger.

The explicitly anarchist manifesto the PLM printed after the failure of the Baja raids in 1911 did not mention Chinese. The document held, "The Partido Liberal Mexicano recognizes that every human being, by the simple fact of coming to life, has the right to enjoy each and every one of the advantages that modern civilization offers, because these advantages are the product of the effort and sacrifice of the working class in all ages."[65] Although the PLM never publicly retracted the earlier anti-Chinese plank, the differences between the 1906 and 1911 documents illustrated the evolution of the PLM's political presentation. The timing of this change is crucial. Jason Chang wrote that as Mexico "burst into revolt in 1910, anti-Chinese politics became intertwined with the articulation of a state-sponsored brand of racial nationalism centered on an abstract racial figure, the mestizo."[66] That is, as anti-Chinese politics moved to the front and center of a racialized political discourse during the Mexican Revolution, the PLM articulated a distinct vision of revolutionary interracial antistatism.

Race and racism took various forms in revolutionary Mexico. For instance, Francisco Villa's manifesto "contained a radical nativist program." Before they would be eligible to own land, immigrants would be required to be naturalized Mexican citizens for twenty-five years. Citizens of the United States and China would simply be ineligible to naturalize.[67] The Villiasta forces singled out American and Chinese residents in the state of Chihuahua as the "Chinamen and the white Chinamen, that is the Americans . . . the only ones responsible for all the misfortunes of this country." Mobs in northern Mexico also attacked the "business places of the Syrians, or the Arabs, as they are called in this country and who are particularly hated by the natives."[68] Villa's leading English-language biographer wrote, "Villa never explained his hatred for the Chinese, which contrasted so strongly with his admiration of the Japanese. In all probability, he shared the xenophobic attitude that many northern Mexicans evinced toward Chinese immigrants. That attitude was owing partly to racism and resentment of an alien culture and partly to the fact that many Chinese were merchants who came into the most direct contact with Mexicans, who blamed the Chinese for the high prices of the merchandise they were selling."[69]

As Mexicans in Los Angeles negotiated the racism whites directed toward them and the city's broader racially diverse working class, some similar attitudes surfaced. Racial positioning proved to be part of Mexican American community formation. On the back page of an issue of *El Correo Mexicano*, the American Dye Works suggested in a short advertisement that Mexican workers could escape the aspersion of "Grisers" that Anglos leveled at them through the use of dye products on their clothes. That Anglos categorized Mexicans in the city and that Mexicans pushed back against this through organizing and individual practices is apparent. Mexicans also pushed against others in Los Angeles's diverse working class. Next to this advertisement a short article ran for Pablo R. García's barbershop. After giving the price for a shave and a cut, the article read, "It is very sad that Japanese barbershops are patronized by our people [*gente de nuestra raza*], when it is well known that the Japanese do not appreciate anything since they are not of our blood and it is a mistake to help another nation." On this same page, a Japanese shop owner pledged to treat Mexicans well in his store.[70]

The PLM in Los Angeles

In August 1907 Thomas Furlong, along with two employees of his private detective firm and two Los Angeles police detectives, arrested Ricardo Flores Magón, Antonio Villarreal, and Librado Rivera in a house on East Pico Street without a warrant. The men put up a tremendous fight, fearing they would be spirited across the border to a certain death. The *Los Angeles Times* celebrated the capture of the men and noted that detectives "tracked [them] from one end of the Western Hemisphere to the other, with the fate and welfare of a great nation hanging in their capture." The article continued, "For three years the officers have searched for the men. From the jungles of Southern Mexico to the frozen acres of Hudson Bay." Mexico's ambassador to the United States, Enrique Creel, underscored the importance attached to this event when he traveled to Los Angeles upon hearing the news.[71]

The kidnapping of Western Federation of Miners (WFM) leaders William Haywood, Charles Moyer, and George Pettibone remained fresh in the minds of the labor and radical movement in the United States at the time of the PLM leaders' capture. The fate of the WFM men captivated the Left after officials in Colorado and Idaho colluded in their arrest and illegally transported them across state lines in 1906. Nationally, the socialist, labor, and anarchist press carried a steady stream of articles, and the local movement in Los Angeles organized a number of rallies throughout the year and a half that the WFM men sat in jail awaiting trial. Haywood was the first tried and the first acquitted in 1907. Pettibone's trial came next; the jury returned the same not-guilty verdict. The state declined to try Moyer after these two embarrassing failures.[72]

The risk that the American officials would permit Mexican agents to take the men across the border drew obvious parallels. *Common Sense* noted that "local labor in the political and economic field seems to realize the threatening danger in a case equal in importance to the Moyer-Haywood-Pettibone case, which made through precedent kidnapping legal and refusal of habeas corpus between state and state, while the present incident might create the same precedent of legalizing the kidnapping of champions of labor between nation and nation, making labor's bondage truly international by outlawing and disfranchising the toilers."[73] This declaration placed the Mexicans' cause on equal ground with that of the Anglo labor leaders, and local leftists now had something close to home to fight for. After the men lingered for eleven months in the Los Angeles County Jail, *Common Sense* saw the case of the Mexican rebels as "an excellent inter-nation parallel to the inter-state Moyer-Haywood affair."[74] The paper also connected the arrest of the Mexican rebels to events in Mexico when it declared its opposition to the "introduction of Mexican justice and Colorado mine-owners' methods for Cananea purposes into this state of ours."[75]

The broad-based community support for the PLM immediately became apparent after the men's arrests, and it continued to build as they sat in jail. The Socialist Party organized a meeting in Burbank Hall on September 1 to publicize the case. A. R. Holston, one of the socialist attorneys representing the men, spoke, as did Lázaro Gutiérrez de Lara, followed by comrades Newerf, Sanftleben, Lauff, and Rafael Carmona. A "short talk in Spanish to a strong delegation of Mexican labor at the meeting was interpreted to the American comrades by our foreign correspondent," Alfred Sanftleben. *Common Sense* reported that on the same afternoon as the meeting in Burbank Hall "our Mexican Brethren of toil held an open-air meeting at the Plaza."[76]

Supporters of the PLM raised legal defense money, used their media to spread word of the injustice, and held protests and meetings. One thousand people, roughly half Mexican, attended another in the series of mass meetings that November. Plainclothes detectives and uniformed officers also joined the gathering. A band opened the event by playing the "national hymn of Mexico." The rousing evening included performances by a "Mexican string band" and "fifteen or twenty Mexican children on the stage," which "lent picturesqueness to the scene." After a speaker addressed the crowded hall in Spanish, John Murray read several letters of support, including one from "the aged" abolitionist and suffragist Caroline M. Severance. A. R. Holston then spoke forcefully about "the despotism that is driving the workers of the world into one camp regardless of color, race or creed."[77]

A consortium of members of the PLM, Socialist Party, Socialist Labor Party, and IWW Local 12 formed the Mexican Defense Funds Committee in Los Angeles in 1908 "in order to centralize all actions, concentrate all efforts and simplify all procedures" in organizing the legal defense of the imprisoned men. In January 1908, George Pettibone traveled to Los Angeles, hoping that the climate would help him recuperate from the toll that imprisonment in Idaho exacted on his body. While in the city, he stopped by the jail with the famed attorney Clarence Darrow to visit and offer his support to the imprisoned PLM leaders. The prisoners remained in Los Angeles County Jail until the authorities extradited them to Arizona in March 1909.[78]

Coalition Building and Internationalism

The growth of the socialist and anarchist movements in Los Angeles undergirded its ability to support the jailed Mexican rebels and created a broad-based community of solidarity. The local movement reflected immigration patterns to Los Angeles, and each increasingly diversified. The immigration process itself and then experiencing racial and ethnic diversity in Los Angeles greatly expanded the complexion and outlook of movements. When people gathered in Los Angeles's streets and meeting halls, their knowledge of the world and the international movement infused their gatherings.

Anglos led the Socialist Party in Los Angeles, but it offered an umbrella under which ethnic/language locals formed. By 1909 the city's Socialist Party had Hungarian, Russian, German, and Mexican branches in addition to the English-language local. These branches organized according to language and country of origin, but this did not make them insular. For example, in February 1909 the Russian Branch of the Socialist Party held an "educational international meeting" that featured a "musical program, addresses, recitations in English, Russian, German, Spanish, and Hungarian." The "Russian and German socialist singing societies" also entertained the crowd.[79] The internationalism of the "language locals" fostered intergroup ties in the United States; members contributed and participated as they could in politics abroad.

In January 1909 the "Russian Colony in Los Angeles" wrote a letter to the "Labor Unions of Los Angeles" informing the broader community of its upcoming protest against the looming extraditions of Christian Ansoff Rudowitz and Jan Janoff Pouren to Russia. The two men faced extradition for the "false charge of murder" among other charges stemming from the unrest in Russia in 1905. The Russian group warned the labor community that "this extradition will not alone affect Rudowitz and Pourin. If these men can be taken under false charges, no political refugee can longer find a haven in this land that has hitherto always offered a shelter to those fleeing despotic power." The parade started at Eighth and Main Streets and marched to the plaza, where the participants filled the air with "music and speeches." This protest doubled as a memorial for those killed on St. Petersburg's 1905 Bloody Sunday.[80]

After the demonstration, Peter Rubens reported in the city's AFL weekly, the *Citizen*, "Many have come to these shores to escape despotisms akin to that under Russia is suffering today. . . . Turkey and Persia even are entering upon reforms. Russia remains inexorable." Rubens concluded with an assurance, certainly intended to appease conservative labor, that people "wrongly interpreted" the orator Onton Cherbak, "which," he said, "we regret exceedingly. No incendiary, or other threats were made. [Cherbak] said nothing about Russians revolting against the government of this country under any circumstances."[81] Cherbak's membership in the International Committee of the Mexican Liberal Party junta and a press release he signed with a number of prominent anarchists on the committee a few years later indicate that in all probability he did use a good bit of "incendiary" rhetoric.[82] Clearly, Rubens attempted to distance labor from radical public speaking.

The socialist press recorded the event differently: a "committee of local Russian revolutionists issued the call, and labor of many lands responded in splendid solidarity." A procession of "300 marched from 8th and Main streets to the Plaza singing revolutionary songs." A crowd of two thousand then gathered to listen to speeches in English, German, Yiddish, Hungarian, Spanish, and Russian from representatives of the Socialist Party, Socialist Labor Party, IWW, and the Jewish Socialist-Territorial Labor Party of America. The day culminated with the singing of the "La Marseillaise" in "the many tongues of the crowd assembled." *Common Sense* remembered the protest and memorial as the "most significant international demonstration" in Los Angeles's history, and the paper's editors hoped that "this incident in the history of local international labor will be a spur for future solidarity and class conscious activity."[83] In January 1909 U.S. Secretary of State Elihu Root found Rudowitz's charges to be politically motivated and he declined to extradite him. The community celebrated its victory but remembered that "Jan Janoff Polren [*sic*] still languishes in New York, and our Mexican friends are in the Los Angeles county bastile."[84]

In February 1909 the Los Angeles Socialist Party nominated Fred Wheeler, one of the two Anglo organizers in Oxnard in 1903, as its mayoral candidate amid internal disputes within the city organization. While the Anglo local struggled through the infighting, the ethnic/language locals continued to function. The "Finns, the Germans, [and] the Hungarians have the most powerful socialist organizations, and the best disciplined, in their native countries, and the most powerful self-sustaining socialist organizations and self-supporting party owned socialist press in this country."[85] The Mexican branch grew as well, connected to PLM growth. Lázaro Gutiérrez de Lara traveled through the PLM network on a lecture tour. He visited Santa Maria, San Francisco, Albuquerque, Yuma, and Phoenix, spreading the socialist message and organizing against Porfirio Díaz.[86]

Solidarity sustained leftist movements, and local ad hoc purpose-based organizing committees gave it its most tangible form. People from diverse backgrounds and different organizational affiliations came together to work on causes they believed just. Most viewed their participation in local efforts as part of their participation in a global movement. Local leftist publications certainly represented it this way. At the same time that socialists in Los Angeles read about large-scale protests of unemployed workers in Berlin, Germany, the Social Science Club held a "Bloody Sunday" commemoration. The meeting filled Mammoth Hall to commemorate the deaths of protesters in St. Petersburg at the hands of czarist forces in 1905. The crowd listened "earnestly" to what precipitated "the slaughter of the unarmed people by the bullets of the minions of the autocrat." The speakers drew parallels "with the slaughter of the people of Monterrey, Nueva Leon, by Bernardo Reyes in connivance with the autocrat of the republic of Mexico."[87]

In similar terms to G. W. Woodbey's organizing, African Americans continued to increase their visibility to white leftists when they joined the cause. In 1908 the Reverend L. Milton Waldron, president of the Negroes' National League, wrote a letter to Eugene V. Debs, who was running as the Socialist Party's presidential candidate, for an explanation of the party's views on the Republican Party's nomination of William Howard Taft. *Common Sense* published Debs's reply, under the title "Not Racial but Class Distinction," in which he elucidated the party's views: "The Socialist Party knows that the great mass of Negroes are ignorant and it is the only party that refuses to traffic in that ignorance."[88] In 1910 the *People's Paper* reported that "Negroes Embrace Socialism" and noted that "at a mass meeting of the amalgamated negro organizations of Oklahoma, held at Chickasaw, resolutions charging the old parties with neglecting the interest of the negro race and calling upon the negroes of the state to support the entire Socialist ticket, were adopted by a large majority."[89] The paper did not report on these events again. Outside this paradigm, the *People's Paper* ran a short newswire about the lynching of an African American man in McHenry, Mississippi, without comment. The man, Patrick Husband, stood accused of "assaulting two daughters of Balton

Rouse, a well known planter" when "one hundred armed men caught the negro and shot him to death."[90]

The affinities of anarchists continued to fuel the strongest interracial solidarities. In July 1910, *Mother Earth* informed its readers about "our energetic comrade" T. Takahashi's newspaper the *Proletarian*, published in Chicago in Japanese and English. The article in the most prominent English-language anarchist magazine in the country stated that Takahashi "strives to acquaint his readers with the modern ideas of Anarchism and to free them from jingoism." *Mother Earth* printed an excerpt of an article from the *Proletarian* that read: "Recent conditions prevailing among the Japanese workers on the western coast are deplorable. A vast throng flocked in front of an employment agency seeking a job even in mid-summer. The active anti-Japanese movement for the last three years has been effective enough to drive them out of certain districts and concerns. The movement employs a cowardly and sneaking method, even using means of violence. Japanese are attacked in day time openly on the streets of the western metropolis and no one interferes." The article closed with "Let us unite! Not only in words, for unless our unity develops into action, the emancipation of wage slaves cannot be accomplished. Salvation lies in the unity of workmen regardless of race or color!"[91]

One of the clearest examples of solidarity between anarchists in the United States and Japan came through the international effort to save the life of Kōtoku Shusui and his comrades from execution by the Japanese state. Crucially, the linkages between the movements came through personal connections. Kōtoku met Leopold Fleischmann while the war correspondent was in Japan covering the Russo-Japanese War. Fleischmann then put Kōtoku in touch with anarchists in California. This blossomed into Kōtoku traveling on the West Coast of the United States for roughly six months in 1905 and 1906.[92]

The most interesting aspect of his visit is that he managed to negotiate any divisions between American or European immigrant radicals and the Japanese community. Kōtoku wrote articles for *Nichibei Shimbun* (*Japanese American News*), gave speeches, attended study groups, and helped form the Shakai Kakumeito (Social Revolutionary Party). He met with "the atheist Kidder, with the socialist Eitel, with the Swedish anarchist Widen, with the American anarchist Pyburn, with the socialist organizer George Williams, with Anthony of the IWW, and with a series of others, and, of course with Albert Johnson."[93] In Oakland he met with members of the newly formed IWW local.

The *People's Paper* reprinted an article in 1911 from the *Socialist Woman*, edited by Josephine Conger-Kaneko, that summarized Kōtoku's agitation for its Anglo readership. It read in part that Kōtoku felt "the futility of political action in their native country where the universal franchise is unknown, he became a 'direct actionist,' something akin to the I. W. W.'s in this country" after his visit to the United States.[94]

Kōtoku used his time to study the American situation:

> The street-corner speeches of the local white men's socialist party have also again and again been broken up by the police. Of course, the police do not have the authority to prohibit these speeches. But they always find all sorts of pretexts for their obstruction. Needless to say, speech and press for atheism or anarchism are always subjected to the most severe shackling. One comrade, a white, told me in his indignation: "America is a land of liberty for the rich and the religionists. The way the workers are persecuted and oppressed here makes America not the tiniest bit different from Russia or Japan. Just look, look at the scars over shoulders! That's from the beating the police gave me." How can liberty exist, how can popular rights exist in a place where the capitalist class exists, where the landlord class exists![95]

Upon returning to Japan, Kōtoku resumed agitating in his home country, which eventually led to his arrest and a death sentence along with his partner Kanno Sugako and ten other comrades. The radical press around the world and in the United States published an array of appeals. Hutchins Hapgood, Leonard Abbott, Emma Goldman, Hippolyte Havel, Sadakichi Hartmann, Alexander Berkman, and Dr. Ben L. Reitman signed one of the most widely published, which appeared in many publications including the *Industrial Worker* and funneled donations through *Mother Earth*.[96]

Leftists in Los Angeles supported their Japanese comrades with equal enthusiasm. In January 1911 the Socialist Proletariat Club of Los Angeles organized a "Monster Protest" in support that the German Socialist Maennerchor (Men's Choir) opened in song. At the protest meeting a number of local socialists, IWW members, and anarchists spoke out against the looming executions. The IWW attorney Fred Moore spoke in English along with Charles Sprading. Fernando Velarde traveled from Phoenix, Arizona, to express solidarity on behalf of the PLM in Spanish. Leopold Fleischmann concluded the evening telling of "his acquaintance with the Japanese Socialists" and reading from his personal correspondence with Kōtoku.[97] Expressions of solidarity reached beyond North America. In Ancona, Italy, an anarchist group, called the *circoloanarchico* "Kutoki," formed.[98] Ultimately, the efforts failed to spare their lives. Upon Denjiro Kōtoku's death, Emma Goldman remembered him as "a man of brilliant mind, an able writer, and the translator of some of the works of Karl Marx, Leo Tolstoy, and Peter Kropotkin."[99]

Internationalism and Its Limits

■ ■ ■

In 1910 an article in the IWW newspaper the *Industrial Worker* asked, "Who Is the Foreigner?" D. Bond declared that there are two nations in the world and asked readers, "Do you belong to the nation that lives by working, or to the nation that lives by owning?" The article continued: "'Workingmen of all countries, unite.' That means unite in your own nation. The Chinaman, Jap, Mexican, Italian, Hungarian or Negro who [*sic*] workers, belongs to my nation. He belongs to your nation if you are doing needful work. On the other hand, Rockefeller, Morgan, Carnegie, Taft, Nicholas, Edward, Diaz, Alfonso, do not belong to your nation, no matter where they are born or where they live; no matter where you were born or where you live. No matter what their race; no matter what your race." He continued, noting that President Taft "consulted with the arch-fiend Diaz how best to work the workers on both sides [of] the imaginary line."[100] The acceptance of this outlook and its incorporation into movement practice varied across ideology and institutional structures of the left in Los Angeles. The racist structures organized and enforced in law and popular action continued to affect race relations in Los Angeles. The critiques of Chinese labor from the nineteenth century remained the most accessible frame of reference for Anglo labor and socialists when they sought to understand nonwhite laborers. Leftists formulated the most successful challenges to this racism through the language of internationalism. Socialists, anarchists, and Wobblies sought internationalist or antinationalist ideals to frame their acceptance of non-Anglo workers. This continued for years to come as racism persisted on the Left and throughout society.

CHAPTER 5

ORGANIZING MOBILE WORKERS

Six years after Samuel Gompers rejected the charter application from Oxnard's Japanese Mexican Labor Association in 1903 and after the three consecutive years of failure organizing track laborers in Los Angeles between 1902 and 1904, the American Federation of Labor once again turned its attention to mobile workers in California in 1909. The California State Federation of Labor (CSFL) voted at their annual meeting in 1909 to direct resources toward organizing migrant workers within a new branch of affiliated unions, United Laborers locals, throughout the state. Mobility and skill level structured California and the U.S. West's urban and rural labor force. Changing direction to organize unskilled workers put the trade union inescapably on the path toward organizing nonwhite migrant workers. To find success the AFL would have to account for all three factors: skill level, race, and mobility.

Similar to prior multiracial organizing efforts in Southern California, this new campaign had its champions among dissent in the trade organization. This affected funding and other institutional support that the state organization and city bodies such as the Los Angeles Central Labor Council directed toward the United Laborers campaign. This effort also placed the AFL in the same organizing terrain as the expanding Industrial Workers of the World. Competition between the unions, internal conflicts within the AFL, and the structural difficulties of organizing mobile workers at temporary jobsites all contributed to the California State Federation of Labor's withdrawing support for the United Laborers in 1912 and all of the locals shuttering by 1913.

In Los Angeles the lifespan of the United Laborers organizing campaign was set against the backdrop of the Metal Trades strike in 1910 and the bombing of the Los Angeles Times Building perpetrated by AFL members with the assistance of anarchists. Insurgency reached out into the region with the Partido Liberal Mexican–organized Baja raids and the rolling series of IWW-instigated free speech fights across the West. In the context of the period, organizing mobile workers within the AFL appeared deceptively moderate, but interracial organizing had the potential to radically reshape the AFL. The forces that combined in the United Laborers campaign illustrate the continued importance of the patchwork of local AFL organizers and the flexible coalitions they pulled together in and near Los Angeles. The fleeting moments of success of the campaign in Los Angeles foreshadowed future demographic changes to the AFL brought about through inclusion of the city's racially diverse laborers later in the century.

Labor Mobility and Union Organizing

The federated structure of the American Federation of Labor consisted of local unions electing representatives to city labor councils with state and national bodies in bureaucratic layers above. The configuration of the union allowed both for change and for clinging to the old to occur up and down its hierarchy from individual members of locals to the national president. The handful of influential AFL organizers in Los Angeles with far more racially inclusive views than the national AFL leadership generated local union support for the JMLA in Oxnard and the Mexican Federal Union in Los Angeles. After 1903 the number of migrant workers in California continued to grow, and in 1909 the difficult situation of migratory workers and their perceived threat to traditionally organized urban trades came into focus for some members of the California State Federation of Labor. Excluding workers from the AFL based on race clearly did not prevent immigration from swelling the numbers of nonwhite workers, and it made the decision by Samuel Gompers to deny membership of the JMLA in 1903 even more out of touch with the reality of West Coast labor. However, regret for racism was not a common emotion, especially within the AFL, but some organizers, John Murray for instance, continued to view people as unequal while exhaustively organizing with nonwhites. This was the case when he argued for Japanese exclusion in 1908 and when he rose to become one of Gompers's key advisers during the Mexican Revolution.[1] The United Laborers organizing campaign unfolded within this dynamic of defensive trade-union organizing and continued racism.

In 1908 Andrew Furuseth, a stalwart of racist exclusionism and one of the most powerful labor leaders in California, convinced the national AFL convention to support a resolution to look into organizing mobile workers in the West.[2]

The following year, representatives of the San Francisco Labor Council and the San Jose Labor Council proposed a resolution at the CSFL annual convention to "take some action toward" organizing unskilled migrant workers.[3] Also at the convention in 1909, J. B. Dale, who went on to take a major street-level role in United Laborers organizing, introduced a resolution for "the Committee on Organization [to] be instructed to go carefully into the form of organization that might be useful to agricultural workers with a view of the American Federation of Labor putting forth all the force available to help organize amongst these men."[4] A regional vice president's report noted the same year that affiliated unions in Fresno "have been numerically weakened by our membership leaving for other parts to find work."[5]

The state AFL slowly began to take notice of the mobile army of labor that moved through the fields and back to the city streets. Andrew Furuseth continued to support organizing migratory workers and spoke in favor of Dale's resolution.[6] Furuseth and Olaf A. Tveitmoe, secretary of the San Francisco Building Trades Council, later wrote to Samuel Gompers and the executive council of the AFL about migratory workers in California:

> Under our system of land tenure and machine-worked land, held in large tracts, men are not needed on the land continuously. They are wanted in seed and harvest time. There is, therefore, no stability of employment at farm labor as things are now... In order to obtain anything like steady employment on the land, there would have to be a large number of small holdings, interspersed between the larger ones. This would give a man the chance to work on his own land and on other holdings between times.[7]

As the two men analyzed the structurally difficult position of farm laborers in California's industrial agricultural economy, they continued to hold strongly to their views of protecting urban white workers.

On the surface California's State Federation of Labor's initial movements toward organizing migratory workers offered a small bit of hope that the federation would take a step back from its racist exclusionist policies. The AFL, however, reinforced its position that Asian workers were not welcome. The 1909 state convention celebrated an affiliated local union in the East Bay city of Vallejo that forced a Japanese-owned restaurant to shutter its doors.[8]

The state organization made its view of Asian workers even more clear by including A. E. Yoell in meetings. He represented the Asiatic Exclusion League and was the only non-union member allowed to participate. Yoell attended several annual conventions, though he did not hold voting power. Throughout this period the state federation maintained its position against Asian immigration, as was the case when the Los Angeles COL assisted Japanese workers in Oxnard in

1903. When the California State Federation of Labor launched this direction of organizing, it placed itself inescapably on a path toward organizing non-Anglo labor. However, the decisions it made in the course of the next few years remained consistent with its past. This organizing drive opened the AFL to unskilled and mobile workers, but it did not remove racial barriers, especially for Asians. The United Laborers reinforced Anglo notions of racialized employment, even though some organizers and members of locals worked against these same notions.

The bureaucratic gears of the state federation spun fast enough for the Joint Committee on Migratory Labor (JCML) to form in early 1910, a few months after the October meeting. The committee, charged with providing leadership and insight for the state organization, held its first regular session in April. The CSFL allocated two hundred dollars per month in financing and appointed J. B. Dale and Edward Thompson as paid organizers for this initial period—a significant investment of union resources. At the next state convention in Los Angeles in October 1910, the state body planned to assess the progress of the committee, evaluate its future prospects, and decide "whether the results attained justify the expenditure of money and energy in this direction."[9] The CSFL took a cautious, bureaucratic approach and maintained the ability to change direction and redirect its resources throughout the campaign.

Regional Growth of the Industrial Workers of the World

Migrant workers continued to organize in the face of the AFL's racist exclusionism and general inattention toward unskilled laborers. Japanese farm laborers in California formed particularly strong labor associations that increased their wages and, by extension, wages for all farmworkers.[10] The IWW expanded in California and the Southwest among the multiracial working class in agricultural fields, urban jobsites, and mines. The IWW excelled at organizing in this terrain of mobile labor and varied work. Its membership and influence built slowly in the first few years after the founding convention in 1905, but this obscured the crucial efforts of traveling organizers, which led to increased growth after 1909. Regional expansion of the IWW is attributable to several interlocking factors.

The growth of the IWW in the Southwest is closely connected to Mexican organizing and Spanish-language anarchist networks. As early as 1902 the New York– and Tampa-based Catalan immigrant anarchist Pedro Esteve toured western mines, speaking to workers along the way. He remained an active supporter of the striking miners in Colorado in the run up to the founding convention of the IWW in 1905, in which he participated. In 1903 Mexicans workers led a strike at the Phelps-Dodge copper mine in Clifton-Morenci, Arizona. It was the largest work stoppage in the region at the time and evidenced the radical, independent organizing of Mexican workers. PLM organizers Práxedis Guerrero and Manuel Sarabia both lived and organized in these mining towns where Mexican, Spanish, and Italian anarchists circulated. The Clifton-Morenci strike fed into the strike across the border in Cananea in 1906 where Lázaro Gutiérrez de Lara lived. A few months later the PLM made its first unsuccessful attempt at armed revolt.[11]

In 1906 Fernando Velarde and Rosendo Dorame led the effort to add a Spanish-language section to Phoenix IWW Local 272, one of the first in the region outside of California. Mexicans grew into the majority over the next few years. In 1909 the Phoenix local began publishing *La Union Industrial*, the second Spanish-language IWW newspaper, which continued until 1911. Beginning in 1910 Pedro Esteve edited *Cultura Proletaria* and later its successor, *Cultura Obrera*. Both papers circulated in the Southwest, along with Italian anarchist newspapers and PLM publications.[12]

The influence and organizing skills of the PLM-connected organizers most directly facilitated the growth of the IWW among Mexicans in the region. Organizers such as Fernando Palomares, Fernando Velarde, and Pedro Coria spread the PLM's revolutionary ideals, often simultaneously with the IWW's industrial unionism among Mexicans and Native Americans from northern Mexico and across much of the U.S. West. From the copper mines in northern Mexico and Arizona to California's agricultural fields, radical ideas circulated in Mexican networks.[13]

Fernando Palomares and Juan Olivares, with the help of the Italian Joe Ettor, started a Spanish language newspaper in Los Angeles in 1908. Backed by Los Angeles IWW Local 12, they published *Libertad Y Trabajo*. It included IWW content and the writings of Ricardo Flores Magón, another indication of crossover PLM-IWW organizing. They managed to print only a handful of issues as Palomares's organizing drew him out of the city. Palomares, a Mayo Indian, left Los Angeles and traveled through the well-trod migratory circuit for the next two years from Mexico to the Midwest, Southwest, and up to the Pacific Northwest. In Mexico he met with local PLM supporters, particularly Mayo and Yaqui Indians in the north. In Denver he personally extended his gratitude to Bill Haywood and Charles Moyer for their assistance during the Cananea organizing in 1906. It is also possible that he helped organize Mexican participation in Spokane, Washington's IWW free-speech fight in 1909 toward the end of this trip.[14]

This was part of a shared practice of traveling organizing by white and Mexican IWW agitators. Fernando Palomares's two-year trip was similar to a journey made by Frank Little that began in Arizona in 1908. Little first moved through mining camps in Arizona before coming across to California, where he spoke at a Mojave Desert mine. He then dropped down into southern California, where he spoke to agricultural workers. After several more stops, Little's journey culminated in his joining Palomares, Velarde, and others in Fresno to help form IWW Local 66 in 1909, the year before the Fresno free-speech fight.[15] By 1908, new IWW locals had formed outside of Los Angeles and Phoenix in San Diego and in the inland citrus town of Redlands, the Imperial Valley town of Holtville, and the Arizona copper town of Globe. These locations illustrate the appeal of the IWW across different industries, from agriculture and mining to infrastructure projects like building roads or laying gas lines in developing cities.

The national IWW leadership directed attention and limited financial resources to the region. In February 1909 Bill Haywood planned to travel to Los Angeles to give a Sunday night lecture. An advert for the gathering cried, "We must hurry. And the Mexicans, and the Russians, and the workers of the world o'er are demanding in no [un]certain tones 'the right to liberty, life, and the pursuit of happiness.'" It continued: "Does it need imagination to conjure up Cripple Creek, Victor, Telluride, Alabama, Glasgow, St. Petersburg?" Haywood could not make it to town to deliver the lecture, but J. B. Osborne, the blind socialist orator from Oakland, quite ably replaced him. Haywood managed to make his way to the state a few weeks later, and his lecture tour took him through the expanses of Southern California: Rialto, San Bernardino, Hemet, El Centro, Brawley, Upland, Redlands, Santa Ana, San Diego, Escondido, Anaheim, Pasadena, Santa Monica, San Pedro, Sawtelle, and Santa Maria.[16]

The industrial unionism of the IWW proved to be remarkably adaptable. Workers organized under the IWW banner in the range of western employment from miners to farm laborers, in cities and rural areas, at the point of production and away during slack periods of unemployment. The flexibility of the organizing model fed its strong base in the western United States that did not always manifest in steady dues-paying and card-carrying members. Shunned by the AFL and drawn to the IWW, migratory workers constituted one of the IWW's core constituencies culturally and in terms of numbers. Members celebrated mobility as much in the cultural life of the union as in its organizational practices. The classic song "Hallelujah, I'm a Bum!" was but one example of the union's holding the migratory worker up and drawing strength from his condition:

O, why don't you work
Like other men do?
How in hell can I work
When there's no work to do?
[Chorus] Hallelujah, I'm a bum! Hallelujah, bum again!
Hallelujah, give us a handout To receive us again.
O, why don't you save
All the money you earn?

If I did not eat I'd have money to burn.
[Chorus]
O, I like my boss
He's a good friend of mine;
That's why I am starving out in the breadline.
[Chorus]
I can't buy a job
For I ain't got the dough,
So I ride in a box-car
For I'm a hobo.
[Chorus]
Whenever I get
All the money I earn
The boss will be broke
And to work he must turn.
[Chorus][17]

Popular songs aside, IWW organizing connected organizing migratory workers to its racial and linguistic components.

The IWW published union material in a remarkable range of languages—including newspapers in at least eighteen languages other than English—and it remained open to all races.[18] Through this openness many Wobblies held onto to views of the relative organizability of workers according to race.

At the IWW's third annual convention in 1907, George Speed, rather than standing in the way of the inclusion of Japanese workers, argued that they were so well organized that the IWW should not waste their limited resources attempting to include them in the industrial union:

> The Japanese in their work, like all other people come to this country and necessarily hang together like one man, as a solid body, and the same thing is true of the Greeks; in San Francisco they are solid and hang together like one man and if one gets fired, the whole bunch quits.... Now, I say the whole fight against the Japanese is the fight of the middle class of California, in which they employ the labor faker to back it up. That is really the position of the fight there against the Japs and while I know that condition, it is practically useless for the present time and under present conditions for the Industrial Workers of the World to take any steps there to organize these men under the present state of things and prejudices that array our organizers, without going outside and if we organize the men who are already in California into the I.W.W. we will do well for the present and I think it would retard our own development.[19]

When the matter was put to vote, Speed stood as the sole vote against directing union resources toward Asian workers.

At mid-decade, in 1916, directly before American entry into World War I and during IWW Agriculture Workers' Organization campaign, Speed testified before the Commission on Industrial Relations: "In the last two or three years while the average migratory worker has had no sense of organization whatever—the Japs and Chinese have a far better sense of organization than has the native American, and the result is when he eliminates the native out of a given locality he gets better conditions and wages than the native worker does." Speed continued, "I have met with them and seen them and talked to members of it. And I know this, that while a good many people in the State object to the Jap and Chinese, I want to say, as far as I am concerned, one man is as good as another to me; I don't care whether he is black, blue, green, or yellow, as long as he acts the man and acts true to his economic interests as a worker."[20] There are many other examples of race-based thinking permeating the thought of IWW members and many others on the Left, though the difference between this thought and the virile racism seen in the AFL and the Asiatic Exclusion League is that the majority of radicals held Mexicans, Italians, and Japanese as exceptionally willing to organize based on what was understood as their racial characteristics. This discussion most commonly occurred at the local level in the IWW, with organizers either choosing to cooperate with Asian workers or deciding against cooperating with anti-Asian agitators. An example of the latter occurred in Redding, north of Sacramento, when local Wobblies refused to help drive Chinese out of the city.[21]

Living, working, and organizing in this racially diverse region certainly did not eliminate racism or at least a strongly racialized way of viewing individuals by IWW members. One example of how this operated came in an attempt at Wobbly humor. Ned Bond in Imperial, California, wrote "The Hobo's Vindication" in the *Industrial Worker*: "I have given my last four-bit piece to a lame hobo and then stole my dinner from a Bench-legged Chinaman."[22] An oral history by the Wobbly Joseph Murphy recalled another: "I organized a group of Hindus in Marysville, California. We had one bunch that wouldn't cooperate. They used a rag dipped in water instead of toilet paper, so I took turpentine and poured it into their water. When they went to use the rag for toilet paper, they had an unpleasant experience."[23]

More commonly, Japanese workers formed their own organizations with promising results. The *Industrial Worker* noted, "Japanese laborers in California are pushing the work of organization. They may be organized solidly before their white fellow worker."[24] The Commission of Immigration in California reached a similar conclusion in 1911: "The Japanese (as farm workers) were best of all, but in late years have shown less willingness to work hard. Moreover, by securing control of the situation they have reduced the workday from twelve to eleven hours, and by means of strikes have raised the wages of all races."[25]

In Southern California the IWW won one of its first victories in the Imperial Valley in 1910. In Brawley, the "farm hand reigned supreme (and to hear some fellows talk it was impossible to organize him), there, as in Spokane, the floater, the revolutionary worker understanding the surroundings, the conditions, etc., proceeded to get a hall that would meet the emergency in that district. The result was that every worker in the district came there, and the result was that they were able to dictate terms to the farmer." When T. J. O'Brien celebrated this IWW success, he first discussed the difference between labor in the West and the East: "In this western country the conditions differ a great deal from those of the east. A majority of the workers in this part of the country do not know what a home is. The only home most of us have is the roll of blankets which we carry on our backs."[26]

The prominent socialist Austin Lewis argued that the diverse pool of migratory workers responded to IWW teachings on industrial unionism because "the I.W.W. began to interpret the mind of the unskilled and nomadic laborers."[27] Similarly, the historian Hyman Weintraub observed, "The problem of organizing hundreds of thousands of workers who are continually traveling from Oklahoma to Canada, and from Canada to southern California, never remaining for more than a few days in any one place, completely independent and roving and working at their own free will, tied to no particular location—this problem seemed insurmountable organizationally except for the I.W.W."[28]

The growth of the IWW, just as the AFL began the United Laborers organizing drive, increased tension and competition between the two unions across the region and in Los Angeles. Mexican workers also elevated the pressure on the AFL by increasing their demands at jobsites from within the IWW and apart from either organization. For example, on March 2, 1910, one hundred Mexican workers on the Los Angeles-Pacific Railway went on strike for a pay increase from one dollar to a dollar fifty. Their employer did not meet their demand, yet their effort did not go unnoticed.[29] The *Industrial Worker* took note of this short, independent job action and sympathetically portrayed the "Mexican 'cholo,'" imported by railroad interests, as working for "starvation" wages for their families and as being the "poorest paid laborer in the country." The IWW paper, in supporting their failed strike, also described Mexican workers as "poor, ignorant," and knowing "nothing but manual labor."[30] These characterizations continued sympathy and support but also furthered racialized understandings of Mexican workers expressed in English by a white member of the syndicalist union.

In summer 1910 the expansion of the San Diego IWW gave Mexicans a stronger voice in the union. Fernando Palomares and others with similar PLM ties laid the groundwork for the IWW among laborers in San Diego beginning in late spring. This resulted in Public Service Local 378. In August, Mexicans in the local working for the gas company digging trenches for new lines went on strike over race-based pay differences. Anglos received $2.25 compared to the two dollars paid to Mexican, Greek, and Italian workers for a nine-hour day. The Italians joined them, along with some of the Anglos and Greeks, for a total of about sixty men off the job. The *Industrial Worker* gave the strike prominent coverage through correspondence from the local organizers, which changed the tone of the newspaper's coverage. The laborers won the strike; they would all now be paid $2.25 for a day's work, regardless of race.[31]

During this agitation Laura Payne Emerson rose to prominence in the San Diego IWW; the city assumed an important supporting role in the PLM's military action in Baja California that began that winter. Another mark of regional IWW expansion came in Phoenix, Arizona, a city's whose local had around five hundred members in 1910. Attempting to build on the progress in San Diego and elsewhere, the seemingly ever-present Wobbly Frank Little argued that the IWW should work harder to organize Mexican workers in the Southwest.[32] Gearing up for the free-speech fight in Fresno in 1910, Little wrote, "We have a bunch of agitators" in town, including "English, Mexican, German, and Japanese." Little continued, "The papers have announced that the A.F. of L. will organize the laborers—that is, the white slaves. They are going to run the Japanese out of the country."[33] In contrast, IWW organizers in Fresno, while celebrating the local Armenian, Greek, Italian, Mexican, German, and Russian workers, noted, "We omit the Japanese because they are already fairly well organized. All these different nationalities have their eyes now focused on the I.W.W."[34]

The United Laborers

As the IWW expanded its membership and increased its agitation in Los Angeles and the Southwest through grassroots participation, the California State Federation of Labor continued to appoint representatives to the Joint Committee on Migratory Labor, reaching a total of twelve members. The committee decided to begin on the ground organizing in Northern California's Alameda County with two dedicated full-time organizers to build upon its strong union base in the Bay Area. From here, the committee planned first to expand its organizing to other cities with the hope that "they may soon become self-supporting."[35] Committee members envisioned the final phase of their organizing reaching lesser towns and agricultural workers directly in the fields throughout the state. Each new United Laborers local would be chartered with the AFL and fit into city and state union bureaucracies.

Andrew Furuseth and Olaf. A. Tveitmoe spoke of the targets of the campaign favorably, "By what name are these landless, homeless men who travel from place to place, seeking opportunity to obtain remunerative labor, to be called if not 'migratory'? They have been called 'hoboes' by others until many of them have accepted the appellation." Furuseth and Tveitmoe promised to "help them to make the name respected."[36] The organization planning took into accounts that laborers concentrated in cities and towns between periods of employment, often in rural areas. The JCML adapted the United Laborers structure from the normal policy of membership being tied to an individual local to one that recognized labor mobility. Each United Laborers local would honor a "mutual arrangement to exchange cards and transfer membership from any one to another of these locals."[37]

At this point in time the organizing effort was top-down and bureaucratic, but it began with sufficient funds, and the JCML members seemed to recognize the unique challenges they faced. Yet the CSFL leadership had a flawed understanding of the long-term challenges of organizing mobile labor seen through their lack of an extended financial commitment past their initial investment of resources. The state federation sought to create self-sustaining and financially stable locals, an understandable goal, but one that worked against the reality of mobile labor. Already in 1910, with the organizing drive still in its infancy, the state body ordered each new branch to "contribute their share to the necessary expense of organizing the migratory laborers of the state."[38] The lack of permanent employment made regular payment of dues by a regular membership base nearly impossible.

United Laborers organizing in Los Angeles took its first steps forward in the tense autumn of 1910. The city's organized skilled workers squared off against the Merchants and Manufacturers Association in a wave of strikes that began in the spring. In June the city's metal-trade workers walked off the job in support of an eight-hour workday and a wage increase. Clashes between strikers and police resulted in several hundred arrests by the fall. The CSFL and San Francisco labor council had supported the efforts in Los Angeles.[39] Then came one of the most infamous days in the history of Los Angeles. On October 1 a bomb ripped through the Los Angeles Times Building, killing twenty-one people and injuring scores more. Just two days later the California State Federation of Labor opened its annual meeting in Los Angeles. The layers of AFL bureaucracy pooled their resources to support the metalworkers in their assault on Los Angeles's open shop and disavowed any union connection to the blast. The AFL also continued to advance the United Laborers campaign among unskilled workers. Organizing unskilled workers was not the primary focus of the AFL that fall, but it continued with vigor nevertheless.[40]

The AFL's split focus can be seen in the way that state organizer J. B. Dale divided his time in Los Angeles. He arrived before the CSFL meeting and "spent the past few weeks in Southern sections of the state looking over the field for future work" on behalf of the JCML before assisting the striking tradesmen in the city. The JCML reported its limited progress to the 1910 convention in Los Angeles: "The greater part of the past year was taken up in preparatory work. During the early part of the year there was some uncertainty about our ability to finance the project, but we have now an assured income to carry on this great work for the coming year without interruption."[41] Organizing migratory workers continued to be a second-tier effort of the CSFL, but in light of the expense of supporting the metal trades strike in Los Angeles, any continued financial support for United Laborers organizing was an important victory for the JCML.

During the state federation meeting the CSFL organized a parade of fifteen thousand through Los Angeles as a show of strength and solidarity for the striking workers.[42] Typically, workers marched behind banners identifying their union local with as much pomp and circumstance as they could muster. But in this parade an unlikely ally joined the trade unions: "After some agitation therefore numbers of the foreign unskilled expressed their willingness to parade with the organized trades. They did so to the number of about two thousand, almost all Mexicans. It was the first time in the history of the Coast that this class of labor had paraded with the organized trades." Austin Lewis, a leading California socialist, later remembered these workers as "painfully, almost ludicrously, out of place." The trade unions paraded "with their crafts organization banners and the national flag at the head of each division. But what emblem could the unskilled workers carry? The fact, however, as usual produced its own expression and the Mexican workers paraded under the Marxian adjuration 'Workers of the World Unite.' The craft organizations expressed themselves in trade mottoes and national flags; the unskilled with their mass-organization could find no other expression than a statement of that solidarity which their condition demanded."[43] The willingness of the two thousand Mexican workers to join the parade that day grew out of the years of Mexican organizing in Los Angeles and the borderlands by the PLM, IWW, socialists, and the AFL.

Cooperation between the Partido Liberal Mexicano and the AFL helped swell the number of Mexican workers in the streets and eventually in the United Laborers. After the parade, in November, the PLM organ *Regeneración* publicly began laying the groundwork for the United Laborers by editorializing on the importance of the union to its readership. The paper appealed to the possibility of the new union increasing wages and the respect of foreign workers. Given the radical outlook of the paper and its readership, its writers inserted their own politics into their support by stating that the AFL planned to employ the tactics of the revolutionary unions in Europe and take the form of an industrial union. The paper referenced the same strands of French syndicalism that also partially

CHAPTER 5

inspired the IWW. Unequivocally, the AFL was not considering such a sea change in its structure, but it is interesting to note that at the 1913 CSFL meeting one participant commented on the strength of syndicalism while dismissing the IWW.[44]

Internal political dynamics within the PLM influenced how the group cooperated with the AFL. In fall 1910, before the Baja raids that winter, the PLM still had socialist and anarchist leaders, which helped it achieve its broadest community of solidarity. The breadth of local support for the United Laborers in Los Angeles also speaks to the continued influence of socialists within the craft-labor movement in the city. Further, the PLM did not concede its politics or autonomy to the AFL body by supporting this organizing drive. Even the socialist members of the PLM did not shy away from trying to influence the direction of the United Laborers to bring it in line with their own vision. Once organized, local union members would have the ability to push the direction of their own union from within. The PLM supported the United Laborers in 1910, but it spoke about the new union with goals and motivations that were not unified.

The first formal public organizing meeting for the United Laborers in Los Angeles took place on November 8, 1910, and *Regeneración, People's Paper,* and the *Citizen* all covered the event. *Regeneración's* joining with Los Angeles's socialist and trade union papers indicates the broad political coalition supporting the union. At this meeting it became clear that the two leading socialists in the PLM, Lázaro Gutiérrez de Lara and Antonio Villarreal, most strongly supported the unionization campaign within the PLM. They spoke at the meeting along with fellow PLM member Librado Rivera and AFL-affiliated Charles M. Feider. The Mexican men served as the union's temporary officers at the inaugural meeting, at which eighty workers signed union cards.[45] The *Citizen* claimed that "De Lara, as speaker and educator in his Sunday afternoon meetings on the Plaza, and the valiant paper 'Regeneracion,' of Magon, Villarreal, Rivera, and Figueroa, paved the way for the good work. Thus they repay the assistance rendered them in a time of need."[46] The paper referred to the AFL support of the PLM leaders after their arrest in 1907 and through their legal struggle and imprisonment.

After this first meeting Librado Rivera probably refused his appointment to the trade union for political reasons. His anarchism did not square with the values of the trade union even if it organized Mexican workers, but more pressing was the impending invasion of Baja California. Gutiérrez de Lara and Villarreal poured their effort into the union in the fall as others in the PLM planned the Baja insurrection. Librado Rivera later recalled this moment as a crucial split within the PLM, with Gutiérrez de Lara and Villarreal drifting toward Francisco Madero and "*Gomperiana.*" *Regeneración* reported on the United Laborers in a series of articles written by Villarreal. As internal conflict simmered, the close participation of PLM members undoubtedly lent the AFL credibility with the workers they sought to

118

bring into the fold.[47] Villarreal also continued to speak about the Mexican revolution on behalf of the PLM. He journeyed to Oxnard the same week as the first United Laborers meeting and gathered a "good collection" for the group.[48]

In December the United Laborers hosted a "Gran Meeting Internacional" at Italian Hall to mark the kickoff of its broader organizing campaign in the city. The announcement of the meeting communicated to Spanish readers that the meeting answered the call of a declaration "in favor of the organization of wage laborers of all nationalities that live in the United States at the last national convention of the American Federation of Labor. They [the AFL] will step up their activities in Los Angeles in order to carry out this beautiful idea that strengthens unionism and improves the situation of the workers." It continued: "Towards this end, on the night of next Wednesday, December 14, in Italian Hall, on the corner of North Main and Macy, an international meeting especially dedicated to Mexican and Italian workers will be held."[49]

The speakers included Austin Lewis and Antonio Villarreal. Ludovico Caminita, the former editor of Paterson, New Jersey's Italian anarchist paper *L'Era Nuova*, who had recently relocated to Los Angeles, joined the men on the stage. They addressed the audience in English, Spanish, and Italian, respectively.[50] Rather strange bedfellows at first blush to be sure, but Los Angeles commonly produced temporary solidarities between organizations. Disagreements in political ideology, vehement as they might have been, often left room for cooperation. Further, Caminita brought with him cooperative organizing experience from Paterson, New Jersey, where anarchists organized within and with the IWW, roughly comparable to PLM and IWW crossover.[51]

United Laborers organizing continued the public cooperation between the PLM and Los Angeles labor and potentially obscured their military planning for the now-imminent Baja raids. Additionally, the very act of organizing mobile labor in Los Angeles was quite radical even if the AFL leadership failed to recognize it. *Regeneración*, behind Villarreal's pen, celebrated the success of the event, stating that a large number of Mexicans and Italians formed a Trabajadores Unidos (United Laborers) local. Its secretary, Amelio Velarde, directed the correspondence of this group, and it obtained a charter as AFL Local 13097. Propaganda in *Regeneración* focused on organizing for an eight-hour day and expanding the union's membership by turning its three hundred current members into active propagandists. *Regeneración* and the other papers gave it prominent coverage during the winter of 1910–11. Guadalupe Viramontes took over as secretary in March. The PLM connection also reached beyond Los Angeles. In March the Grupo Regeneración in Tulare called itself "Journaleros Unidos."[52]

The unshakable legacy of AFL exclusion hung over the broad coalition supporting the United Laborers in Los Angeles. An article in *Regeneración* directly addressed its Mexican readership skeptical of the AFL's newfound interest in organizing Mexican workers in light of its long anti-Chinese history. The article, rather than claiming that the United Laborers opened the doors of the AFL to all races, drew lines of separation between Chinese and its Mexican readers: "If you do not enroll, if you do not join the Union, then within a short period of time all the jobs will be as badly distributed as in Mexico and then the same workers unions will force the government to throw you out of the United States as they did with the Chinese. Would this be flattering for our people [*nuestra raza*]?" The article then asked Mexicans to "unite!" and join the union.[53]

After the kickoff of the United Laborers in Los Angeles, the State Federation of Labor added Juan Ramirez to their payroll as an organizer in February 1911. Ramirez began his paid work almost two months after United Laborers 13097 organized in late fall 1910, stepping into the space vacated by the three PLM members now occupied by the beginning of the Mexican Revolution. Ramirez, a member of Blacksmith Local 282 in Los Angeles, came from a union family. His father immigrated to Southern California from Sonora, Mexico, in the 1860s; the *Citizen* remembered the elder Ramirez as a community leader in San Gabriel before moving to San Bernardino to work in the produce business around the turn of the century. Ramirez's father and seven siblings, spread across Los Angeles and San Bernardino, facilitated some of the personal connections he drew upon while organizing. The younger Ramirez was the most active and visible Mexican American in the Los Angeles Central Labor Council, and its members elected him to the organization's executive board in July 1911.[54]

Juan Ramirez sought to build on the initial success generated by the PLM men by branching out into Los Angeles's early sprawl. He reported: "I spent some time in the beach cities of Long Beach organizing Migratory Labor; San Pedro, organizing the Lumber Handlers, and in Redondo, organizing the Lumber Handlers. The Migratory Labor of Long Beach were affiliated with the Local in Los Angeles, while the work in San Pedro and Redondo resulted in the organization of locals in both cities affiliated with the International Longshoremen's Union; also, in the city of San Pedro, [was] a Fishermen's Union with a membership of 160." His work in Los Angeles resulted in the organization of seven new unions for a total of ten with an inclusive membership of 1,919.[55] Ramirez reported to the CLC in the end of September 1911 on his successful unionizing efforts of railroad companies in Los Angeles. He also looked to rally union voters to the poll for the October primary to vote for the Socialist Party ticket that included Job Harriman.[56]

Through their growth United Laborers locals continued to reflect the racial and national order within Los Angeles trade unions. The campaign enthusiastically included Eastern European, European, and now more Mexican workers while excluding Asians. The AFL and the Socialist Party organized with African Americans concurrently to the United Laborers, though not on the same scale. In 1911 Los Angeles's Socialist Party nominated an African American, George Washington Whitley, for city council, and the AFL-affiliated paper the *Citizen* provided him with much-needed publicity. Whitley led the Afro-American League, six thousand members strong at the time. That same year, the CLC cooperated with the Afro-American League on a limited organizing drive for black workers. Socialists and the AFL in Los Angeles supported African American organizing, on the street and at the polls, on a handful of occasions, but the Left more broadly remained mostly unconcerned with the struggles of Los Angeles's African American community.[57]

This was not the case with Harrison Gray Otis, the powerful publisher of the *Los Angeles Times*. While Otis's opposition to labor and his attempts at maintaining an "open shop" in Los Angeles made him the sworn enemy of Left, he was popular among African Americans for his views on race. Otis also viewed Chinese immigrant labor as an effective counter to agitators. Racism on the Left, Otis's racial views, and his position to enjoy the benefits of divisions among workers functioned together to create an additional level of complexity in alliance formation in Los Angeles.[58]

Another shift away from the radical roots at the beginning of United Laborers' organizing in Los Angeles with socialist and anarchist participation occurred at the Labor Day parade in 1911. Just shy of a year after two thousand Mexicans marched behind the "Workers of the World Unite!" banner, Mexicans now marched behind a Mexican Flag at the parade.[59] Juan Ramirez remembered it as "beyond a doubt, the greatest demonstration of Organized Labor ever witnessed in Southern California . . . the fact that each man who toils is recognized as a co-worker with the same rights and privileges, regardless of creed or color, carrying out the policy of the American Federation of Labor, is bringing about solidarity, both industrially and politically, that will bring better conditions to the working class."[60]

Los Angeles IWW member Harry Weinstein wrote about the same parade in the *Industrial Worker*. He celebrated the ten thousand workers who marched, but he ridiculed the fact that they marched behind banners "advertising the Bosses' products." Socialists marching in the parade in support of Job Harriman's mayoral campaign, "carrying the United States flag, which floats over every jail, bull pen and capitalist hell hole in this country," drew his ire. He also noted "another sad spectacle," Mexican workers marching behind "the same flag which floated over Mexico when Diaz tried to crush the Mexican Revolution. And the same flag which is being used by Madero and his hirelings to arouse so-called patriotism."[61] The dramatic difference in Mexican participants' choice of symbols in the two parades marked a patriotism unleashed by Díaz's exit and encouraged by Madero. The symbolism also fit well within nationalist frames of internationalism. Along with what participants surely felt as racial and national pride, marching behind the Mexican national symbol fit within trade union organizers' vision of racial and national categorization. It also separated the group of Mexicans marching in the parade from the now public anarchism of the Partido Liberal Mexicano.

United Laborers' organizing continued in the northern half of the state as well. P. Sioris had received the blessing of the Joint Committee on Migratory Labor to take over as the full-time organizer in 1910. In February 1911 he planned a meeting of migratory laborers attended by four hundred. He quickly moved to shore up community support by contacting representatives of the foreign-language press and immigrant community. His work resulted in favorable articles in Italian, "Slavonian," and Greek, as well as a sermon in a Russian church. For all the apparently positive work throughout the state that winter, when Sioris followed the workers to Fresno in June 1911, he met with the regional vice president in the State Federation of Labor, Tom Seaward, to "fix plans to furnish more white laborers to the farmers in place of the Japanese." He enthusiastically organized United Laborers locals for Mexican and Greek workers, all the while trying to push Japanese workers out. Sioris recalled that "there are more than five thousand Japanese and Chinese still employed, and only systematic work can accomplish the task of sweeping out the Japanese and putting in their places white laborers." He proposed to the federation to fund an office in Fresno to continue the organizing of the Greeks and Mexicans, and to reach out to Italians, Russians, and Germans.[62]

In October 1911 the United Laborers' organizing drive produced three thousand dues-paying members statewide. This number diminished, however, when "many members shortly after joining drift[ed] away to other parts of the state wherever work [could] be found."[63] The fact that United Laborers members held transferable union cards did not seem to help. With few branches of the union yet in existence, workers did not have the option of joining a branch during every part of their working lives, nor did they have the ability to pay dues while unemployed.

The growth of United Laborers locals through 1911 came from the considerable effort of organizers working in migrant laborer communities and the substantial time and financial resources the CSFL invested in the northern and southern halves of the state. Juan Ramirez alone received $490 as salary for his organizing efforts in 1911. The budget for the JCML reached $200 a month from April 1911 for a total of $1,200 at the time of the October 1911 meeting. The effort to organize migratory workers in total received $1,690 of the $1,816 organizing budget of the CSFL in 1911. Further, the overall budget of the JCML reached $2,934 in 1911. This covered the salaries of Edward Thompson, P. Sioris, J. B. Dale, and T. C. Seaward. In 1912 the JCML had a budget of $2,062, and Juan Ramirez received

122

$385 in wages for his organizing efforts that year. In addition, Los Angeles's CLC consistently supported the organizing drive in its local district with its own financial resources.[64]

Despite the range of support and resources funneled into the United Laborers drive, it ultimately produced few lasting results, and organizing ceased in 1912. Most of the locals disbanded that year, while some survived into 1913. Despite such promise and energy at their inception, the unions dissipated quietly. Samuel Gompers reflected on the failure of the United Laborers in a letter to the state convention in 1912: "Its maintenance must be the members themselves. A patronizing attitude would react and prove the undoing of the entire project to help them help themselves."[65] If we look at the return investment for the AFL in merely financial terms, Gompers's bureaucratic rationale makes sense. For example, the two United Laborers chapters in Los Angeles, 13097 and 13149, contributed a scant $2.25 and $9.00 to the State Federation of Labor in affiliation fees in 1911.[66]

The JCML reported on the failure:

> During the brief absence of Organizer Juan Ramirez of Los Angeles, the union of United Laborers in that city disbanded for the reason, it is said, that not sufficient support was given them by other unions. This, it may be said, is the same reason advanced by all laborers' unions in the State for their failure to build up more rapidly. While the charge is no doubt substantiated by facts, there should be no mistaken notion upon this point, for if the organization of migratory laborers is ever going to be really successful and a power in the land, it must learn to depend upon its own strength rather than the support of other unions.[67]

J. B. Dale reflected on the failure of the United Laborers at the 1912 state convention as well, offering a warning to his colleagues. He stated that "these men look to organized labor for help, and if the trade-unionists turn him aside, the I. W. W.'s will surely take advantage of the occasion and with promises, like pie crust, made to be broken, will lure him into their camp and teach him to hate the labor movement as organized by the American Federation of Labor."[68]

The following year, Dale analyzed the situation again: "Delegates, the time has come when the truth must be told though the heavens fall. The organized men in this State have not rallied to this work with the enthusiasm and with the whole-hearted determination that the work deserves. We criticize the I. W. W.'s and their methods of appealing to the prejudices of this man when, as a matter of fact, if we had done or would now do our full duty by him he would respond fully and would willingly assume his share of the burden of organization, thereby wholly disarming the I. W. W.'s."[69] Dale fervently believed in organizing migratory labor, at least in defense against IWW encroachment.

Austin Lewis, one of the more astute contemporary observers, attributed the failure of the United Laborers, at least in part, to laborers themselves: "He sees in the United Laborers an attempt to keep him in a perpetually subordinate position[....] This man sees; or thinks he sees, in the United Laborers an attempt to bring him into permanent subjection as a member of the unskilled class, and to discipline and control his union by the united forces of the associated crafts either in the Central Labor Council or in the Building Trades."[70] Lewis argued that the AFL premised its organizational efforts directed at the unskilled on the belief "that this class of workers must be organized for the benefit of the skilled craftsman whose province they threaten to invade." Lewis continued that "one fact stands out most clearly, that the organization of that class of labor is regarded as a most essential and indeed vital matter by the officers of the organization [AFL], and that the menace from unskilled to the regularly organized trades is at once a terror and an incentive."[71]

This, in turn, led mobile workers to embrace syndicalist tactics: "The unskilled must help themselves and the only way that they can do so is by forming an organization apart and distinct from that of the skilled workers, one which is in fact the antithesis of that of the skilled worker in concept and design."[72] Their power to accomplish just that came from their not being "subject to the ethical and patriotic concepts which have drugged the minds of the organized skilled workers. They have no illusions about the value of political action, for they have no vote."[73] Their lack of cooperation with the AFL was because they "know that there is no identity of interest between themselves and the craft organizations; that the latter will use them when it is convenient to do so, otherwise they will repudiate them or will refuse to make any effort to help them gain better conditions."[74]

From its start the United Laborers campaign placed the trade union into competition with the IWW on an unfavorable terrain. The delegates at the state federation meeting took note of the threat and the direct competition of the IWW at the 1910 convention: "After repeated efforts it has been impossible to this date to organize the laborers—that is the Migratory Workers—and the blame for this can be laid directly to the door of the so-called Industrial Workers of the World."[75] The 1911 state convention noted that the *Industrial Worker* editorialized the following:

> There are nearer ten million than three million migratory workers in America and they will not organize under the American Federation of Labor for the purpose of protecting the skilled workers, nor because they are dangerous to society. They will organize into one red union of the workers, known as the I. W. W., will overthrow present society and make the craft unions dance to their music whether they like it or not. Sacred contracts won't be worth the paper they are written on when the migratory workers get next to their power.

Any time they allow any sleek labor fakirs to make catpaws out of them for the purpose of "protecting society" or aristocratic labor, that minute they "foul their own nest."

A speaker at the convention responded, "It will be seen by the foregoing that our friends, the Industrial Workers of the World, are hard to please. They damned us because we did not try to organize and uplift migratory workers, and now they damn us because we do."[76]

Austin Lewis argued that the AFL's organizational premise proved difficult when applied to unskilled workers. He stated that if "these men constituted a craft, the work of organizing them in the A. F. of L. would not be so difficult, for the scope of their employment being limited, they could, without more than ordinary difficulty, be brought into such a position that a union would appear advantageous to them. Moreover, if they really constituted a specific craft with recognized limitations on the scope of their employment, the A. F. of L. would not be very anxious to organize them."[77] He also described an "undercurrent of hostility towards the American Federation of Labor among the unskilled of the West. . . . Occasionally, indeed, at the meetings of the Industrial Workers some one gets up and proposes to 'scab the A. F. of L. out of existence.'"[78] He argued that unskilled workers held this belief because they recognized that a craft union's goal is to "secure a monopoly . . . to a limited number of men who belong to the union."[79]

Edward Thompson, an organizer with the CSFL, recalled a similar, if less hostile, attitude among the men he encountered during his first efforts at organizing the United Laborers. They were "heterogeneous as to language, intelligence, experience and standards of life; they are hard to approach, suspicious of my motives, heartsore at the failures of the past along lines of organization and doubtful of the efficiency of Unions from the standpoint of the unskilled."[80] The state federation offered relatively little to the migratory worker. During the United Laborers campaign one delegate to the state convention noted that the AFL was not trying to change migratory patterns of workers that "would involve an alteration of the system . . . we are trying to deal with things that are."[81]

This period of AFL history saw some dissent spurred by the expansion of the IWW. At the national AFL convention in 1912, delegates from the United Mine Workers lobbied unsuccessfully in favor of resolutions favoring industrial unionism. Throughout this period the IWW attracted the sympathies of AFL men, some of whom were dual cardholders. The San Diego AFL vice president reported in 1913, "It will take years before we can convince the public and a great many of our members that we have cleaned our ranks of adherents of the I. W. W.'s. To the best of my knowledge there is not a single member of Organized Labor in this district who is also a member of the I. W. W.'s, though we have quite a few who parade their radicalism by claiming that they are sympathizers, but they do not have the courage of their conviction to join those disrupters and stand before the world in their true light."[82] This marked a more direct competition between the two unions and organizational models, but it also illustrated the flexibility of local organizing.

■ ■ ■

California's agricultural economy pulled workers to sites of production across the state. Owing to the seasonal requirements of this, labor workers continued migrating to find employment and often resided in cities like Los Angeles while unemployed during the winter. The first goal of the California State Federation of Labor when it provided funds for the United Laborers campaign was to prevent these workers from taking the skilled union jobs of white men in the cities. This points to the slippery nature of "skill" and inherent difficulties of maintaining boundaries between trades. Even so, the trade union's reliance on local organizers and the participation of multiracial workers themselves, newly christened as members of the AFL, opened the AFL to new forms of interracial solidarity. Continued racism in the AFL was not the primary cause of the failure of the United Laborers. Mobility met the limits of bureaucratic organizing and the flexibility required by workers in the transnational West to survive. The fleeting potential of the United Laborers gave way to its failure a few years after the disappointing conclusion to the PLM-led incursion into Baja California. However, the deeply rooted practices of interracial and transnational affinity continued to give focus to working-class culture in the region, and these practices fueled the growth of the IWW. They found still broader outlets in PLM militancy at the beginning of the Mexican Revolution.

CHAPTER 6

THE BAJA RAIDS

Organizing and insurgency ignited California and the borderlands between 1910 and 1912. On October 1, 1910, during the AFL metal-trades strike, an early morning explosion ripped apart the Los Angeles Times Building. When the dust settled, the coroner counted twenty-one dead with many more finding their way to the hospital. The raucous IWW-initiated free-speech fight in Fresno kicked off eight days later, on December 9, 1910. Having gained experience the previous winter in the free-speech fight in Spokane, Washington, the organization had prepared through the summer and fall. In September the *Industrial Worker* began asking for people to start gathering in Fresno. Many responded, including a large group from Los Angeles. On Christmas Day a bomb exploded at Los Angeles's Llewellyn Iron Works, one target of the craft labor actions in the fall, elevating tension still further. Then came the Partido Liberal Mexicano's military incursion into Baja California in January 1911. These interconnected events reached some sort of conclusion in 1912 with the IWW-led free-speech fight in San Diego in February and at the trial of PLM leaders in Los Angeles in July.[1]

From armed insurgency to grassroots community organizing, the spectrum of the Left engaged in a range of actions during this period. Along with a distinct militancy directed against employers, Los Angeles's elite, and the Mexican state came broad solidarities across political ideologies and race. Among the connections cultivated in Los Angeles's labor and radical community, one strand of events in this dynamic period bore fruit 140 miles south of Los Angeles in Baja California and fed the outbreak of the Mexican Revolution.

CHAPTER 6

The PLM and its leaders have long captured the imagination of historians in Mexico and the United States. The Baja raids constitute the group's most contested legacy. Interpretations ranged from accusations of treason and filibustering to sympathetic portrayals of the PLM's influence as a precursor of the Mexican Revolution. This chapter maintains a narrow focus on the central themes of this book to examine the regional coalition building and transnational support structure for the Baja raids pieced together by the PLM. The international character of the raids remained unmatched until antifascist organizing during the Spanish Civil War a quarter century later, with its interracial dimension still more significant.

The racial diversity of participants increased the overall number of rebels and contributed to the effectiveness of the military force. But conflicts between rebels and then with the adventurers and interlopers who crossed the border contributed to questions over the legitimacy of the raids. These conflicts arose as it became clear that the Baja California front was a sideshow to the Mexican Revolution and that the PLM leaders in Los Angeles, though they had many supporters and sympathizers, did not exert direct control over militias anywhere else in Mexico.

The participation of at least a dozen military veterans had a similar effect of increasing the combat effectiveness of the rebel army, while some veterans contributed to contention in the ranks. An important minority of rebels gained military experience in their travels through the networks of empire. Of the men active in the rebel ranks in Baja California, at least two fought in the Anglo-Boer War on opposing sides, some fought in the Spanish-American War for the United States, and still others served in the U.S. military during a period when the country increasingly reached beyond its borders into Latin America, the Caribbean, and the Pacific. By pointing guns at the Mexican state—most for the cause of liberty—using skills acquired in the racist conflicts of colonial states, they created a moment of imperial contradiction in Baja California.

Though this moment offered great promise to radicals, it ended in military failure, bitter disputes among contemporaries, and a complex historiography.[2] Claudio Lomnitz argued more broadly that the "ideological prominence of the Partido Liberal Mexicano was in inverse proportion to its military significance" in the Mexican Revolution.[3] The Baja raids marked the highpoint of PLM military influence. The lasting historical significance of the Baja raids rests in the multiracial and transnational composition of the fighting force and their supporters, which constituted international strands in a national revolution in Mexico. As Devra Weber observed, the "1917 Russian Revolution would later eclipse the memory that, from the vantage point of 1911, revolutionary possibilities were toward the south, in Mexico."[4]

Border Revolts against Porfirio Díaz

People moved freely through the borderlands in the late nineteenth and early twentieth centuries. They carried forward connections from before U.S. conquest, created new ties, and continued to instill this space with a coherency of its own, a condition that revealed the limitations of state power in the region.[5] Cross-border communities in the borderlands also challenged the nationalisms of both countries, regardless of their political actions. It is not surprising, then, that dissidents staged the most serious threats to Porfirio Díaz's regime in this space. In 1890 Francisco Ruíz Sandoval led a failed uprising. The specifics of Sandoval's personal history prove difficult to parse. According to Elliot Young, "Sandoval was either a seasoned Central or South American revolutionary general or a disgruntled junior officer in the Mexican Army." However, the rebel held Chilean citizenship. The failure of the Sandoval-led effort resulted in his deportation to Laredo, Texas, where he lived in exile.[6]

Two years later Catarino Garza led a rebellion from Texas that turned into the "longest lasting and most serious threat to the Porfirian regime" up until that point.[7] Garza formulated a plan for moderate political reforms, and the composition of this rebellion foreshadowed the racial diversity seen in the PLM-led effort in the next century. Mostly Mexicans, from Mexico or Texas, made up the Garza force, but "a few supporters were of Anglo or Italian heritage or had a mixed Anglo Mexican background."[8] Young argued, "The real danger Garza posed for both governments was the transnationality that he and his movement represented."[9] The rebels pointed to and exposed the weaknesses of both nation-states.

This period continuously contained strands of the transnational as the movement of people created new ways of thinking, worldviews, and movements. In 1891 the Scottish anarchist Tom Bell "tried some propaganda work in Mexico" that he wrote about decades later and believed unsuccessful, though, and gains are probably more attributable to factors other than a lack of interest in radical politics in Mexico.[10] The next year, in 1892, conflict between a younger generation against the technocratic *científicos* was a "watershed for Mexico's intellectual and political classes."[11] Ricardo Flores Magón and others that would form the PLM participated in the protests that year. Conflict and insurgency continued intermittently through to the Baja raids and Mexican Revolution.

The PLM attempted to spark revolution in Mexico through military action on three occasions: 1906, 1908, and 1910–11. The first came in 1906 a few months after the suppression of the Cananea mining strike. This attempt largely channeled through Club Liberal Libertad in Douglas, Arizona. Prisciliano Silva also took an active role from the liberal club in El Paso. Silva contacted Francisco Madero looking to cooperate, but Madero strongly opposed revolution at the time; he remained committed to constraining opposition within Mexico's limited legal political process. Authorities learned of the PLM plot and arrested several instigators in Arizona before they could act. A separate PLM-aligned force attacked a customs house in Jiménez, Chihuahua. Federal forces quickly rebutted the challenge, and the surviving rebels escaped back across the border. In Veracruz, the two separate liberal clubs mustered a combined force of one thousand with many indigenous in the ranks, but they too were defeated by federal forces, who then exacted revenge on their villages.[12]

The PLM's precarious legal position, its goal of overthrowing the Mexican government, and limitations in communication across distance reinforced its practice of organizing into a loose network of liberal clubs. This tactic was in tune with the PLM leaders' understanding of Mexico under Díaz and the potential course of revolution. They genuinely expected revolution to break out simultaneously across Mexico given the proper spark.[13] The PLM's international, interracial, and multilingual affinities grew from these beliefs and practices. Organizing in this direction increased after the failures of 1906 and as the PLM leaders spent more time in the United States, some of it in prison, which also worked to limit hierarchy in the collection of liberal clubs.

The PLM's second attempt at revolution came in 1908 and even more clearly reflected the activation of its network than the 1906 attempt. With Ricardo Flores Magón in jail in Los Angeles charged with neutrality violations, his partner, María Brousse, smuggled a letter out of jail with the help of Ethel Duffy Turner and Elizabeth Trowbridge when the trio visited him. Turner remembered:

> One time John [Kenneth Turner] came and told Elizabeth and me that we had a task to perform. We went to the jail and María, who was the sweetheart of Ricardo, was there, and the three of us went in to interview the men, Ricardo Flores Magón, Antonio Villarreal, and Librado Rivera. . . . There was only one guard there in the jail, and he walked from our end up to the far end of the corridor. As we were sitting at the near end, it took him a couple of minutes to get back. As soon as he started his walk, Ricardo dropped a piece of paper and pushed it below the iron mesh. María dropped her purse, and as she picked up her purse she picked up the paper. Elizabeth and I had spread our long skirts on either side of María to hide what she was doing. It was a success. The guard didn't catch us. After we left, we could hardly walk down the street, Elizabeth and I, we were so excited—what a pair we were!—because those were the plans for the 1908 Revolution.[14]

María sent these plans to supporters in liberal clubs on both sides of the border. The initial thrust was to come from the El Paso liberal club and Prisciliano Silva,

Prisciliano Silva. (National Archives at Kansas City, Records of the Bureau of Prisons)

but authorities discovered the plot through informers as they did in 1906. A number of arrests followed on both sides of the border and the planned actions elsewhere fizzled.[15]

When U.S. authorities arrested Silva in El Paso, he was carrying a copy of the Italian anarchist newspaper *Cronaca Sovversiva*. When police searched his home, they discovered a trunk that contained a "large number" of copies of the February 22, 1908, issue, largely dedicated to Mexico and the PLM, so they realized Silva distributed the paper regionally.[16] Silva's connections to Italian anarchists and his position as one of the strongest military leaders in Chihuahua, which became the crucial theater of action during the revolution in 1910, made him the most important PLM anarchist outside of the group in Los Angeles.

Also in 1908 Elizabeth Darling Trowbridge, Ethyl Duffy Turner, John Kenneth Turner, Lázaro Gutiérrez de Lara, John Murray, María Brousse, Frances and P. D. Noels, Hattie Shea, Manuel Sarabia, and others formed a tightknit group that aimed to influence American public opinion in favor of the Mexican cause. This broad effort resulted in the publications *The Border, El Defensor del Pueblo*, and, most significant, serialized articles by John Kenneth Turner in the *American Magazine* that exposed the brutal forms of labor in Porfirio Diaz's Mexico. These articles, later published as *Barbarous Mexico*, drew "sensational" comparisons to Anglo American's conceptions of African American slavery.[17]

Apart from publishing, Práxedis Guerrero and Manuel Sarabia organized in the Arizona mining towns of Douglas, Morenci, Metcalf, Miami, and Globe. They built support for the PLM by forming local liberal clubs and labor organizing. Other on-the-ground organizers in these years included Enrique Flores Magón, Antonio de P. Araujo, Tomás Sarabia, and Fernando Velarde. Their efforts built support for the PLM's failed 1908 attempt at revolution and helped expand the ranks of the IWW in southern California and Arizona among Mexican workers.[18]

Through surveillance U.S. federal authorities obtained a letter that connected the PLM to other anarchists in the broader movement in 1908: "It is clearly indicated by this code letter that these people are real anarchists and they have a connection possibly with not only the few anarchists of the United States, but with European anarchists. The code letter was written by Ricardo Flores Magoon [sic], who is now in jail at Los Angeles, Cal."[19] Ricardo Flores Magón encouraged solidarity within the anarchist movement, specifically its Spanish- and Italian-language speakers, and workers' movements more broadly. He wrote in 1908 that anarchists should "cultivate international relations, but not with governments but with workers' organizations from all over the world whether they are simple trade-unionists, socialists, or anarchists."[20] These connections supplemented the direct revolutionary assistance the PLM received from comrades in and near Los Angeles. However ineffective, the 1908 rebellion had strong transnational anarchist and socialist connections that continued to increase toward 1910.

Preparation and Coalition Building

On August 3, 1910, Ricardo Flores Magón, Librado Rivera, and Antonio Villareal walked out of prison in the Arizona Territory after three years in custody for neutrality violations related to their failed 1906 attempt at revolution. The men returned to Los Angeles, secured an office where many of them lived, and worked on *Regeneración*. Mexican agents monitored the group, but the extent of the upheaval in Los Angeles that fall probably provided the PLM with some degree of cover as U.S. authorities focused on the bombings and strike activity.[21]

In fall 1910 the PLM reached the highpoint of its support and influence in the United States and Mexico. The propaganda work of John Kenneth Turner, Lázaro Gutiérrez de Lara, Ethyl Duffy Turner, and John Murray Jr. had reached a broad audience and helped shape sympathetic Anglo perceptions of the oppressed in Mexico. The solidarity network in Los Angeles expanded through the PLM leaders' prison terms and now radiated across the country into the global labor and radical movement. This supplemented PLM support among Mexicans in Los Angeles that stretched through the borderlands into Mexico. The clearest indication of the group's direct intellectual reach at this point were the twenty thousand subscribers to *Regeneración* predominantly in the U.S. Southwest and Mexico.[22]

The Mexican participants in the Baja insurrection largely came from Southern California and Arizona. Their involvement grew out of the years of organizing by PLM walking delegates among Mexican and indigenous people in the region, part of the interlocking organizing tradition of the PLM and IWW. The closeness between the PLM and IWW continued even as the national bureaucracy of the IWW, the General Executive Board (GEB), attempted to shield itself from legal trouble by formally distancing itself from the PLM and revolutionary cross-border activities. The IWW, however, lacked the organizational hierarchy to enforce official pronouncements, and the cosmopolitan workers who fell in with the syndicalist union often maintained multiple affiliations or none at all. Many simply joined and supported causes as they saw fit, living and practicing a culture of affinity.[23]

The Mexican and U.S. governments recognized that the connections between PLM and IWW organizing and their membership overlapped, so they targeted the IWW in the Southwest as they did the PLM the entire time its leaders lived in the United States. In December 1910 the *Industrial Worker* reported that Mexican members of the IWW in San Diego were "constantly being dogged by secret service men from Mexico and . . . watched by the 'patriotic' American police departments all along the border." The secretary of IWW Local 13 in San Diego tried to create a public separation between the organizations not present in the practice of individual members when he wrote, "The I. W. W. at San Diego has no connection with the Mexican revolution, even though the capitalist newspapers do try to 'make' stories to that effect."[24]

The local had obvious incentive to avoid being publicly linked to the cross-border revolutionary activities, but it did not hide its organizing with Mexican workers throughout the borderlands. While Fernando Palomárez helped organize Mexican workers in San Diego in July, the *Industrial Worker* published a call for solidarity: "Let's organize the Mexican revolutionists on this side of the border and help the oppressed on the other side."[25] Palomárez's organizing in San Diego that summer and fall is one of the clearest examples of the intertwining of the PLM and IWW directly before the Baja raids. Another came when the Scottish immigrant anarchist Tom Bell moved to Phoenix, Arizona, in 1910 and learned that the IWW local had more than five hundred Mexican members. When the revolution erupted, "the I.W.W. Mexicans in Phoenix plunged into it at once, going over the border almost in a body."[26] These actions largely erased the distinction between organizing Mexicans workers in the United States within the IWW and against Porfirio Díaz. Those involved viewed taking up arms against

Díaz and forming industrial unions in the United States as intertwined strands in their revolutionary movement.

Throughout Mexico and the borderlands, dispersed, locally based PLM organizing continued through *club liberales*. Ethel Duffy Turner recalled that in "every place they had formed these clubs for arming and organizing."[27] Ricardo Flores Magón later testified that the junta coordinated with liberal forces in "Sonora, Chihuahua, Coahuila, Tamaulipas, Sinaloa, Durango, San Luis Potosi, La Honda, Tlaxcala, Vera Cruz, Yucatan, Tabasco, and Jalisco."[28] However, in 1910 the junta only directed forces in Baja, and even this filtered through the distance from Los Angeles; Ricardo never went to Baja California to participate directly in the fighting.

Support from the transnational anarchist movement turned the Baja raids from a minor front in the Mexican Revolution into a moment of global significance for anarchists. Anarchist assistance also expanded the geographic reach of participants beyond the Southwest and Mexico. One of the most prominent anarchist groups in the United States and, indeed, the world was the Italian organization in Paterson, New Jersey, Il Gruppo Diritto all'Esistenza, which published *L'Era Nuova*. Members of this organization fervently backed the Mexican struggle and the PLM before it publicly declared its anarchism. In the fall of 1910 the former *L'Era Nuova* editor Ludovico Caminita traveled to Los Angeles to join with the PLM, an indication of the strength of the connection between the two organizations. Often controversial, Caminita brought with him connections from his years in the Italian anarchist movement on the East Coast, but also the burden of its internal conflicts.[29]

Ludovico Caminita and former Il Gruppo Diritto all'Esistenza member Vittorio Cravello, who had relocated to Los Angeles a few years before the Baja raids, were two key provocateurs in a long-standing factional dispute between the Paterson group and the Italian anarchists who published *Cronaca Sovversiva* in Barre, Vermont, along with its most prominent member Luigi Galleani. Galleani, the leading figure of the *anti-organizzatore* in the United States, was "unalterably opposed to political parties, federations, labor unions, and all other forms of organization."[30] The strength of his personality alone led to bitter conflict, but he often accused people who directly challenged his opinions of being untrue to the cause or outright traitors—traits, incidentally, shared at least in part by Ricardo Flores Magón. In ideological contrast, Il Gruppo Diritto all'Esistenza advanced a social anarchism and organized with the IWW. Both groups participated and invested in the Baja California campaign and the Mexican Revolution more broadly. Their previous conflicts did not limit this support, nor did such conflicts affect the willingness of Italian anarchists in both camps to travel to Baja California and fight, but tensions boiled over along these preexisting lines in June

1911 and continued through a protracted war of words in the anarchist press and public meetings for another year.[31]

Separate tensions surfaced publicly in Los Angeles directly before the insurrection began, indicating lasting ruptures within the loose anti-Díaz alliance. In December 1910 Ricardo wrote an article in *Regeneración* about Francisco Madero that read in part:

> Governments have to protect the right of property above all other rights. Do not expect, then, that Madero will attack the right of property in favor of the proletariat.... Owners are men who have helped him with money to build their revolutionary groups, owners are the group leaders, owners have been many of the agitators and propagandists. It is the party of the bourgeoisie, friends, and with it we would only manage to tighten our chains. Open your eyes. Remember a phrase, simple and true and as truth indestructible: The emancipation of the workers must be the work of the workers themselves.[32]

Ricardo more publicly expressed his anarchist vision for Mexico at the same time that the thawing political situation began opening alternative paths beyond opposition to Díaz.[33]

In the same issue of *Regeneración* as Ricardo's article on Madero, the English page editor Alfred Sanftleben prefaced a communiqué from Madero: "It makes it also clear why the Mexican Liberals join hands with the middle-class revolutionists of these days, the rising middle class needing the guarantees of free speech, free press and free assemblage for the fulfillment of the mission of their class, and the toiler needing the same factors to educate and uplift."[34] Neither the newspaper nor the junta maintained ideological uniformity, and this breadth of opinion reflected the different authors and readership of the Spanish and English sections. The English page during this period remained consistently more moderate and conciliatory than the Spanish pages reflecting Sanftleben's outlook. But Sanftleben, an anarchist in the vein of his friend Gustav Landuer, backed away because this disagreement and Ethel Duffy Turner assumed the editorial duties of the English page.[35]

With the course of military action set, Turner remembered that while she worked on *Regeneración*, her husband, John, "was buying up all the guns he could find."[36] A. G. Rogers, the publisher of the *People's Paper*, assisted John Kenneth Turner in buying arms. Rogers bought nearly fifty army surplus Springfield rifles of dubious quality from a store selling them as "cozycorner ornaments" for $1.98 each. Finding the correct ammunition for the outdated arms proved difficult.[37]

A key part of the PLM's legal strategy rested in the belief that it would not violate American neutrality laws if fighters crossed the border unarmed, the same laws the three PLM leaders finished serving their time for violating in August.

CHAPTER 6

Ethel Duffy Turner recalled that the guns purchased in Los Angeles "were shipped to the border labeled as tools or implements for the farmers."[38] These weapons crossed the border through the PLM's affinity network. While a teenager, Josefina Amador carried rifles across the border hidden in her skirt while pushing a niece along in a pram.[39] The PLM also transported arms and supplies from Los Angeles to a farmer in Holtville, Jim Wilson, sympathetic to its cause. Wilson then took them in a wagon to the border, where PLM members already in Mexico offloaded them. Indeed, A. I. McCormick, the U.S. district attorney for the Southern District of California, testified before Senate hearings organized by Albert Fall:

> The difficult thing in our prosecution was to prove that the expedition was of a military character, and in that connection I may state that the Magonistas were constantly advised by the best attorneys, who posted them on the neutrality laws, and for that reason they kept everything absolutely secret which had anything of a military character attached to it at all. In other words, their idea was, "you go down to the Mexican line and do not be a soldier or indicate in any way that you are a soldier until after you get across the line. Then you will find so and so and will immediately receive your gun and ammunition."

Assistant U.S. Attorney Dudley Robinson testified before the same hearing that the PLM "clearly thought in their operations, since the trial at Tombstone three or four years ago, that they had now found a way to get around the law, so that if they sent these men down there and did not give them arms" they would not be violating neutrality laws and thus be left unhindered by American authorities.[40]

However, a few days before fighting began the *People's Paper* openly solicited its readers to donate guns for the revolt: "It is perhaps not well understood that the revolutionists are sadly in need of arms and all who are desirous of assisting the patriots in their attempts to free their country from its present brutal domination are asked by *Regeneración* to contribute as they can."[41] Scant other public rumination of the PLM's military plans reached the printed page in English or Spanish before the raids. Revolutionary planning tended to occur through clandestine channels, while above ground, labor organizing continued unabated.

The Baja Raids

The PLM fit within the prerevolutionary political terrain of "liberal" opposition to Porfirio Díaz. In the fall of 1910 Francisco Madero, now in a much stronger position than the junta in Los Angeles, forced an agreement to begin this attempt at revolution on November 20, but it began slowly. Amid rumblings across the country, the initial thrust from Los Angeles came when Práxedis Guerrero left for Chihuahua, Mexico, where he led a small, PLM-affiliated force in taking the town of Casas Grandes on December 28. The core member of the PLM died in a firefight in nearby Janos two days later, and his death deeply affected those in Los Angeles. Despite an uneven start, Mexico entered a period of open warfare that winter.[42]

The military action of the Los Angeles–based PLM filtered through the Holtville IWW office in January. A small force led by PLM members José María Leyva and Simon Berthold slipped across the border to join a dozen Mexicans waiting on the other side. Each of these two men had a long history of regional activism. María Leyva participated in the agitation in Cananea in 1906 and held a card to the AFL-affiliated Hodcarriers Union in Los Angeles. Berthold, born in Mexico to a German immigrant father and Mexican mother, was active in Los Angeles's IWW ranks while working an AFL organized trade. This small group of *insurrectos*, fewer than twenty, gained control of Mexicali on January 29, with the town's jail warden the only casualty. The *Imperial Valley Press* referred to the jail under the warden's charge as a "relic of barbarism" after the rebels liberated it. Reflecting the region, the prison held many Anglos who ran afoul of the law in Mexico along with Mexican citizens. News of the victory quickly spread through the popular and movement press as well as through radical affinity networks, and several hundred people eventually converged on Baja California to join the rebels. The first influx of reinforcements arrived in February during a lull in local combat. As volunteers crossed the border, events elsewhere in February affected the outcome of the insurrection in Baja California.[43]

The PLM-affiliated anarchist Prisciliano Silva led the most powerful armed group in Chihuahua, Mexico, in February 1911. Silva's militia captured Guadalupe, a small town east of the city of Chihuahua, while forces under Francisco Madero also fought in the region. Madero contacted Silva, asking for assistance, which he provided. The two groups then arranged a meeting at which Madero attempted to get Silva to sign on to his side. Silva refused. Madero's forces then arrested him and disarmed his most loyal troops.[44]

When news of this reached Los Angeles, Ricardo Flores Magón printed a scathing attack of Madero in *Regeneración*, calling him a "traitor to the cause of liberty." The sidelining of Silva and then Madero's continued success that winter provided an outlet to political divisions within the PLM and between the PLM and the broader anti-Díaz movement. After Ricardo's article attacking Madero screamed across the front page of *Regeneración*, he simply declared on the bottom corner of the same page of newsprint that Antonio "Villarreal is no longer a member of the Junta."[45] Villarreal had left Los Angeles to join Madero in Chihuahua. Villarreal's name had a recognizable currency as a member of the PLM's junta and a signatory of the PLM's 1905 program penned in St. Louis. Many liberals joined him and Madero, some under "false pretenses," which further reduced PLM influence in the region.[46]

The break with Madero had lasting consequences on the ability of the PLM to maintain its breadth of support north of the border and to influence events in Mexico. The open military action of the PLM had already frightened away some moderate supporters in the United States, but splitting with the reformist Madero opened these cleavages still wider. International anarchist and regional radical support filled in the gaps as labor and many socialists in the United States withdrew. Volunteers continued to arrive in Baja California, but PLM connections to forces fighting elsewhere in Mexico became increasingly precarious after Madero's arrest of Prisciliano Silva stifled the strongest PLM-aligned anarchist voice in the crucial revolutionary state of Chihuahua. The PLM leadership remained in Los Angeles, growing increasingly distant from the fluxing center of power in Mexico, now rapidly consolidating around Madero.

In Baja California that February, after the fight for Mexicali, Stanley Williams, a member of the Holtville IWW local, who had helped organize the opening of the raids from Los Angeles, crossed the border with around thirty men, mostly IWW volunteers, "consisting of white men and negroes."[47] The newly arrived formed a separate unit from María Leyva's, a "foreign legion," and elected Williams their officer. Williams had served in the U.S. Army during the Spanish-American War, which bolstered his credentials for the position. Under advisement from the PLM leadership in Los Angeles, Williams replaced Leyva after some infighting. Leyva eventually left to join with Madero.[48]

Newcomers to the international battalion grew to include additional IWW members and anarchists from across the United States and Canada. Many of the radicals were European immigrants from England, Russia, Germany, Sweden, and France, with Italians of special note. Australians and Boers also joined the fight. The PLM in Los Angeles kept in close contact with the leadership of the South Asian Ghadar movement based in San Francisco, although no formal military cooperation came of it after "a frontline visit convinced Pandurang Khankhoje, head of Ghadar's 'action committee' and a personal friend of the Magón brothers, that the plan was not feasible."[49] One person remembered seeing a Chinese man who owned a local restaurant fighting. Authorities arrested a Japanese man attempting to cross the border to join with eight Mexican and four Anglo companions. Other significant local participants included Native Americans: Cocopah, Diegueño, Kiliwa, and Papai.[50]

The participation of African Americans is especially remarkable, although a firm number is difficult to determine. Rumors circulated that PLM recruiters promised participants 140 acres of land and money payable upon victory, but it did not originate from an official PLM recruiting strategy. These claims surfaced after the fighting to question the motivations of some who came to fight, especially African Americans. Assistant U.S. Attorney Dudley Robinson testified:

African American Rebels in Baja California, 1911. (San Diego History Center)

"One colored man who was a valiant fighter said he was promised two horses and a couple of guns and some revolvers" for his participation. The man, a veteran of the U.S. Army, "was given the privilege of always carrying two revolvers."[51] This man's clear acceptance in the ranks and the timing of the African Americans who came to fight in February, in the first wave of IWW reinforcements, seems to indicate that many shared radical commitments with the PLM and IWW.

The international influx soon surpassed Mexican and local indigenous participants who made up fewer than half of the combatants in Baja California by late February. Support from radicals north of the border and abroad bolstered the number of troops and further internationalized the Baja California front of the Mexican Revolution after the PLM split with Madero, a crucial moment in the political life of the group. The international influx also led to conflicts among the rebels. Internal tension over tactics, leadership, and personalities fueled the split of divisions between (predominantly) Mexicans under Simon Berthold and the international force under Stanley Williams. Yet the reality of combat reworked the force in its own way. In fighting during April, federal troops fatally shot Williams while he led seventy men against more than four hundred Mexican regulars. The rebel force inflicted heavy casualties, but they suffered one more of their own, an African American "insurrecto." The next week federal forces killed Berthold.[52]

Despite the loss of life, volunteers continued to cross the border to join the fight. The rebels elected Jack Mosby to succeed Berthold and the Welsh adventurer Caryl Ap Rhys Pryce to succeed Williams. Both Mosby and Pryce had prior military experience. Mosby fought in the Second Boer War against the British, the Thousand Days' War in Panama, and served in the U.S. Marine Corps before deserting and joining the IWW. The adventurer Pryce fought in the Second Boer War for the United Kingdom and had further military experience from the corners of the British Empire in India and Western Canada. While Pryce did not hold radical political commitments, with his military experience he assumed a leadership position.[53]

In contrast, Mosby made his motivation for fighting clear when he moved to expel adventurers and soldiers of fortune from the unit under his command; they allowed only those who fought for liberty to remain. The Anglo IWW member Sam Murray, a U.S. Navy veteran who served on the battleship *Oregon* during the Spanish-American War, recalled Mosby as "easy and informal." He also remembered that the men, as a sign of equality, did not salute their elected "officers."[54] At least twelve of the participants had deserted from the American military and flowed through the U.S. West before finding their way to Baja California—a signal of their loyalties but also of the weaker American state before World War I.[55]

As events on the ground progressed in the spring, a group of anarchists formed the "International Committee of the Mexican Liberal Party Junta" in May. "Spanish, Italian, Russian, Polish, Australian, and American comrades" attended the first meeting.[56] They issued a press release through the Associated Press from Juárez, Mexico, on May 18, 1911, signed by:

(Italy)
L. Caminita, Vittorio Cravello, Andrea La Morticella
(Mexico)
Ricardo Flores Magón, A. L. Figueroa, A. M. Ojeda, F. Velarde, Francisco Martinez [Fernando Palomárez]

(United States)

WM. C. Owen

(Germany)

Rudolph Wirth

(Russia)

A. P. Cherbak, P. H. Leiffert

(Poland)

K. Jozefoski, W. Lazicki[57]

This statement listed some of the PLM's most prominent anarchist supporters in Los Angeles. Anarchists across the country stepped up their support of the PLM and the fighters in Baja through fundraising and meetings. The Spanish- and Italian-speaking anarchist community in New York City provided a particularly high level of support. "El Comite 'Pro-Comunistas Mexicanos,' de New York" organized an international meeting at the Cooper Union in English, German, Italian, Yiddish, Spanish, and "other languages."[58]

Radicals in San Diego, including women, also supported activities in Baja California. They turned their city into a safe base of support out of the reach of Mexican troops. Much of the assistance filtered through the city's IWW, an additional result of the labor organizing by Fernando Palomárez and the others the prior summer. Laura Payne Emerson proved the most vocal in San Diego. She crossed the border into Tijuana after the IWW and PLM forces captured it and wrote about her experiences in the IWW paper *Solidarity*. Further shoring up San Diego solidarity, Kasper Bauer followed up his "defense of internationalism" refuting socialist support for Japanese exclusion in 1907 by arranging for Emma Goldman to speak at a rally in San Diego the day before rebel forces took Tijuana in May.[59]

It was a male crowd and masculine revolution in Baja, even though at least one woman, Margarita Ortega, joined the fighting. Ortega served as the "link between the combat forces" of the PLM in Baja California: "An able horsewoman and an expert in the use of firearms, Margarita crossed the enemy lines and smuggled arms, munitions, dynamite, whatever was needed, to the comrades on the field of action." Many other *soldaderas* fought throughout Mexico over the course of the revolution.[60] More broadly, "Women played crucial roles in these social networks and also in labor and political conflicts. They were not only in charge of a female sphere of labor but were activists in their own right and were recognized as such within the PLM."[61]

In early May federal troops seriously wounded Mosby in a skirmish, and he returned to Los Angeles to convalesce. Shortly afterward the PLM leadership in Los Angeles ordered the two separate divisions in Baja to join together and march on Ensenada. The roughly 250 troops under Rhys Pryce, of which only ten were

Laura Payne Emerson (San Diego, 1918)

Mexican, took their own initiative, walked to Tijuana, and seized the city on May 9. The PLM leaders realized the geographical distance between themselves and the troops in Tijuana and, rightly, worried about the political distance between themselves and Pryce.[62]

They reacted by calling even more loudly for international anarchists to travel to Baja California. Ricardo Flores Magón wrote to Pedro Esteve in New York on May 3 calling for "anarchists from all parts of the world go to Baja California to

Margarita Ortega

support the expropriation of the land and machinery." Magón claimed that they would find the "earth precious, the mines rich, and the ports magnificent. In the hands of libertarians," he said, "Baja California has the resources to bring the revolution through Mexico and even the entire world because it is very large, but sparsely populated."[63]

On May 22 Ricardo again wrote to Esteve, stating concern about the composition of their forces in Baja California and the potential influence that an international anarchist brigade could exert in this theater of combat: "Not only a gun is needed, but we must also to sow the idea. We are in possession of a vast territory, and we need the presence of a strong libertarian division, that is, com-

CHAPTER 6

posed of pure libertarians, in order to emancipate the unconscious" among their own troops. He continued:

> Our fighting columns of are not comprised of pure libertarians, but they are mixed. The truth is that there are men that are emancipated and anarchists, but generally they do not understand our ideals completely, that they will be happy if they arrive in possession of land, and it is for the possession of land they struggle. It is already difficult to get them to ignore the right of property; But our ambition is to wake them up even more to ensure success and avoid a reaction. . . . The comrades of the special division would go to the camps of the other comrades, fraternize with them and teach those who know nothing, as well as make special efforts to instruct the peasants on the advantages of common land cultivation.[64]

On May 20 *Regeneración* had publicly called for people in their solidarity network to travel to Baja California to set up a colony, suggesting that all that they would need could be produced from the land—that they could put their anarchist ideas into practice. The newspaper made clear the interracial dimensions of this call by listing the names of people killed fighting thus far: "Camilo J. Jiménez, Simón Berthold, Antonio Fuertes, William Stanley, Rosario García, José Espinosa, T. L. Wood, J. C. Smith, Jesús R. Pesqueira, Miguel Hernández, José Flores, y otros más."[65] On May 28 around 30 anarchists, mostly Italian insurrectionists in Luigi Galleani's camp, answered the call and descended on Tijuana from Vancouver, Kansas, Nevada, Washington, Wisconsin, and Pennsylvania. What they found in the dusty desert town would be the source of the most virulent recriminations in the months to come.[66]

Three days later, on May 31, thirty-five years of rule by Porfirio Díaz ended with him boarding a ship bound for Paris. Francisco Madero then sent Juan Sarabia and Jesús Flores Magón to Los Angeles from Mexico to negotiate an end of hostilities with the junta. The core anarchist members of the PLM refused the overture, and shortly after this meeting, on June 14, the Los Angeles police arrested Ricardo and Enrique Flores Magón, Librado Rivera, and Anselmo Figueroa for violating neutrality laws. Three days later the PLM first division of mostly Mexicans, which had remained in Mexicali, surrendered to federal troops after the commander accepted Madero's overture. In Tijuana the Mexican and indigenous troops also slipped away. By the end of June six hundred federal troops now loyal to Madero recaptured Tijuana from the approximately two hundred remaining rebels after an afternoon battle that killed at least thirty of their ranks. The PLM's late push to shore up their position in Baja California with international anarchists came far too late to serve as a bulwark against Madero's consolidation of power.[67]

144

The Baja Raids

Rebels aboard a Commandeered Train from the S.D. & A.R.Y. Railroad, Owned by John Spreckels. (San Diego History Center)

A subplot of revolutionary interlopers intent on leading a filibustering campaign in Baja California during the fighting that spring also compounded the difficulties of the PLM. As the PLM split with Madero in the early days of fighting, a number of adventurers and others not drawn to fight for the cause of liberty filtered into Baja California along with the committed anarchists and Wobblies. This complicated the coalition on the ground and tainted the rebels with charges of filibustering—of wanting to cleave off Baja California for themselves or the United States—as the broader political situation in Mexico gravitated away from the PLM. The actor and self-promoter Dick Ferris capitalized on the fluidity of the situation with two well-publicized filibustering stunts, the first through pen and press while he lived in San Francisco in February and March, and then again after rebels had taken Tijuana in May while he lived in San Diego. The first evaporated on its own; rebel troops quashed the second effort by running a small group supporting Ferris out of town.[68]

A second aspect of filibustering, apart from Ferris's grandstanding, deserves attention. Claudio Lomnitz referred to the residents of Tijuana as *"conocidos."* In the small town, people knew and interacted with each other daily. Regardless of their intentions or the justness of their cause, the international anarchists who arrived to fight in Baja California were an outside force. When the motley group of radicals arrived and turned their guns against the state, many local residents feared that it would result in the United States annexing the territory. This fear extended beyond Díaz supporters. One sign of this was in San Diego, when a group of Mexican U.S. residents formed the Sociedad Defensores de la Integridad Nacional (Society for the Defense of National Integrity) to protect their interests. When the PLM issued its calls for international anarchist participants, it made it clear that they were not fighting for Mexican national interests. The PLM's anarchist goals of using Baja California to put its ideals into action by seizing and collectively cultivating land could be viewed as anarchist filibuster, especially as Madero ascended and the continued large-scale interests of American businesspeople and corporations. Nationalism made it difficult for most to see beyond the framework of Baja California's being part of either Mexico or the United States.[69]

Recrimination

The defeat of the rebel forces in Tijuana and the arrest of the PLM leaders in Los Angeles effectively ended the PLM's ability to directly participate in the Mexican Revolution. These twinned events also conscribed the PLM to fighting two distinct battles outside of Mexico for the next few years. As its leaders struggled against the U.S. court system for their freedom, conflicts forced them to defend the trueness of their cause and their legitimacy as anarchists in the face of vicious attacks by other anarchists. Confrontation shifted from Baja California to courthouses and streets in Los Angeles and out through the affinity networks that brought so many to fight in the first place.

What greeted the group of Italian anarchists in Tijuana at the end of May was a far cry from the insurrection of global significance that they envisioned and, indeed, traveled thousands of miles to risk their lives in. Tijuana in 1911 could only claim a population of about one thousand. The town's limited economy consisted of shops and services mostly dedicated to cross-border tourism, and its political importance in Mexico was even smaller.[70] Apart from realizing that they arrived in an outpost of the revolution, this group chaffed at the organizational disarray they entered, a lack of ammunition, and little contact with the junta in Los Angeles. Eight of the Italian anarchists left after a single day in Mexico and immediately began publicizing their experiences in the anarchist press.

These eight men first penned a letter critical of what they saw in Tijuana and posted it to *Cronaca Sovversiva* and *L'Era Nuova*. The junta in Los Angeles learned of the letter, and they immediately telegraphed *L'Era Nuova*, requesting that it refrain from publishing it, but they did not telegraph *Cronaca Sovversiva*. Without the request, *Cronaca Sovversiva* printed the letter signed by Ernesto Teodori, Guglielmo Galcotti, Filippo Perrone, Vincenzo Cipolla, Sam Rizzo, John Longo, Pasquini Guglielmo, and Aristide Paladini on June 17. The men chastised the radical press for misinforming them about the Mexican Revolution. They arrived in Tijuana believing that a social and economic revolution was well underway but saw no evidence of it in this isolated corner of the country and argued that anarchists should focus their attention and financial contributions elsewhere.[71]

In lieu of the letter of dissent, *L'Era Nuova* published a letter from Ludovico Caminita on June 24, in the same issue that announced the arrest of the junta in Los Angeles. Caminita wrote to his Paterson comrades that he had just returned from Tijuana that morning and thus spoke from personal experience of the dynamic there in the days before federal troops retook the city. Without stating clearly the content of the men's grievances, Caminita argued that they based them on a brief sojourn to Baja California, which prevented them from knowing the full course of events where they visited, let alone across Mexico. Motivated to communicate directly with Italian anarchists at the outset of the disagreement, Caminita added a regular Italian-language column to *Regeneración* on July 8 and a separate four-page Italian edition beginning July 15, 1911.[72]

Despite their best attempts, the PLM and Caminita failed to contain the fallout generated by the disgruntled men, and eventually the transnational anarchist movement expressed their grievances in meetings and on the page. The situation became grave enough that the Liberty Group (Grupe Frayhayt), Ferrer Association, Unión de Fogoneros, Círculo de Trabajadores de Brooklyn, *Mother Earth*, and *Cultura Proletaria* organized a convention in Brooklyn in August 1911 to publicly clear the air. This meeting brought together a large part of New York's radical community; the Spanish immigrant anarchist Jaime Vidal presided. Debate at the convention focused on finding consensus on whether or not the Mexican Revolution generally and the events in Baja California specifically amounted to a social revolution. This greatly concerned the anarchist participants and supporters, as it would be anathema to their politics to actively side with one or another political faction in a battle for state power.

Emma Goldman spoke and continued her support of the PLM from her time in California. Bernard Sernaker, a well-known Jewish anarchist in New York, spoke in support from his position as the Liberty Group's delegate, and the Unión de Fogoneros carried over its energy from early protests to continue its support. Those in attendance at the Brooklyn meeting unanimously agreed that the upheaval in Mexico constituted a broad social revolution and thus deserved the full support of anarchists. Shortly after this meeting the organizing committee Pro-Revolución Mexicana held a large outdoor meeting in Union Square at which William Thurston Brown, Emma Goldman, Ben Reitman, and Jaime Vidal all spoke. An incredibly strong show of support to be sure, but it failed to settle the discord.[73]

The issue simmered through the autumn until the Gruppo Autonomo in Boston called another convention in December over what they called the "Mexican Question." The first speaker to take the podium, Egidio Girardi from Brighton, told the anarchists in the crowded hall (most of whom were Italian) that the events transpiring in Mexico did not resemble a socialist or anarchist revolution. He also claimed that those associated with the PLM were simply not anarchists. His speech at once pointed to his views about what a revolution should look like and what role leaders should play in a popular revolt. Well versed in the anarchist canon, he slightly blunted his own criticism by drawing upon Peter Kropotkin's *Words of a Rebel* from memory: "Every upheaval by the people brings the social revolution closer."[74] Anarchists often used this line of thought to justify support of popular upheavals not explicitly anarchist in character. In fact, he warned against those who would abandon their support of the Mexican struggle because of this infighting.

When the delegates assessed the Mexican Revolution, they unavoidably reconciled their visions of social and economic revolution with their understanding of Mexico. Drawing a comparison, Luigi Galleani stated that he sympathized with the republican revolt in Portugal and the upheaval underway in China, but sympathizing with these struggles did not equate to organizing the grassroots support they provided the PLM. Galleani described Portugal and China as bourgeois revolutions in strikingly Marxist language and argued that since events in Portugal and China lacked a proletarian component, radicals did not feel compelled to take up financial collections in support, let alone travel to participate. He supported Kropotkin's belief that any unrest with a strong popular component could lead to social revolution and should be supported, but he saw no such thing in Mexico because he did not know of strikes by urban industrial proletarians. He characterized the situation in Mexico as being at an elite level, between Madero and Bernardo Reyes, and that the "proletariat has thus far failed to detect any hint of revolutionary idealism."[75]

Galleani correctly observed events in Mexico for the most part but failed to understand them. Across the spectrum of revolutionary protagonists, including Madero, urban insurrections had failed. Even in the "pioneer regions" of the revolution in Chihuahua, Durango, and along the Durango and Coahuila border, attempts to seize towns were unsuccessful. Rebels shifted to a "rural strategy," and industrial workers organized as such did not constitute a major force in this stage of the Mexican Revolution. Alan Knight characterized the spring 1911 revolutionary push in these states as "rural, popular, and significantly agrarian."[76] Galleani failed to see the revolutionary potential of rural Mexico.

Galleani also compared Mexico to other Latin American countries with radical movements—Peru, Chile, Brazil, and Ecuador—when he quite ridiculously claimed that radicals in Mexico had never published an "anti-clerical newspaper, let alone a socialistic one and *Regeneración* has never fired a dart at the big conventional lies—religious, political, economic, or moral." He carried this reasoning so far as to even dismiss that radicals were fighting in Mexico at all. Even if they were, he still saw the group in Los Angeles deterring the cause because it "claimed a patent over the popular movement."[77] This criticism was equally as bound up in the Italian anarchists' understanding of Mexicans as in their own thoughts about anarchist praxis.

Another Italian anarchist at the meeting, Raffaele Guzzardi, criticized the PLM and Mexicans generally when he questioned who consumed the twenty thousand issues of *Regeneración* that he believed circulated weekly. He held that between 80 percent and 90 percent of Mexico's population were illiterate and so they could not be the primary consumers of the paper: "The whole thing is produced, not for Mexico, but to create the impression among subversives around the world that there is a social revolution under way when in fact there is not and there cannot be." John Longo from Pioche, Nevada, one of the eight cosigners of the original letter, echoed this sentiment when he wrote, "[I went] there to see for myself and was convinced: convinced that the Mexican people are in a rudimentary condition, resistant to anarchist or social ideas, illiterate, slavish, religious and loyally patriotic."[78]

While much of this criticism is demonstrably false, even at the time, it was probably also heartfelt and true to their limited experiences. Throughout the spring of 1911, coverage in *L'Era Nuova*, *Cronaca Sovversiva*, and *Regeneración* focused on the entirety of revolutionary events in Mexico. The newspapers often discussed Baja California, but on the whole this did not take precedence over the descriptions of events transpiring across Mexico. As anarchists arrived in Baja California, many must have expected this theater to be more central to the revolution than the frontier that it was.

A connected disagreement surfaced only in vague language at the meeting. Giovanni Rossi spoke representing Italian anarchists from Portsmouth, West Virginia, and complained that the PLM declined his group's offer of "revolutionary assistance of a character which this is not the place to specify." Rossi chastised the PLM for declining their offers of assistance in bombings and assassinations, tactics perfectly at home in urban insurrections that would have been woefully out of place in the rural battlefields in Baja California or elsewhere in Mexico.[79] Clearly, the Boston convention failed as miserably as the Brooklyn meeting to settle the Mexican question.

The discord also spread to European anarchist circles, most significantly through the pages of *Les Temps Nouveaux* in France, edited by Jean Grave, which became another focal point of international debate over the legitimacy of the Baja raids. The Parisian paper started as a strong supporter of the PLM. In May it carried sympathetic articles about the PLM and Mexican Revolution more broadly and took up a collection. Its editors also vouched for the PLM by writing that "we associate ourselves with the campaign" and noted that Michel Petit contributed five francs to those in Los Angeles.[80]

Transatlantic information lag, attributable to the reliance on mail carried by steamers rather than telegraph, contributed to misunderstandings. In July, after the rebels surrendered Tijuana, *Les Temps Nouveaux* published an article by Jean Humbolt, a French correspondent credited as "H," who had joined with a revolutionary group in El Paso in April before being arrested for neutrality violations. After his release in May the French anarchist crossed the line into Juarez, which Madero's forces had captured, and wrote that here he lost any illusions that he may have had about Madero's reformist credentials. The paper also noted the arrest of the PLM leaders in Los Angeles and early signs of repression in Mexico by Madero, writing that the struggle continued by those holding the PLM's "Land and Liberty" flag.[81]

Out of step with reality of the PLM's legal situation, the same July 1 issue published a letter from "G. B." requesting that they form a committee to consolidate correspondence with the PLM to assist the large number of comrades who wished to travel to join the fight in Mexico. It was not until July 8 that the plea for international volunteers, issued by the PLM leadership before the fall of Tijuana, appeared in the French paper. It had been dated May 20.[82]

The first signal of the developing controversy in Europe came on July 22 when the newspaper noted that it was receiving contradictory information about the direction of the Mexican Revolution over its "social revolutionary" character. On August 19 *Les Temps Nouveau* published an article by Manuel G. Garza dated July 20 that noted the PLM legal difficulties and cautioned that the PLM could not financially assist French anarchists who wished to make the journey.[83]

In September L. Morel, whom *Les Temps Nouveau* editors introduced as a militant who's sincerity they trusted, dismissed the notion that a social revolution was underway in Mexico, criticized the PLM for exaggerating, and warned away the comrades "who are leaving from around the world" to join the revolution in Mexico.[84] The paper's view of the events in Baja turned still further in the next issue, when E. Rist claimed that the PLM led a colonization effort in Baja California rather than fight for revolution. Rist noted the geographical isolation of the peninsula and its arid climate. He then cautioned readers not to mistake the many indigenous people on both sides of the border for "conscious revolutionaries." He recalled Élisée Reclus's characterization of indigenous people as "great children" and claimed they were "ignorant of the modern world" so they could not lead the way in a social revolution.[85]

The chronicler of global anarchism, Max Nettlau, believed that the criticism in *Les Temps Nouveaux* arose from the disappointment of a group of Parisian anarchists who had traveled to fight in Mexico but did not find the fighters they had planned on connecting with. Nettlau laid blame for this on the character of conflict in the Mexican Revolution. Most anarchists, and certainly those who traveled from France, looked for and failed to see a "barricade revolution" reminiscent of Garibaldi, rather than understand the multilayered rural, guerilla-style conflict underway. Nettlau was more damning in his assessment of the broader anarchist movement, in which many found it "incomprehensible that *Regeneración* expressed feelings of strong affinity for social-revolutionary Native Americans."[86] *Cronaca Sovversiva* certainly fed the French paper's criticism as well when *Les Temps Nouveaux* published an article by Antonio Cavalazzi, a writer for *Cronaca Sovversiva* who had publicly argued with Caminita's writing in the Italian edition of *Regeneración* in November 1911. Rist's criticism and Nettlau's insights, however, reveal how the racist and conceptual limits of their revolutionary imagination surely contributed as well.[87]

Coverage in *Les Temps Nouveaux* was not uniformly negative. The prominent Spanish anarchist Fernando Tárrida del Marmol wrote an article supporting the PLM in February 1912. He drew much of his information from Voltairine de Cleyre's writings on the PLM, some of which *Mother Earth* had published. In the spring of 1912 Ricardo Flores Magón, Enrique Flores Magón, and William C. Owen at last directly engaged the attacks in the French paper. Eventually, and a further indication of the importance of the issue in the anarchist movement, Peter Kropotkin personally intervened by writing *Les Temps Nouveaux* in defense of the PLM efforts in Baja California. The international expansion of this debate elucidates the role of the anarchist press as a tool of consensus building in a dispersed movement. It also points to important differences in individual understandings of anarchism across the global movement.[88]

William C. Owen, the strongest Anglo supporter of the PLM after it publicly embraced anarchism, offered an interesting rebuttal to some he believed mischaracterized Mexicans. He wrote that "unquestionably the American worker's ignorance of Mexican affairs is due largely to his conceit, since he looks down on the Mexican as an illiterate. That is a profound mistake. In Mexico, as in Asiatic countries, news travels with astonishing rapidity—by word of mouth—and it is the most important news. The Mexican peon is in blissful ignorance of the sort of trash with which Hearst drugs our proletariat, but with all the more force is he able to concentrate on the news that vitally affects his own life."[89]

Owen continued this conversation:

The Anarchist revolutionary movement has had, for years, its stronghold among the Latin races, and for thoroughly sound, fundamental, racial reasons. The Latin does not love work for work's sake, as so many Anglo-Saxons seem to do, in accordance with the philosophy of commercialism, which is that the production of commodities is the one end and aim of life. The Latin may love money, but he loves pleasure more. He may profess devotion to law and order, but he has an instinctive antipathy to strong, centralized Governments, preferring to be his own policeman both in defense and attack; for which reason he is generally looked on by the Anglo-Saxon as a may-be violent and undesirable citizen. But I regard it as certain that these racial traits will bring him into sympathy with the Mexicans, to whom he is also bound by the great tie of a common language, spoken from Texas, in North America, to Cape Horn.[90]

The intellectual background of Owen's defense of Mexicans through inherent "racial traits" came from his reading of Herbert Spencer. Years earlier Owen described his politics as "evolutionist" in the vein of Spencer. This supported his belief that workers—for whom he used broad racial terms to denote—possessed the potential to develop into desirable members of the labor and radical movement. His positive view of evolution did not overly focus on winners or losers but instead on individual growth through the process of struggle, and it textured his clear racism directed at Chinese workers in the late nineteenth century and his less prejudiced understanding of non-Anglos later in his life.[91]

Mexican socialists like Antonio Villarreal and Lázaro Gutiérrez de Lara, now split from the PLM, shared a dim view of Mexico as a "backward country with only incipient industrialism and a largely 'feudal' countryside," which pushed socialism to the end of "a long process of progressive economic development"—one of the reasons that they so easily slid toward Madero, though Gutiérrez de Lara also held up the civilized character of Aztecs, Toltecs, Zapotecs, and Maya against the inferiority of Spanish blood. Claudio Lomnitz argued that "Lázaro thus echoed eugenicist thinking of the day and made it his own while inverting its valuation of Spanish and Indian races." "Scientific" racism proved malleable and had a broad currency.[92]

Ricardo Flores Magón and his comrades in the PLM first developed their anarchism by reading the European canon in Camilo Arriaga's library in Mexico City, particularly from strands of anarchism focused on unequal land distribution, and then melding it with their experiences in Mexico. The group distinguished itself among anarchists to the extent that they placed indigenous people and land at the center of their vision of anarchism, freedom, and revolution. The PLM's anarchism was "a unique synthesis of European anarchist thought (with a heavy emphasis on Kropotkin) and an idealized—or imagined—conceptualization of indigenous cultural patterns characteristic of agrarian Mexico."[93] The land component of the PLM's anarchism also had similarities to the Italian anarchist Errico Malatesta's attention to rural, nonindustrial workers and reflected their opposition to the land consolidation carried out under the Mexican president Porfirio Díaz and foreign companies.[94]

The PLM members and the many thousands who read *Regeneración* or otherwise encountered anarchism in Mexico and the borderlands possessed the local knowledge to transform the anarchism they read or talked about to meet their needs through a syncretic process. When the global anarchist community assessed the social revolutionary potential of Mexicans from afar, it filtered through individual understandings of Mexicans as much as that of the different anarchisms being created through struggle. Debate about the Baja raids and the Mexican Revolution in anarchist circles slowly sputtered to a halt in the spring of 1912 without a clear conclusion across the diffuse movement networks.

The End in Los Angeles

Throughout the recriminations in the transnational anarchist movement, confrontation continued in the courthouse and on the streets of Los Angeles. The PLM and IWW participants in the Baja raids awaited trial in Los Angeles along with the McNamara brothers (accused of bombing the Los Angeles Times Building) and H. B. Connors, F. Ira Bender, and A. B. Maple, charged with plotting to dynamite the Los Angeles Hall of Records while it was under construction by the anti-union Lewellyn Iron Works. Agitation in the city reached beyond these sensational criminal cases. Peter Casterano, an anarchist and IWW member, also sat in jail. The *Industrial Worker* reported that the "I. W. W. boy is doing 90 days for diosrderly [*sic*] conduct, which means that he beat up a scab at the aqueduct."[95]

Jack Mosby and two others "who helped keep the red flag flying in Mexico for over six months" faced a judge in Los Angeles first. The three men had their habeas corpus writ on July 24, "a memorable day in the annals of the federal court in Southern California." The IWW press reported, "The court room was so jammed by revolutionists, to the surprise of the judge, who made the statement that if he knew that there would be such a crowd, he would have made other arrangements." This marked their fourth hearing without charges being filed. Authorities released them the next day after another hearing—before arresting them again "on a trumped up charge of robbery." All the while, E. J. Lewis, a lead IWW organizer in Los Angeles, gathered "the biggest crowds ever assembled to hear an I. W. W. speaker" in the city. Local IWW secretary Harry Weinstein proudly boasted, "A. F. of L. boys who are getting wise to themselves are coming in by leaps and bounds."[96]

The IWW achieved exceptional growth in Los Angeles the summer after the Baja raids. It sold five hundred copies of the *Industrial Worker* weekly and held seven meetings a week. Meeting locations varied, but on Sundays people rallied at regular gatherings in "one of the largest halls in town." As it organized workers in the city, the local also raised funds for the defense of the Wobblies and the PLM leaders on trial. These efforts often took the form of mass protest meetings. One featured H. W. Wright, Fred Moore, and Ed Lewis. The IWW also organized picnics, which took on a more social and family-oriented flavor. Though supporters filled the streets and courthouse, some tension arose between a few Anglo Wobblies in Los Angeles and the PLM by late summer. E. J. Lewis wrote to the *Industrial Worker* in August, complaining that the paper carried only stories regarding the junta at the expense of information about the imprisoned Anglo Wobblies (Mosby, Leflin, and Reed). He also complained that the defense committee neglected the men by directing money raised by the IWW toward the PLM. IWW support continued uninterrupted despite this brief surfacing of discontent.[97]

In the winter of 1912 the IWW turned its attention to its free-speech fight in San Diego initially fed by veterans from Baja California. Many of the non-Mexican volunteers had stayed in San Diego after being released by the U.S. troops who had detained them as they returned to the United States after defeat in Tijuana. A further influx of more than one hundred Wobblies traveled on a train from Los Angeles to participate. The free-speech fight was characterized by bloody, vigilante-led violence against those participating and by the kidnapping of Emma Goldman's partner Ben Reitman. Laura Payne Emerson and George Washington Woodbey both took active roles.[98]

As the IWW faced a violent crackdown in San Diego, the Holtville IWW Local 439 faced repercussions for their participation in the Baja raids. William C. Owen wrote in London's anarchist journal *Freedom* that "American officials have been engaged in kidnapping their [Mexican] members and handing them over to the Mexican authorities, to gain the blood-money paid by Madero's Government, which offers 100 dollars for the apprehension of every private, and 500 dollars for that of every officer engaged in armed insurrection." In January 1912 "a mob of brave and respectable citizens" set fire to the Holtville IWW local's empty meeting hall. The sheriff arrested twelve IWW members shortly thereafter. This marked the regional extension of the violent vigilantism witnessed in San Diego against the IWW and its supporters.[99]

For all of the discord among anarchists, the radical community in Los Angeles remained largely unaffected. That spring Ludovico Caminita left Los Angeles to return to Paterson. On his way east he went on a speaking tour of the country, "Texas, Kansas, Oklahoma, Illinois and other states," on behalf of *Regeneración* and the Mexican cause generally. Notwithstanding the fact that one of the primary Italian anarchist antagonists of the PLM, Ernesto Teodori, lived in Los Angeles, Italian anarchists in Los Angeles continued their support of the Mexican group unabated. *Regeneración* reported on an "Italian picnic" attended by one hundred of the "free-thinking element of the Italians." They collected funds for the defense of IWW organizers Joseph Ettor and Arturo Giovannitti, arrested during the 1912 strike in Lawrence, Massachusetts.[100] Recall that Ettor had lived in Los Angeles and organized for the IWW in the same community, making this support direct and personal.

Crowds in Los Angeles enthusiastically continued their support at the trial of Ricardo Flores Magón, Enrique Flores Magón, Librado Rivera, and Anselmo Figueroa on conspiracy charges in June 1912. The PLM supporters present wore "the red badge of the Mexican Liberal Party" in the court room. "Every morning as we began the trial we would turn around toward the back of the room and face a solid phalanx of the wearers of the red." It is possible that the earlier tension between the Anglo and Mexican supporters briefly resurfaced at the beginning of this trial when Mexicans filled the courtroom benches almost entirely. If this was the case, local Anglo Wobblies soon forgot their discontent and joined in their support. Mr. Robinson recalled:

> Known members of the I. W. W. were seen mingling with the crowd—numerous men who were identified by our officers and investigators as having participated in the rioting at San Diego. Some of them were men who had been in Lower California in the revolution, and one whom I personally recognized was a member of the gang that was prosecuted here for an attempt to dynamite the Hall of Records, and among them were more dangerous labor union agitators, the "wrecking crew" of the labor union gang here in Los Angeles. The I. W. W.'s and the labor union men became more and more numerous, and toward the end of the trial they just about equally balanced the Mexicans who were in the court room and corridors.[101]

After the jury returned guilty verdicts on the men, an even larger number of supporters turned their sentencing hearing into the latest confrontation with the state. When the judge handed down twenty-three months' jail time, the uproarious crowd forced the bailiffs to take the men "down through the post-office department and up an alley to the county jail." Those inside then filed onto the street, joining the large crowd assembled outside. Outrage at the sentence boiled over when some in the crowd rushed the building en masse. Officers met them with their clubs: "Among the 17 or 18 who were arrested were some women. One

CHAPTER 6

woman had a baby in her arms, but nevertheless she managed to claw the officer." This was Lucía Norman, Ricardo Flores Magon's daughter-in-law. The men now faced a sentence of twenty-three months in McNeil Island, a federal penitentiary in west-central Washington State.[102]

■ ■ ■

The lack of military or political success of the cosmopolitan army should not constrain the historical legacy of the PLM-led insurgency in Baja California. Historians have considered the PLM's role as a "precursor" to the Mexican Revolution and its broader impact in Mexico and United States.[103] But viewing the PLM from the limiting confines of national historiographies obscures the broader importance of its organizing. The PLM functioned as a funnel of interracial internationalism during the outbreak of the Mexican Revolution by channeling financial and material resources and people through Los Angeles. The flows of people and ideas back out through the connected movement, in turn, increased the scale of discord and broadened the historical legacy of the Baja raids. The Baja raids are an example of the potential of militant cosmopolitan revolutionary action. They are also a cautionary tale of the difficulties of bringing such a diverse group together—on the front lines of battle and mediated through the global movement—with an impulse for internationalism yet little understanding of the distinct cultural and ideological differences in their shared revolutionary movement.

Defeat in Baja California affected surviving participants less severely than it did the PLM as an organization. The racially diverse military force that took up arms against the state in Baja California gave an outlet to the militant interracial impulses circulating through the region. Defeat in Baja California forced a re-channeling of focus, but the culture of affinity was not tied to a single moment of revolutionary fervor. The depth of these cultural practices influenced interracial labor organizing and continued regional militancy as the decade wore on.

CHAPTER 7

A CULTURE OF AFFINITY

A poor economy in 1914 amplified the perennial unemployment patterns of winter. In Los Angeles a band of four hundred men formed an unemployed "army" and encamped on the bank of the Los Angeles River. The group, part of a nationwide movement known collectively as "Coxey's Army," planned to go "eastward soon and join Coxey at Cleveland and others along the way." This movement constituted a reprise of Coxey's first attempt in 1894 at creating a mass organization of the unemployed. The men in Los Angeles did not make it to Ohio. In fact, they did not leave the city. Los Angeles police raided the camp and arrested the Anglo, German, Italian, Mexican, Russian, Scandinavian, and Slavic men that the *Los Angeles Times* recognized as constituting the movement. One of the group's leaders, Morris Rose, characterized the group as an independent movement insisting that they "do not belong to the I.W.W., although there may be a number of members of that organization in our ranks."[1]

After the Baja raids the radical movement in Los Angeles continued to organize, bringing large numbers of people into the street in a multitude of forms, often not organizationally affiliated. The Industrial Workers of the World, Partido Liberal Mexicano, and an even greater number of unaffiliated radicals and sympathizers contributed to a multicentered local movement that generated dramatic moments of street confrontation and an institutional presence in the half-decade or so before the United States entered World War I. Los Angeles also increased its importance as a publishing center for Spanish-language radical newspapers. These vital community-building pages increased Los Angeles's visibility and significance

CHAPTER 7

in the global movement. In these years the local movement successfully weathered internal conflicts before World War I–era repression reshaped its ability to act and to formulate its own terms of struggle. Outside of the city, Los Angeles–based radicals continued to participate directly in moments of outright insurrection in Texas and Arizona.

After the Baja Raids

Leftists in Los Angeles faced significant setbacks in the wake of the Baja raids. The failure of the invasion of Baja California, the arrest of the PLM leaders, and their imprisonment marked a turning point in which the ability of the PLM to influence events in Mexico almost entirely evaporated. The PLM's organizing ability in Los Angeles and the borderlands declined more gradually toward World War I at the same time that its intellectual stature increased in the global movement. Another local setback came on the electoral front.

In the summer and fall of 1911 after the rebels surrendered Tijuana, socialists and their supporters in Los Angeles poured their collective resources into Job Harriman's mayoral campaign as the Socialist Party candidate. Overall Socialist Party membership in Los Angeles reached around eight thousand in 1911 before it entered into an electoral alliance with the Union Labor Party. Together their numbers amounted to twenty-six thousand members. Directly before the election, the McNamara brothers unexpectedly pleaded guilty to bombing the Los Angeles Times Building, which worked to discredit Harriman, who had supported the men. Harriman still received 51,796 votes in his losing bid, a strong level of support, but the incumbent mayor George Alexander won the day with 85,739 votes. Los Angeles failed to follow in the path of Milwaukee, which had recently elected the socialist mayor Emil Seidel.[2]

The 1911 election was the Socialist Party's strongest electoral showing in Los Angeles and the highpoint of the party's orientation toward electoral politics. Coupled with the victory of the open shop over the city's trade unions during the 1910–11 AFL strike wave, these defeats marked a watershed moment in city politics and labor movement. However, neither the Socialist Party nor the AFL gave up the fight. Fred Wheeler won a seat on the city council in 1913 for the Socialist Party. Job Harriman ran for mayor again in the same election but finished third and turned away from electoral politics in defeat. Socialists reoriented toward other projects, most notably they directed more resources into the Llano del Rio colony in the high desert north of Los Angeles. In 1914 the Socialist Party and the trade unions ended their cooperation on electoral efforts amid disagreement over affiliation and membership. By 1915 the Socialist Party was no longer a force in Los Angeles city politics. AFL organizing also slid "downhill" toward

World War I. The sum of such eventualities left open the central districts to radical organizing and new voices.[3]

The arrival of Blanca and Juan Francisco Moncaleano in Los Angeles, with their deep connections to Spanish-language-radical networks in Latin America and the Caribbean in late fall 1912, energized the local movement. Juan Francisco also generated substantial conflict within Los Angeles's anarchist community, and he proved to be an active yet divisive individual. Committed anarchists in Colombia, where Juan Francisco worked as a university professor, the couple made a circuitous journey to Los Angeles. They fled the state repression that accompanied their organizing in Colombia, settling in Havana, Cuba. While the Moncaleanos lived in Havana they taught at the Cerro School. About forty students attended this school modeled after the teachings of the Spanish anarchist Francisco Ferrer i Guardia.[4]

Regeneración first introduced Juan Francisco to its readership as a comrade in November 1911. Blanca Moncaleano wrote an article for *Regeneración* titled "*Hacia el Porvenir*," or "Making a Future," published in August 1912 and signed it as "Profesora Racionalista," Havana, Cuba. Cooperation between the couple and those in Los Angeles predated their physically meeting. Correspondence facilitated their solidarity on a more direct and personal level than the facilitating role of newspapers in the global movement. In 1912 the Moncaleano couple traveled from Havana to Mexico with three Cuban friends, all drawn by the Mexican Revolution that continued to unfold.[5]

The couple picked up where they left off in Cuba and joined an effort to organize a rational school in the Yucatán Peninsula. They then moved to Mexico City, where they passed through a handful of small organizations before forming a secret group that published the anarchist newspaper *Luz* (Light). The paper only lasted three issues due to financial constraints, but Madero's repression limited the group even more than their lack of money. Police raided *Luz*'s offices and arrested the members of the group. Rather than sending them to jail, authorities expelled Blanca and Juan Francisco from Mexico, which sent them north to Los Angeles. *Regeneración* noted the raid, continuing the connection and correspondence between the Moncaleano couple and their PLM comrades in Los Angeles.[6]

The Moncaleanos quickly got to work in Los Angeles that fall, and by February 1913 they joined efforts with a group of anarchists to open the International Workers' Home. Juan Francisco Moncaleano, bookstore owner Rómulo Carmona, and the Italian A. R. Vitagliano signed a lease for a large building, the "Orphans' Home," at the corner of Yale and Alpine in 1913. They envisioned it becoming the center of anarchism in Los Angeles. Carmona served as the home's treasurer. With the goal of long-term financial stability, the group retained the option to buy the property outright for fifty thousand dollars.

CHAPTER 7

In this building they created space for radical community-building activities and living: "Every comrade from a foreign land who may immigrate to this city may count on receiving the moral and material support of the International Workers' Home. He will enjoy the following advantages: Sleeping accommodations, hot and cold baths, a library, food, rational instruction, a doctor's services, and those of a corps of interpreters speaking different tongues. The International Workers' Home will do its utmost to get him occupation, by which he may make an independent living." The large property accommodated the rational school, the offices of *Regeneración*, a barber, library, gymnasium, and dormitories. In line with anarchist principles, the various occupants of the building remained autonomous and paid rent voluntarily. Dr. John Creaghe maintained an office in the building. Often referred to by the Spanish equivalent "Juan," Creaghe traveled even more than the Moncaleanos. Born in Ireland, he immigrated to Argentina and traversed the Americas, participating in radical activities throughout.[7]

To celebrate the opening of the building, they organized two large, well-attended conferences. One hundred and fifty people attended the first, and five hundred the second, which forced people to stand outside. The center offered regular classes, including language instruction in "Italian, English, Spanish, French, and Esperanto." People also used the building as a recreational and social center, and it provided space for dances.[8]

These developments in Los Angeles's multiracial and multilingual radical community came at the same time as the specter of even more immigration-fueled cheap labor loomed. The seizure of land in Central America by the United States to construct the Panama Canal proved important in the United States' extending its dominant position in the hemisphere. Preceded by the Spanish-American War, which saw American troops on the ground in Cuba and an extended and brutal occupation of the Philippines, both marked key steps in the United States' becoming a global military power. In Los Angeles, radicals and business leaders alike expected the opening of the Panama Canal and cheap steamship travel direct from Europe to increase the number of new immigrants moving to the West Coast. City leaders viewed new immigrants and radicals as synonymous. While many called for immigration restrictions, the city's anarchists worked to educate and organize. They viewed their educational work and organizing as "endeavoring to forestall the situation."[9]

On the occasion of *Regeneración* moving its offices into the International Workers' Home in 1913, an article titled "Our New Home" made the connection between radical organizing and the opening of the Canal:

It may be mentioned also that the property is situate [*sic*] in what is essentially the Italian quarter, and we have great hopes that the Italians, whose language is so closely allied to Spanish and who feel instinctively that they and the Mexicans are nearly related, will unite with us in making this co-operative effort the success it deserves to be.... In short, the *Latin race* has immense representation in Los Angeles even now, and this will become vastly greater with the opening of the Panama Canal.[10]

Radicals and their publications played a central role in identity construction in the immigrant community. In this case, they used a category broader than national origin by appealing to cultural and linguistic similarities. Tampa, Florida, remains the best-documented example of Cubans and Italians forming broad cultural affinities. This closeness extended through Spanish- and Italian-language radical networks in the United States and elsewhere in the Americas.[11]

The Bureau of Investigation reported that the "principal object" of Spanish-language anarchist paper *Cultura Obrera*, edited by Pedro Esteve, was "to encourage strikes of all kinds among the Latin peoples, Italians and Spanich [*sic*] principally." The bureau also took note of the connection between *Regeneración* and *Cultura Obrera*: An issue "contains a communication from Enrique Flores Magón, formerly editor and publisher of the anarchistic sheet 'Regeneracion.' This letter purports to be written on the eve of his departure to the Federal penitentiary.... It contains exhortations to his comrades and followers to continue in the same course as heretofore."[12] The connections between movements, individuals, and newspapers fed efforts to broaden individual conceptualizations of commonality and difference. This is also evidence of the bureau's beginning to see some of the connections within the Spanish- and Italian-language anarchist networks.

The International Workers' Home invigorated Los Angeles's anarchists that winter, but by May divisions between Juan Francisco Moncaleano and the PLM members running *Regeneración* (as Ricardo Flores Magón, Enrique Flores Magón, Librado Rivera, and Anselmo Figueroa were imprisoned) surfaced. First, an article in *Regeneración* claimed that Juan Francisco had attempted to wrest control of *Regeneración* away from the PLM and turn it into the official paper of the International Workers' Home. In response, *Regeneración* quickly moved its offices out of the building, first to 914 Boston Street and then to more permanent offices at 503 North Figueroa Street. The following month, *Regeneración* carried a full-page article to air their grievances against Juan Francisco, which ranged from his stealing movement funds to committing acts of sexual impropriety with young girls in Mexico. Despite criticism from the Cuban anarchist paper *¡Tierra!* for publishing personal attacks in a public forum, *Regeneración* did not back down from their charges. In August *Regeneración* published a letter from a Cuban comrade accusing Juan Francisco of molesting girls in Cuban rational schools as well.[13]

CHAPTER 7

A greater indication of the importance of the charges is that the editors of *Regeneración* included Romulo S. Carmona in their attack, more significant by far for the local movement than falling out with the recently arrived Moncaleano. Carmona sheltered Ricardo Flores Magón and Modesto Díaz when they first arrived in Los Angeles in 1907 attempting to elude police and after Enrique Flores Magón had married Carmona's daughter Paula. The acting editors of *Regeneración* claimed that Carmona wrote a letter to Ricardo under the pen name Pilar Robledo, stating that he had assumed the editorship of *Regeneración*. The paper also claimed that Moncaleano and Carmona leveraged Enrique by pressuring his wife and children. The couple, in fact, soon divorced. William C. Owen attached his name to the condemnation of Juan Francisco in August. The PLM also charged Rafael Romero Palacios, an active Milwaukee-based PLM fundraiser, with stealing movement funds intended for the group in Los Angeles and signing his name to articles written by European comrades published in various anarchist newspapers.[14]

The veracity of these claims is difficult to corroborate; however, the extent and clarity of the charges against the two men gives them weight, and the relationships were not repaired. At this point Teodoro M. Gaitán, Blas Lara, Antonio de P. Araujo, Alberto Tellez, and Juan Rincón cared for the Spanish pages of *Regeneración* while William C. Owen continued to edit the English section. With Ricardo Flores Magón, Enrique Flores Magón, Librado Rivera, and Anselmo Figueroa imprisoned in Washington, and with Victoriano Huerta overthrowing Madero in Mexico, the PLM was in its weakest position since its leaders arrived in the United States. The PLM, however, was not in a desperate situation. Its financial condition became worse in the coming fall and winter, but anarchists in the United States, Mexico, and globally still supported it. The group managed to increase the page count of *Regeneración* from four to six pages for a short time beginning in the summer of 1913, evidence of at least a reasonable financial situation. The PLM leaders would have understandably worked to maintain control over *Regeneración*, their primary organizing tool. The newspaper was their voice.

Similar to the fallout with Italian anarchists after the Baja raids, the strength of the radical movement in Los Angeles is indicated by its ability to continue mobilizing through such a crisis. Blanca Moncaleano seems to have escaped the charges levied against her husband, and in November 1913 she published the first issue of her new anarchist feminist newspaper *Pluma Roja*. Blanca was at the helm, though Juan Francisco often wrote for the paper. With articles like "For Women and Anarchy," *Pluma Roja* confronted patriarchy more than the male-dominated radical press. The paper also primarily focused its content on theory and Spanish-language anarchist networks without writing about events or disagreements in Los Angeles.[15]

Through the accusations in 1913, *Regeneración* continued to roll off the press, albeit with fewer subscribers from its highpoint right before the Baja raids. Meanwhile two new papers—*Fuerza Consciente* and *Huelga General*—joined *Regeneración* and *Pluma Roja* in Los Angeles. The simultaneous publication of these four newspapers turned Los Angeles into a world center of Spanish-language radical publishing. It also indicated that a substantial amount of local organizational energy involved printing newspapers intended for consumption outside of the city; local circulation alone could not sustain these four newspapers. *Regeneración* and *Huelga General* focused more on local events than the other two papers, though both sought to empower and represent the local movement differently.

The Spaniard Jaime Vidal began *Fuerza Consciente* with the title *Brazo y Cerebro* in New York City in 1912. The newspaper complemented *Cultura Obrera*, published in neighboring Brooklyn and edited by Pedro Esteve. *Brazo y Cerebro* made its broad worldview clear in the first issue. It ran an article updating readers about the Mexican Revolution and a description of living conditions in India. Donations from supporters in Los Angeles connected the first issue of *Brazo y Cerebro* to the West Coast city. The second issue, published in October, furthered the new paper's broad connections with an advertisement for the *Chinese Anarchist News*, edited by Lieu Sun Soil. Anarchists published this paper in China before the revolution in 1911, after which the group took up residence in Tokyo, Japan. By March 1913 harassment from U.S. postal inspectors forced the publishing group to change the name of *Brazo y Cerebro*, so they settled on *Fuerza Consciente*. Support for *Fuerza Consciente* from anarchists in Los Angeles drew Vidal and his comrades to move the paper from New York to Los Angeles in October 1913. It remained in the city until spring 1914.[16]

In July 1913, a month before the first issue of *Huelga General*, *Regeneración* carried an uncredited article on the English page, most likely written by William C. Owen, announcing the new IWW paper. In the article, tension between the IWW in Los Angeles and the PLM is evident: "[*Huelga General's*] editorials will have to be superior to those of '*Regeneración*,' its revolutionary outlook broader" in order to be successful.[17] After the Baja raids, grumblings over prison support for IWW members and PLM leadership found its way to the page, though such sentiment did not seem to be reflected in street-level support. The 1913 conflict involving Moncaleano more directly factored into the present tension, as the Mexican IWW group in Los Angeles remained comrades with Moncaleano.[18]

With *Huelga General*, years of Spanish-language IWW organizing in Los Angeles at last added a local newspaper to its arsenal. José Corona served as director for the new newspaper. The addition of *Huelga General*, more so than *Pluma Roja* or *Fuerza Consciente*, indicates the breadth or, less kindly, factions in the local movement. The Spanish immigrant Aurelio Vincente Azuara wrote for the paper, along with many others in Los Angeles's Spanish-language radical community. *Huelga General* became the third Spanish-language IWW newspaper in the Southwest after the Phoenix IWW local's *La Union Industrial* published in 1910 and 1911, and *Libertad y Trabajo* in 1908. Fernando Velarde was a major force in the Phoenix IWW local and had relocated to Los Angeles to organize with the PLM for the Baja raids. Velarde stayed in the city and worked behind the scenes to get *Huelga General* off the ground. This paper had a short life, running only from August 23, 1913, to September 12, 1914. A supplement to the paper from March 1914 announced that it would not continue because of "insufficient support on the part of the workers." An article noted: "In the first place, the brutal persecution that the members of our organization have been the victims of, in the second place the jailing of our Fellow Workers after the riot of Dec. 25th is sufficient to suspend the paper till we can raise more funds."[19]

Newspapers functioned as foci of the various strands of the radical movement. Participants and sympathizers invested a significant amount of resources into their publication and distribution. Radical newspapers linked local movements regionally and globally and had the power to broadcast disagreements to a large audience. Local movements, in turn, learned and participated in these mediated discussions at their discretion. As important as these forums were to the radical movement, ephemeral or clandestine organizing, job actions, or attempts at armed insurrection illustrated the indirect connection between the page and action.

Wheatland and Rangel-Cline

Labor organizing and radical cross-border activities continued through radical networks established over previous years. In the summer of 1913 two dramatic confrontations of far-reaching importance, one in Wheatland, California, and the other near Carrizo Springs, Texas, took the lives of seven men, with many more wounded. The town of Wheatland lies thirty-five miles north of Sacramento. Ralph Durst and his brother operated a 640-acre ranch ten miles outside of the town center. In 1913 they dedicated a large part of their acreage to growing hops, a cash crop used in beer production. They followed the common practice of advertising for field hands to travel to their farm to work. Advertisements promised "all white pickers" jobs if they arrived before the first of August. Nearly three thousand people responded and made their way to the Durst ranch. The farm had no way of employing or accommodating that many people. Squalid conditions and lower-than-expected wages met those who arrived. As workers held an outdoor meeting to discuss their grievances, the sheriff, supported by a posse of armed local men, confronted the crowd. The ensuing violence resulted in four deaths and reverberated across the West. It is probably the best-recorded of all rural labor disputes in these years, owing to governor Hiram Johnson's commissioning the economist Carlton Parker to study the conditions that led to the violence for the Commission of Immigration and Housing.[20]

The importance of Wheatland comes from two interconnected facts. First, the composition of the workers on the farm varied from single men to families, who Parker estimated to represent twenty-seven different nationalities. The Commission report noted Cubans, Puerto Ricans, Mexicans, Syrians, Japanese, Sikhs, Poles, Greeks, Italians, Lithuanians, and Spanish from Hawaii as the most common ethnic or racial groups on the farm. Second, the character of the organization on the farm typified the manner in which radical ideas circulated. Wheatland was not an official IWW strike. Similar to Fernando Palomares and Frank Little's IWW organizing discussed earlier, many other men traveled regional fields, camps, and railcars spreading the ideals and tactics of the IWW. This was far more important for the continued propagation of the regional culture of affinity than recruiting workers to sign a union card and pay a small amount in dues. Carlton Parker estimated that "at least 400 knew in a rough way the—for them curiously attractive—philosophy of the I.W.W. and could also sing some of its songs."[21]

On the Durst farm, around thirty men formed a temporary IWW local and elected Richard Ford as their spokesman. Ford had formerly held an IWW membership card, but he had not paid dues in some time. This group began agitating for improved living and working conditions, such as better toilet facilities, water to drink in the fields as they labored under the summer sun, lemonade made from lemons and not just citric acid, and a flat rate per pound of hops picked. At the end of an attempt to negotiate, a scuffle occurred. Durst struck Ford and then fired the whole of the negotiating committee on the spot before he ordered them off his property. Durst then asked a deputy sheriff to arrest Ford, but fellow workers intervened to prevent this from happening.

Squalid work conditions and simmering conflict with an undercurrent of radical organizing provided the context for a mass meeting on the farm that same afternoon. Ford and Herman Suhr, among others, took the stage; workers spoke seven languages on the stage during the meeting. While the assembled crowd sang the Wobbly hymn "Workingman, Unite!"—"Shall we still be slaves and work for wages? It is outrageous—has been for ages; This earth by right belongs to toilers, And not to spoilers of liberty"—the sheriff and a posse of eleven other armed men pulled into the farm in two automobiles.[22]

Not surprisingly, accounts of what exactly transpired next vary considerably. The IWW journalist Mortimer Downing wrote that the sheriff rushed the speakers and attempted to arrest Ford. Ford challenged him by asking for a warrant, which the sheriff met with his fist before firing a shot in the air in a vain attempt to disperse the crowd. A woman then grabbed the sheriff, whom he hit with the butt of his weapon before they both fell to the ground. The other armed men began to fire, and the crowd surged toward them, at which point a young English boy in the crowd was shot and killed. A young black Puerto Rican boy grabbed the sheriff's gun and returned fire, killing the local district attorney who had joined the posse, before being shot and killed himself. The names of the English and Puerto Rican boys are unrecorded but their youth noted. The posse retreated, leaving four dead and around twelve wounded, including the sheriff, on the ranch.[23]

The coroner's inquest in nearby Marysville found the strike leaders responsible for the district attorney's death. Courts soon issued warrants and eventually arrested Ford and Suhr, among others. The prominent socialist attorney Austin Lewis represented those arrested for the IWW. A jury found the two men guilty of second-degree murder and sentenced them to life terms. This event garnered national attention from leftists and the general public alike. For example, the African American IWW member Benjamin H. Fletcher wrote to *Solidarity* that his group in Philadelphia held a protest meeting in support of its fellow workers in Wheatland, California, at which Joe Ettor, J. J. McKelvey, and the associate editor of *Il Proletario*, Edmondo Rossoni, spoke.[24]

The extent of the violence in Wheatland that forced the Governor of California to turn his attention to migratory workers stands out. However, the racial composition of the people who were present and the ad hoc organizing fueled by the mobility of radicals joining workers together on that hot summer day was typical. Shortly after the events in Wheatland, another, strikingly different event transpired throughout the extended regional radical networks. In Texas, dedicated revolutionaries, most anarchists or syndicalists, planned to join the Mexican Revolution.

In the closing days of that same summer, in September, a group of around twenty men, many with military experience, attempted to march across the Mexican border from Texas to join the Mexican Revolution. They carried a flag emblazoned with the phrase "land and liberty," the same slogan that rebels raised over Tijuana in 1911. The group rallied at the "Capones Wind Mill" near the town of Carrizo Springs in Dimmit County. They even posed for a group photo before setting out.[25] PLM members had planned the rough outline of the incursion at a meeting in May attended by local PLM-affiliated clubs representing Chihuahua, Coahuila, Durango, Nuevo León, Tamaulipas, and cities in Texas. Comrades in Mexico waited for them to cross the border.[26] The events that followed occurred in slow motion, punctuated with moments of deadly consequence.

Similar to the radical practices in the doomed Baja raids, this small band elected its leadership, choosing José Guerra as leader for twenty-four hours and Silvestre Lómas as their scout for an unspecified period. Lómas was a member of a PLM group in El Paso. He had fought with PLM comrades in Chihuahua in 1911 and had served a one-year sentence in 1911–12 at Leavenworth, Kansas, for these activities. Authorities in El Paso arrested Lómas along with Fernando Palomarez and Rosendo Dorame for neutrality violations in 1912. Dorame had worked on the Phoenix IWW publication *La Unión Industrial*. Jesús María Rangel was one of the primary architects of the group assembled in Texas along with Eugenio Alzalde. Rangel was wounded in Las Vacas, Coahuila in the failed 1908 PLM attempt at revolution. Although this insurrection occurred near the Texas-Mexico border in Carrizo Springs some two thousand miles from Los Angeles, Juan Rincón traveled from San Gabriel, California, to participate. Rincón was part of a San Gabriel group supporting *Regeneración* while the junta served their prison terms in Washington. He worked in the *Regeneración* office before leaving for Texas. Charles Cline, the only Anglo present, was an IWW organizer who had worked with the Brotherhood of Timber Workers in the South.[27]

As the group marched toward the border on September 11, their scout Silvestre Lómas led the way. As he marched out of sight of the others, he signaled trouble by blowing a whistle. Hearing the call, the main party sent four men forward; they found Lómas laying on the ground with bullet wounds. They went forward again when two men came out from behind cover and ordered their surrender. Recognizing their numerical supremacy, the rebels refused, and returned the demand. Sheriff Eugene Buck and Deputy Candelario Ortíz obliged. Taking captives, let alone from law enforcement, was not part of their plan.[28]

Now joined by the rest of their comrades, the rebel group interrogated their two captives, who revealed that they had been in a group of four. The rebels sent out a party in a failed attempt to negotiate with the two remaining officers. When the two groups encountered each other, the officers fired on the rebel's negotiating party but did not inflict any wounds. The two officers who escaped sounded the alarm after the initial confrontation. That night the elected rebel leader, José Guerra, executed ("*ajustició*") Deputy Ortíz for his part in killing Lómas. Reinforcements of Texas Rangers arrived the next day, and the two groups once again made contact. To secure the release of Sheriff Buck, all parties signed a contract stating that the rebels would be allowed to cross the border without hindrance upon the release of their captive. Cline, fluent in Spanish, served as the interpreter for these exchanges. They released the sheriff and prepared to cross the border the next day. While camping and eating deer meat on September 13, a still-larger group, including more Texas Rangers, surrounded the rebels and opened fire without warning. This raiding party shot the young Juan Rincón in the stomach before the rebels had a chance to surrender, which they did in short order. Of the deaths, Rincón's most deeply affected those in Los Angeles, and Antonio de P. Araujo wrote a heartfelt obituary for the young man in *Regeneración*.[29]

CHAPTER 7

The Texan officers marched the surviving rebels to a nearby ranch, where they threatened their captives with lynching, even suggesting that they could pick out the branch upon which they would hang. The restraint of an U.S. Army lieutenant with orders to bring the men before a judge seems to be what spared their lives over a tense few days. The surviving men stood trial before "a jury of farmers to whose interest it is to have cheap labor and against a prosecution that is well prepared—with the whole machinery of the state of Texas being used by the employing class to send our brother to the gallows." Radicals widely believed that the men were "the victims of extreme race and class feeling, fanned by the employing class which recognizes a menace to their cheap labor in the teachings of these men."[30] Local juries convicted three members of the rebel group to sentences ranging from nine to ninety-nine years before authorities moved the trial of the leaders to San Antonio. The PLM and Mexicans more broadly rallied around their comrades awaiting trial. Amid the threat of popular unrest if the state executed the remaining prisoners, Texas authorities delayed their trials, which eventually resulted in Rangel, Cline, and Abraham Cisneros receiving ninety-nine-year sentences. Pedro Perales, Jesus González, and Leonardo Vasquez also received long terms.[31]

The incident became known as Rangel-Cline in the radical imagination; the *Road to Freedom* compared their sentences for attempting to join the Mexican Revolution to the American revolutionary tradition: "for that crime the descendants of George Washington and John Brown have apparently today no mercy."[32] In Los Angeles the Rangel-Cline Defense Committee organized support for the men in Texas under the banner "The Strength of Labor Is the Strength of Labor's Militancy."[33]

Some of the members of the Rangel-Cline Defense Committee were well-known anarchists and socialists, with some associated with trade unions in Los Angeles. Anarchist Vittorio Cravello of AFL-affiliated Clerk's Union 83 served as the committee's secretary. Another anarchist, German immigrant Rudolph (or Robert) Wirth occupied the position of treasurer, and Stanley Gue, also from Clerk's Union 83 and a veteran of the Baja raids, chaired the committee. Gue had been secretary of IWW Local 13 in San Diego in 1911. John Murray Jr. of Typographical Union 174 and the longtime California laborite Frank Roney, now living in Alhambra, joined the committee and personally wrote to ironmoulders' unions in Texas asking for support. The Los Angeles Building Trades Council, the Los Angeles Central Labor Council, and the Socialist Parties of Texas, California, and Los Angeles all endorsed the effort. Rangel and Cline received extensive labor and leftist support for an open act of armed rebellion.[34]

The composition of this committee evidences the extent of solidarity and support in Los Angeles in the years after the Baja raids. Regardless of the fallout, the events in 1911 did not end cooperation among anarchists, Wobblies, socialists, and trade unionists in Los Angeles. Nor did the Baja raids mark the end of popular Anglo and Mexican support for the Mexican revolutionaries in the United States. Comrades rallied to support the Mexican revolutionaries at a time of significant need, but the Rangel-Cline affair and the arrest of some other PLM members in Arizona in August 1914 forced much of the now-limited organizing efforts of the PLM toward legal defense rather than new organizing. A few participants died or were murdered in prison. They served time for killing a deputy, after all, which opened them to retaliatory acts committed or facilitated by guards. Cline served thirteen years of his sentence; after his release he continued to organize, including speaking in Gary, Indiana, in 1926 to a group of Mexican steel and factory workers.[35]

In both Wheatland, California, and Carrizo Spring, Texas, the outbreaks of violence reflected the local contexts of each struggle. Both events, however, fit within the larger history of working-class radicalism that was typically interracial with regional cooperation. The circulation of radical ideas, the mobility of workers, and the presence of militants combined to fuel events ranging from local wage disputes to armed revolutionary activities. Labor and revolutionary organizing continued to operate in close proximity in the region. As these episodes radiated through radical networks, the discontent of workers and the aggression of police exploded on Christmas Day in Los Angeles.

The Christmas Riot and an Army of the Unemployed

In Los Angeles street battles between police and protesters occurred with some frequency during the early twentieth century. In 1903 the *curandera* Teresa Urrea led a large "crowd of Mexican women" in support of the Mexican Federal Union.[36] After the sentencing of the PLM leaders in 1912, a major riot ensued. On January 5, 1913, the *Los Angeles Times* reported, "Several hundred I.W.W.'s and sympathizers, marching behind a red flag carried by two Mexican women of Amazonian proportions, precipitated a riot at Third and Los Angeles streets." The paper continued: "Four arrests were made. A number of heads were cracked."[37] One lasting consequence of the tumult of the bombing of the Los Angeles Times Building, the Baja raids, and regional IWW free-speech fights was that authorities increasingly shifted their focus from their previous "panics regarding white workingmen" generally and instead toward "arresting organized workers and labor radicals."[38] The gathering of unemployed workers and radicals on Christmas Day and then in the Unemployed Army brought both of these foci together and produced the brutal response of city authorities.

Seasonally unemployed workers continued to winter in the city as they had in years past, and organizing efforts continued. For Christmas Day 1913, radicals

CHAPTER 7

planned a large gathering of unemployed workers for the plaza. Organizers extensively publicized the rally, and even the labor-friendly yet mainstream daily *Los Angeles Record* issued a call on its front page: "THE PLACE—THE PLAZA. THE TIME—2 O'CLOCK. THURSDAY AFTERNOON. THE OCCASION—MASS MEETING OF ALL UNEMPLOYED IN LOS ANGELES."[39]

Roughly five hundred people gathered to listen to William C. Owen, Morris Rose, and Juan Francisco Moncaleano, who still had a public presence after the fallout with the PLM. Police intervened in the peaceful meeting, and a melee ensued in which police shot dead Rafaél Adames. The thirty-five-year-old had lived a few blocks from the plaza. Shortly after Adames's death, fellow workers carried his body to the IWW hall on South Los Angeles Street and laid it under a picture of Karl Marx that hung on the wall. Mexican and Anglo members of the IWW shared headquarters at 420 North Los Angeles Street. The *Los Angeles Times* observed, "Two charters hanging upon the wall; one in English, setting forth that the place is rented by the Los Angeles chapter of the Industrial Workers of the World; the other in Spanish, stating the 'Trabajadores del Mundo Unidos' have their headquarters there."[40]

The police apparently believed that they killed two other people, but they could not find the bodies because members of the crowd hid them "somewhere in Sonoratown." Attempting to find "one man shot through the stomach" and "at least a score" of people they believed to be seriously injured, the Los Angeles Police swept through the district, searching restaurants, pool halls, and movie theaters for people who may have been involved. Fearing more violence that evening, the police ordered all bars north of Temple Street cleared. The *Los Angeles Times* reported that the riot injured eleven officers, some seriously. Police made just over seventy arrests that day. The same night, a disturbance broke out in Boyle Heights. It turned out to be unrelated and, in the words of the *Times*, "merely a race affair."[41]

The anarchist writers for *Pluma Roja* remembered Adames as one of their own. He had spoken at a pair of meetings at Mammoth Hall in support of the Rangel-Cline defense effort two months before his death. *Regeneración* recorded that at Adames's funeral at Odd Fellow's Cemetery in Boyle Heights, "Comrades addressed the cosmopolitan army assembled: everyone listened intently and occasionally turned their faces to see their comrades steadfast with the arguments and sweet and vindictive words of the speakers."[42] Anarchists in Los Angeles grieved heavily over the loss of their fellow worker.

The police designated five of the arrestees, Peter Casterano, Armando M. Ojeda, Juan Sanchez, Pedro Coria, and Cesario Andrade, as leaders, holding them on two thousand dollars' bail rather than the five hundred dollars reserved for the others. The *Los Angeles Times* characterized those arrested as a "motley gang of Mexicans, Italians and Americans"[43] and described the thirty-one-year-old Ojeda, active in the IWW and fluent in English, as "a clean shaven young man, with the appearance of a sort of cross between a moving-picture hero and a habitue of the Latin quarter."[44] Peter Castorena, who had been arrested in 1911 after an altercation with a strikebreaker, reportedly told the city committee looking into the riot while he was in jail, "What have I ever got from our government that I should be loyal to it or give it my allegiance?" He continued, "No. I am against all government; I have no use for the American flag. The laws of this country and all its States and cities are made by the capitalists. Instead, they should be made by workingmen, men who know conditions and whose sympathies are with the down-and-out."[45] Police charged a young Italian named Silvio Nutti separately for giving an "incendiary speech" after Adames's death.[46] His charges stemmed from reportedly saying: "We must find out the policemen who killed our brother, Rafael Aldames [sic], and kill and maim him and others if we have to. We must Revolt."[47] Nutti often spoke with the leading radicals in the city, including on one occasion at Italian Hall with Lázaro Gutiérrez de Lara, Juan Francisco Moncaleano, and Fred Moore at a protest meeting in support of León Cárdenas Martínez, a teenager accused of killing a white woman in Texas.[48]

In the week after the violence, the Los Angeles City Council passed a resolution urging the unemployed to stay away from the city that winter. The *California Social-Democrat* ran the resolution under the headline: "There's No Work for You in Los Angeles." It read in part: "That the city council of Los Angeles does hereby warn and advise all non-resident unemployed not to come to Los Angeles with the hope of securing employment."[49] The city also began a crackdown on street speaking. Police Chief Charles Sebastian told the *Times* that the police would "use every means within our power to keep these trouble makers within strict bounds."[50] After the tragic Christmas Day events, William C. Owen wrote that it "now appears that in speaking at the Plaza we had broken an ordinance, and that the police were technically within their rights." But he defended his and the crowd's presence by arguing that the gathering was "widely advertised in the daily papers" and that he spoke because he was asked to do so. He also called upon readers of *Regeneración* to view Adames's murder as part of a pattern of violence on the West Coast, from vigilantes in San Diego in 1912 during the IWW free-speech fight to the Wheatland violence in 1913.[51]

Huelga General reported that authorities released "twenty or thirty" of the people arrested without charges because of difficulty identifying them. The city prosecutor later dropped the charges on sixteen others.[52] Of the roughly "sixty or seventy" men arrested, juries convicted ten. *Regeneración* noted the sentences and argued that the harsh sentence given to Peter Castorena was "beyond doubt, because he attacked Capitalism, Authority and the Church, in open court."[53] *Re-*

generación also wrote that the local IWW fell victim to the Los Angeles "Cossacks" with increased repression after the riot.[54] In the aftermath of the riot, Dr. Paul Edwards argued in the *Los Angeles Times* that the "Mexican I.W.W.'s and others who started the Christmas riots should be punished here then shipped back to their own countries." He continued that the "Christmas riots are a hint of what is coming when we get in the thousands of those coming from Mediterranean ports when our canal is open."[55]

The interracial IWW local and anarchists organized the rally on Christmas Day. In the bitter falling-out between Juan Francisco Moncaleano and the PLM, the Mexican IWW members sided with Moncaleano, which drew them away from the PLM.[56] This tension continued to simmer for the next few years and eventually ended cooperation between the local IWW and the PLM. However, these disagreements did not yet manifest visibly in street-level participation in the radical movement. The broad and strong attendance at the Christmas Day rally and the speakers taking the podium that day are indicative of the resilience of the local movement.

On January 19, 1914, the PLM leaders imprisoned on McNeil Island in Washington—Ricardo Flores Magón, Enrique Flores Magón, Librado Rivera, and Anselmo Figueroa—gained their freedom. The one fortunate condition of their sentences was the prison's location near to the anarchist Home Colony, whose residents supported the men in prison. William C. Owen traveled up the coast on a speaking tour drumming up support for the PLM prisoners and the Mexican cause to welcome his comrades out of prison. The group traveled the short distance to Tacoma, where radicals held a mass meeting in their honor on this first evening of their release. The men spoke in Seattle, Portland, and San Francisco on their way to Los Angeles. The fallout from the PLM conflict with Juan Francisco Moncaleano, Romulo S. Carmona, and International Workers' Home and a now-dire financial situation awaited the PLM leaders upon their return to Los Angeles.[57]

Their first and greatest challenge was raising funds to continue publishing *Regeneración*. The solution for Ricardo and Enrique, their families, and a number of comrades was to form a commune on a farm in Edendale, now the Los Angeles neighborhoods of Echo Park, Los Feliz, and Silver Lake. On the farm they lived a semi-idyllic life on their land, where they gardened and tended to chickens. They also struggled financially to live and to get their paper out, which they published less regularly and mailed to fewer subscribers in these years. And these were indeed difficult years for the PLM. The cold, damp conditions in the Pacific Northwest exacerbated Anselmo Figueroa's tuberculosis, and he died in June 1915 in Arizona. Ricardo and Enrique also faced health crises in 1915. Certainly events in Mexico and now even the local movement in Los Angeles had moved away from the PLM after its leaders walked out of prison.[58]

Owen's trip up the coast to speak and to welcome the junta out of prison caused him to reflect about the state of the labor and radical movements on the West Coast as he saw it that winter. In San Francisco Lucy Parsons organized unemployed women and men. In Seattle the IWW engaged in an active campaign for unemployed workers. Despite this activity, Owen wrote that the "entire Pacific Coast is seething with revolt, but it lacks as yet, the unity which alone can produce results. At present the chief centers of revolt are isolated. Los Angeles is not in touch with San Francisco, and the latter has no direct means of communicating with Portland, Seattle or Tacoma. That is ridiculous and must be remedied. This situation is the more absurd because the West is notoriously the most generous supporter of numerous radical and revolutionary papers published in the East and Europe."[59]

Shortly after writing this article, William C. Owen rather than join the PLM group in Edendale, relocated to Hayward, California, to found the Bakunin Institute along with Mrs. E. Norwood and the Indian revolutionary Har Dayal. The trio announced through *Regeneración* that they had "free of rent, more than six acres of highly productive land and a most commodious house," which they were "using as a propaganda center." At the time, they were making preparations to install a printing press on the property. On May Day 1914 the first issue of *Land and Liberty* rolled off the freshly installed press, and they proudly wrote that they took the title of the publication from the PLM's motto. Dayal served as the head of business administration for the group; W. D. Guernsey served as the treasurer. This effort stood to remedy the situation that Owen observed during his travels.[60]

The group made its politics clear in the first issue, proclaiming "wherever men or women battle for freedom they will find in us a champion, whether that battle is in Mexico or the United States, in Europe or the Orient."[61] Police arrested Dayal in March, before the group released the first issue of the paper, after he delivered a speech at San Francisco's Bohemian Hall. While still editing the English-language page of *Regeneración* that spring, Owen wrote that Dayal's arrest came at the behest of the British government. Soon after, Antonio de P. Araujo wrote strongly against the deportation of Dayal on the front page of *Regeneración* in Spanish.[62]

In Los Angeles, the dust from the Christmas riot had barely settled in March 1914 as word spread about the bloody massacre in Ludlow, Colorado, in which at least seventy-five people lost their lives. The month before the Ludlow Massacre, American forces landed in Veracruz, Mexico. Rampant unemployment amplified the normal seasonal patterns along the West Coast that winter. In Sacramento, California, two thousand unemployed men and "a few women" who were camped in a lot organized as a ragtag unemployed army. Another twenty-five hundred unemployed people camped in Yolo County at the same time.[63]

In an attempt to solve the cyclical unemployment problem, the city of Los Angeles opened a Municipal Employment Bureau in December 1913. Within a year the bureau placed people in 28,860 positions, but the wages remained substandard at one or two dollars a day.[64] As those arrested during the Christmas riot awaited trial, the *Los Angeles Times* reported on a "tramping party of 200 I.W.W. and other nondescript hobos" traveling from Fresno to Los Angeles.[65] By March 1914 a group of roughly four hundred men formed an unemployed "army" in Los Angeles, camping on the bank of the Los Angeles River with an office under the North Main Street Bridge. A self-styled "general," Morris Rosenweig, who spoke at the Christmas Day meeting, claimed leadership of the group. The twenty-two-year-old Rosenweig, better known by the last name Rose, reportedly went by the name "Young Leach Cross" while a prizefighter in Savannah, Georgia.[66]

Rose claimed that 750 men lived in the camp at its peak. Many wore buttons that identified them as members of the "Army Unemployed—Los Angeles."[67] Los Angeles's chief of police, C. E. Sebastion, officially recognized the group on March 20 with the following declaration: "Notice to Officers and to Whom it May Concern: Permission is hereby granted to the 'Army of the Unemployed' to camp on the north side of the Santa Fe Bridge, near the East Side Police Station, beginning Saturday, March 21, 1914, and until such time as this permit may be revoked." With limited financial resources of their own, the men sustained themselves by collecting "donations at street meetings" to buy provisions and published a short-lived newspaper, *Unemployed Worker*.[68]

City officials soon grew tired of such a large group of people camping in the city, and conflict ensued when the unemployed army planned a demonstration on the plaza. The *Los Angeles Times* traded barbs with the liberal *Los Angeles Record* over what Rose said regarding meetings on the plaza after the Christmas riot. The *Record* quoted him as saying, "We will offer no resistance even if we are knocked down, jailed or have our blocks beaten off by police clubs. But we insist on decent treatment." Ever looking to stoke the city's residents against labor, the *Times* reported that Rose had a much more confrontational message: "We have a right to meet at the Plaza and nothing can be done to take that right from us. I do not make any threats, but if the police interfere there is very likely to be another affair like that of Christmas Day." On this point, the *Times* quoted Rose as saying, "We are going to make the whole United States take notice of the problem of the unemployed. We are just starting here. In a few days we move on. If it takes us five years we will get to Washington with a tremendous army, for in five years the problem will be greater than it is today. We do not belong to the I.W.W., although there may be a number of members of that organization in our ranks. We will move eastward soon and join Coxey at Cleveland and others along the way. We mean business."[69]

On the morning of the planned rally, police marched to the river and arrested twenty-seven men for camping illegally. The *Times* reported that the "men who were dragged out of the river bed and hurried to jail yesterday are mostly foreigners. They answered the questions of Judge Williams in the broken accents of the Mexican, the German, Italian, Scandinavian, the Russian and the Slav. With them were two or three boys, who were sent to the Juvenile Court." There could not have been a more typical sampling of the ranks of mobile labor in the West. Anticipating being arrested for "mendicancy," or begging, Rose stayed in the East Side Hotel the night before the rally in a failed attempt to insulate himself from this charge. When Rose and what was left of the army arrived on the plaza, police promptly arrested Rose as well. They justified this charge by his having collected contributions to feed those in the camp. Authorities promptly released some of these men, while others faced the especially hefty bail amount (for someone unemployed) of fifty dollars. They pleaded not guilty and requested jury trials.[70]

Morris Rose did not remain at the helm of the so-called army for long. The men in the army voted him out after the arrests and appointed "Mad" P. H. Buck and "Capt." Frank Kelly as their representatives. The city also briefly made a concession to the group, offering it a place to set up camp on "a vacant lot on Avenue 28." Frank Kelly, accompanied by two others, addressed the city council on March 30 with a proposal that the "army" would work if the city would pay them. The city planned on constructing two tunnels, at West First and West Second Streets, and Kelly proposed that the city put the men to work with unskilled laborers earning a minimum wage of three dollars a day. The group had collectively agreed on these standards at a meeting the previous Sunday in the camp.[71] The men rejected the offer to move to the new location, and the city rejected their offer to work. On March 31 the police moved on the camp again and arrested 110 people, even with around two hundred absent at the time of the raid. The raid occurred without the police chief's formally revoking the permit he personally had issued. When twenty-five officers surrounded the encampment, the men fell into line behind Kelly and marched to the city jail, singing "America" and "La Marseillaise."[72]

Attorney William Francis Ireland, Councilman Fred Wheeler, and others met with the judge in an unsuccessful attempt to arrange the men's release without trial; John Altman from the German Branch of the Socialist Party bought two dollars' worth of tobacco for the prisoners.[73] The situation came to a resolution of sorts after Rose, who continued to organize while being held as an "idle and dissolute person," eventually pleaded guilty to the charge and received a sentence of thirty days, which the judge waived upon his agreement to leave town. The chief of police attempted to secure employment for some of the men, but by that point most of them had jobs or had agreed to leave town. The *Los Angeles Times* reported that those who refused to work for two dollars a day did so on the advice of William Francis Ireland, a Christian socialist. He reportedly said that it was a "sin" to work for that low a wage because "the man who employed them would realize more than that for their labor." Rose's successor, Frank Kelly, alone received the relatively harsh sentence of thirty days, as he "had been the agitating member all along, and his activity had been so pernicious in its malicious intent."[74] The winters that followed brought the same pattern of seasonal unemployment and people flowing into the city, yet not this level of direct confrontation. The first break in this cycle came through "the prosperity born of World War I."[75]

El Rebelde, Rebellion, and Race

In the months and years following the Christmas riot and the forced decampment of the unemployed army in Los Angeles, simmering discontent, disparate organizing, and rebellion—potential as well as realized—fed the radical imagination of workers just as surely as citizens, capitalists, and the state. Los Angeles continued to be a base of radical labor and revolutionary organizing that reached out through regional networks. In the years before the United States entered World War I, Spanish-language organizers affiliated with IWW Local 602 in Los Angeles most actively spread through the region.

The IWW was not a traditional union in organizational structure or in its culture. IWW members did not seek to replicate the AFL, even in a more radical form. Even more important, however, is that the grassroots cultural forms of the IWW in the Southwest, often with quite a bit of anarchism mixed in, provided a diverse framework for action. The IWW as an organization recognized the importance of newspapers—printed in languages that people could read—in connecting members and sympathizers over distances in their diffuse network. The IWW published newspapers in no less than eighteen languages before 1940.[76] After the failure of *Huelga General* in 1914, Los Angeles IWW organizers kept hopes of having their own Spanish-language newspaper alive. They realized this goal in February 1915, when the first issue of *El Rebelde* rolled off the press. It filled the need for Spanish-language IWW newspaper rooted in the Southwest in light of the continued regional IWW activism and the decline of the PLM. *El Rebelde* endured until federal suppression of the IWW in 1917.

The Propaganda League of Mexicans in Los Angeles led the publication effort, and it retained local autonomy over *El Rebelde*. In the words of one of its editors and chief scribes, Aurelio Vincente Azuara, it was "an I. W. W. paper, without being under the control of the G. E. B." (the General Executive Board).[77] José Corona resumed the administrative duties that he fulfilled for *Huelga General*, and the staff of the paper cycled through a small group of dedicated members.[78] By the fifth issue, Armando M. Ojeda, one of the men charged in the aftermath of the Christmas riot, assumed its editorship. Another of the men charged in the Christmas riot and formerly active in the PLM, Pedro Coria, frequently contributed to and edited the paper for a short time as well. Ojeda and Fernando Velarde previously wrote for *La Unión Industrial*, the first Spanish-language IWW paper published in Phoenix. The publishing committee discussed moving the *El Rebelde* from Los Angeles to Phoenix. Those involved in publishing the paper and in IWW Local 602, most notably Fernando Velarde, maintained deep organizing ties in Arizona, but Aurelio Vincente Azuara successfully lobbied the group to keep it based in Los Angeles.[79]

El Rebelde's second issue made clear its editors particularly radical political outlooks, even for an IWW-affiliated paper, and its position in the fallout between the local IWW and the PLM. The paper ran a rousing article signed by *"un anarquista"* calling on the workers of Los Angeles to remember the Christmas riot in December 1913 and the murder of Rafaél Adames.[80] There was no disagreement over remembering the local martyr, but "un anarquista" was most likely a nom du plume of Juan Francisco Moncaleano, who did not join the IWW but supported the local organization and continued as comrade with the paper's publishers after the bitter accusations leveled by the PLM. Understandably, *El Rebelde*'s publishers would have preferred to keep his name off the page.

In 1915 members of IWW Local 602 ascended into the position of the leading Spanish-language organizers in Los Angeles and the region, gaining influence as the PLM's reach decreased. Previously, before and during the Baja raids and even in the few years after, IWW and PLM organizing and membership overlapped and intertwined. Gradually, the distance between the organizations increased, starting with the grumblings over the lack of support for imprisoned IWW members active in the Baja campaign and helped along by the bitter fallout that began with the junta's imprisonment in Washington. Now, though, the distance also increased because the two organizations maintained different foci, and the pages of *El Rebelde* gave voice to a politics distinct from those expressed in *Regeneración*.

El Rebelde's editorial group separated themselves from the PLM most drastically in their view toward the ongoing revolution in Mexico. In general the pages of *El Rebelde* reflected a strong interest in radical labor organizing in Mexico, in places like Aguascalientes and Guadalajara, but not in political power struggles. In two brief articles the newspaper addressed the questions: "Why isn't '*El Rebelde*' focused on the Mexican Revolution?" and "Do the IWW support the Mexican Revolution?" The newspaper's editors laid out their positions, writing that they viewed the revolution over the previous few years as a capitalist development. They reiterated the anticapitalism of the IWW and stated that while the IWW was not giving monetary support to the revolution, they did support labor organizing in Mexico with the goal of emancipating of all workers. The organizers associated with *El Rebelde* avoided the politically fraught strategy of aligning with one of the various political factions active in the Mexican Revolution in favor of grassroots syndicalist organizing in Mexico through the pages of the newspaper and direct workplace organizing.[81]

As the legal assault on what was left of the PLM constricted the group's ability to operate, IWW members continued to take to the field, organizing Mexican workers. Divergent trajectories, supplemented by interpersonal conflicts, provided the context for the reshuffling of the earlier battle between the PLM and the IWW over the International Workers' Home. In the spring and into the early summer of 1915 a handful of articles in *El Rebelde* and *Regeneración* publicly hashed out their differences. In 1915 *Regeneración*'s subscription list had just fewer than four thousand names, down from a high of twenty thousand. *El Rebelde*'s list probably never reached more than two thousand.[82]

The year 1915 was difficult for the PLM. The group struggled to get out *Regeneración*, managing one spring issue and fourteen total that year, markedly down from the regular weekly publication schedule. That solitary spring issue carried a story that lashed out at Juan Francisco Moncaleano, Armando Ojeda, and Fernando Velarde, one similar to the *Los Angeles Times* article after the Christmas riot that referred to Ojeda as having "the appearance of a sort of cross between a moving-picture hero and a habitue of the Latin quarter."[83] Ricardo Flores Magón described Ojeda as "bourgeois with propertied roots, the same as Velarde" and repeated the charges against Moncaleano about his conduct with young girls, ultimately advising his readers not to support IWW organizing in Los Angeles.[84] He pulled no punches in this vicious personal attack; the men were nothing short of "idiots" to Ricardo.[85] *El Rebelde*'s editors responded to this article in one column on its last page, titled "The Excommunication of a Father." They refuted the charges, defending themselves through their own organizing efforts, and notably refrained from making similar personal attacks against Ricardo.[86] It is clear from this point that reconciliation would be difficult, but each group focused the majority of its effort on propagandizing, organizing, and surviving.

Labor organizing and rebellion in the borderlands continued in close connection as they had in years past, especially in Mexican radical networks. A failed plot in Arizona in August 1915 deserves particular attention. The Rangel-Cline affair in 1913 along with outrage at racist laws, lynchings, and the U.S. invasion of Veracruz joined with growing feelings of nationalism by many Mexicans in the Southwest. To Anglos this fed strong feelings of racial animosity and drove rumors of Mexican uprisings, both real and imagined. In August 1914 Teodoro Gaitán, who had co-edited *Regeneración* for a period, traveled to Arizona for work, where authorities arrested him along with fifteen others amid rumors that Mexicans planned on seizing Phoenix and Tempe to use as bases for the Mexican Revolution. Gaitán was soon released, charging that the plot was the product of an agent of the Mexican consulate.[87]

A Culture of Affinity

In winter 1915 word circulated in South Texas about the "plan of San Diego," a plot that envisioned gathering forces against Anglo repression and advocated for African Americans and Native Americans to join the fight. As Basilio Ramos crossed into the United States, officials discovered the plan in a document he carried, which set the date for the start of the rebellion on February 20. No action materialized, however; but the revolutionary plan underwent a significant revision on that day. The new document aimed at nothing short of social revolution for people of all races in the United States. It sought to abolish racism and create modern schools; a multiracial group that included Mexican, German, Italian, and Japanese supporters signed their names to it. For the spring, though, little visibly happened to advance the cause articulated in the document. In July a series of raids on Anglo ranches by Mexicans and a simmering "hidden Tejano civil war" kept the idea of the plan in the public consciousness. A vicious response followed through the fall that claimed the lives of about one thousand Tejanos, Mexican residents of Texas. The racial tensions in Texas spread throughout the borderlands.[88]

In Arizona in 1915, continued unionization attempts in copper mines in Miami, Globe, and Ray stoked Anglo fear and unease alongside rumors of rebellion. The Western Federation of Miners was the largest union in the state's mines with other, more radical ideologies challenging from the margins as IWW and PLM organizers seamlessly flowed through the state, spreading their messages among workers. Fernando Palomarez, former PLM confidant Lázaro Gutiérrez de Lara (who fell out with the group over the Baja raids), and Fernando Velarde all maintained connections to the state's Mexican workers. In June, one hundred Mexican men in Ray held a meeting where they decided to "help Mexico fight the United States" in the event of war between the two countries, which they viewed as imminent. The meeting included "Mexican revolutionaries," but in the end they settled on striking their employer, the Ray Consolidated Copper Company.[89]

In August 1915 a stillborn attempt at revolution arose out of local labor unrest and the long radical tradition of the PLM and IWW that closely resembled the goals of the revised plan of San Diego. Thomas Bell owned a farm at the time near the Gila River outside of Phoenix, where he lived with his family before relocating to Los Angeles in the 1920s. He maintained strong personal connections to leading anarchists around the world, and his account of events in Phoenix illuminates a series of circumstances noted yet not fully understood by contemporaries and historians.[90]

Bell remembered three organizers who "much influenced" Mexican radicals in Phoenix in 1915. Even though he wrote about the events in 1932, Bell chose to keep their names out of print because of the illegal nature of the activities. He described the first as "a shoemaker, and Anarchist, reading everything Anarchist he could put his hands on." He identified the second only as a Yaqui Indian. Bell

179

often hired Yaquis as extra hands to work on his farm, and he described his admiration for the skills and revolutionary zeal of the men: "These Yaquis we found were really farmers like ourselves: they seldom spoke either English or Spanish and we could not talk to them, but they did not need to be talked to: working alongside of us they understood what was to be done and they would take care of our teams just as well as we could." He described Yaqui as not wanting steady employment: "They worked hard and saved their money, but it was not to buy fine shoes and swell hats like so many of the Mexican workers, in reality, the Yaqui came over the border, worked and saved—till he could buy himself a rifle and ammunition: then he was off home again to defend his village in the hills." The last of these three men was from San Salvador. Bell described him as "a highly educated man, who liked to talk literature with me in French . . . [but] he bitterly complained to me about the fashion in which his fellow Spanish-Americans were treated in the United States."[91]

The participants hatched a conspiracy to cut telegraph lines and set fire to all of the railroad bridges leading into Arizona. Afterward a group would raid the Phoenix arsenal to seize arms. This task would be eased with the Arizona National Guard stationed on the border in Texas. With the Mexican population armed, they would then rebel against the local Anglo population, with Pima Indians joining them. The next stage of the plan was to warn all of the Anglos in the Salt River Valley that they would blow up the Roosevelt Dam if "the rebels were pushed too hard." Bell remembered that "Arizona was to be declared part of Mexico again, and it was hoped that the affair might spread to the Mexican population in New Mexico and Texas, and perhaps even to Louisiana, Mississippi, Alabama, and the other states in which the negroes were the majority." The Phoenix radicals devised their plan and then contacted Librado Rivera, now a widower living with his two children at the Edendale PLM commune, asking him to travel to Phoenix. Rivera agreed, but once fully briefed on the plot's details, he "pointed out to them that their scheme was not Anarchist but Nationalist, and that it would inevitably break the relationship between them and the American workers." On this rationale he refused to participate. For his part, Bell doubted the effectiveness of the plan because he believed that local Anglo farmers and ranchers were "accustomed to horses and arms."[92]

This did not put an end to the plot. Librado Rivera managed to persuade the Phoenix radicals to change their plans. They now planned to go to Mexico, join "any of the partisan bands operating in Mexico," and then leave with their guns for Coahuila or Tamaulipas. Rivera wanted to siphon the ample arms in circulation in the Mexican Revolution to benefit what remained of the PLM's cause. Once enough comrades gathered with arms, they would first cross back into Texas to free Rangel and Cline before joining the revolution directly.[93]

Authorities discovered the plot before it could be put into action. One of the Phoenix radicals wrote to a Pima Indian he trusted in Sacaton, Arizona, about changes in the plan to reflect Rivera's influence, but the man could not read. Thinking that the letter he received had "something to do with the payments for a plow he had bought," he gave it to an Indian agent to read for him; the agent then alerted authorities. The others involved in the plan managed to escape, but Librado Rivera was arrested. When they arrested Rivera, the authorities did not know the full extent of the planned uprising. Bell recalled that he sat in jail for about two months before being acquitted of the charges and released, but his arrest never made the local newspaper. Given Rivera's prominence the lack of press coverage is most likely explained by his concealing his true identity from authorities in Arizona. Revolutionary zeal aside, Rivera's idea of turning the plot toward influencing the Mexican Revolution again highlights the different foci of the PLM and the IWW. The PLM continued its focus on events in Mexico and armed revolution, while the IWW worked to organize Mexican workers into unions.[94]

The local press did catch wind of part of the plan. The *Arizona Republican* buried the story "Warlike Rumor Chased Down" on August 16, which included the rumor that Mexicans planned on dynamiting the Roosevelt Dam. A deputy sheriff from Glendale came to Phoenix to spread the word of the plot. Anastacia Ortega, who lived and worked with her husband on an Anglo-owned ranch, had supposedly received a letter from her father in Mexico that "two Mexicans were about to leave for Arizona to blow up the Roosevelt dam." After the sheriff interviewed Ortega, the plot was laughed off, and the paper reported "the rumor turned to nothing [but] a spasm of uneasiness in the town of Glendale."[95] A few weeks later the paper again reported on a rumor of rebellion from Glendale, the "center of all imaginary Mexican disturbances." This time "600 Mexicans" were "nightly and, sometimes, daily" drilling by the Agua Fria River "about to participate in what has come to be known as the 'San Diego plan.'" A sheriff thoroughly investigated the rumor and even made a nighttime trip to the river in case any men gathered, but again, the sheriff and the paper dismissed the rumor.[96]

In September, the *Arizona Republican* once more wrote about a planned uprising. A "band of armed Mexicans" rumored to be congregating from "Miami, Ray, Superior and Mesa, would total three hundred men."[97] The rumor indicated that the group would descend on the prison in Florence to break out eleven imprisoned Mexicans, "arrested at Ray ten days ago for 'revolutionary activities,'" in addition to five other Mexicans awaiting execution. Again, the paper found no evidence to support the rumors: "the entire story is discredited here."[98]

Officials in Arizona never learned the full details of the plot; otherwise, further arrests and criminal prosecutions most certainly would have followed. Even with an actual plot in the works, local reaction and the swirling rumors were based

CHAPTER 7

more on fear and the larger pattern of unrest in the region than any concrete knowledge of the planned uprising. The degree to which the *Arizona Republican* reported on the rumors and then dismissed them is noteworthy in this regard. None of the radical papers referenced these events until Tom Bell wrote about it in a eulogy for Librado Rivera in the *Road to Freedom* in 1932.

Back in Los Angeles, Juan Francisco Moncaleano passed away suddenly after surgery in December 1915.[99] His death did not put the tension between the IWW and the PLM to rest. The next salvo in this unpleasantness came with the arrests of Ricardo and Enrique Flores Magón in February 1916 on federal charges. Prosecutors accused the men of distributing obscene material through the mail for two articles published in *Regeneración* about Carranza and violence in Texas. When a broad group of PLM supporters leaped into action to provide for the legal defense of the PLM leaders, Los Angeles's IWW Local 602 unanimously passed a resolution declaring that they were not going to support the imprisoned men. An article in *El Rebelde* signed by two Anglo members of the IWW local, Ben Wittling and William Baker, justified the local's stance by arguing that the PLM obstructed local IWW organizing and criticized sabotage—held dear to many Wobblies—as a method of struggle, and that the PLM leaders believed that the only way to achieve freedom was by marching on Mexico. The article went so far as refer to *Regeneración* as "*Degeneracion*," referencing degenerate, a slur for homosexuals.[100] Shortly after making this declaration, the IWW local refused to participate in a large protest on the plaza supporting the PLM men.[101]

Out of prison on bail, the core PLM group resumed printing *Regeneración* at Edendale. Still in very difficult financial straits, they were nonetheless more successful with their paper in 1916 than in 1915. The group used *Regeneración* to lay out its case for support and criticized the IWW local for their lack of solidarity. Following a front-page article came two-and-half columns of newsprint listing local groups and individuals in Los Angeles supporting the PLM.[102] *El Rebelde* then struck a slightly conciliatory tone by responding that "I.W.W. members are not personal enemies of the Magón brothers," but still justified their differences and choice to not support the PLM leaders.[103] Although this dispute leached limited movement resources, it mostly seems to have stayed on the page. Again, the PLM continued its effort to survive, and IWW organizers traveled and organized.

■ ■ ■

Radicals in Los Angeles and out through their networks enjoyed their greatest freedom to organize in the years before World War I. This was a period of diverse action through the radical networks connecting through Los Angeles, and organizing spanned a range tactics and locations. The willingness of people to join together and formulate the terms of their struggle according to local conditions is the uniting strand throughout this period—not a single organization or tactic. Organizing in Wheatland, the unemployed army in Los Angeles, and insurrection in Texas and Arizona did not come from the top of bureaucracies. The energy and solidarities driving these events arose out of the difficult working and political conditions in the region. Multiracial coalitions arose in racially diverse spaces seething with discontent and seeping with the ideals of the Industrial Workers of the World and the PLM. People then drew from their own experiences and ideals to channel their actions with the people in their immediate surroundings, supplemented by connections through radical networks. The trend continued for the most racially diverse organizing to concentrate in temporary coalitions without strong hierarchies.

CHAPTER 8

THE CONTOURS OF REPRESSION

World War I erupted in Europe over the summer of 1914, and the United States joined the conflagration almost three years later, declaring war in April 1917. The legal framework for organized and sustained federal repression of radicals on a national scale came after American entry, when Congress passed the Espionage Act in June 1917 and the Sedition Act in 1918 among changes to immigration law.[1] The Espionage Act criminalized the stealing of government secrets, and its broad reach extended to activities that could be construed as an "attempt to cause insubordination, disloyalty, mutiny, refusal of duty, in the military or naval forces of the United States" or that "obstruct the recruiting or enlistment service of the United States."[2] The Sedition Act extended the Espionage Act to include printing or publishing of material deemed to contain "disloyal, profane, scurrilous, or abusive language about the form of government of the United States" or speech that urged a "curtailment of production." The Sedition Act also granted postal inspectors the power to bar material from the mail that they considered falling afoul of the law.[3] This new legal framework criminalized much of the radical press and changed the character of state intervention in leftist activities. To many in power, the Russian Revolution then increased the sense of the urgency behind enforcing these laws.

World War I–era laws expanded and refined the federal repressive apparatus developed over previous decades. Before Congress passed the Espionage and Sedition Acts, radicals in Los Angeles and across the country faced pressure from a mix of local, state, and federal agencies in addition to private detective firms and private citizens; this continued, but the changes in federal law ushered in a stronger role for the federal government in monitoring and policing radicals for an expanded range of offenses. After Armistice in November 1918, California's legislature passed the California Criminal Syndicalism Act in April 1919, aimed specifically at curtailing IWW organizing in the state. This legislation broadened enforcement at the state level.

Radical organizing and its policing contained local, national, and transnational components. These intra- and interstate layers and human mobility provided outlets for evasion and resistance. During the early twentieth century Los Angeles proved to be a place of refuge and repression alike for a wide range of radicals. When the state unleashed the weight of its repressive apparatus during the World War I era, it significantly affected leftist organizing and the free exchange of ideas in the United States, but the results were nonetheless uneven and incomplete. The range of activities coupled with the breadth of the movement's support and participation helped a base survive government repression so that it could begin to rebuild. The sum of this history is a trajectory in which repression shifted between nation-states and between local, state, and federal agencies within the United States while radicals relied on deep local, national, and transnational solidarities to weather waves of repression and attempt to regenerate as they receded. Radicals in Los Angeles drew on their solidarities to navigate state repression during World War I and immediately afterward. Indeed, some of the most severe state responses to radical activities in California and throughout the western United States came after the war ended as the direct federal role in repression receded. In these years most formal leftist organizing focused on legal and prison support for comrades. Repression and the strain of years of struggle also caused internal divisions within the radical movement during this difficult time.

The End of the Partido Liberal Mexicano

Revolutionary organizing across the U.S.-Mexico border and U.S.-Canada border—as well as activities such as smuggling and undocumented immigration—attracted the attention of federal law enforcement well before the United States entered World War I. The legal entanglements of the PLM began before the World War I legal paradigm and provide context for increased federal repression of radicals during the war. Owing to the cross-border nature of their organizing and American interests in Mexico, the PLM leadership faced the sustained attention of the federal government beginning soon after they entered the United States in 1904. The PLM also confronted government at the local and state levels as well as private detective agencies employed by the Mexican government. Legal problems notwithstanding, the United States was a safer, more open jurisdiction in which to organize than Mexico. The U.S. federal government prosecuted PLM leaders in 1909 when a jury in Tombstone, Arizona, found Ricardo Flores Magón, Antonio Villarreal, and Librado Rivera guilty of neutrality violations, a federal crime. After the Baja raids a jury in Los Angeles again convicted Ricardo Flores Magón, Enrique Flores Magón, Librado Rivera, and Anselmo Figueroa of violating neutrality laws in 1912.[4]

The group's next encounter with the federal government came as American entry into the war grew nearer in 1916, when Ricardo Flores Magón, Enrique Flores Magón, and William C. Owen faced charges of sending obscene material through the mail. Government prosecutors charged the men under federal law excluding from mailed materials anything "obscene, lewd, or lascivious" or that incited "arson, murder, or assassination."[5] Before the Sedition Act the federal government often pursued obscenity cases to suppress the anarchist press and other material such as birth-control information. The Post Office also revoked or denied second-class mailing privileges for periodicals to limit the circulation of unpopular ideas. Federal pressure in 1916 extended to other anarchist publications such as Alexander Berkman's San Francisco–based *The Blast*, which had published birth-control information. Postal inspectors excluded it from the mail for the "indecent" articles and stripped the paper's second-class mailing permit because of irregularities in its publishing schedule—caused by the postal service itself.[6]

After the indictments of *Regeneración*'s editorial staff came down in 1916, authorities raided the PLM's Edendale colony on February 18 and arrested the Flores Magón brothers. That same day, María Brouse telegrammed Owen, who was staying at the anarchist Home Colony in Washington State, to inform him of the arrests. Owen initially wanted to face the charges along with his comrades, but Enrique wrote that "we begged him not to do so and although unwillingly, he was kind and honored our wish. By special reasons, we think best for the propaganda to aboid [*sic*] Owen's sacrifice."[7]

While at Home Colony, the Irish-born Dr. John Creaghe, long active in the Argentine anarchist movement and who had maintained offices in the International Worker's Home in Los Angeles, along with the Frenchman Gaston Lance and Lance's wife, provided Owen with assistance and shelter. The group stayed in the Lance residence, which provided excellent cover; the Bureau of Investigation agents recorded, "It is difficult of approach [the residence] without the knowledge in advance of it's [*sic*] occupants." Owen's comrades at Home Colony provided him much-needed support: "Agent at first started to keep them under surveillance, but discovered that there were two other men watching their movements. Agent immediately dropped the matter and went to the hotel, where at 7:25 P.M. Agent received a communication from informant and met the informant at the parlor of the Olympus Hotel for a period of three or four minutes." Even with the help

William Charles Owen. (University of Michigan Library Digital Collections)

of the informant, Bureau of Investigation agents failed to arrest Owen when they made an attempt at the residence. He had escaped by rowboat to Tacoma, where he stayed with the Italian anarchist Eugene Travaglio and his family.[8]

From Tacoma, Owen traveled north to Vancouver, British Columbia, with the help of a man whom the Bureau of Investigation could identify only as "Raheim."[9] The man assisting Owen was South Asian revolutionary Hussein Rahim, a connection that Owen surely gained working with Har Dayal on their newspaper *Land and Liberty*. Rahim had organized a "revolutionary network" in British Columbia and often traversed the border building regional support.[10] Soon after, Owen returned to his native England, where he lived and wrote freely until his death in 1929.

After Owen successfully crossed national borders to his advantage, Enrique and Ricardo Flores Magón faced the obscenity charges in Los Angeles. A jury convicted the pair in June 1916, but a judge released them on bond after a month in jail, pending appeal. In this latest legal struggle of the PLM, supporters, including the leading voices of anarchism and free thought in the United States, organized a fundraising drive, spoke on behalf of the men, and used their publications to rally supporters. Backing for the Flores Magón brothers in Los Angeles consolidated around the Workers International Defense League which proclaimed in 1916 to be "in the service of those captured by the enemy." An appeal printed by the league read, "In Los Angeles the workers and the radicals of all groups and nine different nationalities have organized The Workers Defense League. It is holding mass meetings, sending out protests."[11] As the federal government increased pressure on leftist organizations in 1916, comrades and sympathizers responded by forming organizations for legal representation and prison support. Radicals continued to draw on this infrastructure during the mass arrests that began after American entry in the war.

The arrests in 1916 marked another point on a journey in which the PLM influence decreased in Mexico and the United States but the stature of its leadership grew in international anarchist circles. Throughout the years of increasingly serious legal trouble for the PLM leadership—and Ricardo's declining health—the tight-knit group around them continued to organize, but its direct organizational reach failed to extend much beyond a dwindling number of comrades in Los Angeles. However, the national and transnational support for Ricardo and Enrique Flores Magón increased through their legal struggles, and Ricardo, especially, rose in stature, cementing his position as a significant figure in the global anarchist movement. This occurred as the group's actual organizing impact almost entirely evaporated as if in counterweighted balance.

In 1917 some longtime associates remained active and the PLM continued to attract some new blood in Los Angeles. Ricardo Flores Magón's young son-in-law, Raul Palma, brought fresh enthusiasm as a speaker to the streets of Los Angeles. Police arrested the twenty-year-old for speaking along with Odilón Luna on the plaza in May 1917. While the two spoke in Spanish to "a group of Mexicans," officer Louis Rico arrested each one for being "an idle and dissolute person." After their arrests, authorities amended the local charge to include the federal crime of "being an anarchist, and advocating or teaching anarchy and advocating publicly in the city of Los Angeles, the assassination of public officials, in violation of the Immigration Act of February, 1917." Affidavits by Los Angeles police officers L. J. Lacher, Louis A. Rico, and George A. Cummings substantiated these charges, although Cummings later admitted to the court that he could not speak Spanish.[12]

The federal government used the change in immigration law in an attempt to deport the men for being anarchists—for their ideology rather than their alleged actions or words uttered while speaking on the street. This law extended the 1903 Anarchist Exclusion Act, which prohibited anarchists from entering the United States or naturalizing. Relying on individuals to self-proclaim their anarchism limited the effectiveness of the 1903 law, but its retooling in 1917 and again in 1918 expanded federal power to allow for naturalized citizens who became anarchists after they naturalized to be stripped of their citizenship and deported.[13]

The final legal struggle in the United States for the PLM leadership came in 1918 when Ricardo Flores Magón and Librado Rivera faced charges of violating the Espionage Act, the Trading with the Enemy Act, and Section 211 of the Federal Penal Code with the 1916 charges still under appeal. After a short trial, a jury convicted both men of all charges and sentenced them to twenty and fifteen years, respectively, along with substantial fines.[14] They initially served their time in McNeil Island Penitentiary, but Ricardo received a transfer to Leavenworth Penitentiary in Kansas due to his failing health. Rivera was transferred there shortly after. Enrique Flores Magón served the sentence for mailing obscene materials in Leavenworth as well; he was there when the government began deportation proceedings against him.[15]

These four trials marked the major legal entanglements of the PLM's leaders with the federal government of the United States. The years of intermittent imprisonment and the stress of organizing combined with this new wave of repression to effectively dissolve the PLM. Few, if any, other radical groups based in the United States faced this number of federal prosecutions over such an extended period. The World War I era brought about refinements to existing law and new laws that expanded government power over U.S. residents, but the tools for repression came out of a longer history of policing cross-border radicals that began well before American entry into World War I.

Blanca Moncaleano took her own path to avoid repression after the death of her husband, Juan Francisco. The fate of the PLM leaders was clear to all, especially to Blanca, given her years of activity in the anarchist movement. Now a single mother, Blanca and her children remained in Los Angeles, changed their last name to Lawson, stayed out of sight as best they could, and successfully avoided the dragnet that swept up so many of their comrades.[16]

CHAPTER 8

Navigating Repression: The IWW

State-sanctioned officers of the law and private citizens variously acting within the law and extrajudicially took their toll on the IWW over the years. The IWW faced this combination of forces at their free-speech fights in the West and again in Wheatland, California, in 1913. The state of Utah, of course, executed Joe Hill for murder on doubtful evidence in 1914. As American entry into World War I neared in 1916, the IWW waged an active organizing campaign in the iron mines through Minnesota's Mesabi Range, where a police-supported mob threatened the Italian anarchist Carlo Tresca with lynching before he was later arrested with several IWW organizers in June. A similar mix of lawlessness and law enforcement went awry with deadly consequence in Everett, Washington, a few months later on November 5, 1916, when police confronted IWW members on a ferry, dockside. After the ensuing violence five IWW members and two deputies lay dead. This recurrent theme reached its zenith with the Bisbee Deportation in Arizona in July 1917 after the United States had entered the war and also on August 1, 1917, when a vigilante mob lynched Frank Little, one the West's most active and visible IWW members, in Butte, Montana. Then came the nationwide raids of IWW offices on September 5, during which the Justice Department gathered material to indict 166 members for conspiracy to violate the Espionage Act.[17]

Los Angeles–based IWW members organized in two primary geographical and industrial areas during the run-up to American entry into the war. The IWW created a new industrial union for agricultural workers, the Agriculture Workers' Organization (AWO), amid some disarray and factionalism within the IWW, and after debate over the inclusion of tenant farmers and sharecroppers. The founding meeting took place in Kansas City in 1915 and included representatives from Fresno and San Francisco, but not Los Angeles. The national meeting spawned a California organizing meeting in Sacramento in December 1915 and, in turn, local organizational meetings over the next month or so in Los Angeles, San Bernardino, Redlands, and Santa Ana.[18]

Organizing farmworkers in California continued to be as difficult a task as it was for the AFL during the United Laborers campaign, but the IWW faced different obstacles than the craft union. AWO organizing in California encountered state repression the AFL did not face during its campaign. For instance, in Brawley local police rounded up several local IWW members after a murder in town. Prosecutors did not charge any of the men with the crime, but a jury convicted them of unrelated other charges, and they served sixty-day sentences of hard labor. This prevented the men from organizing during the local melon harvest. Also of importance, AWO organizers faced self-imposed hurdles such as concern over

190

IWW centralization in Chicago and debates over sabotage, which limited their regional effectiveness in 1916.[19]

AWO organizing in California included a group of IWW members and outside sympathizers dedicated to gaining pardon for Ford and Suhr convicted after the Wheatland violence. The direct action wanted to push for pardon through a boycott of California agriculture and, at least, the threat of sabotage in the form of crop destruction. Popular newspapers in the state accused IWW members of setting grassfires in summer 1915; accusations that federal prosecutors used to build their case against the IWW in a few years when mass repression of the organization came by capitalizing on the union's language of sabotage and direct action. In Southern California, a few job actions arose out of the AWO campaign in April 1917. In the inland citrus-belt city of Redlands, Native American, Mexican, Japanese, and white orange pickers collectively walked out. Also, in April, Mexican and South Asian field hands successfully struck to increase their hourly wages from twenty cents to twenty-five cents in Riverside and Claremont.[20]

Probably more important to the local movement than AWO organizing, Los Angeles–based IWW members continued to travel through Arizona mines, spreading the influence of the industrial union in Spanish between 1915 and 1917. Aurelio Vincente Azuara, Pedro Coria, Tomás Martínez, and Fernando Velarde were the most active IWW organizers in Arizona with strong connections to Los Angeles. In September 1916 authorities arrested Azuara and Benigno Medina after a street meeting in Morenci. Azuara had not planned to hold mass rallies or public meetings on this trip; he later remembered, "I was going there to organize them, not to hold any meetings, but it seems to me that they were very anxious to hear the industrial union be explained by a member of the Industrial Workers of the World."[21] Local IWW members in Morenci had printed flyers announcing a rally before Azuara arrived. The vice president of the Arizona Federation of Labor, John Donnelly, was also in Morenci, along with E. J. Moreno, an organizer for the Western Federation of Miners (WFM). The two craft-union men forced Azuara to turn the rally into a debate between them. Azuara accepted their demand and the debate proceeded in front of about five hundred people gathered in the town's plaza. Eventually, Donnelly walked away and called the police on the telephone. A lone officer arrived and waded into the crowd in an attempt to arrest Azuara and Medina. The deputy managed to briefly capture Medina, but the crowd surrounded the pair, unarrested Medina, and prevented the men from being taken into custody. Police nevertheless arrested Azuara and Medina a few days later.[22] After Pedro Coria and John Miller of Local 602 in Los Angeles led a fundraising drive and collected five thousand dollars for their bond, the men gained their freedom in Arizona. Coria had taken over as interim editor of *El Rebelde* in Azuara's absence.[23]

Aurelio Vincente Azuara. (National Archives at Kansas City, Records of the Bureau of Prisons)

IWW members faced occasional arrest in Los Angeles for their local organizing, but their on-the-ground efforts and the pages of *El Rebelde* Local 602 primarily focused on the unfolding mining "revolution" in Arizona in 1916 and 1917.[24] Pedro Coria also extended the Los Angeles local's reach to Tampico, Mexico, in this period. After traveling through Arizona mines organizing, Coria headed for Tampico at the end of 1916 to assist in chartering IWW-affiliated Marine Transport Workers (MTW) Local 100 in January 1917.[25] He returned to the United States before heading to Northern California's Shasta County, where he organized among striking miners in Kennett in September 1917.[26]

This ever-active and dedicated group of IWW members in Los Angeles pushed their organizing priorities up to the national level of the IWW. The Los Angeles local and Aurelio Vincente Azuara drove the organization to invest more resources in organizing Spanish-speaking workers in the United States and abroad. In the summer of 1917 during the Tampico general strike, workers in Tampico contacted Azuara asking if he could send a U.S. IWW delegation to an IWW convention in their city. Around the same time, Azuara wrote to Bill Haywood, informing him that he wanted to call a convention of "all the Latin workers in Central and South America."[27] It is not clear if the IWW sent delegates to the meeting. During the tumultuous summer of 1917 Pedro Coria, Tomás Martínez, and B. Negreira had all taken leadership positions in the Globe-Miami struggle in Arizona.[28] It is possible that Coria made a brief return trip to Tampico. The outlook of *El Rebelde* also reflected the drive to expand the IWW south, and mention of Tampico increased through 1917.[29]

In 1916 and into the spring of 1917 a fantastic revolutionary optimism along with a sense of the increasing consequences of state-sanctioned policing and violence directed at the IWW is apparent in the pages of *El Rebelde*. The weight of repression mounted still further in the summer of 1917. With ongoing agitation in Clifton-Morenci-Metcalf, workers in Jerome, Bisbee, and Trona went out on strike. In Jerome the familiar mix of police and vigilantes corralled more than sixty workers and shipped them to Needles, California.[30] Shortly afterward, in Bisbee, events culminated with the Bisbee deportation in July when a deputized posse forced more than one thousand people of thirty-four nationalities into railcars and dropped them in the New Mexican desert.[31] These incidents, in addition to the lynching of Frank Little in August, deeply shook radicals in Los Angeles, but there is little hint that local IWW members foresaw the changes in policy toward their union being made at the highest levels of the federal government.

The federal raids on the IWW on September 5 resulted from an evolving approach toward policing the IWW over the previous decade that shifted rapidly in 1917. After Congress overrode a presidential veto to pass the Immigration Act of 1917 in February, Woodrow Wilson, on the day the United States declared war on Germany, issued an executive order aimed at curtailing antiwar activities of German immigrants. Justice Department officials initially used these powers with discretion against the IWW, making just a few arrests of specifically targeted individuals. Beginning in the spring, federal troops, the National Guard, and federalized National Guard troops moved through the West to put down strike activity in the name of protecting wartime production. Federal troops arrived in Arizona and Montana in July 1917. The War Department granted local commanders sweeping powers to achieve these goals through internal policy decisions and legal interpretations, not new laws.[32]

The growth of the Military Intelligence Division (MID), tasked with protecting wartime production, resulted from these internal decisions. The MID surveilled the IWW and other perceived threats in parallel with the Bureau of Investigation. The MID expanded its number of agents and informants during the war, collecting voluminous information about people in and near Los Angeles. The federal government attempted to connect German money to IWW organizing nationally, a connection they failed to document. Shortly after a series of cabinet meetings in the wake of the Bisbee deportation, Woodrow Wilson signed off on a "total assault" of the IWW, in the words of historian Eric Chester.[33] This plan united western states and the federal government against the IWW, and the Espionage Act would be the legal tool in a coordinated assault.

The September 8, 1917, issue of *El Rebelde* reported that Post Office had rejected their second-class mailing permit. The issue also included a few lines squeezed onto the bottom of the front page informing readers that their offices had been "assaulted" on September 5. The group published one more issue, on September 22, with dueling headlines on the Justice Department raids of IWW offices nationwide and the continuing struggle of mine workers in Arizona.[34] Then the paper fell silent. A grand jury in Chicago indicted 166 IWW members on September 28 for conspiracy to obstruct the draft under the Espionage Act, among other lesser charges. Bill Haywood and others at the national level of the IWW decided to take the fight to the courtroom. They hired lawyers and urged those indicted to turn themselves in.[35]

On the morning the indictments came down and police moved in, Pedro Coria had just returned from an organizing trip to Shasta County and slept in. While walking to the office, he ran into some other members of the Los Angeles local on the street. The fellow workers informed Coria that the police were searching for him. He promptly went into hiding, escaped arrest, and fled to Tampico, Mexico. Police arrested Azuara in the September 28 roundup or shortly thereafter. Other IWW members arrested in Los Angeles during this sweep included James Elliott, Charles McWhirt, and Glen Roberts.[36]

Of the 160 people arrested, 116 stood trial in Chicago, with Aurelio Vincente Azuara among them. The Chicago trial began in April 1918 with a lengthy jury selection process and lasted more than four months, yet it took the jurors only an hour to find the one hundred people still charged guilty on all counts. In August the presiding judge sentenced ninety-five Wobblies to prison terms ranging from one year to as many as twenty years for senior leadership. Azuara, along with fourteen others, including William Haywood, received the harshest sentence of twenty years.[37]

In December 1917, just a few months after the initial federal indictments in September, a bomb exploded in Sacramento outside the governor of California's official residence. Police arrested a number of IWW members; authorities attempted to connect the union to the blast, eventually expanding to further mass arrests and the harassment of IWW members across California. In April 1918 IWW member A. R. Harvey wrote from San Francisco to Warren Lamson of the Los Angeles IWW local about affairs in a letter confiscated by federal agents: "They are picking men up by the hundreds here; they pinched about two hundred and fifty last Saturday. They raid rooming houses south of Market St. Regularly, from what I understand LA is about the least affected by this dealous [*sic*] frenzie for the Cause of Democracy."[38] In this case local police handled street-level disruption and the federal government used its powers over the mail to surveil communication. The composition of the IWW in Los Angeles made the type of raids Harvey described in San Francisco less likely. The strength of the Los Angeles IWW lay in its members organizing at jobsites elsewhere, not in a mass organization in the city. This also made targeted repression more successful in Los Angeles.

Authorities proved unable to link the union to the explosion, but undeterred, federal prosecutors in Sacramento convened a grand jury and secured indictments of IWW members for violating the Espionage Act. The federal government tried forty-six members or suspected sympathizers of the organization beginning in December 1918 in the Sacramento trial, the most important wartime IWW trial aside from the now-concluded proceedings in Chicago.[39] Seeing the mass convictions in Chicago, the defendants in Sacramento chose a different legal strategy than the national leaders had in Chicago. They decided to forgo legal representation and refused to participate in the proceedings against them. The men chose a "silent defense," a decision that contributed to factional discord within the IWW a few years later. The tactic produced the same result for the men charged without the same financial burden on the union as the Chicago trial had been. The jury returned guilty verdicts for all charged and on all charges in January 1919 with little deliberation.[40]

Of those convicted in Sacramento, Mortimer Downing and Felix Cedeño were the two most important to Los Angeles. Downing had joined the IWW in 1905 in Los Angeles and remained active in the city's local over the years, although at the time of his arrest he lived in San Francisco. The jury sentenced Downing to ten years in Leavenworth. Cedeño contributed to *El Rebelde* and went on a national fundraising tour for the paper in 1916.[41] The jury sentenced him to two years in the Kansas prison also, where they joined the PLM leaders and their comrades convicted in Chicago.[42]

The federal assault on the IWW achieved its purpose. It significantly disrupted the union's ability to organize during the war. It drew its limited funds toward legal defense and away from forming new unions. It interrupted the publication of the union's many newspapers, the vital communication tools of the multilingual and dispersed organization. The federal government's orchestrated effort to suppress the union also generated discord within the IWW that contributed to its split in 1924. It is not surprising that United States government could exert such force during wartime, but the degree of resilience exhibited by the union is perhaps surprising.

A little more than a year after the federal government forced the Los Angeles group to shutter *El Rebelde* and hauled away its editor in handcuffs in September 1917, the first issue of a new Spanish-language IWW periodical began in December 1918.[43] Based in Chicago, *La Nueva Solidaridad* featured voices familiar to IWW Spanish speakers with near constant updates on organizing in and near Los Angeles. For example, Pedro Coria penned a letter to *La Nueva Solidaridad* in January 1919 from El Paso calling on readers to remember the enthusiasm of the now-imprisoned Azuara, Tomás Martínez, and Felix Cedeño, along with their Anglo comrades.[44] Fernando Velarde also contributed a few articles to the new paper.[45]

Coria signing a letter with his real name from within in the United States was either a ruse or a taunt to the federal agents that everyone knew still pored over every line of radical publications. After Coria evaded arrest in 1917 the Bureau of Investigation actively attempted to locate him for the next few years. In November 1917 the bureau dispatched agents to search for him in the unlikely locations of the offices of the newspapers *El Heraldo de Mexico* and *El Correo Mexicano*. Agents also inquired about his whereabouts at "different news stands selling Mexican papers" and among locals on San Fernando Street in Los Angeles. They learned that Coria had traveled to Tampico through San Antonio, where he wrote to his cousin Manuel Sotelo to join him directly after the September round up.[46] By December bureau agents understood that Coria had become a fixture at the offices of the Tampico anarchist newspaper *Germinal*.[47] This connection speaks of the larger revolutionary circuits throughout Mexico, the United States, and the borderlands. Ricardo Treviño, the first editor of *Germinal*, had been a member of a PLM group in San Antonio.[48] Given the disruption of the organization, it seems that not even all of Coria's comrades knew of his whereabouts at this point. In a January 1918 letter to Manuel Sastre in Los Angeles, J. Pujol from the Chicago IWW office randomly slipped in the out-of-context sentence "Where is Pedro Coria?"[49]

Pedro Coria's decision to flee the American justice system turned out not only to benefit his own freedom but also to contribute directly to the expansion of the IWW in Mexico. After Coria helped charter the first IWW local in Mexico, petroleum workers in Tampico also organized under the IWW banner. Over the next two years IWW locals chartered in Torreón, Cananea, Mapimí, and Pachuca, among other places. Not one to lay down the struggle, the indefatigable Coria wrote to the Chicago office in April 1918 saying they he had yet to receive the official charter for the new IWW-affiliated oil-workers union in Tampico. Vincent St. John wrote to Pedro Coria, who was still under indictment, later in 1918, using Coria's real name and asking for address update in Tampico. The IWW office in Chicago was in disarray from the federal prosecutions, but it maintained a minimal level of function. By 1919 Mexico had a national IWW body to further coordinate local organizing efforts. Coria continued to organize actively for the IWW in Mexico, and in 1920 he led the syndicalist faction in a split from communist-influenced members. In connected organizing, north of Tampico in González, the U.S. Consul believed many of the key leaders of an IWW farm had come from Los Angeles.[50]

With other local Los Angeles leaders arrested, having fled, or lying low, Alfonso Cordoba and Manuel Sastre became the leading public faces of IWW organizing in Los Angeles. They assumed this position at great risk to themselves. With the Sacramento trial ongoing and with the result of the Chicago trial clear to all, the men took great risk in attaching their names to articles in *La Nueva Solidaridad* regardless of what they wrote. That Cordoba wrote about the lack of justice in the United States and in favor of workers continuing to agitate with the "ideal of love toward all humanity" and then signed his name from the Los Angeles local's office illustrates his level of commitment to fellow workers.[51]

Manuel Sastre had a similar life story to Aurelio Vincente Azuara's. Sastre emigrated from Pozaldez, Spain, in 1908. He worked as a laborer in the Panama Canal Zone before entering the United States through San Francisco in 1910. Sastre joined the IWW soon after his entry, in 1911, and lived a typically mobile life before basing himself out of Los Angeles. In 1918 he worked as a laborer for a shipbuilding company in San Pedro. Although not indicted in either the Chicago or Sacramento cases, Sastre still chose to remain mostly underground and kept a very low profile in Los Angeles through most of 1918. This did not mean he stopped organizing. He still spoke for the IWW, and BI agents found him to be well known in Bakersfield's Mexican community. Sastre signed his name to an article in the first issue of *La Nueva Solidaridad* in November 1918.[52]

Continuing local activism mixed with difficult working conditions led to a strike of citrus workers in Covina that extended to other nearby communities in February 1919. Local papers reported that the IWW infiltrated the local citrus groves as part of an orchestrated campaign with "Russian Bolshevik agitators." Local San Gabriel Valley newspapers and the Los Angeles Times hurled "Bolshevik," "Russian," and "I.W.W." as epithets with tales of invading outsiders, stoking the fire of a conservative counterattack.[53] Manuel Sastre later claimed in an interview with a BI agent that he first went to Covina looking for work. The reality of the situation more closely resembled prior IWW agricultural organizing at places like Wheatland and more recently in the AWO. A handful of dedicated activists like Sastre allied with discontented workers. Notably, the union printed material in English, Spanish, and Japanese. On January 22 workers presented to William Hoogendyke, the manager of the Charter Oak Citrus Association, their demand to increase wages to four dollars for an eight-hour day. Hoogendyke brushed the request aside, and the workers called for a strike across the entire orange belt. At the beginning of the strike Manuel Sastre grabbed Hoogendyke's arm while the manager physically confronted a boy. Nearby police arrested Sastre. He served

CHAPTER 8

thirty days in Los Angeles County Jail and was forced to pay a thirty-dollar fine for his involvement in the incident.[54]

On February 1 hundreds of supporters of the striking workers gathered in Los Angeles's Walker Hall. The IWW local held another meeting the next night, on February 2, attended by six hundred people. Indicative of the more settled work patterns of citrus workers and community support they received, the number of women and children present as well as a speech by a local elementary school-teacher caught the attention of journalists and an MID agent. Despite the family environment, an air of repression hung over this meeting. The first speaker announced that the police and Justice Department had denied them permission to hold the meeting, but they had defied that order. The speaker also "cautioned" those in attendance "not to say anything detrimental to the government but they could think whatever they liked." Only one of the speakers, Webber, was introduced by name.[55]

The agitation and strike activity soon spread to Azuza, Duarte, Monrovia, Pomona, and Glendora. While a precise number of workers withholding their labor power is difficult to determine, a local newspaper reported on February 3 that around five hundred or six hundred Mexican workers in the Pomona Valley had refused to work. The packinghouse in Monrovia also closed briefly for lack of supplies. The strike and agitation spread with mixed success into San Dimas, La Verne, and then still farther out into Upland, Redlands, and Riverside. Hoping to support the workers as the strike spread, Warren Lamson of the Los Angeles IWW sent an urgent telegram to the San Francisco IWW asking if they could send financial assistance and two Japanese organizers to Covina. The BI intercepted the telegram at the Fresno relay.[56]

The backlash of the growers reached its peak on February 5 when a vigilante mob descended upon what they had labeled the "Russian house" where a number of Russian Jewish organizers or sympathizers had taken up residence in Covina. The mob, which had grown to 150 cars and four hundred people, forced the residents of the dwelling onto a waiting truck, but when the driver learned of his proposed cargo, he refused the job. This gave the unwilling passengers an opportunity to speak to the crowd and sing "La Marseillaise" before another truck arrived with a driver willing to carry human freight down to Boyle Heights. Sheriff's deputies present at the scene allowed it progress without hindrance; later, a U.S. district attorney compared the afternoon's events to the Bisbee deportation, arguing that since a federal judge ruled that the Arizona events did not violate federal law, neither did the events in Covina, California. In the end, the sheriff and vigilantes worked together to keep further organizing at bay. Two arrests in Pomona, six in Azusa, and seven in Covina further contributed to ending the strike.[57]

IWW organizing did, however, continue in Los Angeles. At a fundraising meeting for strikers on February 16 two "husky officers stood at the entrance to the hall, and a number of plain clothes men sat among the audience."[58] At another meeting at the end of the month, on February 28, five hundred people listened to speakers at Turner Hall before they cleared the floor to dance. As the meeting turned from business to social release, a Bureau of Investigation agent assisted by two deputies turned to Fred C. Spayde, a reporter for the *Los Angeles Times*, to identify Manuel Sastre, whom they arrested for violating the Espionage Act. Bureau agents attempted to connect Sastre to recent fires in Modesto and Mateca, in a replay of earlier IWW arrests during the war, but in the end they did not find enough evidence to substantiate the charges of violating the Espionage Act, let alone arson. After some interdepartmental wrangling in which local immigration authorities refused to accept Sastre into their custody, the bureau eventually deported Sastre as a foreign national.[59]

Despite the continuation of the difficult legal environment, several other strikes occurred in Los Angeles in 1919. Brickyard workers in Santa Monica walked out in March, and it is possible that the IWW worked to organize brickyard workers elsewhere in 1919. After the February citrus strike, Pedro C. Aguilar, secretary of IWW Local 400 in Azusa, continued to organize citrus workers in his city. On May Day 1919 police broke up an International Ladies' Garment Workers' Union (ILGWU) picnic with "red flags everywhere" and arrested two women.[60] Between carmen, platform workers, and track laborers, enough workers of Pacific Electric Railways walked out to shut down service for a day in August. Although these strike actions did not lead to victories for workers, they did illustrate the continued relevance of organizing and direct action.[61]

Mexico as a Safe Haven

At the same time the criminal justice system targeted radicals across the country for their political activities and ideologies, members of radical groups faced the government as draft-eligible citizens. The federal government also required noncitizens to register under the Selective Service Act, which put them at risk of being quickly drafted if the government changed policy to include them. In total, the federal government called into service 2.8 million of the 23.9 million men who registered with the Selective Service. An estimated four million men evaded the World War I draft. Tens of thousands chose to travel to Mexico for this purpose. Mexico proved a particularly popular option for anarchists, and their flight fit well within their antinational views. In 1918 the Military Intelligence Division noted "a great deal of talk . . . about the slackers who have made their

CHAPTER 8

escape into Mexico where they have colonized to some extent, and it is claimed that the border troubles will increase and become more of a menace all the time."[62]

Los Angeles was a crucial stop in the journey to Mexico for some anarchists, notably young members of the L'Era Nuova group in Paterson, New Jersey. William Gallo, the son of the anarchist couple Ninfa Baronio and Firmino Gallo, whom the BI labeled "a dirty, sneaking cowardly Italian," made the journey. William grew up in the anarchist community in Paterson and joined the struggle as a young man, most publicly as the treasurer of the Young Men's Ferrer Club. Spartaco Guabello, also a member of the club, accompanied the Gallos. Their journey to Mexico took them first to Los Angeles to meet with two of Firmino's friends in the city, L. Chiechi and Michele Fasano. The two prominent Italian anarchists, in turn, connected William with a number of Mexican radicals in Los Angeles who probably helped the men settle in Mexico.[63]

Firmino supported William and Spartaco's effort by wiring fifty dollars to his son in Los Angeles through Western Union. To get to Mexico, the pair traveled from Los Angeles through Del Rio, Texas, where they stopped at the home of B. R. Wilson, the address to which Gallo's father had mailed his son a package containing film, camera, and a pair of binoculars. They made it safely to Mexico, but authorities later arrested them upon their return to the United States, and each served a four-month sentence in Del Rio, Texas. The Bureau of Investigation blandly recorded: "William Gallo, the son of Firmino Gallo, escaped from Paterson to California, thence to Mexico, and later, upon returning to the States, was caught and sentenced to serve four months for evasion of the draft."[64]

These were trying times for anarchist organizations and anarchists personally. In July 1919 Michele Fasano wrote to his friend Firmino Gallo to "encourage the disheartened Gallo," in the words of a BI agent. Fasano wrote, "I am sure that anarchists and sympathizers are more numerous now in America than in the time of Malatesta and Coni. Isn't that sufficient? Of course, according to our wishes this is not sufficient and we wouldn't be satisfied even if a revolutionary movement would be spread over the whole world. Even then we wouldn't say 'yes, but we are not in Anarchy.'"[65]

Other Italian anarchists made their way to Mexico. Nicola Sacco and Bartolomeo Vanzetti traveled by train with a group of Italian anarchists from Boston to Laredo, Texas. They then crossed the border with the help of Mexican anarchists from Monterrey. Perhaps sixty people in Luigi Galleani's camp made this journey, traveling from across the United States. Some Galleanisti had a second motivation for going to Mexico other than avoiding the draft. They went to prepare for what they believed to be imminent revolution in Italy and feared being unable to travel to participate if they remained in the United States. Later, an official in the Department of Justice recorded his belief that anarchists traveled to Mexico to receive explosives training; however, the historian of anarchism Paul Avrich noted that "while little evidence has come to light to sustain this hypothesis, the possibility cannot be ruled out."[66] The first goal of most remained avoiding conscription.

Many of the leftists now living in Mexico added to a vibrant cosmopolitan milieu, most notably in Mexico City and Tampico. They included the Indian nationalist Manabendra Nath Roy, Linn Gale (who published *Gale's Magazine*), the Japanese communist Sen Katayama, and Jewish socialist Roberto Haberman. Pedro Coria, Primo Tapia, and others with ties to the PLM and IWW in Los Angeles fit into this scene as well. The affinities cultivated to facilitate the global revolution sustained people personally through these difficult years.[67] Many of these international travelers also learned from revolutionary Mexico in a period of global turmoil. M. N. Roy's "experience with the Mexican Revolution helped him comprehend the ways in which fates were linked and objectives were shared in the struggle against racial capitalism. His experience in Mexico expanded his conception of a worldwide struggle for freedom."[68]

Crucially, many of those who fled to Mexico in the 1920s came from elsewhere in Latin America. Cuban revolutionary Julio Antonio Mella lived and organized in Mexico between 1926 and his murder in 1929. Nicaragua's Augusto César Sandino lived in Tampico between 1923 and 1926 before returning to his home country to fight. A group of Venezuelan students exiled for agitating against their government made their way to Mexico, as did Peruvian Victor Raúl Haya de la Torre. Radicals began to see new connections between capital, class, and race in Mexico, which in turn filtered back out in the global revolutionary conscious.[69]

Serving Time and the Postwar Continuation of Repression

After World War I drew to an end with the Armistice in November 1918 and then the signing of the Treaty of Versailles in July 1919, leftists in the United States continued to face a hostile environment for organizing. As those convicted during the wartime crackdown languished in prison, state legislatures passed new laws to extend wartime repression into the 1920s. In April 1919 the California legislature created an even more effective legal apparatus to confront radicals than the federal legislation passed during the war. California's Criminal Syndicalism Act outlawed doctrines advocating the use of violence, sabotage, or other criminal acts to change society. The law included restrictions on simply joining an organization that advocated such means, and it aimed squarely at the resurgent IWW and its perceived connection to Bolshevism, exemplified by the strike activity in Covina's orange groves shortly before the legislature passed the bill.[70] By February 1920 authorities had arrested thirty people for engaging in criminal syndicalism in Los Angeles, twenty-five in Stockton, and nineteen in Oakland, among lesser numbers throughout the state. In September 1919 a grand jury in Los Angeles secretly indicted IWW members in the city. Raids carried out by the Justice Department followed, but the men faced state prosecutions. After the first wave of arrests the number of detentions climbed to 504 through 1926.[71]

Leftists in Los Angeles and elsewhere in California responded by continuing to engage in radical activities, but the situation forced most aboveground organizing toward the legal and emotional support of their imprisoned comrades. On the legal front, a range of sympathizers, including the socialist attorney Austin Lewis, formed the California Civil Liberties Union to help with the courtroom fight against this legislation. When Austin Lewis wrote to Mrs. Orlow Black in July 1920 about the organization's formation, he described its primary purpose as supporting those convicted under California's criminal syndicalism law and to repeal the legislation.[72]

Prison support activities included the IWW's "Prison Comfort Club," which sent imprisoned members sundries such as socks, underwear, dried fruit, and tobacco: all banal necessities of day-to-day life that became dear in prison.[73] Nicolaas Steelink, arrested in October 1919 and among the first men convicted under the Criminal Syndicalism Act, fared better in prison than many. He wrote to Mary Gallagher that he did not have dependents outside and that friends, in addition to the District Defense Committee in San Francisco, supported him through visits and a monthly allowance of three dollars. He passed the time working in San Quentin State Prison's furniture factory packing boxes and even managed to buy a typewriter so he could translate the works of a Dutch author he enjoyed. The prison board paroled him in 1922.[74]

Radicals convicted during and after the war spent their time in many prisons, but Leavenworth Penitentiary contained the largest concentration of "political prisoners" in the country. Leavenworth held Ricardo Flores Magón, Enrique Flores Magón, and Librado Rivera; the South Asian revolutionary Tarknath Das; in addition to convicted IWW members such as the African American Wobblie Ben Fletcher. Prisoners faced great hardship, yet they also turned Leavenworth into space for the transmission of radical ideas out through global radical networks, what Christina Heatherton referred to as a "University of Radicalism." Leavenworth functioned similarly to the spaces in Los Angeles, the borderlands, and Mexico in which affinities flourished. The clear hierarchy of the state and its representative guards forced a constellation of radicals into close proximity in the cells, prison library, and yard connections; understandings grew through the hardship. Heatherton argued, "Leavenworth Federal Penitentiary, a container of dissent against racial capitalism and militarism, became a site through which the fluidity of the racial regimes within and across borders was made legible."[75]

Life in the prison was difficult. Aurelio Vincente Azuara wrote to Mary Gallagher from Leavenworth in 1921 that his time in prison had taken a toll on his health. However, like Steelink, he counted himself as fortunate because he did not have dependents outside the walls. In prison he had persistent ear infections that he believed would require surgery, and he had lost most of the sight in his right eye. Despite the hardship, he offered his advice to gain the freedom of the IWW men. He asked Gallagher to organize a publicity campaign, highlighting the stories of one prisoner each week that could be distributed to the surviving IWW press and internationally in Europe and Latin America.[76] Tomás Martínez and Aurelio Vincente Azuara both maintained their organizing zeal in Leavenworth and reached an audience outside through *La Nueva Solidaridad*, which published their letters as well as poems penned by Azuara.[77]

Citizenship status continued to have meaning in prison. Azuara and Martínez were both foreign nationals; Azuara held Spanish citizenship, Martínez Mexican. The U.S. government attempted to deport Martínez in 1920, but the attorney Harry Weinberger contested the proposed deportation on the grounds that Martínez had fought in the Mexican Revolution under General Angeles and would be executed by Carranza. As the case made its way through the courts, Tomás Martínez died in the custody of immigration officials on December 3, 1921, due to complications from surgery. He had contracted septicemia while still in Leavenworth the previous year. President Harding commuted Azuara's and a few other IWW prisoners' sentences on December 30, 1922, in a deal that brought his release after agreeing to being deported to Spain.[78]

Enrique Flores Magón had stepped out of Leavenworth in September 1920, but Ricardo Flores Magón and Librado Rivera remained incarcerated. While Enrique faced lengthy deportation proceedings upon his release, Ricardo died in prison in November 1922. In his failing health Ricardo served as the prison's librarian, along with an Anglo conscientious objector from Chicago and Taraknath Das. Das, along with Har Dayal, with whom William C. Owen worked at the Bakunin Institute in Hayward, were two of the leading figures in the Ghadar movement. At his trial, Das took the blame for distributing a bomb-making manual, supposedly instructions from Russian revolutionaries, on the Pacific Coast.[79] Flores Magón's failing health notwithstanding, rumors swirled that the true cause of his death was murder. His comrade and cell mate in Leavenworth, Librado Rivera, remembered "many discolorations on the body" and said that he "always had a strong suspicion that ill treatment by the guards had a good deal to do with the death."[80] Recently, the historian Christina Heatherton brought these accusations out of the realm of innuendo and made a strong circumstantial case that a prison guard murdered Ricardo in retaliation for a Mexican inmate killing a guard at the prison.[81]

Comrades arranged for Ricardo's body to be transported from Kansas to Los Angeles, where they held a "great reception." They refused an offer from the Mexican government for a grand public funeral in Mexico City, but they did allow the Mexican railroad union, which Tom Bell described as "a very militant and radical union," to transport the body to Mexico City. Along the way they made stops "for propaganda at all the big towns," culminating in a large funeral in Mexico City.[82] The U.S. government eventually deported Enrique on March 21, 1923, along with Therese and four of his children.[83] Ricardo's death and Enrique's deportation signaled less a seismic shift and more the resting point of PLM decline, but its legacy lived on.

The Retreat of the IWW in Los Angeles

In the winter of 1922–23 the IWW managed to return to agitation both on the job for better working conditions and away from the jobsite with the goal of freeing their imprisoned comrades. Police arrested twenty-seven IWW members over a five-month period in Los Angeles and San Pedro for criminal syndicalism in 1923, the largest single prosecution in the state under the law.[84] When brought to court, the committed members of the organization made no effort in their own defense, similar to the Sacramento trial a few years earlier. The judge asked each in turn "if he would renounce his membership in the I.W.W. and tear up his red card." All responded with "a very firm, vehement 'no.'" Given the political climate and the flexibility of the law, membership in the union constituted sufficient evidence to convict them. When authorities loaded the handcuffed men onto a bus to San Quentin, one of their supporters, Mary Gallagher, remembered that "they went into the buses singing and sang all the way up to Richmond . . . and went into prison singing. That was the type of men they were." They also brought their organizational strength with them to prison. In Gallagher's words: "While these men were in prison in California they maintained their organization the same as the Leavenworth prisoners had done. All questions were put to a vote and their attitudes to each other were on an organizational basis. When these men wanted to protest against a condition which seemed unbearable to them, they put on a hunger strike. Several such strikes took place in San Quentin; one lasted 21 days, and to it is attributed many of the reforms later instituted in that prison."[85]

The arrests in San Pedro resulted from a concerted effort to tamp down resurgent IWW organizing at the port, at least partially by card carriers and sympathizers converging on the city as they had in prior actions. In April 1923 workers at the port walked off the job, reported to be around three thousand, a number large enough to affect operations. Strikebreaking techniques ranged from the importation of scabs to the mass arrests of strikers. Authorities even arrested and confiscated the papers from an attorney representing IWW members. The strike failed after a week when most workers returned to the job. IWW membership tripled during the strike, reaching fifteen hundred in Los Angeles County. After the conviction of twenty-seven strike leaders in Los Angeles the IWW called another strike. It was an insignificant job action that nonetheless illustrated the continued presence of radical agitators at the port.

The next winter, vigilantes and the police combined forces against the IWW in San Pedro. Arrests and raids of suspected Wobblies followed. Members of the Ku Klux Klan took their own initiative: Klansmen circled the block in automobiles while police raided the IWW office. June brought other violent attacks on Wobblies. As around three hundred people gathered at a fundraising event for two union members killed in accidents, vigilantes, some in navy uniform, burst in and wreaked havoc on persons and property. They burned several children, including nine-year-old May Sundstedt, with scalding-hot coffee when they attacked the union hall and kidnapped several adults. May Sundstedt's mother succumbed to her injuries a few days later. They transported the kidnapped men to the then-remote Santa Ana Canyon, tarred and feathered them, and left them to find their own way back.[86]

After the violence in San Pedro, the American Civil Liberties Union, characterized as the "pink-tea adjunct of the I.W.W.," held a street meeting in San Pedro. The attorney Leo Gallagher and writer F. Moffet both spoke at the rally. Gallagher stated from the podium that un-uniformed police officers participated in the violence. After Gallagher led the crowd in singing a "wobbly song" local police arrested and charged him with violating Judge Charles Busick's July 1923 restraining order barring all IWW members from violating California's Criminal Syndicalism Act.[87] Police arrested Moffet for violating the Criminal Syndicalism Act as well. The wealthy socialist Kate Crane Gartz accused the San Pedro Police Department of failing in its duties by letting the violence occur, and the IWW believed that the "exalted ruler" of the San Pedro chapter of the Elks Club, James Dodson, the local attorney and businessman Lloyd Mix, and Sergeant William Webber organized the violent vigilante assault.[88] IWW organizing at the port in San Pedro was the most significant job action by the union near Los Angeles before or after the war.

During this period a nationwide effort to gain pardon for radicals still imprisoned on federal charges gathered strength. The campaign followed Warren Harding as he traveled the country in 1923. In California, wherever Harding's train stopped, concerned citizens were there to ask for pardon. The organizing committee in Los Angeles arranged for a pilot to fly over Harding's boat on his planned trip to Santa Catalina Island, dropping leaflets and carrying a banner "demanding release of the prisoners." As Mary Gallagher remembered, the president did not make it down the coast: "Poor Harding never arrived. He died in San Francisco and I was very angry with him for upsetting our plans."[89] In the fall of 1924 the millionaire Rudolph Spreckels and Charles Sprading spoke at a crowded meeting in Los Angeles's Philharmonic Auditorium in favor of Senator Robert La Follette's efforts to restore rights after the measures taken during World War I. Around 1924 a shift took place in organizing and prosecutorial discretion as authorities increased their use of the Criminal Syndicalism Act to prosecute communists and turned their attention away from the IWW.[90]

These years proved incredibly difficult locally and nationally for the IWW. In 1924 the organization went through a factional schism "between 'decentralists,' supported by many anarchists, and 'centralists,' supported by the Communist Party."[91] The first group formed under what it termed the "emergency program" or the "E.P." The second became known as the "4-trey," after their office address of 3333 West Belmont in Chicago.[92] The sides drew lines over whether or not imprisoned members should accept conditional pardons for their release. They also conflicted over the growing influence of communism and the organization's centralization.[93] The longtime Los Angeles IWW member Mortimer Downing was "one of the most violent opponents" of accepting conditional pardons, and he opposed its centralization. After "some violent altercations in Chicago" the emergency program moved to Los Angeles.[94] The spirit of the culture of affinity continued, but federal and state government efforts during and after World War I brought about the end of the PLM and greatly curtailed the ability of the IWW to act upon their ideals. The years 1923 and 1924 represented the low point from which radicals in Los Angeles and out through the networks tried to rebuild their movement before the Great Depression, and the growth of communist organization restructured leftist politics and the terrain of struggle. The IWW never recovered. It could still claim anywhere between twelve thousand and seventeen thousand card-carrying members in 1925, but by 1930 its ranks fell to between three thousand and eight thousand.[95]

■ ■ ■

The repression of radical movements in the name of the nation before, during, and after World War I greatly constrained their ability to organize and act. The U.S. government from the federal to the local levels tailored its repressive tools to meet the distinct challenges posed by the varied actors in radical organizing. The street-level repression of radicals also generally included nonstate actors working with at least the tacit consent of government officials. This history of IWW and anarchist repression during this dark period in U.S. history is national, regional, state-level, and local. Indeed, as flight to Mexico illustrates, it also contains important transnational dimensions.

Mortimer Downing. (National Archives at Kansas City, Records of the Bureau of Prisons)

The deeply rooted practices of working-class resistance that elicited such a fierce response also facilitated the movement's survival. As radicals fought to survive state repression, the depth of radical infrastructure came to fore: from wealthy sympathizers to underground anarchist networks. Continued organizing in support of imprisoned comrades and in job actions illustrated the relevance of radical ideals to the lives of thousands of residents in the region. In Los Angeles state power proved far more effective when directed at individuals and organizations than it did at erasing the ideals fueling movements from the working-class imagination. The ability to rebuild a transnational movement in the wake of repression illustrates the depth of the radical cultural practices of affinity—although, in the end, radical movements in the United States could not effectively counter the power of the state.

CONCLUSION

REGENERATION, DECLINE, AND REORDERING THE LEFT

Is it my fault that in the Days of Death
I happen to be born, when hope seems sinking
For all the human race? Should I, with bated breath,
A coward, lay me down, life-blinded blinking?

—Alfred Sanftleben, "Hope Deferred,"
August 24, 1930

The state repression unleashed during World War I and after reconfigured the landscape of radical movements across the country; however, nascent organizing through these dark years kept hope alive for a brighter day. In Los Angeles anarchists slowly reemerged between 1922 and 1924 as the harsh repression of the IWW continued. The 1920s brought the most important period of industrial and suburban development in Los Angeles history. New radical organizing faced the shifting spatial landscape of the rapidly developing city. The structural reconfiguration of Los Angeles through dispersed industrial development and white suburbanization compounded internal movement dynamics altered by the Russian Revolution and the emergence of Communist Parties in the United States and Mexico. Combined these factors reordered local solidarities and alliances in the 1920s.

The seizure of power by the Bolsheviks in 1917 began a years-long process of change on the left. Anarchists, syndicalists, and socialists had to reckon with the worker's state and with a growing number of communists within their own communities and movements. The Left met the news of the revolution in the dark days of World War I with near-universal elation. It captured the radical imagination like never before—certainly more than the outbreak of the Mexican Revolution

Conclusion

at the turn of the decade. Even anarchists initially believed this was a moment of true potential that they could influence and should support.

In the few years after the October Revolution anarchists based in the United States and Mexico tended to highlight the revolutionary potential of what they understood had occurred in Russia: a democratic upwelling of workers. Mexican anarchists and syndicalists, the dominant actors on the left, "interpreted" the events in Russia through their own ideals, emphasizing the newly formed workers' councils while they celebrated the revolution as a "magnificent example of direct action (*acción directa*) carried out by an active minority."[1] Anarchists and syndicalists in the United States commonly understood the revolution on similar terms. The IWW leadership in the United States, for example, celebrated the revolution with "unrestrained enthusiasm" when they learned of it while in jail in Chicago awaiting trial after the nationwide raids in 1917.[2]

Given the evolving process of the Russian Revolution, geographical distance, and slower speed that news traveled, the shift from support to critique occurred over a few years. The rupture between Bolsheviks and anarchists—marked in Russia by the arrest of anarchists and then the violent repression of the Kronstadt Rebellion in 1921—took its own course in the United States, Mexico, and throughout the global movement. Anarchist criticism of the Soviet state achieved a degree of visibility by early 1919. The German anarchist Rudolf Rocker became one of the Bolsheviks' most prominent opponents when he published his essay "Soviet System or Dictatorship?" in 1920.[3]

Timing and context mattered. Emma Goldman, Alexander Berkman, and 247 other deportees arrived in Russia in 1920 after a treacherous voyage on the *Buford*. Goldman and Berkman found a welcome reception, even gaining a brief audience with Lenin, and enjoyed a privileged position traveling the country. The pair, like many others, changed their view of the Revolution after the violent suppression of the Kronstadt Rebellion in March 1921 "which had called for the restoration of civil liberties and democratic soviets in the place of one-party rule."[4] Ricardo Flores Magón, too, shifted from extreme praise for Lenin in the final issue of *Regeneración* in 1918 to criticism in early 1921.[5] Kenyon Zimmer described the shifting interpretations among anarchists: "As the Russian Communist Party consolidated its hold on power, its relationship with the anarchists deteriorated. The soviets, trade unions, and factory committees in which anarchists placed so much hope were transformed into appendages of centralized Communist power, and workers' control gave way to 'one-man management' and militaristic 'iron discipline' in the workplace."[6] As the worker's state became increasingly authoritarian, anarchist critiques grew stronger.

Changing assessments of the revolution caused great conflict within the IWW, and "as the Russian regime bureaucratized, Wobblies began to fragment in their attitude toward Soviet rule."[7] With the IWW prisoners now convicted and sure to lose their final appeal before the U.S. Supreme Court in 1921, William Haywood jumped bail and fled to Russia the same month as the Kronstadt Rebellion.[8] Conflict over the IWW's relationship to the Soviet state contributed to the organization's split in 1924. These internal—and necessary—movement conflicts came at the worst possible time. The anarchist movement and the IWW had suffered severe disruption during and after the war. Now, as they attempted to rebuild their movement, radicals had to reconcile their libertarian ideals with the new reality in Russia, which generated great internal strife. During this process Communist Parties in the United States and Mexico slowly emerged to challenge existing organizations and ideologies.

On the whole, the size of the anarchist movement in the United States stabilized in the 1920s after declining during World War I. The Italian movement even achieved some growth in the United States in this often-neglected period of anarchist history. Historians have generally assumed that the remnants of the anarchist movement that survived World War I–era repression and deportations were dealt their final blow by the Johnson-Reed Immigration Act of 1924. The act's imposition of new quota-based immigration restrictions limiting Southern European and Eastern European migrants denied the Jewish and Italian anarchist movements—the anarchist movements' two largest segments—new supporters. This process, however, was more complex than previously assumed. Kenyon Zimmer argued that the "new legislation choked off anarchism's supply of potential new adherents as the American state's growing administrative capacity enabled the government to more effectively—though never completely—control its borders."[9] Yet he also shifted prior understandings by detailing the persistence of the movement's Yiddish and Italian wings into the 1930s: "The collapse of America's Yiddish and Italian anarchist movements did not occur until the end of the 1930s and resulted less from state repression or rival ideologies than from the tragedy of the Spanish Civil War and the end of mass transatlantic migration. Immigration created anarchists in America, and in its absence, their numbers atrophied."[10]

Immigration patterns and movement dynamics in Los Angeles gave this history a local form. Immigration restrictions in the 1920s exempted Mexico even as the decade brought about attempts to regulate the United States' southern border. A multiethnic English-language group, a Yiddish group, Spanish-language groups, and an Italian group were the largest segments of the city's anarchist movement. Immigration restriction affected the Yiddish and the Italian groups far more than the English and Mexican groups. Yet by 1930 the anarchist movement and the IWW were almost entirely absent from street-level organizing in Los Angeles. What remained were components of an intellectual movement unable to accomplish more than to publish material or host sporadic meetings. Anarchists mostly worked within other organizations and trade unions, like the International Ladies' Garment Workers' Union, to influence jobsite-based organizing as the 1920s wore on. Massive unemployment during the Great Depression failed to draw people toward the anarchist or syndicalist cause in the 1930s. The Communist Party better harnessed this discontent than the earlier actors on the radical left in Los Angeles. Through these years the generation of anarchists aroused to action by the Haymarket tragedy died, and younger radicals took the lead in the movement, changing the personal face of the Left in Los Angeles.

The Postwar Regeneration of Radical Los Angeles

In an atmosphere of intense pressure on anarchists, the IWW, and other radicals, leftists created another organization to challenge capitalism. The American branch of the Communist Party was founded in 1919, and a chapter formed in Los Angeles in the early 1920s. One sign of the local party's growth came in the struggle for control of the Walt Whitman School, a modern school affiliated with the Francisco Ferrer Association. The nationwide leader of the modern-school movement, William Thurston Brown, led the effort to found the school in Los Angeles in 1919 after helping to create schools in Salt Lake City in 1910 and Portland in 1911. The school closed its doors in 1922 or 1923, an event the anarchist press recalled as a "severe defeat."[11] Marion Bell placed the blame for the demise of the school at the feet of the rising influence of the Communist Party: "The Communists were taking over and there was terrible quarreling."[12]

More intra-left infighting occurred, but for most of the 1920s the Communist Party in Los Angeles functioned "as much as a social organization as a political party."[13] The party's base in the 1920s lay among Jewish residents of Boyle Heights, where it maintained a co-op on Brooklyn Avenue. It functioned as a local community center much like other radical spaces in prior years, with rooms for meeting, a restaurant, and a barber. Communist street speakers in Los Angeles also fit into the tradition of socialists, IWW, and PLM, but the suppression of radical speaking on the plaza and downtown pushed most communist speaking into surrounding residential neighborhoods. Although it had a primarily Jewish membership base at this point, there were visible strands of the regional cosmopolitan organizing tradition in local communist organizing. Sen Katayama, the one-time associate of Kōtoku Shusui, settled in Los Angeles for a spell after spending time in Mexico. He organized for the Communist Party in both locations. It took the better part of the decade before the organization became a leading actor in local radical organizing. Until then the Communist Party germinated as the anarchist movement struggled onward.[14]

Conclusion

Children at the Walt Whitman School in Boyle Heights. (Southern California Library for Social Studies and Research, Los Angeles, California)

In the early 1920s a number of anarchists moved to Los Angeles and infused the city with new energy, immediately contributing to increased organizing. Lizzie and Tom Bell moved to Los Angeles from Phoenix around 1920. They brought with them friendships with members of the PLM and IWW in Arizona as well as personal connections to many of the most well-known anarchists of the fin de siècle. An anarchist of long standing, Bell was "a widely traveled and well read man, with a good knowledge of half a dozen languages." Years earlier, he "chained himself securely to a lamp-post in Paris during a free speech fight and he had the poor minions at their wits end, while he talked to the crowd until his voice gave out."[15] Bell grew into an old sage of the movement during these years and contributed to the formation of the Libertarian Group in 1922.

While initially a Jewish organization, Libertarian Group members "realized the necessity of an English movement." A member claimed that by the group's second year in existence it had gathered the "largest selection of Anarchist English literature of any group in existence."[16] Yiddish-based Jewish organizing benefited from new arrivals as well. In 1923 former members of the Jewish anarchist Clarion Colony in Utah, founded around 1913, came to Los Angeles and established the Kropotkin Literary Society (KLS), a branch of the Workmen's Circle. The Russian-born Joseph Spivak also arrived in Los Angeles in 1923 from New York.

Mortimer Downing, who led the Emergency Program faction of the IWW after his time in Leavenworth, returned to the city in 1924, where he had joined the IWW nearly two decades earlier.[17]

The Libertarian Group balanced its organizing between gathering financial support for IWW and Russian prisoners and running a "Free Workers Forum" starting in 1923. During its "four years of continual functioning," Spivak remembered in 1927, it did "more for the development of the free thought than any other means of propaganda." Spivak went so far as to claim, "It will not be exaggerating to state, that this Open Forum has made Anarchism in Los Angeles popular."[18] The Open Forum ran as a speaking series with a specific goal: "Whatever the topic of the evening is, we always bring our Anarchist views into it." Indicative of the group's reach, it printed ten thousand copies of a pamphlet containing Mollie Steimer's "Letter from Russia," of which it sold three thousand copies in Los Angeles.[19] Spivak quickly became comrades with Tom Bell through the Libertarian Group, and he joined the IWW. He also wrote for the *Road to Freedom* and *Fraye Arbeter Shtime*. Strongly anticommunist, he became a Stirnerite after the Russian Revolution.[20] The Open Forum stood as one of the primary venues for leftist organizing in the city in mid-decade, indicative of a shift away from street-level or jobsite-based organizing.

As anarchist organizing took new steps forward, Joseph Spivak suffered a great personal loss when his wife, Manya, passed away in 1926. The *Road to Freedom* remembered her as "one of our most active comrades" and offered the editors sympathies to her family and friends.[21] As personal a tragedy as it may have been, it soon became political. Her survivors wanted her gravestone at the Jewish cemetery in East Los Angeles, Home of Peace, to read, "A brave and noble woman, an ardent advocate of Anarchism. She inspired her comrades to enthusiasm and remains in their hearts a tender memory." But the president of the cemetery, a member of the Better America Federation, had the word "Anarchism" filled in with concrete; he would not allow a word "that threatens to overthrow our government."[22]

The reinvigoration of the Spanish-language radical movement also came in 1923 and 1924 when the circulation of the IWW newspaper *Solidaridad* grew because of increased Mexican immigration to the United States.[23] The newspaper continued as *La Nueva Solidaridad* in 1920, also published in Chicago. In Los Angeles in the winter of 1924, P. Mares Velasco served as the secretary for the newly formed anarchist group Obreros Libres, based in Belvedere Park. It engaged in a propaganda campaign to create a federation out of the many small, fractured groups of Mexican anarchists still active in Southern California. Indicating the continued importance placed on newspapers to draw together a dispersed movement, Obreros Libres aimed to publish a Spanish-language anarchist newspaper in Los Angeles, though it is doubtful that any issues rolled off the press. One of the group's flyers appealed directly to Mexicans, as it quoted the Italian anarchist Errico Malatesta.[24] Anarchism clearly reached beyond the PLM in Los Angeles's Mexican community, but former members of that organization continued to serve as a point of reference to the movement.

Enrique Flores Magón returned to organizing in Mexico after his deportation and maintained his connections to the global movement. Enrique remembered, "[When I] came back to Mexico in 1923, I threw myself into the struggle heart and soul, together with my wife Therese."[25] While living in Mexico City in 1924 Enrique wrote to his friend, the veteran Los Angeles anarchist Stephanus Fabijanović, "I am corresponding with 514 labor syndicates, several Federations (local and State ones), over one hundred independent propaganda groups, and well over four thousand comrades in Mexico, besides many others in all South America, U. S., England, Germany, Japan, Spain, France, Italy, Etc." That year, he and Therese traveled through Mexico on a propaganda tour, visiting "all the workers' syndicates and going from factory to factory, advising the toilers not to [get] mixed up with politicians and, much the less, take sides in the present political strife between Obregón and de la Huerta, but to let them fight it alone. The task has been a dangerous one, for we have aroused the ire of the eternal president of the Mexican Regional Labor Conference." Rafael García traveled with the pair in Mexico for part of this tour. When García left Mexico he traveled first to Louisville, Kentucky, and then "around California for a while." When he reached his home in Los Angeles, García wrote to Enrique, chiding him for not responding to correspondence from their mutual friend Fabijanović.[26]

Through the 1920s the prospects of the Communist Party in Mexico competed with promise of the revolution "as a socialist project under which the state redistributed the national wealth through agrarian reform and the expropriation of foreign-owned natural resources."[27] The legacy of the PLM's agrarian-based anarchism, in turn, influenced the direction of the nascent Communist Party through individual and ideological continuity. Primo Tapia de la Cruz, a former IWW and PLM member, joined the Mexican Communist Party (PCM) in 1921. José Valades, a PCM leader until his expulsion in 1922, remembered that the PCM was "under the influence of anarchism and vice versa" between 1919 and 1924.[28] Mexico saw its own period of reconciliation of the legacy of past movements in the shifting landscape of the left after the Russian Revolution in which the anarchism of the PLM and the IWW's syndicalism played important roles.

While Therese and Enrique Flores Magón lived in Mexico, their eldest daughter remained in Los Angeles. In June 1924 Therese traveled back to the city to be at Esperanza's side, as she had just given birth. Unable to return to the United States, Enrique stayed in Mexico with the couple's three youngest children: Pete, Joe, and "little" Henry. Low on funds, the couple relied on money sent from their

Conclusion

daughter and their longtime comrade Rafael García to pay for Therese and their "two oldest children, Stelle and James" to make the trip. She ran out of money in the city and did not have enough to pay for passage back to Mexico. Enrique wrote to Fabijanović, "Therese has no money to come back home to us and she has gone to work—or is about to work—to the fruit picking in order to get the money for her passage back." While his wife and children faced hardship in Los Angeles, Enrique wrote that they planned to remain for some time, "for in this poor Mexico life is impossible." The IWW in Los Angeles helped support the couple. It took up a collection for them at an IWW picnic held at Rose Hill Park. A group of anarchists in Los Angeles also gathered funds. Together they raised thirty dollars and sent it to Enrique in August 1924.[29]

Through these difficult financial times, Enrique Flores Magón antagonized Mexican authorities. While visiting the "Peasants Syndicate Ricardo Flores Magón" in Melcher Ocampo, Guautitlán, in the fall of 1924 the group ran into trouble.[30] He and several comrades met in a house in the afternoon, planning for a public gathering the next day. That evening, "a group of drunk soldiers, two policemen and a lieutenant, broke into the home of Felipe P. Cervantes, and aiming their guns to the breasts of the men, women, and children," hauled them to jail. Police released the men on bail, and they issued this appeal: "And it is up to you, comrades and fellow workers everywhere, to come to their rescue agitating in their behalf through our papers in all languages, and by sending your protests to Plutarco Elias Calles, President of the Mexican Republic."[31]

Back in Los Angeles, the efforts of the Libertarian Group over the few years previous culminated in its opening a new institutional space for anarchism on Brooklyn Avenue in Boyle Heights a few blocks from the Communist Co-op. It housed the group's library and had space available for meetings. The anarchist group had a second goal. It sought to build "a new society within the old and intolerable one—to start a free colony near Los Angeles." Aaron Rogat negotiated with real estate companies on behalf of the Libertarian Group to buy land on which it planned to build a colony within fifteen or twenty miles of Los Angeles. There is no evidence that the group moved past this stage. These efforts show a willingness and the financial ability to institutionalize that at least equaled earlier years, but the colony, in particular, also evidences an inward focus in the movement.[32]

In the winter of 1927 a new Mexican anarchist group formed and created the Libertario Centro in central Los Angeles. It joined the Libertarian Group and the Kropotkin Literary Society as one of the three largest anarchist organizations in the city. The group had the funds to rent a meeting hall near the city center and to publish a Spanish-language newspaper. Joseph Spivak characterized its members as "one hundred per cent proletarian." Members focused their energy on "educating their members and to Anarchist propaganda among the Mexican population." They also assisted "various Anarchist institutions" with financial support and have "done quite some work" on behalf of Sacco and Vanzetti. The group even promised Spivak they would "run an entertainment" for the English-language anarchist newspaper, the *Road to Freedom*. It cooperated broadly with the other anarchist organizations in Los Angeles while organizing Mexican workers.[33]

The Mexican anarchist group's efforts brought life to the Confederación de Uniónes Obreros Mexicanos (CUOM) in Los Angeles in 1927, the realization of the confederation attempted three years earlier in 1924. It had twenty-two local chapters the next year with around three thousand members. The CUOM by far surpassed any other anarchist labor-organizing effort in this period. Other anarchists in the city focused on propaganda rather than forming worker-led organizations. Similar to prior efforts to organize agricultural workers by the AFL and the IWW, the CUOM survived only a couple of seasons, but this latest anarchist-led effort "helped spur the formation of the first permanent Mexican agricultural union."[34]

Street-level protests began to reemerge in Los Angeles in the late 1920s, especially on behalf of imprisoned anarchists Nicola Sacco and Bartolomeo Vanzetti, but police allowed leftists much less space to operate. Before a protest in support of Sacco and Vanzetti in August 1927, police preemptively arrested "all the active members of the conference." This did not stop hundreds of people from turning up at the plaza: "The police were forced to be represented in full force. They had to recall all the men from their vacation to guard the city and prevent the demonstration." Anarchists and remaining IWW members attended this demonstration with a growing number of communists. Police arrested Mortimer Downing, the anarchist Pietro Gandolfo, and two communists. Authorities released Downing but detained Gandolfo with the communists. They charged the Italian under the alien anarchist law, and he faced deportation. International Ladies' Garment Workers' Union organizer and anarchist Anna Sosnovsky served as point-woman for a campaign on his behalf.[35]

In October 1927 anarchists held a conference in Los Angeles with the "purpose of bringing our various language speaking groups together." Members of "English, Spanish, Italian, Jewish, and Russian groups" from the city attended and discussed organizing tactics for creating a stronger movement. Charles Sprading suggested that "we have to use new methods if we want to succeed. Our propaganda must be done in an indirect way. We ought to call ourselves Libertarians and try to do propaganda in every field." Sprading had entered local politics in the 1920s and this fit well within his outlook, but many anarchists did not think highly of his views. Enrique Flores Magón wrote dismissively of Sprading to Stephanus Fabijanović the previous year: "I am not surprised about Sprading becoming a politician, for I never thought much of him."[36]

At the conference, Anna Sosnovsky strongly disagreed with Sprading as she lectured on the history of anarchism in the United States. She argued: "We must not fear to do open propaganda as Anarchists. To call ourselves Libertarians will not solve the problem. Indirect methods in our work will bring little results." Mortimer Downing "outlined the plan for local activities," while Tom Bell urged his comrades to concentrate on English-language organizing. Wanda Tiger, the secretary of the conference, wrote: "It is a recognized fact that the English speaking Anarchists movement throughout the United States is in a difficult position and the time is ripe that steps be taken to overcome this evil. It is high time to make a systematic effort to acquaint the masses with our ideal."[37]

The conference served as a catalyst for a new radical center, the Libertarian Center, which had a meeting hall, a library, and other rooms in Boyle Heights a few blocks from the prior location. Anarchists used the building for educational work and to provide space for the regular Monday night lectures of the Free Workers Forum, in its sixth year in 1928. One writer noted that the conference also resulted in "co-operation and harmony" between the various active language groups in the city. Continuing local cooperation at a second conference the following year (1928), the coalition of anarchists in Los Angeles resolved to support the organizing of Mexican anarchists: "The sense of the conference is to encourage the co-operation of the Libertarian Center with other language groups and also to encourage the activities of the Spanish group in their work among the Spanish workers of Los Angeles and vicinity."[38]

The IWW managed spurts of organizing in the late 1920s as well, and the young Byron Kitto emerged as one of the most energetic members during this period. He went to Boston as an official representative of the IWW in 1927 to assist in the ultimately doomed last-minute attempts to save the lives of Sacco and Vanzetti. He then traveled to Colorado during the statewide coal strike, where authorities arrested him. Once out on bail, he came to Los Angeles to await trial; in Los Angeles he led the effort to form a local committee to support the Colorado efforts. Mary Gallagher remembered that his "disregard for fine oratory made his speeches more convincing. His hurried, youthful declamation interspersed with current slang phrases lent fire to his address as he described the horrors he had seen in the homes and the environment of the Colorado strikes." He returned to Colorado to face the charges after a month in Los Angeles. A jury convicted him; and he caught pneumonia after being transferred to jail and then contracted tuberculosis during his time in prison. After serving out his sentence, he returned to Los Angeles aboard a freight train, where he fought his illness for two and a half years before eventually succumbing in March 1931. As a fitting end to the life of an itinerate IWW organizer, his comrades held memorial services for him in Los Angeles and San Francisco, California, and Lafayette and Columbine, Colorado.[39]

The Emergency Program faction of the IWW had been based in Los Angeles since 1924, but without a public voice. Mortimer Downing led the fundraising effort to finance a new IWW newspaper. It went to press in 1927 with the title *New Unionist*. The first issue of the new paper called for workers to "Strike as One for Sacco-Vanzetti." The paper also continued Los Angeles's and the IWW's connection to Mexican radicalism by publicizing the arrest of Librado Rivera and others in the group Hermanos Rojas in Tamaulipas, Mexico.[40]

Librado Rivera remained active in Mexico after his release from American prison and deportation in 1923. In 1927 Mexican authorities arrested Rivera and his comrades at the offices of the paper *Sagitario* in Tampico. The *Road to Freedom*'s editors wrote fondly of their friend: "Rivera is an old fighter and was active in this country where he spent more than five years in jail in Leavenworth Penitentiary, whence he was released to be deported to Mexico, where he took up the fight again."[41] Rivera joined the group that published *Sagitario* soon after his deportation from the United States. In the newspaper, Rivera was "unsparing in his criticism of Calles and Obregón, especially as regards their brutal and inhuman campaign of extermination against the Yaquis." His attention to indigenous struggle continued from the height of PLM organizing.[42]

The *Road to Freedom* published a letter from Librado Rivera while he sat in Andonegui Penitentiary, Tampico, "this socialist Bastille" of the Calles administration. Rivera declared: "Since the very moment that the present Calles administration in agreement with the ex-president Alvaro Obregon declared a war of extermination against the Yaqui Indians a year ago, I have been writing against this infamous crime. . . . This infamous massacre of human beings has continued since September, 1926, and to the present time there is no sign to be stopped. And as 'Sagitario' took the task in denouncing this government's crime that was the cause to put me behind bars."[43] Mexican authorities released Rivera after seven months, in large part because of the intense international protests organized on his behalf by anarchists. The newspaper *Cultura Proletaria* took the lead in this campaign, while in Los Angeles Aaron Rogat organized a fundraiser for him.[44]

The two anarchist conferences and all the other organizing resulted in tangible successes, but the radical community continued to fluctuate and reform in the late 1920s. Tom Bell wrote that in this "old town of Los Angeles, though the great mass of those Jewish comrades who before the Russian Revolution thought themselves Anarchists have melted away into support of the Bolsheviki or into despair."[45] Despite the efforts to integrate the various language groups of Los Angeles's anarchist community, members of the Yiddish group seemed content to organize among themselves. The Kropotkin Literary Society had "about 60 members" in 1927 when Rudolf Rocker and Saul Yanovsky, the former editor of *Fraye Arbeter Shtime*, visited Los Angeles on a lecture tour. This same year, Joseph Spivak criticized the group for being "extreme right in their psychology and go with the right Socialist wing hand in hand in every question." Spivak also chastised the KLS for not aiding the *Road to Freedom* because it made "the same mistake as all the foreign language speaking groups, in not being interested in the English propaganda."[46] In 1928 the KLS organized lectures by "three different former Anarchist editors" in Yiddish; between 150 and six hundred people attended the talks. At the end of the last lecture the group asked for those in attendance to attend the weekly English-language anarchist meetings, but only five did so the next week. Bell characterized this with clear frustration: "Anarchism which deals with American conditions rather than those of their native land, which is suited to American psychology rather than to Jewish, leaves them cold."[47] The organization of these groups indicates the persistence of language and/or ethnic organizing by anarchists in the 1920s. Most sought to build affinities between groups, but some organizations maintained distinct organizational priorities and could be insular.

Tom Bell contrasted this tendency with the growing number of people moving toward English-language organizing: "The English-speaking group here contains people of American, English, Scotch, French, German, Italian, Mexican, Serbian, Lithuanian, and Russian birth or extraction. And, of course, many Jews. They unite not to put forth a 'selfish nationalist psychology,' but to influence the people of the country they live in." Further, Bell argued, "I do not think that my ability to deal with them is due merely to the fact that I am an 'Anglo-Saxon' myself. I come across comrades of foreign birth—Jews, Germans, what-not—who are just as skillful in their approach and as successful in getting a hearing. It is not a question of the country in which he really 'lives'—of what language he thinks in, of papers he reads, of what literature he is steeped in, of where his interest lies, of his acceptance of the idea that he is one of its people—no longer a member of a superior race." He concluded, "I used to talk English with a Scotch accent: now I am sure my accent is distinctly Jewish. The bulk of my friends and comrades have been Yiddishers." But he believed that the high proportion of Jews in the American anarchist movement hindered the development of what he characterized as a "'native' libertarianism."[48]

Alfred Sanflteben continued to work diligently, as he had for decades, to foster his vision of cosmopolitanism locally and in his column "International Notes" in the *Road to Freedom* in the 1920s. For example, he wrote "in Peking and in Shanghai Korean anarchists amongst the folks in exile who devote their lives to the translation and publication of the anarchist classics." He also brought the recent trial of nine Korean anarchists by the Japanese forces occupying Seoul, which the occupying force renamed Hang Tchen, to the attention of his English-language audience.[49] Sanflteben persisted in connecting English readers to the world movement through his pen.

The Reordering of Radical Los Angeles

The late 1920s into the 1930s brought a generational shift in the anarchist community as the life cycle of fin de siècle radicals ended. Tom Bell struggled with this issue in 1928 when he commented on the appearance of the new anarchist newspaper *Rising Youth*, "I am not one of those propagandists who have failed so wretchedly or become so discouraged that in their sixties they think their experience worth less than nothing and stand willing to hand over the guidance of the movement to the young just because the young are youthful." On the other hand, he wrote, "I have no respect for the old merely because it is senile. The Anarchist-Communism of Kropotkin was developed in his Conquest of Bread at least fifty years ago. To my own knowledge it has been dead for at least twenty-five years. What can we do with it now? *Give it a decent and honorable burial*." He concluded with, "Let us bury it with all due respect. And then let the mourners gather round the grave and start a new and different anarchism—a libertarian movement suited to the time and the place, a libertarianism of the present day here in America."[50]

The multiethnic anarchist movement faced competition on many fronts. The rise of fascism divided Italians. The growing influence of Zionism among Jews surely stripped anarchism of new adherents. Many Jews joined the Communist Party, making up around half of its membership ranks in its first two decades of existence. Kenyon Zimmer found that the growth of anti-Semitism in the United States also "coupled with increasing persecution of European Jewry and the promise of the Balfour Declaration, contributed to a dramatic rise in support for Zionism. The growth of both of these movements came in part at the expense of anarchism."[51] Andrew Cornell argued "that the anarchist movement was placed in competition with, and came under attack by, the communists and the fascists immediately after having been repressed in the Western democracies was of grave significance."[52] The 1920s into the 1930s brought the regeneration and then decline of the anarchist and syndicalist movements, while the Communist Party gradually found its footing in the United States and Mexico.

Interracial organizing continued, but the IWW and anarchists increasingly found themselves displaced and on the outside of tangible local-labor organizing. In the Imperial Valley, long home to Mexican and Anglo IWW organizing in Holtville and Brawley, the Trade Union Unity League (TUUL), organized by the Communist Party in 1928, assisted the Mexican Mutual Aid Association in organizing strikes in 1928 and 1930. The multiracial strike saw eight thousand Mexicans, Filipinos, and Chinese workers, including women and children, "militantly picketing."[53] The Communist Party also increased its position among Mexicans in Los Angeles during this period. The party organized two demonstrations in the summer of 1929; each drew crowds of more than two thousand.[54]

On March 6, 1930, the Communist Party and the TUUL led a march as part of their "Organize the Unemployed Campaign." Nationally more than a million people took to the street that day; estimates of the crowd in Los Angeles reached around ten thousand.[55] During these years communist labor organizing picked up where earlier efforts left off in their willingness to work with the region's cosmopolitan laborers. Carey McWilliams remembered one meeting of walnut workers in the early 1930s during communist-led organizing campaign directed at agricultural workers: "I saw faces which I shall never forget. It was a huge meeting, with a dozen or more nationalities being represented. The Chairman was a Russian girl, eighteen years old, who used a hammer for a gavel, and presided as a veteran. The remarks of the speakers had to be translated into many languages: Russian, Armenian, Spanish. But the impression I carried away from the meeting, as of many similar meetings, was of superb faces, a sea of faces: strong, impressive, unforgettable."[56]

In Los Angeles, African Americans organized with the Communist Party in a formal way in greater numbers than with anarchists, socialists, or craft unions. African Americans participated in the communist-led street demonstrations in 1930 across the country and locally in Los Angeles. Later, during the Great Depression, Thomas "Ace" Walton, "a black leader of the Los Angeles Unemployed Council, organized demonstrations (which were often violently suppressed) against the discriminatory administration of the county relief program."[57] Ishmael Flory, a graduate of UC-Berkeley, also participated in Los Angeles's Communist Party and joined the National Students League, a student organization at UCLA. When Langston Hughes moved to Los Angeles in the early 1930s, he lived with Loren Miller, and they both joined the city's John Reed Club.[58]

Through the 1920s the old-guard IWW and anarchists in Los Angeles continued to develop their criticism of the Soviet Union and the Communist Party in their city, which laid the intellectual groundwork for the anticommunist left in the following decades. Nationally, "Communism, fascism, and Zionism all outflanked libertarian socialism among America's immigrants, and for several years, the public face of the anarchist movement was reduced to the struggle to save the lives of Sacco and Vanzetti—a struggle that forced anarchists into unhappy alliances with Communist and liberal allies."[59]

These conflicts also took local form. On one occasion Tom Bell criticized the communist paper the *Daily Worker* for practicing the "same yellow journal fashion as Hearst does his. Not the slightest care that the stuff should bear any resemblance to the truth." He gave as an example: "Does a brute of a cop beat a Communist in Los Angeles? Next day you can read of 'Communists in Los Angeles Battle the Police.'" He also characterized communists in Los Angeles as being primarily Russian, "the men to whom Communism had became [*sic*] not only a matter of principle but also a matter of patriotism," but he argued that "the old movements if not American were always international."[60]

The onset of the Great Depression hit the anarchist movement in Los Angeles hard, cashed-strapped as it was in the best of times, and institutions withered. Bell wrote to Alexander Berkman: "Despite the devoted efforts of quite a number of good comrades I am afraid that this year we shall not be able to achieve much in a financial way. I am sure that is not because—certainly not because—they are working less; but because the general financial situation in the city is so bad, so very bad. Unemployment is widespread. No, the unemployment does not seem to arouse the workers as some of us always thought it would do."[61]

The Open Forum continued from the previous decade as the primary remaining English-language anarchist institution in Los Angeles. In June 1931 the group held a banquet to honor Alexander Berkman, who had not set foot in the United States since his deportation in 1919. With great joy Tom Bell described the event to his friend Berkman in a letter: "Yes, it was a great event, the finest we have had here for quite a while. No, not the biggest, because when we get up the Arrestanten Ball, with dancing and such attractions we get a bigger crowd. But last night was the most enthusiastic most heart-warming we have had for a very long time. We held it in our own hall. The publicity was almost all by invitation circular." The group charged only fifty cents to attend the gathering because "times are hard." These gatherings were mostly social affairs attended by activists who had struggled alongside each other for decades; they maintained the radical community that struggled forward into the 1930s. Berkman's "own pupil," I. Kushner, spoke first at the gathering. Bell wrote that "Kushner was at one time an opponent of mine in regard to Russian affairs; his own common-sense in the long run brought him round. No, he remains a Socialist Party man; but he does much excellent work among them and is thoroughly disillusioned about the USSR." Upton Sinclair declined to attend with sharp words for Berkman's anti-Soviet criticism.[62]

The month after this banquet, the Open Forum organized a protest meeting: "Quite a lot of different bodies are in it—at least nominally—from the Armenians, the social Revolutionaries to the IWW." The group held it in the hall of the American Civil Liberties Union. Joe Ettor was the biggest draw, and he spoke along with a new young Socialist Party secretary named Busick, Mortimer Downing, and Thomas Bell. Bell recalled about the famous IWW organizer, "Joe is not an Anarchist, but is quite strongly opposed to Communism." Opposition to communism brought them together, and Bell had recently given a lecture titled "The

Failure of the Five Year Plan."[63] Tension developed before this meeting between various factions, upon which Bell reflected: "Unfortunately the Socialist Party had allowed the affair to fall into the hands of the Civil Liberties Union. Its director wanted to arrange the affair entirely his own way, as an ordinary meeting of the Sunday forum. We put up a fight and broke off with him, but unluckily Joe Ettor came to me to say that he had already advertised it among the Italians." Despite this a "very fair crowd" attended.[64] Ettor eventually "became a wealthy man in the wine industry" in California, but one longtime Wobbly supporter remembered that "he never lost contact with the I.W.W. and would go to their meetings and keep in touch with their work."[65]

Though this event drew a crowd, the general decline of the previous dominant groups in Los Angeles was clear. As Tom Bell saw the situation in 1931: "The Socialists have picked up a bit but it has been mainly due to one or two active young members. The IWW survives only a few devoted old guards who will not let it go down altogether so long as they are alive; but they are making up the split that took place several years ago."[66] Bell also wrote:

> The other radical bodies are mere vestiges of what they used to be. It saddens to go to a Wobbly affair: Mortimer Downing keeps together a score in the emergency section, but there does not appear to me more than a dozen in the other lot. They are gone. The communists have a large proportion of the young Russian-Jewish element. With a lot of what is not very different from nationalism influencing them, but they have also much devotion—developed here in the last three years or so—and are going to jail freely. Bitter intolerance, blind faith, much ignorance, but devotion beyond question.

Always the cosmopolitan, Bell ended his letter with "a young Korean comrade has just come in to talk to me; I must close."[67]

In the 1930s the Kropotkin Literary Society's membership fluctuated and the new membership consisted of mostly Jewish arrivals to Los Angeles. Spanish and Italian anarchists also organized with the society in "very small groups."[68] Joe Ettor and Mortimer Downing, along with the Libertarian Group in Los Angeles, organized a convention of the industrial unions in the United States with the hope of moving past the IWW to start a new umbrella organization of industrial unionism. The IWW local in Los Angeles attempted to organize WPA and aqueduct workers in 1930s, but this too met with little success. The Socialist Party in Los Angeles fared better, but it also found it difficult to raise money to sustain itself. Rose Pesotta's work in the ILGWU was the most successful jobsite-based organizing by an anarchist in Los Angeles in the 1930s. She helped organize Mexican dressmakers who walked off the job in 1933.[69]

William Trautmann, one of the most prominent men in the foundation of the IWW, lived in Los Angeles in 1931 and worked with Mary Gallagher and her husband to organize a theater group for unemployed artists. The theater group became part of the California Theater Guild, "which afterwards was submerged in the Federal Theater Project." Gallagher remembered that Trautmann became very interested in New Deal policies: "He took a great interest in the Roosevelt Administration," and "was in constant communication with officials of the W.P.A."[70] In the early 1930s Alfred Sanftleben took an active interest in more immediate local concerns and worked at Goodwill Industries supervising disabled workers.[71]

The 1930s brought difficult times in Mexico as well. In 1933 an aging Enrique Flores Magón wrote to his longtime friend and comrade Ralph Chaplin asking if he could write a regular column for the *Industrial Worker*. He had fallen on difficult times and asked for support. Sick and without work because he was blacklisted, Flores Magón recalled that we was "too known to go under assumed names, as I did in [the] U.S. in factories, shops, fields, mines and wherever I worked." He wrote to his comrade that "there was a day when at 4 o'clock P.M. I had not been able to bring home a piece of bread; my children were still without breadfast [*sic*]. Their lips were white and trembling." He did receive some assistance from an old friend, Juan José Ríos, "who was under [Flores Magón] in 1906, at the head of the group of conspirators at San Juan del Rio" in Zacatecas. In 1933 José Ríos served as Secretary of the Interior for President Pascual Ortiz Rubio, and Enrique wrote, "He likes me and remembers when we were in the same boat, as rebels against Porfirio Díaz.[72]

Many of the aging members of the PLM maintained their activism into this decade. Tom Bell recalled of Fernando Velarde in the early 1930s that "his fine family all of them are still active in the I.W.W. movement."[73] This included his son Guillermo, leader of the Confederación de Uniónes de Campesinos y Obreros Mexicanos (CUCOM), which brought forward the efforts of the CUOM a few years earlier. Guillermo maintained IWW membership while leading the CUCOM. This new organization received assistance from the Confederación Regional Obrera Mexicana (CROM). At the end of 1935 a new Spanish-language anarchist newspaper briefly surfaced in Los Angeles, titled *El Luchador*. The paper's connection to earlier Mexican anarchism was clear in an article about the PLM in the paper's third issue as well as an English page edited by members of the Libertarian Center.[74]

In 1933, longtime member of the Los Angeles left Stephanus Fabijanović died from stroke complications. Born in 1868 in what became Yugoslavia, he lived a typically mobile life. He did not attend school, but he learned the trade of baker, and after finishing compulsory military service he began his life of travels. He first

Conclusion

met his friend Alfred Sanflteben in Zurich in 1894. They met again in London in 1897, the year Fabijanović came to the United States. Fabijanović "crossed the country in every direction, ever studying, as occasion offered, working at his trade, belonging to its union to the end, serving it often in responsible positions of trust." The man's "many wanderings led him to Canada, Mexico, the Far East, and Australia." He met his wife at a rally in Seattle where Emma Goldman spoke. The couple then settled in Los Angeles: "Here they have suffered bitter hunger in the years of busted prosperity, but also read the best of books."[75]

His comrades held his funeral as the ILGWU were out on strike. Alfred Sanftleben wrote, "The comrades came in good numbers to the funeral hall, Comrade [Mortimer] Downing speaking for organized labor, Slovak [Sanftleben] for the outcasts and as mere man. At the crematory Slovak spoke once more, followed by old faithful [Tom] Bell who tendered parting greeting on behalf of the ever dwindling number of the old guard."[76] Reflecting on the difficult times in the early 1930s, Alexander Berkman wrote to Bell from Nice, France: "It is only that one has not the energy and vitality to take a more active part in the movement, nothing to compare with the vitality of past years. But such is life. Moreover, it is time to give the new generation a chance. If they would only grab it!"[77]

■ ■ ■

The radical movement in Los Angeles demonstrated its resilience after World War I by publishing newspapers, forming broad coalitions, and speaking publicly to advance its ideals. The commitment of individuals, the strength of solidarity networks, the incorporation of the movement's affinity practices into regional working-class culture, and the continued relevance of radical alternatives to the state and capitalism prolonged the anarchist and syndicalist movements into the 1920s and 1930s. However, the public face of these movements obscured their slow decline. Anarchists and the IWW exerted much less influence in local labor organizing or on the street level politics in Los Angeles than in past decades; they gradually moved to the sidelines throughout the 1920s, taking positions as intellectual forces on the left in opposition to capitalism, the state, and now communism and fascism. Having lived through the organized mass slaughter of World War I and the resurgence of nationalism that birthed fascism in the 1930s, many aging radicals surely believed that their dream of a better world had died before their own passing.

It would be a mistake to assume that anarchism died along with this generation of its proponents. A small number of anarchists carried their ideals forward. In Los Angeles anarchism remained an intellectual current in the pages of the *Roman Forum*, a new periodical published in the city. Rudolf Rocker moved to Los Angeles in the 1930s, drawn by supporters in the Kropotkin Literary Society, out

Conclusion

of which formed the Rocker Publications Committee. The group translated and published his seminal monograph, *Nationalism and Culture*, in 1937. In a chapter examining the connection between scientific racism and European nations Rocker wrote, "Belief in race becomes the most brutal violence to the personality of man, a base denial of all social justice."[78] When Rocker turned seventy in 1943, the Rocker Publications Committee printed a booklet to record the occasion. After thanking the KLS, *Freie Arbeiter Stimme*, the Stelton Modern School Group, and the Associated Roman Forums for support, it drew readers' attention to the "host of others among Eastern Americans, British, German, Spanish, Portuguese, Scandinavian, Dutch, and even Chinese groups can not be overlooked."[79] Although Rocker moved to the East Coast, the remnants of the KLS stayed together into the 1940s. Small groups of Mexican anarchists also continued to meet in the 1940s and 1950s, and the IWW held group picnics into the 1940s.[80]

While it is possible to trace currents of anarchist organizing forward in time, the rich cultural tradition of mutual solidarity is the most important lasting contribution of early-twentieth-century radicalism in Los Angeles. Anarchists, syndicalists, and socialists brought interracial, multilingual, and international organizing to the center of regional working-class culture through their struggle to bring their visions of a new social and economic order into reality. As these movements declined, future activists retranslated these practices into interracial labor and civil rights organizing that continued through the century. This book illustrates that the pull of cooperation could be stronger than the will for division for many residents of Los Angeles. A culture of affinity is their legacy.

NOTES

Abbreviations

Archives of Labor	Archives of Labor and Urban Affairs, Wayne State University, Detroit
Bancroft	Bancroft Library, University of California, Berkeley
CA State	The California State Library, Sacramento, California
IISH	The International Institute of Social History, Amsterdam, Netherlands
Labadie Collection	Joseph A. Labadie Collection, Special Collections Library, University of Michigan, Ann Arbor
NARA	National Archives and Records Administration, Archives I, Washington D.C.
NACP	National Archives at College Park, Maryland
NAR	National Archives at Riverside, California
Post Office Records	Records of the Post Office Department; Entry 40, Records Relating to the Espionage Act, World War I, 1917–1921; Records Group 28; NARA
Urban Archives	Urban Archives Center, California State University, Northridge

Introduction

1. *Regeneración*, April 26, 1913.

2. "Pedro Coria to W. H. Westman," June 28, 1961, Industrial Workers of the World Collection, box 17, folder 43, Archives of Labor.

Notes

3. "Letter from Pedro Coria," March 2, 1946, Industrial Workers of the World Collection, box 17, folder 42, Archives of Labor.

4. McWilliams, *Southern California Country*, 315.

5. Fogelson, *Fragmented Metropolis*; Davis, *City of Quartz*; Sitton and Deverell, *Metropolis in the Making*.

6. Monroy, *Rebirth*; Sanchez, *Becoming Mexican American*; Deverell, *Whitewashed Adobe*; Flamming, *Bound for Freedom*; Sides, *L.A. City Limits*; Modell, *Economics and Politics*.

7. Kurashige, *Shifting Grounds of Race*, 12.

8. Bernstein, *Bridges of Reform*; Wild, *Street Meeting*.

9. Kurashige, *Shifting Grounds of Race*, 12.

10. Edwards, *Practice of Diaspora*, 4.

11. Horne, *Black and Brown*, 72.

12. Garcia, *A World of Its Own*, 6, 7; Lipsitz, *Dangerous Crossroads*.

13. McWilliams, *Factories in the Field*, 217.

14. Here the notion of "articulation" advanced by Stuart Hall is helpful. See Grossberg, "On Postmodernism and Articulation"; Hall, "Notes on Deconstructing."

15. Zimmer, *Immigrants against the State*, 4. Original emphasis.

16. Contemporary sociologists define social movements "as collectivities acting with some degree of organization and continuity outside of institutional or organizational channels for the purpose of challenging or defending extant authority, whether it is institutionally or culturally based, in the group, organization, society, culture, or world order of which they are a part." See Snow, Soule, and Kriesi, *Blackwell Companion*, 11.

17. *Common Sense*, February 6, 1909.

18. *Industrial Worker*, January 15, 1910.

19. *Mother Earth* 11, no. 6 (August 1916): 576.

20. Day, *Gramsci Is Dead*, 14.

21. Löwy, *Redemption and Utopia*, 148–49.

22. Bullock and Jennings, *Walter Benjamin*, 40; Löwy, *Redemption and Utopia*, 97, 100.

23. Levy, *Gramsci and the Anarchists*, 229; Anderson, "Antinomies of Antonio Gramsci"; Genovese, *Roll, Jordan, Roll*; Scott, *Weapons of the Weak*.

24. Kelley, "We Are Not What We Seem"; Scott, *Domination*.

25. Scott, *Art of Not Being Governed*, x.

26. Ibid., 38.

27. Goethe, *Elective Affinites*; Howe, "Max Weber's Elective Affinities"; Löwy, *Redemption and Utopia*; McKinnon, "Elective Affinities."

28. Swedberg, *Max Weber Dictionary*, 83.

29. Anderson, *Under Three Flags*, 2.

30. Kropotkin, "Anarchism."

31. Owen, *Anarchism Versus Socialism*, 10–11.

32. Graeber, *Fragments*, 6.

33. Cohn, *Underground Passages*, loc. 263–65.

34. Faure, "Affinité."

35. Bookchin, *Spanish Anarchists*, 178.

Notes

36. Kinna, "Anarchism."

37. Solnit, *Paradise Built in Hell*. Other useful studies are Bamyeh, *Anarchy as Order*; Day, *Gramsci Is Dead*.

38. Berlin, *Many Thousands Gone*, 66.

39. Linebaugh and Rediker, *Many-Headed Hydra*, 181.

40. Ibid., 228.

41. Frykman, "Mutiny on the Hermione," 177.

42. Trotter, *Coal, Class, and Color*, 112; Corbin, *Life, Work, and Rebellion*; Gutman, *Work, Culture, and Society*; Lewis, *Black Coal Miners*; Montgomery, *Fall of the House of Labor*.

43. Mellinger, *Race and Labor*, 167.

Chapter 1. Economic Development, Immigration, and the "Labors of Expropriation"

1. Testimony of Aurelio Vincente Azuara in "U.S. vs. Haywood, et al., 1918," Industrial Workers of the World Collection, box 114, item 1, Archives of Labor.

2. Andrew Furuseth and O. A. Tveitmoe, "Letter to American Federation of Labor," in "Proceedings of the Twelfth Annual Convention of the California State Federation of Labor," Bakersfield, California, October 2–6 1911, 77, CA State.

3. Linebaugh and Rediker, *Many-Headed Hydra*, 42.

4. Madley, *American Genocide*, loc. 181–83.

5. Hernández, *City of Inmates*, 9.

6. Igler, *Industrial Cowboys*, 116.

7. Ibid.; Peck, *Reinventing Free Labor*; Sackman, *Orange Empire*; Street, *Beasts of the Field*; Truett, *Fugitive Landscapes*.

8. Pitt, *Decline of the Californios*; McWilliams, *Factories in the Field*, 24; Igler, *Industrial Cowboys*, 60–61, 182; Heilbroner, *Worldly Philosphers*, 188.

9. Igler, *Industrial Cowboys*, 61.

10. Ibid., 63; Street, *Beasts of the Field*, 184.

11. Garcia, *World of Its Own*, 28.

12. Gutiérrez, *Walls and Mirrors*, 41–42.

13. Ibid., 41; Sanchez, *Becoming Mexican American*, 21–22; Lewis, *Iron Horse Imperialism*; Orsi, *Sunset Limited*; Street, *Beasts of the Field*, 575; Murray, *Canadian Pacific Railway*, 86.

14. Erie, *Globalizing L.A.*, 47–50.

15. Fogelson, *Fragmented Metropolis*, 20, 121.

16. Erie, *Globalizing L.A.*, 50.

17. Ibid., 53; Fogelson, *Fragmented Metropolis*, 108–34.

18. Erie, *Globalizing L.A.*, 53–54, 57; Fogelson, *Fragmented Metropolis*, 112–18.

19. Erie, *Globalizing L.A.*, 47.

20. Ibid., 51–2; Fogelson, *Fragmented Metropolis*, 118; Garcia, *World of Its Own*, 25.

21. Davis, "Sunshine and the Open Shop," 97.

22. Ibid., 99; Erie, *Globalizing L.A.*, 61–62.

23. Erie, *Globalizing L.A.*, 61–63; Fogelson, *Fragmented Metropolis*, 119.

Notes

24. Wild, *Street Meeting*, 17–19.

25. Modell, *Economics and Politics*, 22.

26. Lee, *At America's Gates*; Kurashige, *Shifting Grounds of Race*; Modell, *Economics and Politics*; Ngai, *Impossible Subjects*; Garcia, *World of Its Own*; Gutiérrez, *Walls and Mirrors*; Monroy, *Rebirth*; Sanchez, *Becoming Mexican American*; Crosby, "Italians of Los Angeles"; Lothrop, "Italians of Los Angeles"; Sokoloff, *Russians in Los Angeles*; Vorspan and Gartner, *History of the Jews*; Flamming, *Bound for Freedom*.

27. Garcia, *World of Its Own*, 35.

28. Parker, *Casual Laborer*, 173.

29. Testimony of Aurelio Vincente Azuara in *U.S. vs. Haywood et al.*, 1918, Industrial Workers of the World Collection, box 114, item 1, Archives of Labor.

30. Benton-Cohen, *Borderline Americans*, 100, 225; University of Arizona, "The Bisbee Deportation 1917: A University of Arizona Web Exhibit," http://www.library.arizona.edu/exhibits/bisbee.

31. Kern, *Culture of Time and Space*.

32. Peck, *Reinventing Free Labor*, 47.

33. Ibid., 80.

34. Lee, *At America's Gates*, 6.

35. Street, *Beasts of the Field*, 408.

36. Ibid., 407.

37. Wild, *Street Meeting*, 24.

38. This number differs from the nativity figure from census data in table 1. Changes in census categories and undercounts underrepresented Mexicans. See: Sanchez, *Becoming Mexican American*, 90; Monroy, *Rebirth*; Weber, *Dark Sweat, White Gold*, 54; Wild, *Street Meeting*, 30.

39. Garcia, *World of Its Own*, 77; Gutiérrez, *Walls and Mirrors*, 40, 43; Sanchez, *Becoming Mexican American*, 43; McWilliams, *North from Mexico: The Spanish-Speaking People of the United States* (New York: Greenwood Press, 1990), 197; Benjamin, "Rebuilding the Nation," 470.

40. Igler, *Industrial Cowboys*, 133; Crosby, "Italians of Los Angeles"; Lothrop, *Chi Siamo*; Igler, *Industrial Cowboys*, 136; Lothrop, "Italians of Los Angeles," 36; Lothrop, *Fulfilling the Promise*; Wild, *Street Meeting*, 28–29.

41. Kurashige, *Shifting Grounds of Race*, 18.

42. Flamming, *Bound for Freedom*, 47–50, 62, 70–78, 96.

43. Kurashige, *Shifting Grounds of Race*, 81–82.

44. Hernández, "Hobos in Heaven," 440.

45. Monroy, *Rebirth*, 99.

46. Estrada, *Los Angeles Plaza*; Wild, *Street Meeting*.

47. McEuen, "Mexicans in Los Angeles," 76, 70.

48. *El Mosquito*, August 25, 1906.

49. *El Correo Mexicano*, March 14, 1914.

50. McEuen, "Mexicans in Los Angeles," 70, 76.

Notes

51. *El Correo Mexicano*, March 14, 1914.

52. "Corn husks for tamales, acorns from Nogales, Sonora, dried meat from Baja California, fresh cheese from Mocorito, and tomatoes from Mochis, Sinaloa State, Mexico." *El Correo Mexicano*, March 14, 1914.

53. Kurashige, *Shifting Grounds of Race*, 72.

54. Box 2776, file 10110, Military Intelligence Division, Department of War, Record Group 165, NACP.

55. Estrada, *Los Angeles Plaza*, 293n80.

56. Kurashige, *Shifting Grounds of Race*, 72.

57. Sides, *L.A. City Limits*, 6.

58. Wild, *Street Meeting*, 33.

59. Flamming, *Bound for Freedom*, 64.

60. Wild, *Street Meeting*, 31.

61. Nicolaides, *My Blue Heaven*, 25.

62. Kurashige, *Shifting Grounds of Race*, 34.

63. Nicolaides, *My Blue Heaven*, 41.

64. Weber, *Dark Sweat, White Gold*, 55.

65. Deverell, *Whitewashed Adobe*, 154.

66. Flamming, *Bound for Freedom*, 214.

67. Davis, *City of Quartz*, 227–28.

Chapter 2. Creating Connections through Radical Practices

1. Interview with Marion Bell in Avrich, *Anarchist Voices*, 30.

2. Anderson, *Imagined Communities*.

3. Kuhn, *Radical Space*, 5, 6.

4. For a discussion of the AFL political participation see Greene, *Pure and Simple Politics*.

5. Stimson, *Labor Movement in Los Angeles*, 33, 43, 194.

6. *Citizen*, January 20, 1911.

7. Perry and Perry, *Los Angeles Labor Movement*, 21.

8. Laslett, *Sunshine Was Never Enough*, 83–152; Perry and Perry, *Los Angeles Labor Movement*, 193–236.

9. Stimson, *Labor Movement in Los Angeles*, 286–88.

10. *Citizen*, April 9, 1909.

11. Hirsch, *Empire of Nations*.

12. Greenstein, Lennon, and Rolfe, *Bread and Hyacinths*, 37; Stevens, *Radical L.A.*, 45.

13. *Common Sense*, March 23, 1907; *Common Sense*, February 20, 1909; Lomnitz, *Comrade Ricardo Flores Magón*, 79, 133.

14. *Common Sense*, February 20, 1909; *Common Sense*, February 27, 1909; *Common Sense*, March 20, 1909.

15. Zimmer, *Immigrants against the State*, 37.

16. *Common Sense*, February 20, 1909.

Notes

17. Ibid.

18. *Citizen*, March 3, 1911; *Common Sense*, March 23, 1907; Cross, *Labor Movement in California*, 274.

19. *Common Sense*, March 23, 1907.

20. Kraft, "Job Harriman's Socialist Party," 49; Stimson, *Labor Movement in Los Angeles*, 362; Laslett, *Sunshine Was Never Enough*, 54.

21. Greenstein, Lennon, and Rolfe, *Bread & Hyacinths*, 116–21; Murrah, "Llano Cooperative Colony," 92.

22. *Industrial Worker*, January 8, 1910, 2.

23. Shor, "Virile Syndicalism."

24. "Fred Thompson to Nick Steelink," October 23, 1977, box 10, folder 11, Fred Thompson Papers, Archives of Labor; Foner, "Reverend George Washington Woodbey," 154.

25. *International Socialist Review*, September, 1917.

26. Archives of Labor, Fred Thompson Papers, box 14, file 9; Botkin, *Frank Little and the IWW*.

27. Chaplin, *Wobbly*, 195.

28. Rosemont, *Joe Hill*, 237.

29. *Industrial Union Bulletin*, March 2, 1907; Weber, "Wobblies," 265; Zimmer, "Whole World Is Our Country," 238.

30. *Common Sense*, September 23, 1905; *Common Sense*, July 28, 1906; *Industrial Worker*, April 30, 1910; Weintraub, "I.W.W. In California," 22–23, 281.

31. "Rips the Mask from 'Unemployed' Riots," *Los Angeles Times*, December 27, 1913; *El Rebelde*, May 12, 1917; *New Unionist*, May 7, 1917.

32. Parker, *Casual Laborer*, 189.

33. Rosemont, *Joe Hill*, 126.

34. Teiser, *Ethel Duffy Turner*, 22.

35. *El Mosquito*, August 25, 1906; Kanellos, "Spanish-Language Anarchist Periodicals," 71.

36. *Regeneración*, February 22, 1913.

37. Guglielmo, "Transnational Feminism's Radical Past," 12.

38. "Mailing List—Regeneración," case 1071, box 60; Federal Court Records, Southern District of California, Southern Division (Los Angeles), Criminal Case Files, Records Group 21, NAR; "Mailing List—La Jacquerie," 1920, case file 61-4184, Bureau of Investigation Case Files, 1908–1922, Records Group 65, NACP; Davis, "Sunshine and the Open Shop," 105–7.

39. "*Circular*," n.d., Max Nettlau Papers, folder 3374, IISH; *Road to Freedom*, October 1, 1926; *Road to Freedom*, December 1928; *El Luchador*, February 1, 1936.

40. *Regeneración*, January 3, 1914; Estrada, *Los Angeles Plaza*.

41. Wild, *Street Meeting*, 148–75.

42. *Regeneración*, April 13, 1913.

43. *Industrial Worker*, June 24, 1909.

44. *Common Sense*, June 30, 1906; *Common Sense*, June 15, 1907.

45. Estrada, *Los Angeles Plaza*, 135.

46. *Los Angeles Times*, December 28, 1913.

Notes

47. *California Social-Democrat*, March 28; *California Social-Democrat*, April 4, 1914; "'Unemployed' Threaten More Bloody Rioting," *Los Angeles Times*, March 21, 1914; "'Hobos' Pleas Are Postponed," *Los Angeles Times*, April 1, 1914; Perry and Perry, *Los Angeles Labor Movement*, 13–15.

48. Bird, Georgakas, and Shaffer, *Solidarity Forever*, 44–45; Brissenden, *I.W.W.*, 338.

49. Street, *Beasts of the Field*, 539.

50. Lomnitz, *Comrade Ricardo Flores Magón*, 144.

51. Amato, *On Foot*; Rebecca Solnit, *Wanderlust*.

52. Lomnitz, *Comrade Ricardo Flores Magón*, 212.

53. File 50527, Post Office Records; File 50267, Post Office Records.

54. File 49864, Post Office Records.

55. File 49387, Post Office Records.

56. File 50058, Post Office Records.

57. *Regeneración*, November 26, 1910; *Regeneración*, April 1, 1911; *Regeneración*, December 4, 1915; *Regeneración*, November 11, 1916.

58. *Huelga General*, March 7, 1914.

59. "IWW Newspapers," Mapping American Social Movements, University of Washington, http://depts.washington.edu/iww/newspapers.shtml; *El Rebelde*, February 5, 1915; *El Rebelde*, March 18, 1916.

60. *El Rebelde*, March 18, 1916; *El Rebelde*, June 24, 1916; *El Rebelde*, March 17, 1917.

61. *Regeneración*, September 14, 1912; *Regeneración*, February 10, 1912.

62. Shaffer, "Havana Hub," 53.

63. *Regeneración*, April 1, 1911.

64. Albro, *Always a Rebel*, 33.

65. Henkin, *Postal Age*, 21.

66. Ibid., 22.

67. Albro, *Always a Rebel*, 50; Poole, *Land and Liberty*, 117; United States Congress, House of Representatives, Communist and Anarchist Deportation Cases, "Hearings before a Subcommittee of the Committee on Immigration and Naturalization," 66th Congress, 2nd Session, April 21 to 24, 1920, 109; "Mailing List—Regeneración," case 1071, box 60; Federal Court Records, Southern District of California, Southern Division (Los Angeles), Criminal Case Files, Records Group 21, NAR; Sandos, *Rebellion in the Borderlands*, 59.

68. *Road to Freedom*, June 1932.

69. "Mailing List—Regeneración," case 1071, box 60; Federal Court Records, Southern District of California, Southern Division (Los Angeles), Criminal Case Files, Records Group 21, NAR; *Industrial Worker*, June 3, 1909.

70. "Letter from C. A. Whitney to *The Blast*," May 30, 1916, Alexander Berkman Papers, folder 112, IISH.

71. *Freedom* (New York), August 1933.

72. "Note from Walter Sheridan to Alexander Berkman," June 19, 1916, Alexander Berkman Papers, folder 112, IISH.

73. McEuen, " Mexicans in Los Angeles," 88.

74. Kanellos, "Spanish-Language Anarchist Periodicals," 71.

Notes

75. McEuen, "Mexicans in Los Angeles," 88.

76. *Germinal,* June 14, 1917; File 47701, Post Office Records; Shaffer, "Tropical Libertarians."

77. File 47474, Post Office Records.

78. "Memorandum to Mr. Bielaski," January 22, 1918, Bureau of Investigation Case Files, 1908–1922, Records Group 65, microfilm 1085, case OG 56693, roll 413, NACP; Wilson, "I.W.W. in California," 40.

79. *Cogito, Ergo Sum,* September 15, 1908.

80. *Cultura Proletaria,* July 23, 1910.

81. *Common Sense,* January 12, 1907.

82. Ibid., November 24, 1906.

83. Ibid., October 26, 1907.

84. Ibid., July 25, 1908.

85. *People's Paper,* January 13, 1911; Franck, *Vagabond Journey*; Peter Kropotkin, "Autobiography of a Revolutionist," *Atlantic Monthly* 83, no. 395 (1899).

86. *People's Paper,* January 27, 1911; Johnson, *Revolution in Texas,* 61; Turcato, "Italian Anarchism," 413; Dubofsky, *We Shall Be All,* 188.

87. Mormino and Pozzetta, *Immigrant World of Ybor City,* 97.

88. Anderson, *Under Three Flags,* 96n65.

89. "Communist and Anarchist Deportation Cases," 109.

90. "W. H. Yoakum RE: 'Cultura Obrera,' Spanish Newspaper, I. W. W. Activities," June 13, 1918, Bureau of Investigation Case Files, 1908–1922, Records Group 65, microfilm 1085, case OG 56693, roll 413, NACP.

91. "Edward Fulton to William C. Owen," July 8, 1928, William C. Owen Archive, folder H. J. Stuart, IISH.

92. *Citizen,* February 19, 1909.

93. *Common Sense,* March 30, 1907.

94. Shaffer, "Tropical Libertarians," 303.

95. Shaffer, "Latin Lines and Dots."

96. Rosenthal, "Radical Border Crossers," 63.

97. *Road to Freedom,* December 1926.

98. Ibid.

99. Zimmer, *Immigrants against the State,* 4–5.

100. Conolly-Smith, *Translating America,* 290n32.

101. Stamm, "Space for News," 60.

102. Shaffer, "Havana Hub," 76.

Chapter 3. Solidarity and the Legacy of Exclusion

1. Jew, "Anti-Chinese Massacre of 1871"; Zesch, *Chinatown War.*

2. Saxton, *Indispensable Enemy.*

3. Hernández, *City of Inmates,* 85.

4. Street, *Beasts of the Field,* 451.

5. Stimson, *Labor Movement in Los Angeles,* 227–8.

Notes

6. Federal Writers' Project, *Unionization of Migratory Labor*; Federal Writers' Project, *Oriental Labor Unions and Strikes*, 209, 227.

7. Almaguer, *Racial Fault Lines*, 187; Street, *Beasts of the Field*, 443, 452.

8. *People's Paper*, March 28, 1903.

9. Street, *Beasts of the Field*, 446.

10. Ibid., 446–49; Almaguer, *Racial Fault Lines*, 189–90.

11. *People's Paper*, March 28, 1903; Street, *Beasts of the Field*, 451.

12. *Ventura Free Press*, March 6, 1903, quoted in Street, *Beasts of the Field*, 808; *People's Paper*, March 28, 1903; Murray, "Foretaste of the Orient," 74; Street, *Beasts of the Field*, 451, 455–57, 808n35.

13. *People's Paper*, March 28, 1903; Street, *Beasts of the Field*, 454–57.

14. *People's Paper*, March 28, 1903; Street, *Beasts of the Field*, 458.

15. *People's Paper*, April 4, 1903; "Bloody Union Rioting and Hail of Bullets," *Los Angeles Times*, March 24, 1903; "Labor Trouble Still Brews at Oxnard," *Los Angeles Times*, March 27, 1903; Street, *Beasts of the Field*, 458.

16. "Outlook at Oxnard Blue Last Night," *Los Angeles Times*, March 26, 1903.

17. "Labor Trouble Still Brews at Oxnard."

18. Murray, "Foretaste of the Orient," 75; *People's Paper*, April 4, 1903; "Singular Outrages Allowed in Oxnard," *Los Angeles Times*, March 29, 1903; Street, *Beasts of the Field*, 460.

19. "Oxnard," *Los Angeles Times*, March 28, 1903. "The Strike Breakers: A Story Containing More Recent History than Fiction," n.d., John Murray Papers, box 1, Bancroft.

20. Murray, "Foretaste of the Orient," 75.

21. "Singular Outrages Allowed in Oxnard."

22. "Labor Situation Grave at Oxnard," *Los Angeles Times*, March 25, 1903.

23. Street, *Beasts of the Field*, 461.

24. *People's Paper*, April 4, 1903.

25. *People's Paper*, April 4, 1903; *People's Paper*, April 18, 1903.

26. *People's Paper*, April 18, 1903.

27. *People's Paper*, April 4, 1903.

28. "Indorsed Rioting," *Los Angeles Times*, March 26, 1903.

29. *Oakland Tribune*, April 21, 1903. Qtd. in Federal Writers' Project, "Oriental Labor Unions."

30. *People's Paper*, April 4, 1903.

31. Murray, "Foretaste of the Orient," 79.

32. "Encourage Small Industries," *Los Angeles Times*, March 25, 1903.

33. *Los Angeles Socialist*, May 2, 1903.

34. Escobar, "Chicano Protest and the Law," 208.

35. *People's Paper*, May 2, 1903; Stimson, *Labor Movement in Los Angeles*, 267.

36. *People's Paper*, May 2, 1903; Garcílazo, *Traqueros*, 95–102; Wollenberg, "Working on El Traque"; Friedricks, "Capital and Labor in Los Angeles"; Stansbury, "Organized Workers," 287; Gomez-Quinones, *Mexican American Labor*, 78.

37. *People's Paper*, May 2, 1903; Monroy, *Rebirth*, 8. On Teresa Urrea see Irwin, *Bandits, Captives, Heroines, and Saints*; Vanderwood, *Power of God*.

38. *People's Paper*, May 2, 1903.

Notes

39. "Fiesta Plot at a Finis," *Los Angeles Times*, May 12, 1903.

40. Stimson, *Labor Movement in Los Angeles*, 250.

41. Ibid.

42. *People's Paper*, May 9, 1903.

43. *Los Angeles Socialist*, May 16, 1903.

44. *People's Paper*, May 2, 1903.

45. "Another Defeat for Trouble-Promoters," *Los Angeles Times*, April 30, 1903.

46. Escobar, "Chicano Protest and the Law," 208.

47. *People's Paper*, May 2, 1903.

48. Ibid.

49. "Another Defeat for Trouble-Promoters."

50. *People's Paper*, April 18, 1903; *People's Paper*, May 2, 1903.

51. Flamming, *Bound for Freedom*, 73–78.

52. "Another Defeat for Trouble-Promoters."

53. "New Schemes of Agitators," *Los Angeles Times*, May 3, 1903.

54. Street, *Beasts of the Field*, 462–43.

55. Murray, "Foretaste of the Orient," 78.

56. "Are to Bolt the Caucus," *Los Angeles Times*, July 28, 1902.

57. *People's Paper*, June 13, 1903.

58. Ibid.

59. *People's Paper*, April 18, 1903; "Gompers Slaps Japs," *Los Angeles Times*, May 24, 1903; Street, *Beasts of the Field*, 567.

60. *People's Paper*, June 13, 1903.

61. *People's Paper*, August 29, 1903.

62. "Agitating Peons," *Los Angeles Times*, April 13, 1904.

63. Stimson, *Labor Movement in Los Angeles*, 267.

Chapter 4. Internationalism and its Limits

1. *Mother Earth*, July 1907.

2. *Mother Earth*, November 1907; Goldman, *Living My Life*, 400–402.

3. *Common Sense*, March 23, 1907.

4. Lothrop, *Chi Siamo*, 13; Lothrop, "Italians of Los Angeles"; Estrada, *Los Angeles Plaza*, 95.

5. Bufe and Verter, *Dreams of Freedom*, 347.

6. Fredrickson, *Racism*, 5–6. Original emphasis.

7. *Common Sense*, July 1, 1905.

8. *Common Sense*, July 15, 1905.

9. Ibid.

10. *Common Sense*, September 23, 1905.

11. *Common Sense*, October 28, 1905.

12. *Common Sense*, July 28, 1906; *Common Sense*, June 30, 1906; *Common Sense*, April 21, 1906; Weintraub, "I.W.W. in California," 17, 281.

Notes

13. *El Mosquito*, May 4, 1906; *El Mosquito*, August 25, 1906.

14. *El Mosquito*, August 25, 1906.

15. *El Mosquito*; Stimson, *Labor Movement in Los Angeles*, 306.

16. Weber, *Dark Sweat, White Gold*, 110.

17. *Common Sense*, January 12, 1907.

18. *Common Sense*, February 20, 1909.

19. Turner, *Ricardo Flores Magón*, 138; Weber, "Wobblies," 188–226.

20. *Common Sense*, June 30, 1906.

21. *Common Sense*, May 4, 1907.

22. *Common Sense*, March 23, 1907.

23. *Mother Earth*, November 1909.

24. *Common Sense*, May 25, 1907.

25. *Common Sense*, June 15, 1907.

26. Ibid.; Foner, *Black Socialist Preacher*, 23, 243.

27. *Common Sense*, May 25, 1907.

28. Flamming, *Bound for Freedom*, 25–26.

29. *Common Sense*, January 12, 1907.

30. *Common Sense*, February 9, 1907.

31. *Common Sense*, February 16, 1907.

32. *Common Sense*, February 1, 1908.

33. *Citizen*, June 19, 1908.

34. *Citizen*, July 17, 1908. The article was credited to the *United Mine Worker*.

35. *Citizen*, November 18, 1910.

36. *Emancipator*, November 1906.

37. *Emancipator*, May 1907.

38. Wayne, *Women's Rights*, 57.

39. *Emancipator*, November 1906.

40. Ibid.; Konishi, *Anarchist Modernity*.

41. *People's Paper*, September 21, 1907.

42. *Common Sense*, March 2, 1907.

43. *People's Paper*, September 14, 1907; Lee, "Hemispheric Orientalism."

44. McWilliams, *Factories in the Field*, 139.

45. Albro, *Always a Rebel*, 7; Lomnitz, *Comrade Ricardo Flores Magón*, 83; Weber, "Wobblies," 202.

46. "Ricardo Flores Magón to Harry Weinberger," May 9, 1921, Max Nettlau Papers, folder 3400, IISH.

47. "*Program y Manifesta*," *Regeneración*, July 6, 1906.

48. *Regeneración*, November 14, 1914; *Regeneración*, November 28, 1914; Axelrod, "St. Louis"; Salerno, *Red November, Black November*, 83; Turner, *Ricardo Flores Magón*, 72.

49. *Regeneración*, April 15, 1906; *Mother Earth*, April 1911; Albro, *Always a Rebel*, 50; Poole, *Land and Liberty*, 117.

50. "Ricardo Flores Magón to Harry Weinberger," May 9, 1921, IISH.

51. Ibid.; Hernández, *City of Inmates*, 110.

Notes

52. Hernández, *City of Inmates*, 110; "Thomas Furlong Director (Furlong's Secret Service Co) to M. E. Diebold, *Consul Mexicano*," St. Louis, Missouri, November 23, 1906, Diego Abad de Santillan Papers, folder 381, IISH; Records of the Department of Justice, Records Group 60, Straight Numerical File 90755, box 713, NACP; Albro, *Always a Rebel*, 32; Raat, *Revoltosos*, 190–91; Turner, *Ricardo Flores Magón*, 14.

53. *Regeneración*, July 6, 1906.

54. Ibid., October 22, 1910. Plank 15: "Es inútil declarar en el Programa que debe dares preferencia al mexicana sobre el extranjero, en igualdad de circunstancias, pues esto está ya consignado en nuestra Constitución. Como medida eficaz para evitar la preponderancia extranjera y garantizar la integridad de nuestro territorio, nada parece tan conveniente como declarar ciudadanos mexicanos á los extranjeros que adquieran bienes raíces."

55. *Regeneración*, October 22, 1910. Plank 16: "La prohibición de la inmigración china, es, ante todo, una medida de protección á los trabajadores de otras nacionalidades, principalmente á los mexicanos. El chino, dispuesto por lo general á trabajar con el más bajo salario, sumiso mezquino en aspiraciones, es un gran obstáculo para la prosperidad de otros trabajadores. Su competencia es funesta, y hay que enitarla en México. En general, la inmigración china no produce á México el menor beneficio."

56. Chang, *Chino*, loc. 718–19.

57. *Ibid.*, loc. 778–80.

58. Ibid., loc. 706–7.

59. Ibid., loc. 1995–97.

60. Hart, *Revolutionary Mexico*, 6–7.

61. *Common Sense*, October 12, 1907.

62. *Regeneración,* September 3, 1910.

63. *Regeneración,* October 8, 15, and 22, 1910. The translations continued sporadically until Alfred Sanftleben resigned. *Regeneración* printed his resignation letter on December 24, 1910.

64. Lomnitz, *Comrade Ricardo Flores Magón*, 256, 275–6.

65. *Regeneración*, September 23, 1911; Bufe and Verter, *Dreams of Freedom*, 139.

66. Chang, *Chino*, loc. 219–20.

67. Katz, *Pancho Villa*, 593.

68. Ibid., 626.

69. Ibid., 630. See also Delgado, "At Exclusion's Southern Gate"; Lee, "Orientalisms in the Americas."

70. *El Correo Mexicano*, March 14, 1914.

71. "Nip Revolutionists in Los Angeles Den," *Los Angeles Times*, August 24, 1907; Albro, *Always a Rebel*, 84.

72. Brissenden, *I.W.W.*, 170–75; Dubofsky, *We Shall Be All*, 99–105; Foner, *History of the Labor Movement*, 45–59.

73. *Common Sense*, September 21, 1907.

74. *Common Sense*, July 25, 1908. The other parallel was the case of Manuel Sarabia, who was arrested by Arizona Rangers without warrant and illegally deported to Mexico in June 1907. His supporters forced his return to the United States. See Albro, *Always a Rebel*, 81–84.

Notes

75. *Common Sense,* September 21, 1907

76. Ibid.

77. *Common Sense,* November 16, 1907;

78. *Common Sense,* January 25, 1908.

79. *Common Sense,* February 6, 1909.

80. *Citizen,* January 22, 1909.

81. *Citizen,* February 5, 1909.

82. *Regeneración,* May 27, 1911.

83. *Common Sense,* January 30, 1909; *Common Sense,* February 27, 1909.

84. *Common Sense,* February 20, 1909.

85. *Common Sense,* February 27, 1909.

86. Ibid.; *Common Sense,* March 20, 1909; *Common Sense,* April 3, 1909.

87. *Common Sense,* January 25, 1908.

88. *Common Sense,* September 19, 1908.

89. *People's Paper,* November 4, 1910.

90. *People's Paper,* December 21, 1907.

91. *Mother Earth,* July 1910.

92. *Man!,* December–January, 1936–37.

93. Elison, "Kōtoku Shūsui," 449.

94. *People's People,* February 17, 1911 (this issue named the periodical *Progressive Woman*).

95. Kōtoku Denjirō, *Diary of a Voyage to America,* qtd. in Elison, "Kōtoku Shūsui," 451.

96. *Industrial Worker,* November 24, 1910.

97. *People's Paper,* February 3, 1911.

98. Antonioli, *Dizionario Biografico,* 2:68.

99. Goldman, *Living My Life,* 474.

100. *Industrial Worker,* January 15, 1910.

Chapter 5. Organizing Mobile Workers

1. Andrews, *Shoulder to Shoulder?* 17.

2. Daniel, *Bitter Harvest,* 78.

3. "Proceedings of the Tenth Annual Convention of the California State Federation of Labor," San Rafael, California, October 4–8 1909, California History Room, CA State, 45.

4. Ibid., 56.

5. Ibid., 72.

6. Ibid., 55.

7. "Proceedings of the Twelfth Annual Convention of the California State Federation of Labor," Hill's Theatre, Bakersfield, California, October 2–6, 1911, California History Room, CA State, 77.

8. Ibid., 72.

9. "Proceedings of the Eleventh Annual Convention of the California State Federation of Labor," Los Angeles, California, October 3–7, 1910, California History Room, CA State, 45.

Notes

10. Federal Writers' Project, *Oriental Labor Unions and Strikes*, 7.

11. *Doctrina Anarquista-Socialista*, July 30, 1905; Carey, "Vessel, Deed, Idea," 56; Casanovas i Codina, "Pedro Esteve," 73; Salerno, *Red November, Black November*, 50; Acuña, *Corridors of Migration*, 109, 112–18; Mellinger, *Race and Labor*, 33–58; Gordon, *Great Arizona Orphan Abduction*, 229; Lomnitz, *Comrade Ricardo Flores Magón*, 133.

12. *La Union Industrial*, October 7, 1911; *Cultura Proletaria*, May 7, 1910; "Memorandum to Mr. Bielaski," January 22, 1918, Bureau of Investigation Case Files, 1908–1922, Records Group 65, microfilm 1085, case OG 56693, roll 413, NACP.

13. Weber, "Wobblies," 265; Weber, "Different Plans," 10–28.

14. *Revolt*, March 16, 1912; Weber, "Wobblies," 225, 227; Turner, *Ricardo Flores Magón*, 159.

15. Struthers, "IWW Internationalism," 79; Botkin, *Frank Little and the IWW*.

16. *Citizen*, February 5, 1909; *Common Sense*, February 20, 1909.

17. *Songs of the Workers*.

18. Cole, Struthers, and Zimmer, "Introduction," in *Wobblies of the World*, 18.

19. Industrial Workers of the World, "Proceedings," 403–4; Weintraub, "I.W.W.," 8.

20. U.S. Commission on Industrial Relations, *Industrial Relations*, 5:103.

21. Weintraub, "I.W.W.," 278.

22. *Industrial Worker*, February 26, 1910.

23. Bird, Georgakas, and Shaffer, *Solidarity Forever*, 51–52.

24. *Industrial Worker*, October 1, 1910.

25. Federal Writers' Project, *Oriental Labor Unions and Strikes*, 7.

26. *Industrial Worker*, February 26, 1910.

27. Lewis, "Drift in California."

28. Weintraub, "I.W.W.," 59.

29. "Mexicans Go on Strike," *Los Angeles Times*, March 2, 1910; Cross, *Labor Movement in California*, 281.

30. *Industrial Worker*, May 7, 1910.

31. Ibid., *Industrial Worker*, August 20, 1910; *Industrial Worker*, September 3, 1910.

32. *Road to Freedom*, June 1932; Mellinger, *Race and Labor*, 89; Weintraub, "I.W.W.," 117.

33. *Industrial Worker*, June 11, 1910.

34. *Industrial Worker*, November 2, 1910.

35. "Proceedings, Eleventh Annual Convention," 54.

36. "Proceedings, Twelfth Annual Convention," 77.

37. "Proceedings, Eleventh Annual Convention," 54.

38. Ibid., 62.

39. Laslett, *Sunshine Was Never Enough*, 56–57.

40. Stimson, *Labor Movement in Los Angeles*, 373–74.

41. "Proceedings, Eleventh Annual Convention," 54–55.

42. *People's Paper*, November 11, 1910.

43. Lewis, "Basis of Solidarity."

44. *Regeneración*, November 5, 1910; "Proceedings of the Fourteenth Annual Convention of the California State Federation of Labor," Fresno, California, October 6–11, 1913, California History Room, CA State, 73.

Notes

45. *Regeneración*, November 5, 1910; *Regeneración*, November 12, 1910; *People's Paper*, November 11, 1910; *Citizen*, November 11, 1910.

46. *Citizen*, November 11, 1910.

47. Letter Librado Rivera to Nicolás [Bernal?], May 12, 1924, Diego Abad de Santillan Papers, packet 234.

48. *People's Paper*, November 11, 1910.

49. *Regeneración*, December 10, 1910.

50. Ibid.

51. Zimmer, "Cosmopolitan Crowd."

52. *Regeneración*, December 3, 1910; December 17, 1910; December 31, 1910; March 25, 1911.

53. *Regeneración*, December 3, 1910

54. *Citizen*, August 2, 1912; "Proceedings, Twelfth Annual Convention," 68; "Minutes: Los Angeles County Central Labor Council Executive Board and Council Meetings," February 3, 1911, and July 26, 1912, Urban Archives.

55. "Proceedings, Twelfth Annual Convention," 68.

56. *Citizen*, September 29, 1911.

57. *Citizen*, September 1, 1911; Stimson, *Labor Movement in Los Angeles*, 336, 364; Douglas Flamming, "African-Americans and the Politics of Race in Progressive-Era Los Angeles," in *California Progressivism Revisited*, ed. William Deverell and Tom Sitton (Berkeley: University of California Press, 1994), 220; Stevens, *Radical L.A.*, 72.

58. Flamming, *Bound for Freedom*, 52–56; Street, *Beasts of the Field*, 386.

59. *Industrial Worker*, September 21, 1911.

60. "Proceedings, Twelfth Annual Convention," 68.

61. *Industrial Worker*, September 21, 1911.

62. "Proceedings, Twelfth Annual Convention," 69.

63. Ibid., 77.

64. Ibid., 103, 106–8; "Proceedings of the Thirteenth Annual Convention of the California State Federation of Labor," Germania Hall, San Diego, California, October 7–12 1912, California History Room, CA State, 98, 105; "Minutes: Executive Board."

65. "Proceedings, Thirteenth Annual Convention," 66.

66. "Proceedings, Twelfth Annual Convention," 103, 106–8; McEuen, "Mexicans in Los Angeles," 27.

67. "Proceedings, Thirteenth Annual Convention," 97; Lewis, "Organization of the Unskilled," part 1, 876.

68. "Proceedings, Thirteenth Annual Convention," 86.

69. "Proceedings, Fourteenth Annual Convention," 68.

70. Lewis, "Organization of the Unskilled," part 1, 881.

71. Ibid., 877.

72. Lewis, "Organization of the Unskilled," part 2, 960.

73. Ibid., 962.

74. Lewis, "Organization of the Unskilled," part 1, 880.

75. "Proceedings, Eleventh Annual Convention," 48.

76. "Proceedings, Twelfth Annual Convention," 101.

Notes

77. Lewis, "Organization of the Unskilled," part 1, 878.

78. Lewis, "Organization of the Unskilled," part 2, 956.

79. Ibid., 959.

80. "Proceedings, Eleventh Annual Convention," 52.

81. "Proceedings, Twelfth Annual Convention," 77.

82. "Proceedings, Fourteenth Annual Convention," 56, 50.

Chapter 6. The Baja Raids

1. *Industrial Worker*, September 24, 1910; Dubofsky, *We Shall Be All*, 188; Wilson, "I.W.W.," 12; Estrada, *Los Angeles Plaza*, 140.

2. Lomnitz, *Comrade Ricardo Flores Magón*, 329–35; Blaisdell, *Desert Revolution*; Cánovas, *Ricardo Flores Magón*; Ceballos, *¿Se Aproderará Estados Unidos?*; Cockcroft, *Intellectual Precursors*; López, "El Poblado Fronterizo de Tijuana"; Santillan, *Ricardo Flores Magón*; Turner, *Ricardo Flores Magón*.

3. Lomnitz, *Comrade Ricardo Flores Magón*, 319.

4. Weber, "Wobblies," 191.

5. Truett and Young, "Making Transnational History"; Young, *Catarino Garza's Revolution*, 3.

6. Young, *Catarino Garza's Revolution*, 78–86.

7. Ibid., 98.

8. Ibid., 189.

9. Ibid., 4.

10. *Road to Freedom*, June 1932.

11. Lomnitz, *Comrade Ricardo Flores Magón*, 52.

12. Albro, *Always a Rebel*, 58–64.

13. Lomnitz, *Comrade Ricardo Flores Magón*, 268.

14. Teiser, *Ethel Duffy Turner*, 11–12.

15. Albro, *Always a Rebel*, 107.

16. "W. H. H. Llewellyn to Attorney General Charles Joseph Bonaparte," October 24, 1908, Straight Numerical File 90755, box 713, Records of the Department of Justice, Records Group 60, NACP.

17. Lomnitz, *Comrade Ricardo Flores Magón*, 179–91; Streeby, *Radical Sensations*; Turner, *Barbarous Mexico*.

18. Lomnitz, *Comrade Ricardo Flores Magón*, 243, 249; Weber, "Wobblies," 200.

19. "Llewellyn to Bonaparte," October 24, 1908.

20. Albro, *Always a Rebel*, 103.

21. Teiser, *Ethel Duffy Turner*, 22.

22. Lomnitz, *Comrade Ricardo Flores Magón*, 179–91; Sandos, *Rebellion in the Borderlands*, 58–59.

23. Lomnitz, *Comrade Ricardo Flores Magón*, 320; Weber, "Different Plans"; Weber, "Wobblies."

24. *Industrial Worker*, December 22, 1910.

Notes

25. *Industrial Worker*, July 16, 1910.

26. *Road to Freedom*, June 1932.

27. Teiser, *Ethel Duffy Turner*, 13; "Notes on the Life of John Kenneth Turner," Ethel Duffy Turner Papers, box 1, folder: Notes on the Life of John Kenneth Turner, Bancroft.

28. Investigation of Mexican Affairs, Preliminary Report and Hearings of the Committee on Foreign Relations, United States Senate, Pursuant to S. Res. 106, S.Doc.285, 66th Congress, 2nd Session, 2 vols., May 24, 1920, 2514. Hereafter "Mexican Affairs."

29. Avrich, *Anarchist Voices*, 502; Zimmer, "Anarchist, Informant, Fascist, or American?"

30. Pernicone, "War among the Italian Anarchist," 79.

31. *Al Compagni*, August 20, 1909, Max Nettlau Papers, folder 3379, IISH; Avrich, *Sacco and Vanzetti*, 52; Lomnitz, *Comrade Ricardo Flores Magón*, 269.

32. *Regeneración*, December 10, 1910; Bufe and Verter, *Dreams of Freedom*, 355.

33. As early as November 1907 the PLM newspaper *Revolución* published a short biography of Peter Kropotkin, calling him a "Russian Hero" (November 23, 1907).

34. *Regeneración*, December 10, 1910.

35. Lomnitz, *Comrade Ricardo Flores Magón*, 288.

36. Teiser, *Ethel Duffy Turner*, 24.

37. "Mexican Affairs," 2511.

38. Teiser, *Ethel Duffy Turner*, 24.

39. Weber, "Wobblies," 190.

40. "Mexican Affairs," 2508; "Interview of Sam Murray by Ethel Duffy Turner," January 11, 1955, Ethel Duffy Turner Papers, folder: Joe Hill, box 1, Bancroft Library, University of California, Berkeley.

41. *People's Paper*, January 27, 1911.

42. Lomnitz, *Comrade Ricardo Flores Magón*, 269; Bufe and Verter, *Dreams of Freedom*, 356; Teiser, *Ethel Duffy Turner*, 23.

43. *Imperial Valley Press*, March 25, 1911; Blaisdell, *Desert Revolution*, 39, 48; Lomnitz, *Comrade Ricardo Flores Magón*, 321; Turner, *Revolution in Baja California*, 6.

44. Hart, *Revolutionary Mexico*, 243; Lomnitz, *Comrade Ricardo Flores Magón*, 335; Turner, *Revolution in Baja California*, 20.

45. *Regeneración*, February 25, 1911.

46. Lomnitz, *Comrade Ricardo Flores Magón*, 335.

47. "Mexican Affairs," 2515.

48. Blaisdell, *Desert Revolution*, 74–77; Lomnitz, *Comrade Ricardo Flores Magón*, 321.

49. Zimmer, "Forgotten Revolution"; Ramnath, *Haj to Utopia*, 46, 66–67.

50. Horne, *Black and Brown*, 135; Lomnitz, *Comrade Ricardo Flores Magón*, 320; Turner, *Revolution in Baja California*, 35.

51. "Mexican Affairs," 2509; Blaisdell, *Desert Revolution*, 44–45.

52. *Imperial Valley Press*, April 15, 1911; *Industrial Worker*, April 27, 1911; "Mexican Affairs," 2508; Blaisdell, *Desert Revolution*, 39, 51, 74–75, 82, 109; Lomnitz, *Comrade Ricardo Flores Magón*, 320–21; Griswold del Castillo, "Discredited Revolution."

53. "Mexican Affairs," 2509; Humphries, *Gringo Revolucionary*; Blaisdell, *Desert Revolution*, 99; Vanderwood, "Writing History with Picture Postcards."

Notes

54. "Interview of Sam Murray," Bancroft Library.

55. "Mexican Affairs," 2515; *Imperial Valley Press*, June 17, 1911; Blaisdell, *Desert Revolution*, 181.

56. *Regeneración*, May 20, 1911.

57. Ibid., May 27, 1911.

58. *Cultura Proletaria*, June 17, 1911.

59. "Fred Thompson to Nick Steelink," October 23, 1977, box 10, folder 11, Fred Thompson Papers, Archives of Labor; Foner, "Reverend George Washington Woodbey"; Blaisdell, *Desert Revolution*, 123.

60. *Regeneración*, June 13, 1914; *Regeneración*, April 29, 1911; *Regeneración*, December 23, 1911; Fuentes, "Battleground Women"; Poniatowska, *Las Soldaderas*; Turner, *Revolution in Baja California*, 66–67; Weber, "Keeping Community," 221–22.

61. Weber, "Wobblies," 215.

62. "Ricardo Flores Magon to Eulalio A. Basa and Joaquin Ramos," May 4, 1911, Archivo Electrónico Ricardo Flores Magón, http://archivomagon.net/obras-completas/correspondencia-1899-1922/c-1911/cor323; Blaisdell, *Desert Revolution*, 110–11; *Industrial Worker*, June 8, 1911; "Jack Mosby Badly Injured," *New York Times*, May 3, 1911.

63. "Ricardo Flores Magón to Pedro Esteve," May 3, 1911, Archivo Electrónico Ricardo Flores Magón, http://archivomagon.net/obras-completas/correspondencia-1899-1922/c-1911/cor324; *L'Era Nuova*, June 24, 1911; *Regeneración*, May 20, 1911; Blaisdell, *Desert Revolution*, 124; Turner, *Revolution in Baja California*, 44–45.

64. "Ricardo Flores Magón to Pedro Esteve," May 22, 1911, Archivo Electrónico Ricardo Flores Magón, http://archivomagon.net/obras-completas/correspondencia-1899-1922/c-1911/cor325.

65. *Regeneración*, May 20, 1911.

66. *Cronaca Sovversiva*, September 11, 1911; *Regeneración*, February 24, 1912; *Il Contropelo*, February, 1912; Presutto, *La rivoluzione dietro l'angolo*, 48.

67. Blaisdell, *Desert Revolution*, 180–81; Lomnitz, *Comrade Ricardo Flores Magón*, 329.

68. Lomnitz, *Comrade Ricardo Flores Magón*, 363; Taylor, "Magonista Revolt in Baja California"; Griswold del Castillo, "Discredited Revolution."

69. Lomnitz, *Comrade Ricardo Flores Magón*, 326–27, 351.

70. Herzog, *Where North Meets South*, 107; Vanderwood, *Juan Soldado*, 85–86.

71. *Cronaca Sovversiva*, June 17, 1911; Samaniego López, "El Poblado Fronterizo de Tijuana"; Presutto, *La rivoluzione dietro l'angolo*, 50–69.

72. *L'Era Nuova*, June 24, 1911; The separate Italian edition of *Regeneración* continued until October 28, 1911 and the Italian language column through April 6, 1912.

73. *Cultura Proletaria*, August 19, 1911; *Cultura Proletaria*, September 2, 1911.

74. *Cronaca Sovversiva*, January 6, 1912; Peter Kropotkin, *Words of a Rebel* (Montreal: Black Rose Books, 1992).

75. *Cronaca Sovversiva*, January 6, 1912.

76. Knight, *Mexican Revolution*, 175–79.

77. *Cronaca Sovversiva*, January 6, 1912.

78. Ibid.

Notes

79. Ibid.

80. *Les Temps Nouveaux*, May 20, 1911; *Les Temps Nouveaux*, May 27, 1911; *El Luchador*, February 1936.

81. *Les Temps Nouveaux*, July 1, 1911.

82. *Les Temps Nouveaux*; *Les Temps Nouveaux*, July 8, 1911.

83. *Les Temps Nouveaux*, July 22, 1911; *Les Temps Nouveaux*, August 19, 1911.

84. *Les Temps Nouveaux*, September 23, 1911.

85. *Les Temps Nouveaux*, September 30, 1911.

86. Max Nettlau, "Anarchist Activities in Mexico," Max Nettlau Papers, IISH, 456–57.

87. *Les Temps Nouveaux*, July 1, 1911; *Les Temps Nouveaux*, August 19, 1911; *Les Temps Nouveaux*, September 30, 1911; *Les Temps Nouveaux*, November 18, 1911; *Regeneración*, February 3, 1912; *Cronaca Sovversiva*, February 17, 1912; Presutto, *La rivoluzione dietro l'angolo*, 84–85.

88. *Les Temps Nouveaux*, February 3, 1912; *Les Temps Nouveaux*, April 27, 1912; *L'Era Nuova*, May 11, 1912; Nettlau, "Anarchist Activities in Mexico"; Presutto, *La rivoluzione dietro l'angolo*, 122.

89. *Freedom* (London), February, 1912.

90. *Freedom* (London), March, 1912.

91. W. C. Owen, "The Coast Crisis: An Argument Justifying Socialists Anti-Chinese Agitation," *Labor Enquirer*, March 6, 1886.

92. Lomnitz, *Comrade Ricardo Flores Magón*, 256, 128–29.

93. England, "Magonismo," 244.

94. *Regeneración*, October 1, 1910; Lomnitz, *Comrade Ricardo Flores Magón*, 202; Malatesta, *Fra Contadini*.

95. *Industrial Worker*, August 10, 1911; Stimson, *Labor Movement in Los Angeles*, 373–74; Greenstein, Lennon, and Rolfe, *Bread and Hyacinths*, 55.

96. *Industrial Worker*, August 10, 1911.

97. Ibid.

98. Shanks, "I.W.W. Free Speech Movement"; Dubofsky, *We Shall Be All*, 197–97; Foner, *Black Socialist Preacher*, 27–30.

99. *Freedom* (London), February 1912.

100. *Regeneración*, March 9, 1912; *Regeneración*, July 8, 1911. He also spoke in New York City: see *Mother Earth*, April 1912.

101. "Mexican Affairs," 2518.

102. "Revolutions in Mexico: Hearing before a Subcommittee of the Committee on Foreign Relations," United States Senate; Pursuant to S. Res. 335, 62nd Congress, 2nd session, G.P.O., 1913, 252; Lomnitz, *Comrade Ricardo Flores Magón*, 457; MacLachlan, *Anarchism and the Mexican Revolution*, 47.

103. Cockcroft, *Intellectual Precursors*; Knight, *Mexican Revolution*, 45–47.

Chapter 7. A Culture of Affinity

1. "'Unemployed' Threaten More Bloody Rioting," *Los Angeles Times*, March 21, 1914. The *Los Angeles Times* reproduced portions of the article from the *Los Angeles Record*.

Notes

2. Kraft, "Fall of Job Harriman's Socialist Party," 49; Laslett, *Sunshine Was Never Enough*, 54; Stimson, *Labor Movement in Los Angeles*, 362.

3. *Citizen*, March 19, 1909; *Citizen*, June 9, 1911; Laslett, *Sunshine Was Never Enough*, 59–60; Stimson, *Labor Movement in Los Angeles*, 224–25.

4. Shaffer, *Anarchism and Countercultural Politics*, 183–84.

5. *Regeneración*, November 18, 1911; *Regeneración*, August 3, 1912.

6. *Regeneración*, September 14, 1912; Hart, *Anarchism*, 111–14; Shaffer, *Anarchism and Countercultural Politics*, 183–84; Shaffer, "Tropical Libertarians," 308.

7. *Regeneración*, February 22, 1913; *Regeneración*, February 8, 1913; O'Toole, *Poor People of the Earth*.

8. *Regeneración*, February 22, 1913.

9. Ibid.

10. *Regeneración*, February 8, 1913 (emphasis added).

11. Mormino and Pozzetta, *Immigrant World of Ybor City*; Shaffer, "Tropical Libertarians."

12. Bureau of Investigation Case Files, 1908–1922, Records Group 65, microfilm 1085, case OG 56693, roll 413, NACP.

13. *Regeneración*, May 10, 1913; *Regeneración*, May 24, 1913; *Regeneración*, June 21, 1913; *Regeneración*, August 9, 1913, 2; Shaffer, "Tropical Libertarians," 308.

14. *Regeneración*, August 9, 1913; Lomnitz, *Comrade Ricardo Flores Magón*, 438; Shaffer, "Tropical Libertarians," 309; Bufe and Verter, *Dreams of Freedom*, 363.

15. *Pluma Roja*, June 27, 1915; *Pluma Roja*, November 5, 1913; *Regeneración*, February 22, 1913.

16. *Brazo y Cerebro*, June 22, 1912; *Brazo y Cerebro*, October 22, 1912; *Cultura Obrera*, February 15, 1913; *Fuerza Consciente*, August 9, 1913; *Fuerza Consciente*, October 15, 1913; *Fuerza Consciente*, November 15, 1913; *Fuerza Consciente*, March 7, 1914.

17. *Regeneración*, July 19, 1913.

18. Sandos, *Rebellion in the Borderlands*, 137.

19. *Huelga General*, March 7, 1914; *Huelga General*, February 21, 1914; Mellinger, *Race and Labor*, 131.

20. Parker, *Casual Laborer*, 179.

21. Ibid., 189, 173; Hall, *Harvest Wobblies*, 50; Dubofsky, *We Shall Be All*, 293; DiGirolamo, "Women of Wheatland."

22. Downing, "Case of the Hop Pickers"; Hall, *Harvest Wobblies*, 48–51; *Songs of the Workers*.

23. Downing, "Case of the Hop Pickers."

24. Hall, *Harvest Wobblies*, 53; Cole, *Ben Fletcher*, 65.

25. *Regeneración*, November 1, 1913.

26. Lomnitz, *Comade Ricardo Flores Magón*, 418.

27. *Regeneración*, November 1, 1913; *Regeneración*, November 16, 1912; *Industrial Worker*, February 22, 1912; Albro, *Always a Rebel*, 106; Foley, *White Scourge*, 109; Mellinger, *Race and Labor*, 135.

28. *Regeneración*, November 1, 1913.

29. Ibid.

Notes

30. *Road to Freedom*, March 1925.

31. *Regeneración*, November 1, 1913; Lomnitz, *Comrade Ricardo Flores Magón*, 422.

32. *Road to Freedom*, March 1925.

33. "Appeal from Rangel-Cline Defense Committee by Victor Cravello," n.d., John Murray Papers, box 1, folder: John Murray Miscellaneous Correspondence, Bancroft.

34. *Industrial Worker*, August 19, 1911, 3.

35. Lomnitz, *Comrade Ricardo Flores Magón*, 440, 53; Vargas, *Proletarians of the North*, 156.

36. *People's Paper*, May 2, 1903.

37. "Clubs, Guns on Foaming Riot," *Los Angeles Times*, January 6, 1913.

38. Hernández, "Hobos in Heaven," 446.

39. Reprinted in the *Los Angeles Times*, December 27, 1913.

40. "Rioters Must Face the Law."

41. "'Mass Meeting' of I.W.W. Ends in Bloody Rioting," *Los Angeles Times*, December 26, 1913; "Rioters Must Face the Law," *Los Angeles Times*, December 28, 1913; "'Unemployed' Threaten More Bloody Rioting"; Escobar, "Chicano Protest and the Law," 214; Estrada, *Los Angeles Plaza*, 147–54; *Regeneración*, January 3, 1914.

42. *Regeneración*, January 31, 1914; *Regeneración*, October 26, 1913; *Pluma Roja*, February 1, 1914.

43. "Rioters Herded Back to Cells," *Los Angeles Times*, December 30, 1913.

44. "'Mass Meeting' of I.W.W. Ends in Bloody Rioting."

45. "Rips the Mask from 'Unemployed' Riots," *Los Angeles Times*, December 27, 1913.

46. *Regeneración*, January 3, 1914.

47. "Rioters Must Face the Law"; The *Los Angeles Times* misspelled his last name as Luti. The man in question was Silvio Nutti, a well-known anarchist in the city.

48. "La España Salvaje," Max Nettlau Papers, folder 3384, IISH.

49. *California Social-Democrat*, January 3, 1914.

50. "City Will Suppress Riotous Anarchists," *Los Angeles Times*, December 26, 1913.

51. *Regeneración*, January 3, 1914.

52. *Huelga General*, February 21, 1914.

53. *Regeneración*, February 28, 1914.

54. *Regeneración*, January 24, 1914.

55. Paul Edwards, "Unworthy Foreigners," *Los Angeles Times*, December 27, 1913.

56. Sandos, *Rebellion in the Borderlands*, 137.

57. *Regeneración*, January 24, 1914; *Regeneración*, January 31, 1914.

58. Lomnitz, *Comrade Ricardo Flores Magón*, 443; MacLachlan, *Anarchism and the Mexican Revolution*, 50.

59. *Regeneración*, February 14, 1914; *Regeneración*, January 31, 1914.

60. *Regeneración*, February 14, 1914.

61. *Land and Liberty*, May 1, 1914.

62. *Regeneración*, April 4, 1914; *Regeneración*, April 18, 1914.

63. *California Social-Democrat*, March 21, 1914; *California Social-Democrat*, March 28, 1914.

Notes

64. Perry and Perry, *Los Angeles Labor Movement*, 12.

65. "Rioters Must Face the Law."

66. "'Hobos' Pleas Are Postponed," *Los Angeles Times*, April 1, 1914.

67. Perry and Perry, *Los Angeles Labor Movement*, 14.

68. *California Social-Democrat*, March 28, 1914.

69. "'Unemployed' Threaten More Bloody Rioting."

70. Ibid.

71. "'Gen.' Rose Ousted as Chief of the Loafers," *Los Angeles Times*, March 31, 1914.

72. *California Social-Democrat*, April 4, 1914

73. Ibid.

74. "Rose Pleads Guilty; Driven Out of Town," *Los Angeles Times*, April 11, 1914; "Vainly Spews Green Venom," *Los Angeles Times*, April 9, 1914.

75. Perry and Perry, *Los Angeles Labor Movement*, 15.

76. Cole, Struthers, and Zimmer, "Introduction," in *Wobblies of the World*, 16.

77. "U.S. vs. Haywood, et al., 1918," Industrial Workers of the World Collection, box 114, item 1, Archives of Labor.

78. *El Rebelde*, February 5, 1915.

79. "*U.S. v. Haywood, et al.*, 1918," Archives of Labor.

80. *El Rebelde*, February 20, 1915.

81. *El Rebelde*, March 18, 1916, 2.

82. Sandos, *Rebellion in the Borderlands*, 59; "IWW Newspapers," Mapping American Social Movements, University of Washington, http://depts.washington.edu/iww/newspapers.shtml.

83. "'Mass Meeting' of I.W.W. Ends in Bloody Rioting."

84. *Regeneración*, March 6, 1915, 2.

85. Ibid.

86. *El Rebelde*, March 15, 1915, 4.

87. *Regeneración*, August 22, 1914; *Regeneración*, September 12, 1914; Lomnitz, *Comrade Ricardo Flores Magón*, 433.

88. Johnson, *Revolution in Texas*, 74–85; Lomnitz, *Comrade Ricardo Flores Magón*, 435–36; Sandos, *Rebellion in the Borderlands*, 83–84.

89. Mellinger, *Race and Labor*, 145–46.

90. Horne, *Black and Brown*, 161; Luckingham, *Minorities in Phoenix*, 29; Mellinger, *Race and Labor*, 157; Truett, *Fugitive Landscapes*, 171.

91. *Road to Freedom*, June 1932.

92. Ibid.

93. Ibid.

94. Ibid.

95. *Arizona Republican*, August 16, 1915.

96. *Arizona Republican*, August 28, 1915,

97. *Arizona Republican*, September 16, 1915.

98. *Arizona Republican*, September 15, 1915; *Bisbee Daily Review*, September 17, 1915.

99. Sandos, *Rebellion in the Borderlands*, 197n56.

100. *El Rebelde*, March 18, 1916.

Notes

101. *El Rebelde*, April 1, 1916.

102. *Regeneración*, May 13, 1916.

103. *El Rebelde*, May 20, 1916.

Chapter 8. The Contours of Repression

1. Higham, *Strangers in the Land*; Preston, *Aliens and Dissenters*; Lubow, "Espionage Act in Southern California."

2. Espionage Act of 1917, Act of October 6, 1917, ch. 106, §10(i), 40 Stat. 422, *codified at* 18 U.S.C. §§ 793–98.

3. Sedition Act of 1918 (Pub.L. 65–150, 40 Stat. 553, enacted May 16, 1918).

4. MacLachlan, *Anarchism and the Mexican Revolution*, 46.

5. Ibid., 60.

6. *Blast*, May 1, 1916, 4–5; *Blast*, July 1, 1916, 2–3; Zimmer, "Whole World Is Our Country," 272.

7. "Enrique Flores Magón to Wm. Gerkee," August 26, 1917, OG 60191, Bureau of Investigation Case Files, 1908–1922 (National Archives Microfilm Publication M1085, roll 418), NACP.

8. "Agent Bryon re: Wm. C. Owen," March 6, 8, 9, and 11, 1916, OG 1363, Bureau of Investigation Case Files, 1908–1922 (National Archives Microfilm Publication M1085, roll 283), NACP.

9. "Agent Bryon re: Wm. C. Owen," March 6, 1916, OG 1363, Bureau of Investigation Case Files, 1908–1922 (National Archives Microfilm Publication M1085, roll 283), NACP. For more on Lance, see Avrich, *Anarchist Voices*, 295.

10. Chang, *Pacific Connections*, 127.

11. "Workers International Defense League, Appeal by Edgcumb Pinchon," May 15, 1916, Subject Vertical Files: Anarchism—Flores Magón, Ricardo, Labadie.

12. "Argument of Counsel, In RE: Raul Palma," June 15, 1917, John Murray Papers, folder "Mexicans in Los Angeles," Bancroft.

13. Zimmer, "Whole World Is Our Country," 311; Preston, *Aliens and Dissenters*, 33.

14. MacLachlan, *Anarchism and the Mexican Revolution*, 76–92.

15. Streeby, *Radical Sensations*, 254.

16. Kanellos, "Spanish-Language Anarchist Periodicals," 73.

17. Pernicone, *Carlo Tresca*, 90; Dubofsky, *We Shall Be All*, 341, 406–7.

18. *El Rebelde*, December 26, 1915, 1; *El Rebelde*, February 4, 1916, 1; Hall, *Harvest Wobblies*, 85.

19. Hall, *Harvest Wobblies*, 95–96; Daniel, *Bitter Harvest*, 86.

20. *El Rebelde*, April 14, 1917, 3; Hall, *Harvest Wobblies*, 92–93; Garcia, *A World of Its Own*, 43; Whitten, "Criminal Syndicalism," 14.

21. Testimony of Aurelio Vincente Azuara in "*U.S. v. Haywood et al.*, 1918," Industrial Workers of the World Collection, box 114, item 1, Archives of Labor.

22. Ibid; *Copper Era*, September 1, 1916, 1; *El Rebelde*, October 7, 1916; Acuña, *Corridors of Migration*, 196.

23. *El Rebelde*, October 7, 1916, 1.

Notes

24. *El Rebelde*, January 6, 1917, 1; *El Rebelde*, July 7, 1917, 1.

25. *El Rebelde*, February 3, 1917; Caulfield, "Wobblies and Mexican Workers," 57.

26. *El Rebelde*, September 8, 1917, 1; *El Rebelde*, September 22, 1917, 3.

27. "*U.S. v. Haywood* et al., 1918," Archives of Labor.

28. Caulfield, "Wobblies and Mexican Workers," 67.

29. *El Rebelde*, August 11, 1917, 1, 3.

30. Caulfield, "Wobblies and Mexican Workers," 67; Whitten, "Criminal Syndicalism," 16.

31. Benton-Cohen, *Borderline Americans*, 198–238.

32. Chester, *Wobblies in Their Heyday*, loc. 135–145; Dubofsky, *We Shall Be All*, 402.

33. Chester, *Wobblies in Their Heyday*, 154.

34. *El Rebelde*, September 8, 1917, 1; *El Rebelde*, September 22, 1917, 1.

35. Chester, *Wobblies in Their Heyday*, 41.

36. "Pedro Coria to W. H. Westman," June 28, 1961, Industrial Workers of the World Collection, box 17, folder 43, Archives of Labor; George, I.W.W. Trial, 10; "Names of Those Arrested to Date," *International Socialist Review* 18, no. 5–6 (1917): 270.

37. "Statistics and records of sentences," Industrial Workers of the World Collection, box 128, folder 4, Archives of Labor.

38. "A. R. Harvey to Warren Lamson," April 29, 1918, file 10110, box 2776, Military Intelligence Division, Records Group 165, NACP.

39. Dubofsky, *We Shall Be All*, 406–7.

40. Chester, *Wobblies in Their Heyday*, 281.

41. *El Rebelde*, June 24, 1916, 4.

42. *La Nueva Solidaridad*, January 31, 1919, 1.

43. *La Nueva Solidaridad*, December 7, 1918.

44. *La Nueva Solidaridad*, January 31, 1919, 2.

45. *La Nueva Solidaridad*, July 19, 1919, 4; *La Nueva Solidaridad*, August 16, 1919, 1; *La Nueva Solidaridad*, September 6, 1919, 1.

46. "RE: Pedro Coria," November 30, 1917, OG 6771, Bureau of Investigation Case Files, 1908–1922, NACP.

47. RE: Pedro Coria," December 3, 1917, OG 6771, Bureau of Investigation Case Files, 1908–1922, NACP; *Germinal*, February 28, 1918, 4.

48. Aguilar, "Peripheries of Power," 45.

49. "RE: Manuel Sastre," February 4, 1918, OG 96994, Bureau of Investigation Case Files, 1908–1922, NACP.

50. "Chief to H. G. Clabaugh," April 30, 1918, OG 6771, Bureau of Investigation Case Files, 1908–1922, NACP; "R. H. Van Deman to Mr. Bielaski," April 6, 1918, OG 6771, Bureau of Investigation Case Files, 1908–1922, NACP; Caulfield, "Wobblies and Mexican Workers," 57; Shaffer, "Tropical Libertarians," 311; DeShazo and Halstead, "Los Wobblies Del Sur," 3–4, 25–26, 31; Rosenthal, "Moving," 80.

51. *La Nueva Solidaridad*, November 31, 1919, 2.

52. "RE: Manuel Sastre," February 26, 1919, OG 96994, Bureau of Investigation Case Files, 1908–1922, NACP; "RE: Rubio and Manuel Sastre," November 23, 1918, OG 96994,

Notes

Bureau of Investigation Case Files, 1908–1922, NARA CP; *La Nueva Solidaridad,* November 30, 1918, 4; "Writes Period to Red Career," *Los Angeles Times,* October 23, 1919.

53. "Bolshevist Conspiracy Bared," *Los Angeles Times,* January 31, 1919; Van Valen, "Bolsheviki and the Orange Growers."

54. "RE: Manuel Sastre," February 26, 1919, OG 96994, Bureau of Investigation Case Files, 1908–1922, NACP; *La Nueva Solidaridad,* February 15, 1919, 1, 4; Van Valen, "Bolsheviki and the Orange Growers," 40.

55. "B. M. Crogan to G. P. Reiman," February 2, 1919, box 4; Military Intelligence Division (Los Angeles), Records Relating to Plant Protection, 1917–1919, Record Group 165, NAR.

56. "RE: Waren Lamsen and Orange Pickers Strike in Covina District," August 11, 1919, OG 229401, Bureau of Investigation Case Files, 1908–1922, NACP; Garcia, *World of Its Own,* 43; Van Valen, "Bolsheviki and the Orange Growers," 41.

57. *La Nueva Solidaridad,* March 1, 1919, 4; Garcia, *World of Its Own,* 43; Van Valen, "Bolsheviki and the Orange Growers," 44–46; Whitten, "Criminal Syndicalism," 23.

58. "Small Collection for Citrus Workers," *Los Angeles Times,* February 17, 1919.

59. "RE: Manuel Sastre," February 6, 1919, OG 96994, Bureau of Investigation Case Files, 1908–1922, NACP; "Manuel Sastre," February 22, 1919, OG 96994, Bureau of Investigation Case Files, 1908–1922, NACP; "Allen, Justice," February 28, 1919, OG 96994, Bureau of Investigation Case Files, 1908–1922, NACP; *La Nueva Solidaridad,* October [n.d.], 1919, 1; "Writes Period to Red Career."

60. "Picnic Here Ends in Riot," *Los Angeles Times,* May 2, 1919; Whitten, "Criminal Syndicalism," 27.

61. *La Nueva Solidaridad,* April 12, 1919, 3; *La Nueva Solidaridad,* September 6, 1919, 4; Monroy, *Rebirth,* 215; Deverell, *Whitewashed Adobe,* 141.

62. "I. W. W. Anarchists," December 30, 1918, File 10110, box 2776, Military Intelligence Division, Records Group 165, NACP; La Botz, "American 'Slackers,'" 564; Chambers, *To Raise an Army;* Keith, *Rich Man's War,* 57–58.

63. OG 289495, Bureau of Investigation Case Files, NARA CP; "Report," Case File 61-4625, Bureau of Investigation Case Files, 1908–1922, Records Group 65, NACP.

64. "Report," Case File 61-4625, NACP.

65. "Michele Fasano to Fermino [*sic*] Gallo," Case File 61-4625, Bureau of Investigation Case Files, 1908–1922; Records Group 65; NACP.

66. Avrich, *Sacco and Vanzetti,* 58–72, 103; Avrich, *Anarchist Voices,* 110, 117, 129, 156.

67. La Botz, "American 'Slackers,'"; Yamanouchi, "Letters and Manuscripts of Sen Katayama."

68. Heatherton, "Color Line and the Class Struggle," 61; Taibo, *Bolcheviques,* 31–38.

69. Carr, "Radicals, Revolutionaries and Exiles."

70. Whitten, "Criminal Syndicalism," 23.

71. For an overview of cases see: "IWW General Defense Committee Calif branch. Digest of Calif Criminal Syndicalism Cases (1926)," Ralph Chaplin Papers, Labadie; "California and Criminal Syndicalism," *One Big Union Monthly,* April 2, 1920; Upton Sinclair, "Civil Liberties in Los Angeles," *Industrial Pioneer,* August 1923; Gallagher, *Interview with Mary Gallagher,* 42.

Notes

72. "Austin Lewis to Mrs. Orlow Black," July 9, 1920, Austin Lewis Papers, box 1, folder: Outgoing Correspondence, Bancroft.

73. "Misc Letters," Ralph Chaplin Papers, folder: Gallagher, Mary E.—Letters from Prisoners—IWW, Labadie; Whitten, "Criminal Syndicalism."

74. "Nicolaas Steelink to Mary Gallagher," October 9, 192, Ralph Chaplin Papers, folder: Gallagher, Mary E.—Letters from Prisoners—IWW, Labadie Collection.

75. Heatherton, "University of Radicalism," 563.

76. "Aurelio Vincente Azuara to Mary Gallagher," September 21, 1921, Ralph Chaplin Papers, folder: Gallagher, Mary E.—Letters from Prisoners—IWW, Labadie Collection.

77. *La Nueva Solidaridad*, October [n.d.], 1919, 2; *La Nueva Solidaridad*, November 30, 3.

78. Inmate 112895, RG 129 Records of the Bureau of Prisons, National Archives, Central Plains Region; Inmate 13102, RG 129 Records of the Bureau of Prisons, National Archives, Central Plains Region; *Bisbee Daily Review*, February 1, 1920; Kohn, *American Political Prisoners*, 86; D. J. Alperovitz, "I.W.W.S Killed," http://www.academia.edu/11211699/I.W.W.s _Killed.

79. Bose, *Indian Revolutionaries Abroad*, 123; Brown, *Har Dayal*, 128; Chaplin, *Wobbly*, 256; MacLachlan, *Anarchism and the Mexican Revolution*, 91, 101; Puri, *Ghadar Movement*, 129.

80. *Road to Freedom*, June 1932.

81. Heatherton, "University of Radicalism," 571–76; Wood, "Death of a Political Prisoner."

82. *Road to Freedom*, June 1932; Lomnitz, *Comrade Ricardo Flores Magón*, 500–508.

83. Kohn, *American Political Prisoners*, 114.

84. The case was McClennigan et al. Los Angeles, CA case 186, trial 77 June 4, 1923. Those arrested included G. J. Terrill, Charles Andrews, Hugo Cedeholm, J. B. Childs, Joseph Clohessy, H. C. Duke, Ernest Erickson, James P. Gordon, Francis Hart, H. R. Hansen, J. C. Hollis, Pierre Jans, J. J. Johnson, T. O. Kleiberg, Walter Kohrs, James Lalonde, Thomas Lyons, G. Lindfors, William Minton, Francis McClennigan, John Pugh, J. C. Robinson, George Roeschlau, Leo Stark, C. J. Sullivan, Charles Jim Smith, Leo Stark, and C. J. Sullivan. See: "Digest of Calif Criminal Syndicalism Cases (1926)," 45–46.

85. Gallagher, *Interview with Mary Gallagher*, 71–72.

86. Van Valen, "Cleaning up the Harbor"; Stevens, *Radical L.A.*, 142–64; Nelson, *Workers on the Waterfront*, 60–61; Laslett, *Sunshine Was Never Enough*, 79–82.

87. Whitten, "Criminal Syndicalism," 59.

88. "Newspaper Clipping," July 7, 1924, and "Newspaper Clipping," n.d., Max Nettlau Papers, folder 401, IISH.

89. Gallagher, *Interview with Mary Gallagher*, 47.

90. Ibid., 77; "Newspaper Clipping," September 4, 1924, Max Nettlau Papers, folder 401, IISH.

91. Zimmer, *Immigrants against the State*, 168.

92. http://www.iww.org/culture/official/dictionary.

93. Zimmer, "Premature Anti-Communists?" 58.

94. Gallagher, *Interview with Mary Gallagher*, 37.

95. Zimmer, *Immigrants against the State*, 168.

Notes

Conclusion

1. Carr, *Marxism and Communism*, 18.
2. Chester, *Wobblies in Their Heyday*, 204.
3. Zimmer, *Immigrants against the State*, 160–63.
4. Ibid., 159; Goldman, *Living My Life*.
5. Hodges, *Mexican Anarchism*, 16–17.
6. Zimmer, *Immigrants against the State*, 158–59.
7. Chester, *Wobblies in Their Heyday*, 204.
8. Ibid., 212.
9. Zimmer, *Immigrants against the State*, 10.
10. Ibid., 13.
11. *Road to Freedom*, August 1927.
12. Avrich, *Anarchist Voices*, 32, 487n97, 487n98.
13. Wild, *Street Meeting*, 178.
14. Wild, *Street Meeting*, 178–79; Monroy, "Anarquismo y Comunismo"; Yamanouchi, "Letters and Manuscripts of Sen Katayama."
15. *Road to Freedom*, February 1932.
16. *Road to Freedom*, October 1927.
17. Frank, "Jewish Farming," 70–71; *Road to Freedom*, August 1927; Gallagher, *Interview with Mary Gallagher*, 37.
18. *Road to Freedom*, October 1927.
19. *Road to Freedom*, March 1925.
20. Avrich, *Anarchist Voices*, 330–31.
21. *Road to Freedom*, August 1925.
22. *Road to Freedom*, July 1926.
23. Caulfield, "Wobblies and Mexican Workers," 72.
24. "Circular," n.d., Max Nettlau Papers, folder 3374, IISH.
25. "Enrique Flores Magón to Ralph Chaplin," January 26, 1933, Subject Vertical Files: Anarchism—Flores Magón, Enrique, Labadie.
26. "Enrique Flores Magón to Stephanus Fabijanović," April 20, 1924, Subject Vertical Files: Anarchism—Flores Magón, Enrique, Labadie.
27. Spenser and Stoller, "Radical Mexico," 67.
28. Hodges, *Mexican Anarchism*, 20; Taibo, *Bolcheviques*, 65–70, 190–92, 263–64.
29. "Enrique Flores Magón to Stephanus Fabijanović," April 20 and August 25, 1924, Subject Vertical Files: Anarchism—Flores Magón, Enrique, Labadie.
30. "Enrique Flores Magón to Stephanus Fabijanović," November 18, 1924, Subject Vertical Files: Anarchism—Flores Magón, Enrique, Labadie.
31. "Appeal from the Ricardo Flores Magón Peasants Syndicate," November 20, 1924, Subject Vertical Files: Anarchism—Flores Magón, Ricardo, Labadie.
32. *Road to Freedom*, June 1926; *Road to Freedom*, October 1, 1926.
33. *Road to Freedom*, October 1927.
34. Weber, *Dark Sweat, White Gold*, 85; Jamieson, *Labor Unionism*, 77–78; Monroy, "Anarquismo y Comunismo," 41; *Road to Freedom*, December 1928.

Notes

35. *Road to Freedom*, October 1927.

36. "Enrique Flores Magón to Stephanus Fabijanović," November 18, 1924, Subject Vertical Files: Anarchism—Flores Magón, Enrique, Labadie.

37. *Road to Freedom*, December 1927.

38. *Road to Freedom*, December 1928.

39. "Biography of Byron Kitto by M. Gallagher, 1955," Industrial Workers of the World Collection, box 23, folder 6, Archives of Labor.

40. *New Unionist*, May 7, 1927.

41. *Road to Freedom*, July 1927.

42. *Road to Freedom*, August 1927; Hodges, *Mexican Anarchism*, 21.

43. *Road to Freedom*, November 1927.

44. *Road to Freedom*, July 1927; *Road to Freedom*, February 1928.

45. *Road to Freedom*, June–July 1928

46. *Road to Freedom*, October 1927.

47. *Road to Freedom*, June–July 1928.

48. Ibid.

49. *Road to Freedom*, November 1, 1926.

50. *Road to Freedom*, June–July 1928.

51. Zimmer, *Immigrants against the State*, 172.

52. Cornell, *Unruly Equality*, 108–9.

53. *Daily Worker* (New York), January 7 and January 17, 1930, in Federal Writers' Project (Oakland, 1938), "Oriental Labor Unions and Strikes"; Weber, *Dark Sweat, White Gold*, 88.

54. Estrada, *Los Angeles Plaza*, 164.

55. Ibid., 165.

56. McWilliams, *Factories in the Field*, 217.

57. Solomon, *The Cry Was Unity*, 268.

58. Flamming, *Bound for Freedom*, 302.

59. Zimmer, *Immigrants against the State*, 167–8.

60. "Thomas Bell to Alexander Berkman," April 5, 1931, Alexander Berkman Papers, folder 10, IISH.

61. Ibid.; "W.P.A. Workers," Industrial Workers of the World Collection, box 178, folder "WPA Workers," Archives of Labor.

62. "T. H. Bell to Alexander Berkman," January 11, 1931, Alexander Berkman Papers, folder 10, IISH.

63. Ibid.

64. "T. H. Bell to Alexander Berkman," February 24, 1931, Alexander Berkman Papers, folder 10, IISH.

65. Gallagher, *Interview with Mary Gallagher*, 17.

66. "T. H. Bell to Alexander Berkman," February 24, 1931, Alexander Berkman Papers, folder 10, IISH.

67. "Bell to Berkman," January 11, 1931.

68. "Morris Nadleman interviewed by Paul Buhle," April 18, 1980, Oral History of the American Left: Radical Histories, tape 171A, Tamiment Library/Robert F. Wagner Labor Archives, Elmer Holmes Bobst Library, New York University.

Notes

69. *Freedom* (New York), October 1933; "Thomas Bell to Alexander Berkman," April 5, 1931, Alexander Berkman Papers, folder 10, IISH; "W.P.A. Workers," Industrial Workers of the World Collection, box 178, folder "WPA Workers," Archives of Labor; Laslett, *Sunshine Was Never Enough*, 132–35.

70. Gallagher, *Interview with Mary Gallagher*, 107.

71. "A Goodwill Plea," February 13, 1933, Max Nettlau Papers, folder 1081, IISH.

72. "Enrique Flores Magón to Ralph Chaplin," January 26, 1933, Subject Vertical Files: Anarchism—Flores Magón, Enrique, Labadie.

73. *Road to Freedom*, June 1932.

74. *El Luchador*, February 1, 1936; Douglas Monroy,"Anarquismo y Comunismo," 41; Weber, *Dark Sweat, White Gold*, 85–86.

75. *Man!*, December 1933.

76. *Freedom* (New York), December 1933.

77. "Alexander Berkman to Tom Bell," May 2, 1931, Alexander Berkman Papers, folder 10, IISH.

78. Rocker, *Nationalism and Culture*, 339.

79. "Testimonial to Rudolf Rocker," ii.

80. Weintraub, "I.W.W. in California," 272.

BIBLIOGRAPHY

Archival Sources

Archives of Labor and Urban Affairs, Wayne State University
  Frederick W. Thompson Collection
  Industrial Workers of the World Collection
Bancroft Library, University of California, Berkeley
  Austin Lewis Papers
  Ethel Duffy Turner Papers
  John Murray Papers
The California State Library, Sacramento, California
  Proceedings of the California State Federation of Labor
The Emma Goldman Papers, Berkeley, California
  The International Institute of Social History, Amsterdam, The Netherlands
  Alexander Berkman Papers
  Diego Abad de Santillan Papers
  Max Nettalu Papers
  Ricardo Flores Magón Papers
  Rudolf Rocker Papers
  William Charles Owen Papers
  Periodical Collection
  Pamphlet Collection
Labadie Collection, University of Michigan Special Collections, Ann Arbor, Michigan
  Agnes Inglis Papers
  Joseph Labadie Papers

Bibliography

Ralph Chaplin Papers
Subject Vertical Files
Los Angeles Public Library
Photograph Collection
Mandeville Special Collections Library, University of California, San Diego
A. I. McCormick Documents
Flores Magón Documents
National Archives and Records Administration
Archives I, Washington D.C.
Department of Commerce and Labor Immigration Service, Immigration and Naturalization Service Records, Records Group 85
Records of the Post Office Department, Records Group 28
National Archives at College Park, Maryland
Records of the Department of Justice; Records Group 60
Bureau of Investigation Case Files, 1908–1922, National Archives Microfilm Publication M1085, Records Group 65
Bureau of Investigation Case Files, 1908–1922; Records Group 65
Military Intelligence Division, Department of War, Record Group 165
National Archives at Kansas City
Records of the Bureau of Prisons, Department of Justice, Bureau of Prisons, Record Group 129. US Penitentiary, Leavenworth, Inmate Case Files, 1895–1957, National Archives Identifier: 571125.
National Archives at Riverside, California
Federal Court Records, Southern District of California, Southern Division (Los Angeles), Criminal Case Files, Records Group 21
Military Intelligence Division (Los Angeles), Records Relating to Plant Protection, 1917–1919, Record Group 165
San Diego History Center, San Diego, California
Southern California Library for Social Studies and Research, Los Angeles, California
Emil and Tassia Fred Collection, 1915–1987
Robert Kenny Collection, 1901–1976
Periodical Collection
Tomás Rivera Library, University of California, Riverside
Sadakichi Hartmann Papers
Urban Archives Center, California State University, Northridge
Minutes: Los Angeles County Central Labor Council Executive Board and Council Meetings
Report of the Proceedings of the Twenty-Eighth Annual Convention of the American Federation of Labor
Ventura County Library
Japanese Mexican Labor Association Collection

Bibliography

Periodicals

Alba-Anarquica. Monterrey, Mexico.

The Blast. San Francisco; New York, 1916–1917.

Brazo Y Cerebro. New York, 1912–1913.

California Social Democrat. Los Angeles, 1911–1916.

The Citizen. Los Angeles.

Cogito, Ergo Sum. San Francisco, 1908.

Common Sense. Los Angeles, 1904–1916.

Il Contro-pelo. Barre, Vermont, 1911–1912.

El Correro Mexicano. Los Angeles.

Cronaca Sovversiva. Barre, Vermont; Lynn, Massachusetts, 1903–1919.

Cultura Obrera. Brooklyn, 1911–1923.

Cultura Proletaria. Brooklyn, 1911.

Doctrina Anarquista-Socialista. Paterson, New Jersey, 1905.

The Dugout. Los Angeles, 1919.

The Emancipator. San Francisco, 1906–1907.

L'Era Nuova. Paterson, New Jersey, 1908–1917.

Il Fil di Fer. Los Angeles.

Freedom. London, 1886–1928

Freedom. New York, 1933–1934.

Fuerza Consciente. New York; Los Angeles; San Francisco, 1913–1914.

Germinal. Tampico, Tamaulipas, Mexico.

Huelga General. Los Angeles, 1913–1914.

Imperial Valley Press. El Centro, California.

Industrial Worker. Spokane, Washington; Seattle; Chicago, 1907–1931.

La Jacquerie. Paterson, New Jersey, 1919.

Land and Liberty. Hayward, California; San Francisco, 1914–1915.

The Libertarian. Los Angeles.

Los Angeles Socialist. Los Angeles.

Los Angeles Times. Los Angeles.

El Luchador. Los Angeles.

Man! San Francisco; Los Angeles; New York, 1933–1940.

Mother Earth. New York, 1906–1917.

El Mosquito. Los Angeles.

New Review. New York.

The New Solidarity. Chicago, 1918–1920.

New Unionist. Los Angeles, 1927–1931.

La Nueva Solidaridad. Chicago; Brooklyn, 1918–1919.

El Obrero Industrial. Tampa, Florida.

The One Big Union Monthly. Chicago, 1919–1938.

People's Paper. Santa Barbara; Los Angeles.

Pluma Roja. Los Angeles, 1913–1914.

Bibliography

El Proletario. Nogales, Sonora.
La Razon. Tijuana, Mexico.
El Rebelde. Los Angeles, 1915–1917.
Regeneración. Los Angeles, 1910–1918.
Revolt. San Francisco, 1911–1912.
Revolución. Los Angeles, 1907.
The Road to Freedom. Stelton, New Jersey; New York, 1924–1932.
Roman Forum. Los Angeles, 1932–1948.
Solidaridad. Chicago; Brooklyn; New York, 1918–1930.
Tribuna Roja. Tampico, Tamaulipas, Mexico.
The Underdog. Los Angeles.
La Union Industrial. Phoenix, 1910–11.
Union Labor News. Los Angeles, 1903–1908.
Verbo Libre. Morelia, Michoacán, Mexico.
La Voz de la Mujer. El Paso, 1907.
The Western Comrade. Los Angeles; Leesville, Louisiana.
Ydea Roja. Michoacán, Mexico.

Government Publications

United States Congress, Senate. Investigation of Mexican Affairs. Preliminary Report and Hearings of the Committee on Foreign Relations, United States Senate. Pursuant to S. Res. 106, S.Doc.285, 66th Congress, 2nd Session, 2 vols., May 24, 1920, LexisNexis U.S. Serial Set Digital Collection, SERIAL-SET-ID: 7666 S.doc.285.

United States Congress, Senate. Revolutions in Mexico. Hearings before a Subcommittee of the Committee on Foreign Relations, United States Senate. Pursuant to S. Res. 335, 62 Congress, 2nd Session, Sept. 7, 9, 11–13, 18, 20, 21, 23–27, 30, Oct. 4, 5, 7–12, Nov. 30, Dec. 10, 12, 17, 19, 1912, Jan. 7–9, 12, 1913.

United States Congress, House of Representatives. Communist and Anarchist Deportation Cases. Hearings before a Subcommittee of the Committee on Immigration and Naturalization. 66th Congress, 2nd Session, April 21 to 24, 1920, 109.

Secondary Sources

Acuña, Rodolfo. *Corridors of Migration: The Odyssey of Mexican Laborers, 1600–1933*. Tucson: University of Arizona Press, 2007.

Aguilar, Kevan Antonio. "Peripheries of Power, Centers of Resistance: Anarchist Movements in Tampico & the Huasteca Region, 1910–1945." MA thesis, University of California, San Diego, 2014.

Albro, Ward. *Always a Rebel: Ricardo Flores Magón and the Mexican Revolution*. Fort Worth: Texas Christian University Press, 1992.

Almaguer, Tomás. *Racial Fault Lines: The Historical Origins of White Supremacy in California*. Berkeley: University of California Press, 1994.

Amato, Joseph A. *On Foot: A History of Walking*. New York: New York University Press, 2004.

Bibliography

Anderson, Benedict. *Imagined Communities: Reflections on the Origin and Spread of Nationalism*. London: Verso, 1983.

———. *Under Three Flags: Anarchism and the Anti-Colonial Imagination*. London: Verso, 2005.

Anderson, Perry. "The Antinomies of Antonio Gramsci." *New Left Review* 100 (November–January 1976–77): 5–78.

Andrews, Gregg. *Shoulder to Shoulder? The American Federation of Labor, the United States, and the Mexican Revolution, 1910–1924*. Berkeley: University of California Press, 1991.

Antonioli, Maurizio, ed. *Dizionario Biografico Degli Anarchici Italiani*. Vol. 2. Pisa: Biblioteca Franco Serantini, 2003.

Avrich, Paul. *Anarchist Voices: An Oral History of Anarchism in America*. Oakland, Calif.: AK, 2005.

———. *Sacco and Vanzetti: The Anarchist Background*. Princeton, N.J.: Princeton University Press, 1991.

Axelrod, Bernard. "St. Louis and the Mexican Revolutionaries 1905–1906." *Bulletin of the Missouri Historical Society* 28, no. 2 (1972): 94–108.

Bamyeh, Mohammed A. *Anarchy as Order: The History and Future of Civic Humanity*. Lanham, Mass.: Rowman and Littlefield, 2009.

Benjamin, Thomas. "Rebuilding the Nation." In *The Oxford History of Mexico*, edited by Michael C. Meyer and William H. Beezley, 467–503. Oxford: Oxford University Press, 2000.

Benton-Cohen, Katherine. *Borderline Americans: Racial Division and Labor Wars in the Arizona Borderlands*. Cambridge, Mass.: Harvard University Press, 2009.

Berlin, Ira. *Many Thousands Gone: The First Two Centuries of Slavery in North America*. Cambridge, Mass.: Belknap / Harvard University Press, 1998.

Bernstein, Shana. *Bridges of Reform: Interracial Civil Rights Activism in Twentieth-Century Los Angeles*. New York: Oxford University Press, 2011.

Bird, Stewart, Dan Georgakas, and Deborah Shaffer. *Solidarity Forever: An Oral History of the IWW*. Chicago: Lakeview, 1985.

Blaisdell, Lowell L. *The Desert Revolution: Baja California, 1911*. Madison: University of Wisconsin Press, 1962.

Bookchin, Murray. *The Spanish Anarchists: The Heroic Years 1868–1936*. Oakland: AK, 1998.

Bose, Arun. *Indian Revolutionaries Abroad, 1905–1922: In the Background of International Developments*. Patna: Bharati Bhawan, 1971.

Botkin, Jane Little. *Frank Little and the IWW: The Blood That Stained an American Family*. Norman: University of Oklahoma Press, 2017.

Brissenden, Paul. *The I.W.W.: A Study of American Syndicalism*. New York: Russell and Russell, 1957.

Brown, Emily Clara. *Har Dayal: Hindu Revolutionary and Rationalist*. Tucson: University of Arizona Press, 1975.

Bufe, Charles, and Mitchell Cowen Verter, eds. *Dreams of Freedom: A Ricardo Flores Magón Reader*. Oakland, Calif.: AK, 2005.

Bullock, Marcus, and Michael W. Jennings, eds. *Walter Benjamin: Selected Writings, Volume 1: 1913–1926*. Cambridge, Mass.: Harvard University Press, 1996.

Bibliography

Cánovas, Agustin Cué. *Ricardo Flores Magón: La Baja California y Los Estados Unidos*. Mexico D. F.: Libro Mex, 1957.

Carey, George. "The Vessel, the Deed, and the Idea: Anarchists in Paterson 1895–1908," *Antipode* 10, no. 11 (1979): 46–58.

Carr, Barry. *Marxism and Communism in Twentieth-Century Mexico*. Lincoln: University of Nebraska Press, 1992.

———. "Radicals, Revolutionaries and Exiles: Mexico City in the 1920s." *Berkeley Review of Latin American Studies* (Fall 2010): 26–30.

Casanovas i Codina, Joan. "Pedro Esteve (Barcelona 1865-Weehauken, N.J. 1925): A Catalan Anarchist in the United States," *Catalan Review: International Journal of Catalan Culture* 5, no. 1 (1991): 73.

Caulfield, Norman. "Wobblies and Mexican Workers in Mining and Petroleum, 1905–1924." *International Review of Social History* 40, no. 1 (April 1995): 51–75.

Ceballos, Rómulo Velasco. *¿Se Aproderará Estados Unidos de America de Baja California? (La Invasión Filibustero De 1911)*. Mexico: Imprenta Nacional, 1920.

Chambers, John Whiteclay. *To Raise an Army: The Draft Comes to Modern America*. New York: Free Press, 1987.

Chang, Jason Oliver. *Chino: Anti-Chinese Racism in Mexico, 1880–1940*. Urbana: University of Illinois Press, 2017. Kindle e-book edition.

Chang, Kornel. *Pacific Connections: The Making of the U.S.-Canadian Borderlands*. Berkeley: University of California Press, 2012.

Chaplin, Ralph. *Wobbly: The Rough-and-Tumble Story of an American Radical*. Chicago: University of Chicago Press, 1948.

Chester, Eric Thomas. *The Wobblies in Their Heyday: The Rise and Destruction of the Industrial Workers of the World during the World War I Era*. Santa Barbara, Calif.: Praeger, 2014. Kindle e-book edition.

Cockcroft, James. *Intellectual Precursors of the Mexican Revolution, 1900–1913*. Austin: University of Texas Press, 1968.

Cohn, Jesse. *Underground Passages: Anarchist Resistance Culture, 1848–2011*. Oakland: AK, 2014). Kindle e-book edition.

Cole, Peter, ed. *Ben Fletcher: The Life and Times of a Black Wobbly*. Chicago: Kerr, 2007.

Cole, Peter, David M. Struthers, and Kenyon Zimmer, eds. *Wobblies of the World: A Global History of the IWW*. London: Pluto, 2017.

Conolly-Smith, Peter. *Translating America: An Immigrant Press Visualizes American Popular Culture, 1895–1918*. Washington D.C.: Smithsonian Institution, 2010.

Corbin, David A. *Life, Work, and Rebellion in the Coal Fields: The Southern West Virginia Miners, 1880–1922*. Champaign: University of Illinois Press, 1989.

Cornell, Andrew. *Unruly Equality: U.S. Anarchism in the Twentieth Century*. Berkeley: University of California Press, 2016.

Crosby, Rosalind Giardinia. "The Italians of Los Angeles, 1900." MA thesis, San Francisco State University, 1983.

Cross, Ira B. *A History of the Labor Movement in California*. Berkeley: University of California Press, 1935.

Bibliography

Daniel, Cletus E. *Bitter Harvest: A History of California Farmworkers, 1870–1941*. Ithaca, N.Y.: Cornell University Press, 1981.

Davis, Mike. *City of Quartz: Excavating the Future in Los Angeles*. London: Verso, 1990.

———. "Sunshine and the Open Shop: Ford and Darwin in 1920's Los Angeles." In Sitton and Deverell, *Metropolis in the Making*, 96–122.

Day, Richard J. F. *Gramsci Is Dead: Anarchist Currents in the Newest Social Movements*. Ann Arbor, Mich.: Pluto, 2005.

Delgado, Grace Peña. "At Exclusion's Southern Gate: Changing Categories of Race and Class among Chinese *Fronterizos*, 1882–1904." In Truett and Young, *Continental Crossroads*, 183–208.

DeShazo, Peter, and Robert J. Halstead. "Los Wobblies Del Sur: The Industrial Workers of the World in Chile and Mexico." Unpublished manuscript. University of Wisconsin, Madison, 1974.

Deverell, William Francis. *Whitewashed Adobe: The Rise of Los Angeles and the Remaking of Its Mexican Past*. Berkeley: University of California Press, 2004.

DiGirolamo, Vincent. "The Women of Wheatland: Female Consciousness and the 1913 Wheatland Hop Strike." *Labor History* 34, no. 2–3 (1993): 236–55.

Downing, Mortimer. "The Case of the Hop Pickers." *International Socialist Review* 14, no. October (1913): 210–13.

Dubofsky, Melvyn. *We Shall Be All: A History of the I.W.W.* Chicago: Quadrangle, 1969.

Edwards, Brent Hayes. *The Practice of Diaspora: Literature, Translation, and the Rise of Black Internationalism*. Cambridge, Mass.: Harvard University Press, 2003.

Elison, George. "Kōtoku Shūsui: The Change in Thought." *Monumenta Nipponica* 22, no. 3/4 (1967): 437–67.

England, Shawn. "*Magonismo*, the Revolution, and the Anarchist Appropriation of an Imagined Mexican Indigenous Identity." In Laforcade and Shaffer, *In Defiance of Boundaries*, 243–60.

Erie, Steven P. *Globalizing L.A.: Trade, Infrastructure, and Regional Development*. Stanford, Calif.: Stanford University Press, 2004.

Escobar, Edward Joseph. "Chicano Protest and the Law: Law Enforcement Responses to Chicano Activism in Los Angeles, 1850–1936." PhD diss., University of California, Riverside, 1983.

Estrada, William D. *The Los Angeles Plaza: Sacred and Contested Space*. Austin: University of Texas Press, 2008.

Faure, Sébastien. "Affinité." In *L'encyclopédie Anarchiste*, edited by Sébastien Faure. Paris: Editions de la Librairie Internationale, 1934.

Federal Writers' Project. *Oriental Labor Unions and Strikes—California Agriculture* (Oakland, 1938). Berkeley, Calif.: Bancroft Library.

———. *Unionization of Migratory Labor, 1903–1930* (Oakland, 1938). Typescript 3–4. Berkeley, Calif.: Bancroft Library.

Flamming, Douglas. "African-Americans and the Politics of Race in Progressive-Era Los Angeles." In *California Progressivism Revisited*, edited by William Deverell and Tom Sitton, 203–28. Berkeley: University of California Press, 1994.

Bibliography

———. *Bound for Freedom: Black Los Angeles in Jim Crow America*. Berkeley: University of California Press, 2005.

Fogelson, Robert M. *The Fragmented Metropolis: Los Angeles, 1850–1930*. Berkeley: University of California Press, 1967.

Foley, Neil. *The White Scourge: Mexicans, Blacks, and Poor Whites in Texas Cotton Culture*. Berkeley: University of California Press, 1997.

Foner, Philip S. *Black Socialist Preacher: The Teachings of Reverened George Washington Woodbey and His Disciple, Reverend G. W. Slater, Jr.* San Francisco: Synthesis, 1983.

———. *History of the Labor Movement in the United States, Volume 4: The Industrial Workers of the World, 1905–1917*. New York: International, 1965.

———. "Reverend George Washington Woodbey: Early Twentieth Century California Black Socialist." *Journal of Negro History* 61, no. 2 (1976): 136–57.

Franck, Harry Alverson. *A Vagabond Journey around the World: a Narrative of Personal Experience*. New York: Century, 1910.

Frank, H. "Jewish Farming in the United States." In *The Jewish People: Past and Present*. New York: Jewish Encyclopedic Handbooks, 1948), 70–71.

Fredrickson, George M. *Racism: A Short History*. Princeton, N.J.: Princeton University Press, 2002.

Friedricks, William B. "Capital and Labor in Los Angeles: Henry E. Huntington vs. Organized Labor, 1900–1920." *Pacific Historical Review* 59, no. 3 (1990): 375–95.

Frykman, Niklas. "The Mutiny on the Hermione: Warfare, Revolution, and Treason in the Royal Navy." *Journal of Social History* 44, no. 1 (Fall 2010): 159–87.

Fuentes, Andrés Reséndez. "Battleground Women: Soldaderas and Female Soldiers in the Mexican Revolution." *Americas* 51, no. 4 (April 1995): 525–53.

Gallagher, Mary. *An Interview with Mary Gallagher on the I.W.W., Tom Mooney*. Berkeley: University of California, Bancroft Library, Regional Oral History Office, 1955.

Garcia, Matt. *A World of Its Own: Race, Labor, and Citrus in the Making of Greater Los Angeles, 1900–1970*. Chapel Hill: University of North Carolina Press, 2002.

Garcílazo, Jeffrey Marcos. *Traqueros: Mexican Railroad Workers in the United States, 1870–1930*. Denton: University of North Texas Press, 2012.

Genovese, Eugene D. *Roll, Jordan, Roll: The World the Slaves Made*. New York: Pantheon, 1974.

George, Harrison. *The I.W.W. Trial: Story of the Greatest Trial in Labor's History by One of the Defendants*. Chicago: IWW, 1918.

Goethe, Johann Wolfgang von. *Elective Affinites: A Novel*. 1809. New York: Oxford University Press, 1994.

Goldman, Emma. *Living My Life*. New York: Dover, 1970.

Gomez-Quinones, Juan. *Mexican American Labor, 1790–1990*. Albuquerque: University of New Mexico Press, 1994.

Gordon, Linda. *The Great Arizona Orphan Abduction*. Cambridge, Mass.: Harvard University Press, 1999.

Graeber, David. *Fragments of an Anarchist Anthropology*. Chicago: Prickly Paradigm, 2004.

Greene, Julie. *Pure and Simple Politics: The American Federation of Labor and Political Activism, 1881–1917*. Cambridge: Cambridge University Press, 1998.

Bibliography

Greenstein, Paul, Nigey Lennon, and Lionel Rolfe. *Bread and Hyacinths: The Rise and Fall of Utopian Los Angeles*. Los Angeles: California Classics, 1992.

Griswold del Castillo, Richard. "The Discredited Revolution: The Magonista Capture of Tijuana in 1911." *Journal of San Diego History* 26, no. 4 (1980): 265–69.

Grossberg, Lawrence. "On Postmodernism and Articulation: An Interview with Stuart Hall." *Journal of Communication Inquiry* 10, no. 2 (June 1986): 45–60.

Guglielmo, Jennifer. "Transnational Feminism's Radical Past: Lessons from Italian Immigrant Women Anarchists in Industrializing America." *Journal of Women's History* 22, no. 1 (2010): 10–33.

Gutiérrez, David. *Walls and Mirrors: Mexican Americans, Mexican Immigrants, and the Politics of Ethnicity*. Berkeley: University of California Press, 1995.

Gutman, Herbert G. *Work, Culture, and Society in Industrializing America: Essays in American Working-Class and Social History*. New York: Vintage, 1977.

Hall, Greg. *Harvest Wobblies: The Industrial Workers of the World and Agricultural Laborers in the American West, 1905–1930*. Corvallis: Oregon State University Press, 2001.

Hall, Stuart. "Notes on Deconstructing 'The Popular.'" In *People's History and Socialist Theory*, edited by Raphael Samuel, 227–40. Boston: Routledge and Kegan Paul, 1981.

Hart, John Mason. *Anarchism and the Mexican Working Class, 1860–1931*. Austin: University of Texas Press, 1978.

———. *Revolutionary Mexico: The Coming and Process of the Mexican Revolution*. Berkeley: University of California Press, 1987.

Heatherton, Christina. "The Color Line and the Class Struggle: The Mexican Revolution and Convergences of Radical Internationalism, 1910–1946." PhD diss., University of Southern California, 2012.

———. "University of Radicalism: Ricardo Flores Magón and Leavenworth Penitentiary." *American Quarterly* 66, no. 3 (September 2014): 557–81.

Heilbroner, Robert. *The Worldly Philosophers: The Lives, Times, and Ideas of the Great Economic Thinkers*. New York: Simon and Schuster, 1953.

Henkin, David M. *The Postal Age: The Emergence of Modern Communications in Nineteenth-Century America*. Chicago: University of Chicago Press, 2008.

Hernández, Kelly Lytle. *City of Inmates: Conquest, Rebellion, and the Rise of Human Caging in Los Angeles, 1771–1965*. Chapel Hill: University of North Carolina Press, 2017.

———. "Hobos in Heaven: Race, Incarceration, and the Rise of Los Angeles, 1880–1910." *Pacific Historical Review* 83, no. 3 (2014): 410–47.

Herzog, Lawrence A. *Where North Meets South: Cities, Space, and Politics on the United States-Mexico Border*. Austin: University of Texas Press, 1990.

Higham, John. *Strangers in the Land: Patterns of American Nativism, 1860–1925*. New Brunswick, N.J.: Rutgers University Press, 1955.

Hirsch, Francine. *Empire of Nations: Ethnographic Knowledge and the Making of the Soviet Union*. Ithaca, N.Y.: Cornell University Press, 2014.

Hodges, Donald C. *Mexican Anarchism after the Revolution*. Austin: University of Texas Press, 1995.

Horne, Gerald. *Black and Brown: African Americans and the Mexican Revolution, 1910–1920*. New York: New York University Press, 2005.

Bibliography

Howe, Richard Herbert. "Max Weber's Elective Affinities: Sociology within the Bounds of Pure Reason." *American Journal of Sociology* 84, no. 2 (1978): 366–85.

Humphries, John. *Gringo Revolucionary: The Amazing Adventures of Caryl Ap Rhys Pryce.* Wales: Dinefwr, 2005.

Igler, David. *Industrial Cowboys: Miller & Lux and the Transformation of the Far West, 1850–1920.* Berkeley: University of California Press, 2001.

Industrial Workers of the World. "Proceedings of Third Annual Convention Industrial Workers of the World: Official Report." 1907. http://www.slp.org/pdf/slphist/iww_conv_1907.pdf.

Irwin, Robert McKee. *Bandits, Captives, Heroines, and Saints: Cultural Icons of Mexico's Northwest Borderlands.* Minneapolis: University of Minnesota Press, 2007.

Jamieson, Stuart Marshall. *Labor Unionism in American Agriculture.* U.S. Department of Labor, Bureau of Labor Statistics. Bulletin 836. Washington: U.S. GPO, 1945.

Jew, Victor. "The Anti-Chinese Massacre of 1871 and Its Strange Career." In *A Companion to Los Angeles,* edited by William Deverell and Greg Hise, 110–28. Malden, Mass.: Wiley-Blackwell, 2010)

Johnson, Benjamin Heber. *Revolution in Texas: How a Forgotten Rebellion and Its Bloddy Supression Turned Mexicans into Americans.* New Haven, Conn.: Yale University Press, 2003.

Kanellos, Nicolás. "Spanish-Language Anarchist Periodicals in Early Twentieth-Century United States." In *Protest on the Page: Essays on Print and the Culture of Dissent since 1865,* edited by James L. Baughman, Jennifer Ratner-Rosenhagen, and James P. Danky, 59–84. Madison: University of Wisconsin Press, 2015.

Katz, Friedrich. *The Life and Times of Pancho Villa.* Stanford, Calif.: Stanford University Press, 1998.

Keith, Jeanette. *Rich Man's War, Poor Man's Fight: Race, Class, and Power in the Rural South During the First World War.* Chapel Hill: University of North Carolina Press, 2004.

Kelley, Robin D. G. "'We Are Not What We Seem': Re-Thinking Black Working-Class Opposition in the Jim Crow South." *Journal of American History* 80, no. 1 (June 1993): 75–112.

Kern, Stephen. *The Culture of Time and Space, 1880–1918.* Cambridge, Mass.: Harvard University Press, 1983.

Kinna, Ruth. "Anarchism: Practice and Politics in Kropotkin's Theory of the State." Paper presented at the European Social Science History Conference, Glasgow, Scotland, April 11–14, 2012.

Knight, Alan. *The Mexican Revolution.* London: Cambridge University Press, 1986.

Kohn, Stephen M. *American Political Prisoners: Prosecutions under the Espionage and Sedition Acts.* Westport, Conn.: Praeger, 1994.

Konishi, Sho. *Anarchist Modernity: Cooperatism and Japanese-Russian Intellectual Relations in Modern Japan.* Cambridge, Mass.: Harvard University Press, 2013.

Kraft, James P. "The Fall of Job Harriman's Socialist Party: Violence, Gender and Politics in Los Angeles, 1911." *Southern California Quarterly* 70, no. 1 (Spring 1988): 43–68.

Kropotkin, Peter. "Anarchism: Its Philosophy and Ideal." San Francisco: Free Society, 1898.

———. "Autobiography of a Revolutionist." *Atlantic Monthly* 83, no. 395 (1899).

———. Peter Kropotkin, *Words of a Rebel.* Montreal: Black Rose, 1992.

Bibliography

Kuhn, Margaret. *Radical Space: Building the House of the People*. Ithaca, N.Y.: Cornell University Press, 2003.

Kurashige, Scott. *The Shifting Grounds of Race: Black and Japanese Americans in the Making of Multiethnic Los Angeles*. Princeton, N.J.: Princeton University Press, 2008.

La Botz, Dan. "American 'Slackers' in the Mexican Revolution: International Proletarian Politics in the Midst of a National Revolution." *Americas* 62, no. 4 (2006): 563–90.

Laforcade, Geoffroy de, and Kirwin R. Shaffer, eds. *In Defiance of Boundaries: Anarchism in Latin American History*. Gainesville: University Press of Florida, 2015.

Laslett, John H. M. *Sunshine Was Never Enough: Los Angeles Workers, 1880–2010*. Berkeley: University of California Press, 2012.

Lee, Erika. *At America's Gates: Chinese Immigration during the Exclusion Era, 1882–1943*. Chapel Hill: University of North Carolina Press, 2003.

———. "Hemispheric Orientalism and the 1907 Pacific Coast Race Riots." *Amerasia Journal* 33, no. 2 (2007): 19–48.

———. "Orientalisms in the Americas: A Hemispheric Approach to Asian American History." *Journal of Asian American Studies* 8, no. 3 (October 2005): 235–56.

Levy, Carl. *Gramsci and the Anarchists*. New York: Berg, 1999.

Lewis, Austin. "The Basis of Solidarity." *New Review*, August 15, 1915.

———. "The Drift in California." *International Socialist Review* 12 (November 1911): 272–74.

———. "Organization of the Unskilled." Part 1. *New Review* 1, no. 22 (November 1913).

———. "Organization of the Unskilled." Part 2. *New Review* 1, no. 23 (December 1913).

Lewis, Daniel. *Iron Horse Imperialism: The Southern Pacific of Mexico, 1880–1951*. Tucson: University of Arizona Press, 2007.

Lewis, Ronald L. *Black Coal Miners in America: Race, Class, and Community Conflict, 1780–1980*. Lexington: University Press of Kentucky, 1987.

Linebaugh, Peter, and Marcus Rediker. *The Many-Headed Hydra: Sailors, Slaves, Commoners, and the Hidden History of the Revolutionary Atlantic*. Boston: Beacon, 2000).

Lipsitz, George. *Dangerous Crossroads: Popular Music, Postmodernism and the Poetics of Place*. London: Verso, 1997.

Lomnitz, Claudio. *The Return of Comrade Ricardo Flores Magón*. New York: Zone, 2014.

Lothrop, Gloria Ricci. *Chi Siamo: The Italians of Los Angeles*. Pasadena, Calif.: Tabula Rasa, 1981.

———. *Fulfilling the Promise of California: An Anthology of Essays on the Italian American Experience in California*. Spokane, Wash.: California Italian American Task Force / Arthur H. Clark Co., 2000.

———. "The Italians of Los Angeles," *Californians* 5, no. 3 (1987): 28–43.

Löwy, Michael. *Redemption and Utopia: Jewish Libertarian Thought in Central Europe; A Study in Elective Affinity*. London: Athlone, 1988.

Lubow, Sylvia. "The Espionage Act in Southern California." MA thesis, University of California, Los Angeles, 1968.

Luckingham, Bradford. *Minorities in Phoenix: A Profile of Mexican American, Chinese American, and African American Communities, 1860–1992*. Tucson: University of Arizona Press, 1994.

Bibliography

MacLachlan, Colin M. *Anarchism and the Mexican Revolution: The Political trials of Ricardo Flores Magón in the United States*. Berlekey: University of California Press, 1991.

Madley, Benjamin. *An American Genocide: The United States and the California Indian Catastrophe, 1846–1873*. New Haven, Conn.: Yale University Press, 2016. Kindle e-book edition.

Malatesta, Errico. *Fra Contadini*. Paterson, N.J.: Tipografia della Questione Sociale, 1898.

McEuen, William Wilson. "A Survey of the Mexicans in Los Angeles." MA thesis, University of Southern California, 1914.

McKinnon, Andrew M. "Elective Affinities of the Protestant Ethic: Weber and the Chemistry of Capitalism." *Sociological Theory* 28, no. 1 (March 2010): 108–26.

McWilliams, Carey. *Factories in the Field*. Boston: Little, Brown, 1935.

———. *North from Mexico: The Spanish-Speaking People of the United States*. New York: Greenwood, 1990.

———. *Southern California Country: An Island on the Land*. New York: Duell, Sloan, and Pearce, 1946.

Mellinger, Philip J. *Race and Labor in Western Copper: The Fight of Equality, 1896–1918*. Tucson: University of Arizona Press, 1995.

Modell, John. *The Economics and Politics of Racial Accommodation: The Japanese of Los Angeles, 1900–1942*. Urbana: University of Illinois Press, 1977.

Monroy, Douglas. "Anarquismo y Comunismo: Mexican Radicalism and the Communist Party in Los Angeles During the 1930s." *Labor History* 24, no. 1 (Winter 1983): 33–59.

———. *Rebirth: Mexican Los Angeles from the Great Migration to the Great Depression*. Berkeley: University of California Press, 1999.

Montgomery, David. *The Fall of the House of Labor: The Workplace, the State, and American Labor Activism, 1865–1925*. Cambridge: Cambridge University Press, 1987.

Mormino, Gary R., and George E. Pozzetta. *The Immigrant World of Ybor City: Italians and Their Latin Neighbors in Tampa, 1885–1985*. Urbana: University of Illinois Press, 1987.

Murrah, Bill. "Llano Cooperative Colony, Louisiana." *Southern Exposure* 1, no. 3–4 (1974): 87–104.

Murray, John, Jr. "A Foretaste of the Orient." *International Socialist Review* 4 (August 1903): 72–79.

Murray, Tom. *Canadian Pacific Railway*. St. Paul, Minn.: Voyageur, 2006.

Nelson, Bruce. *Workers on the Waterfront: Seamen, Longshoremen, and Unionism in the 1930s*. Urbana: University of Illinois Press, 1988.

Nicolaides, Becky M. *My Blue Heaven: Life and Politics in the Working-Class Suburbs of Los Angeles, 1920–1965*. Chicago: University of Chicago Press, 2002.

Ngai, Mae M. *Impossible Subjects: Illegal Aliens and the Making of Modern America*. Princeton, N.J.: Princeton University Press, 2004.

Orsi, Richard J. *Sunset Limited: The Southern Pacific Railroad and the Development of the American West, 1850–1930*. Berkeley: University of California Press, 2005.

O'Toole, Alan. *With the Poor People of the Earth: A Biography of Doctor John Creaghe of Sheffield and Buenos Aires*. Berkeley: Kate Sharpley Library, 2005.

Owen, William C. *Anarchism Versus Socialism*. London: Freedom Press, 1922.

Parker, Carleton H. *The Casual Laborer and Other Essays*. Seattle: University of Washington Press, 1920.

Bibliography

Peck, Gunther. *Reinventing Free Labor: Padrones and Immigrant Workers in the North American West, 1880–1930.* Cambridge: Cambridge University Press, 2000.

Pernicone, Nunzio. *Carlo Tresca: Portrait of a Rebel.* New York: Palgrave Macmillan, 2005.

———. "War among the Italian Anarchists: The Galleanisti's Campaign against Carlo Tresca." In *The Lost World of Italian American Radicalism: Politics, Labor, and Culture,* edited by Phillip V. Cannistraro and Gerald Meyer, 77–98. Westport, Conn.: Praeger, 2003.

Perry, Louis B., and Richard S. Perry. *A History of the Los Angeles Labor Movement, 1911–1941.* Berkeley: University of Californa Press, 1963.

Pitt, Leonard. *The Decline of the Californios: A Social History of Spanish-Speaking Californians, 1846–1890.* Berkeley: University of California Press, 1966.

Poniatowska, Elena. *Las Soldaderas: Women of the Mexican Revolution.* El Paso, Tex.: Cinco Puntos, 2006.

Poole, David, ed. *Land and Liberty: Anarchist Influences in the Mexican Revolution.* Sanday, Orkney: Cienfuegos, 1977.

Preston, William. *Aliens and Dissenters: Federal Suppression of Radicals, 1903–1933.* New York: Harper and Row, 1963.

Presutto, Michele. *La rivoluzione dietro l'angolo: Gli anarchici e aa Rivoluzione messicana 1910–1914.* Foligno: Umbra, 2017.

Puri, Harish K. *Ghadar Movement: Ideology, Organisation and Strategy.* Amritsar, Punjab: Guru Nanak Dev University Press, 1983.

Raat, W. Dirk. *Revoltosos: Mexico's Rebels in the United States, 1903–1923.* College Station: Texas A&M University Press, 1981.

Ramnath, Maia. *Haj to Utopia: How the Ghadar Movement Charted Global Radicalism and Attempted to Overthrow the British Empire.* Berkeley: University of California Press, 2011.

Rocker, Rudolf. *Nationalism and Culture.* Los Angeles: Rocker Publications Committee, 1937.

———. "Testimonial to Rudolf Rocker, 1873–1943." Los Angeles: Rocker Publications Committee, 1944.

Rosemont, Franklin. *Joe Hill: The IWW and the Making of a Revolutionary Workingclass Counterculture.* Oakland, Calif.: PM, 2015.

Rosenthal, Anton. "Moving between the Global and the Local: The Industrial Workers of the World and their Press in Latin America." In Laforcade and Shaffer, *In Defiance of Boundaries,* 72–94.

———. "Radical Border Crossers: The Industrial Workers of the World and Their Press in Latin America." *Estudios Interdisciplinarios de América Latina y el Caribe* 22, no. 2 (2011): 39–70.

Sackman, Douglas Cazaux. *Orange Empire: California and the Fruits of Eden.* Berkeley: University of California Press, 2005.

Salerno, Salvatore. *Red November, Black November: Culture and Community in the Industrial Workers of the World.* Albany: SUNY Press, 1989.

Samaniego López, Marco Antonio. "El Poblado Fronterizo de Tijuana: Emiliano Zapata y la Rivoluzione da Tavolino." *HMex* 66, no. 3 (2017).

Sanchez, George J. *Becoming Mexican American: Ethnicity, Culture, and Identity in Chicano Los Angeles, 1900–1945.* Oxford: Oxford University Press, 1993.

Bibliography

Sandos, James A. *Rebellion in the Borderlands: Anarchism and the Plan of San Diego*. Norman: University of Oklahoma Press, 1992.

Santillan, Diego Abad de. *Ricardo Flores Magón: El Apostol de la Revolucion Social Mexicana*. Mexico, D. F.: Grupo Cultural "Ricardo Flores Magón," 1925.

Saxton, Alexander. *The Indispensable Enemy: Labor and the Anti-Chinese Movement in California*. Berkeley: University of California Press, 1971.

Scott, James C. *The Art of Not Being Governed: An Anarchist History of Upland Southeast Asia*. New Haven, Conn.: Yale University Press, 2009.

———. *Domination and the Arts of Resistance: Hidden Transcripts*. New Haven, Conn.: Yale University Press, 1990.

———. *Weapons of the Weak: Everyday Forms of Peasant Resistance*. New Haven, Conn.: Yale University Press, 1985.

Shaffer, Kirk. "Tropical Libertarians: Anarchist Movements and Networks in the Caribbean, Southern United States, and Mexico, 1890s–1920s." In *Anarchism and Syndicalism in the Colonial and Postcolonial World, 1870—1940: The Praxis of National Liberation, Internationalism, and Social Revolution*, 273–320. Boston: Brill, 2010.

Shaffer, Kirwin. *Anarchism and Countercultural Politics in Early Twentieth-Century Cuba*. Gainesville: University Press of Florida, 2005.

———. "Havana Hub: Cuban Anarchism, Radical Media and the Trans-Caribbean Anarchist Network, 1902–1915." *Caribbean Studies* 37, no. 2 (July–December 2009): 45–81.

———. "Latin Lines and Dots: Transnational Anarchism, Regional Networks, and Italian Libertarians in Latin America." *Zapruder World* 1 (Spring 2014).

Shanks, Rosalie. "The I.W.W. Free Speech Movement." *Journal of San Diego History* 19, no. 1 (Winter 1973): 1–16.

Shor, Francis. "'Virile Syndicalism' in Comparative Perspective: A Gender Analysis of the IWW in the United States and Australia." *International Labor and Working-Class History* 56 (Fall 1999): 65–77.

Sides, Josh. *L.A. City Limits: African American Los Angeles from the Great Depression to the Present*. Berkeley: University of California Press, 2003.

Sitton, Tom, and William Francis Deverell, eds. *Metropolis in the Making: Los Angeles in the 1920s*. Berkeley: University of California Press, 2001.

Snow, David A., Sarah A. Soule, and Hanspeter Kriesi, eds. *The Blackwell Companion to Social Movements*. Malden, Mass.: Blackwell, 2004.

Sokoloff, Lillian. *The Russians in Los Angeles*. Los Angeles: University of Southern California Press, 1918.

Solnit, Rebecca. *A Paradise Built in Hell: The Extraordinary Communities That Arise in Disaster*. New York: Penguin, 2009.

Solomon, Mark. *The Cry Was Unity: Communists and African Americans, 1917–36*. Jackson: University Press of Mississippi, 1998.

———. *Wanderlust: A History of Walking*. New York: Penguin, 2009.

Songs of the Workers: To Fan the Flames of Discontent. 34th ed. Chicago: Industrial Workers of the World, 1980.

Bibliography

Spenser, Daniela, and Richard Stoller. "Radical Mexico: Limits to the Impact of Soviet Communism." *Latin American Perspectives* 35, no. 2 (March 2008): 57–70.

Stamm, Michael. "The Space for News." *Media History* 21, no. 1 (2015): 55–73.

Stansbury, Jeffery. "Organized Workers and the Making of Los Angeles, 1890–1915." PhD diss., University of California, Los Angeles, 2008.

Stevens, Errol Wayne. *Radical L.A.: From Coxey's Army to the Watts Riots, 1894–1965.* Norman: University of Oklahoma Press, 2009.

Stimson, Grace Heilman. *Rise of the Labor Movement in Los Angeles.* University of California Press, 1955.

Streeby, Shelley. *Radical Sensations: World Movements, Violence, and Visual Culture.* Durham, N.C.: Duke University Press, 2013.

Street, Richard Steven. *Beasts of the Field: A Narrative History of California Farm Workers, 1769–1913.* Stanford, Calif.: Stanford University Press, 2004.

Struthers, David M. "IWW Internationalism and Interracial Organizing in the Southwestern United States." In Cole, Struthers, and Zimmer, *Wobblies of the World,* 74–88.

Swedberg, Richard. *The Max Weber Dictionary: Key Words and Central Concepts.* Stanford, Calif.: Stanford University Press, 2005.

Taibo, Paco Ignacio, II. *Bolcheviques: Una Historia Narrativa del Origen del Comunismo en Mexico.* México, D.F.: Ediciones B México, S.A., 2008.

Taylor, Lawrence D. "The Magonista Revolt in Baja California: Capitalist Conspiracy or Rebelion De Los Pobres?" *Journal of San Diego History* 45, no. 1 (1999): 2–31.

Teiser, Ruth. *Ethel Duffy Turner: Writers and Revolutionists.* Berkeley, Calif.: Regional Oral History Office, 1967.

Trotter, Joe William. *Coal, Class, and Color: Blacks in Southern West Virginia, 1915–32.* Urbana: University of Illinois Press, 1990.

Truett, Samuel. *Fugitive Landscapes: The Forgotten History of the U.S.-Mexico Borderlands.* New Haven, Conn.: Yale University Press, 2006.

Truett, Samuel, and Elliott Young, eds. *Continental Crossroads: Remapping U.S.-Mexico Borderlands History.* Durham, N.C.: Duke University Press, 2004.

———. "Making Transnational History: Nations, Regions, and Borderlands." In *Continental Crossroads,* 1–34.

Turcato, Davide. "Italian Anarchism as a Transnational Movement, 1885–1915." *International Review of Social History* 52, no. 3 (December 2007): 407–44.

Turner, Ethel Duffy. *Revolution in Baja California: Ricardo Flores Magon's High Noon.* Detroit: Blaine Ethridge, 1981.

———. *Ricardo Flores Magón y El Partido Liberal Mexicano.* Morelia, Michoacán: Editorial Erandi del Gobierno del Estado Morelia, Michoacán, 1960.

Turner, John Kenneth. *Barbarous Mexico.* Chicago: Kerr, 1911.

U.S. Commission on Industrial Relations. *Industrial Relations: Final Report and Testimony Submitted to Congress by the Commission on Industrial Relations.* 11 vols. Washington, D.C.: U.S. GPO, 1916.

Vanderwood, Paul. *Juan Soldado: Rapist, Murderer, Martyr, Saint.* Durham, N.C.: Duke University Press, 2004.

Bibliography

————. *The Power of God against the Guns of Government: Religious Upheaval in Mexico at the Turn of the Nineteenth Century*. Stanford, Calif.: Stanford University Press, 1998.

————. "Writing History with Picture Postcards: Revolution in Tijuana." *Journal of San Diego History* 33, no. 4 (Fall 1987): 38–63.

Van Valen, Nelson. "The Bolsheviki and the Orange Growers." *Pacific Historical Review* 22, no. 1 (1953): 39–50.

Van Valen, Nelson. "Cleaning up the Harbor: The Suppression of the I.W.W. at San Pedro, 1922–25." *Southern California Quarterly* 66, no. Summer (1984): 147–72.

Vargas, Zaragosa. *Proletarians of the North: A History of Mexican Industrial Workers in Detroit and the Midwest, 1917–1933*. Berkeley: University of California Press, 1993.

Vorspan, Max, and Lloyd P. Gartner. *History of the Jews of Los Angeles*. Phladelphia: Jewish Publication Society of America, 1970.

Wayne, Tiffany K. ed. *Women's Rights in the United States: A Comprehensive Encyclopedia of Issues, Events, and People*. 4 vols. Santa Barbara, Calif.: ABC-CLIO, 2014.

Weber, Devra Ann. *Dark Sweat, White Gold: California Farm Workers, Cotton, and the New Deal*. Berkeley: University of California Press, 1994.

————. "'Different Plans': Indigenous Pasts, the Partido Liberal Mexicano, and Questions about Reframing Binational Social Movements of the Twentieth Century." *Social Justice* 42, no. 3–4 (2015): 10–28.

————. "Wobblies of the Partido Liberal Mexicano: Reenvisioning Internationalist and Transnational Movements through Mexican Lenses." *Pacific Historical Review* 85, no. 2 (2016): 188–226.

Weintraub, Hyman. "The I.W.W. In California: 1905–1931." MA thesis, University of California, Los Angeles, 1947.

Whitten, Woodrow C. "Criminal Syndicalism and the Law in California: 1919–1927." *Transactions of the American Philosophical Society* 59, no. 2 (1969).

Wild, Mark. *Street Meeting: Multiethnic Neighborhoods in Early Twentieth-Century Los Angeles*. Berkeley: University of California Press, 2005.

Wilson, Ione Elizabeth. "The I.W.W. in California, with Special Reference to Migratory Labor (1910–1913)." MA thesis, University of California, 1941.

Wollenberg, Charles. "Working on El Traque: The Pacific Electric Strike of 1903." *Pacific Historical Review* 42, no. 3 (1973): 358–69.

Wood, Andrew Grant. "Death of a Political Prisoner: Revisiting the Case of Ricardo Flores Magón." *A Contra corriente* 3.1 (2005): 38.66.

Yamanouchi, Akito. "The Letters and Manuscripts of Sen Katayama in Mexico, 1921." *Monthly Journal of Ohara Institute for Social Research (Tokyo)*, no. 506 (2001).

Young, Elliott. *Catarino Garza's Revolution on the Texas-Mexico Border*. Durham, N.C.: Duke University Press, 2004.

Zesch, Scott. *The Chinatown War: Chinese Los Angeles and the Massacre of 1871*. New York: Oxford University Press, 2012.

Zimmer, Kenyon. "Anarchist, Informant, Fascist, or American? Self-Representation and the Many Faces of Ludovico Caminita." Paper presented at the European Social Science History Conference, Vienna, Austria, April 23–26, 2014.

Bibliography

———. "'A Cosmopolitan Crowd': Transnational Anarchists, the IWW, and the American Radical Press." In Cole, Struthers, and Zimmer, *Wobblies of the World*, 29–43.

———. "The Forgotten Revolution: North American and European Anarchists in the 1911 Mexican Insurrection." Paper presented to the North American Anarchist Studies Network Conference, New Orleans, January 6, 2013.

———. *Immigrants against the State: Yiddish and Italian Anarchism in America*. Urbana: University of Illinois Press, 2015.

———. "Premature Anti-Communists? American Anarchism, the Russian Revolution, and Left-Wing Libertarian Anti-Communism, 1917—1939." *Labor: Studies in Working-Class History of the Americas* 6, no. 2 (2009): 45–71.

———. "'The Whole World Is Our Country': Immigration and Anarchism in the United States, 1885–1940." PhD diss., University of Pittsburgh, 2010.

INDEX

4-trey, 206

Abad de Santillan, Diego, 62–63
Abbott, Leonard, 104
Adachi, S., 70
Adames, Rafaél, 170–71, 177
affinity: culture of 2–3, 6–13, 15, 36, 46, 48,
    64, 126, 133, 156, 165, 206–7, 226–27;
    network, 136–37, 146; solidarity, 151
African Americans, 2, 25, 30, 47, 82, 166;
    businesses, 32; communism, 222; em-
    ployment 29; IWW, 105, 113; Mexican
    Revolution, 3, 138–39; migration, 24,
    28–29; plan of San Diego, 179–80; so-
    cialists, 87–88, 89, 102–3, 121; unions,
    13, 71–72, 75, 77, 90, 121
Afro-American League, 121
Agriculture Workers' Organization
    (AWO), 113, 190–91, 197
Aguascalientes, Mexico, 177
Aguilar, Pedro C., 199
Alameda County, 115
Alaska, 18, 29
Albanians, 26
Albuquerque, New Mexico, 102
Alexander, George, 40, 158

Altman, John, 175
Alzalde, Eugenio, 167
Amador, Josefina, 136
American Beet Sugar Company, 70
American Civil Liberties Union, 205
American Economist, 56
American Federation of Labor (AFL),
    3–6, 18, 44, 168; building trades, 37;
    IWW, 14, 38, 44, 83, 137, 176, 190, 217;
    newspaper, 51, 52, 101; organizing, 66,
    72, 75; political organizing, 85; race, 14,
    37, 78–80, 82, 90; Socialist Party, 40,
    158; strikes, 127, 158; United Laborers,
    106–26
Amsterdam, Netherlands, 81
Anaconda Copper, 19
Anaheim, California, 111
anarchism, 3–5; anarchist history, 12–13;
    centers, 45, 159, 216; IWW, 134, 176, 215;
    movement, 63–64, 151, 188, 211, 220–21,
    226; networks, 54, 103–4, 201; organiz-
    ing, 36, 41, 87, 214, 218; PLM, 52, 118,
    122, 134, 151–53, 188, 215, 225; repres-
    sion, 189; theory 7–12
Anarchist Exclusion Act (1903), 189
Ancona, Italy, 104

Index

Andrade, Cesario, 170
Anglo-Boer War, 128
Antelope Valley, California, 40
Anthony (of IWW, met with Kōtoku), 103
anti-Chinese movement, 14, 27, 65–66, 96–97, 120
antichinismo, 96
Anti-Citizens' League, 37
anti-organizzatore, 134
anti-Semitism, 221
aqueduct (Los Angeles), 22, 153, 224
Araujo, Antonio de P., 132, 162, 167, 173
Arbayter Ring (Workmen's Circle), 39, 213
Arismendez, F. H., 84
Arizona Federation of Labor, 191
Arizona Republican, 181–82
Armenians, 3, 26, 27, 80, 115, 222–23
Arnold, Charles, 70–71
Arriaga, Camilo, 152
Arteaga, Therese, 204, 215–16
Asians: AFL, 14; laborers, 30, 90; migration, 24, 89; organizing, 72–73, 108–9, 113, 121; racism against, 38, 78, 82, 90, 108–9; South Asians, 138, 187, 191, 202; violence against, 65
Asiatic Exclusion League, 108, 113
Asunción, Paraguay, 58
Atlanta, Georgia, 29
Atlantic Monthly, 60
Australians, 138, 140
Azuara, Aurelio Vincente, 17–19, 34, 163, 176–77, 191, 192, 194, 196–97, 203
Azuza, California, 198

Baba, Kōzaburō ("Joe"), 70
Baginski, Max, 60, 81
Baja California, 6, 14–15, 32, 60, 115, 118, 126, 127–56, 158
Baker, William, 182
Bakersfield, California, 48, 49, 197
Bakunin Institute, 203
Barcelona, Spain, 57, 61
Baronio, Ninfa, 200
Barre, Vermont, 134
Bauer, Kasper, 89, 141
Bazora, Florencio, 93
Bebel, August, 88
Bell, Lizzie, 35, 213
Bell, Marion, 35, 212

Bell, Thomas A., 35, 44, 56, 129, 133, 179–82, 204, 213, 214, 218, 219–26
Bellamy Nationalist Movement, 37
Bellingham, Washington, 92
Belvedere Park, California, 45, 214
Bender, F. Ira, 153
Benjamin, Walter, 8
Berkman, Alexander, 34, 56, 104, 186, 210, 223, 226
Berlin, Germany, 62, 102
Berthold, Simon, 137, 140, 144
Better America Federation, 214
Biddle, Lemuel, 37, 40, 66, 74–75, 77–78, 85
Bisbee, Arizona, 26, 49, 193
Bisbee Deportation, 190, 193, 198
Black, Orlow, 202
The Blast, 35, 56, 186
Bolshevism, 7, 62, 197, 201, 209–10, 219
Bond, D., 5, 105
Bond, Ned, 113
Bontemps, Arna, 33
border (U.S.-Mexico), businesses, 19, 146; crossing, 15, 24, 76, 98–99, 128, 133, 136–38, 140–41, 166–67, 180; organizing across, 42, 93, 110, 135, 164, 185, 189; region, 17, 94, 129–32, 150, 200, 211
The Border (Newspaper), 131
borderlands, 4, 26, 48, 117, 127, 129, 132–34, 153, 158, 178–79, 196, 202
Boston, Massachusetts, 149, 200, 218
Boyle Heights, 15, 30, 45, 46, 170, 198, 212, 213, 216, 218
Brawley, California, 56, 57, 111, 114, 221
Brazil, 62, 149
Brazo y Cerebro, 163
British Columbia, Canada, 92, 187–88
Brooklyn, New York, 147–48, 163
Brotherhood of Timber Workers, 167
Brousse, María, 131
Brown, John, 168
Brown, William Thurston, 148, 212
Buck, P. H., 175
Buford, 210
bum. *See* tramps
Burbank Hall, 44, 46, 53, 81, 87, 99
Bureau of Investigation (BI), 61, 161, 186–87, 193, 196–98, 199, 200
Busick, Charles, 205, 223
Butte, Montana, 49, 190

278

Index

California Civil Liberties Union, 202
California Eagle, 32
California Social-Democrat, 51, 56, 171
California State Federation of Labor (CSFL), 14, 66, 105, 107–9, 116–18, 120, 122, 125–26
California Theater Guild, 225
California Veckoblad, 50
Californios, 20–21
Calles, Plutarco Elias, 216, 219
Caminita, Ludovico, 58, 90–91, 119, 134, 140, 147, 151, 154
Canada, 19, 21, 27, 63, 94, 114, 138, 140, 185, 226
Canadian Pacific Railway Company, 19
Cananea, Mexico, 39, 48, 94, 99, 110, 129, 137, 196
La Capital, 58
Carmona, Paula, 162
Carmona, Rafael, 38, 85, 90, 99
Carmona, Rómulo, 44, 56, 95, 159
Carranza, Venustiano, 57, 182, 203
Carrillo, Vincente, 53
Carrizo Springs, Texas, 49, 164, 166–67
Casa del Obrero Mundial (International House of Labor), 57
Casas Grandes, Chihuahua, Mexico, 137
case del popolo, 36
Casterano, Peter, 153, 170
Cedeño, Felix, 53, 195–96
Central Park (Los Angeles), 46–47
Cerro School, 159
Cervantes, Felipe P., 216
Chamber of Commerce (Los Angeles), 22
Chaplin, Ralph, 42, 225
Charter Oak Citrus Association, 197
Chavez Ravine, 44
Cherbak, Anton P., 101
Chicago trial (IWW), 194–95, 197
Chickasaw, Oklahoma, 102
Chiechi, L., 200
Chihuahua, Mexico, 97, 130–31, 134, 136–38, 148, 166
children: anarchist families, 35, 56, 162, 180, 189, 204, 213, 215–16, 225; indigenous, 42; labor organizing, 166, 197–98, 222; performance, 100; violence toward, 166, 205
Chile, 129, 149

China, 97, 148, 163
Chinatown (Los Angeles), 27, 30, 46, 47, 65
Chinese: anarchism, 62, 138, 163, 227; community, 45, 65, 93; laborers, 6, 26, 27, 67, 90, 121, 122; migration 24, 37, 86; newspapers, 56, 62; organizing, 13, 72, 78, 113, 222; racism toward, 14, 27, 32, 65–66, 95–98, 105, 120, 152; population, 25, 32, 82; violence toward, 65–66
Chinese Anarchist News, 163
Chinese Exclusion Act (1882), 27, 67
Chinese Massacre, 65
Christmas riot (1913), 43, 47, 169, 164, 172–74, 176–78
Chung Sai Yat Po, 56
científicos, 129
Cipolla, Vincenzo, 147
Círculo de Trabajadores de Brooklyn, 147
Cisneros, Abraham, 168
citrus, 3, 20, 24, 27, 28, 42, 111, 191, 197–99
Claremont, California, 191
Clarion Colony, 213
Clifton, Arizona, 48, 109–10, 193
Cline, Charles, 167–70, 178, 180
club liberales, 84–85, 92–93, 129–30, 132, 134
Club Liberal Justicia, 84–85, 92
Coahuila, Mexico, 134, 148, 166–67, 180
Cocopah, 138
Cogito, Ergo Sum, 58
Colombia, 159
Colorado, 99, 109, 173, 218–19
Columbine, Colorado, 219
Commission of Immigration, 113
Commission of Immigration and Housing, 165
Commission on Industrial Relations, 113
Communism, 3–4, 15, 38, 197, 201, 206, 209, 216–17, 221–24, 226
Communist Party, 5, 32, 206, 210–12, 215, 221–22
Comstock Law (1873), 54–55
Confederación de Uniónes de Campesinos y Obreros Mexicanos (CUCOM), 225
Confederación de Uniónes Obreros Mexicanos (CUOM), 217, 225
Confederación Regional Obrera Mexicana (CROM), 225

279

Index

Conger-Kaneko, Josephine, 91, 103
Connors, H. B., 153
Cordoba, Alfonso, 197
Coria, Pedro, 1–2, 15, 53, 110, 170, 176, 191–94, 196, 201
Corona, José, 163, 176
Correo Mexicano, 31–32, 51, 98, 196
Le Courrier Francais, 51
Covina, California, 197–98, 201
Coxey's Army, 37, 156
Cravello, Vittorio, 44, 134, 140, 168
Creaghe, John, 160, 186
Creel, Enrique, 98
Criminal Syndicalism Act (1919), 185, 201–2, 205–6
Cronaca Sovversiva, 131, 134, 146–47, 149, 151
Cultura Obrera, 57, 61, 110, 161, 163
Cultura Proletaria, 58, 110, 147, 219

Daily Worker, 222
Dale, J. B., 108–9, 116, 122–23
Dalmacja, 50
Darrow, Clarence, 100
Das, Tarknath, 202–3
Debs, Eugene V., 102
de Cleyre, Voltairine, 151
Defensor del Pueblo, 131
de Heras, Juan, 51
de la Cruz, Primo Tapia, 201, 215
de la Huerta, Felipe Adolfo, 215
de la Torre, Victor Raúl Haya, 201
Del Rio, Texas, 200
Der Sozialist, 62
Deutsche Zeitung, 51
Diario, 58
Díaz, Modesto, 84, 94–95, 162
Díaz, Porfirio, 105, 121, 146; economic development, 21, 24, 96, 153; organizing against, 84, 91, 93–94, 102, 129–36, 137, 225; repression by, 82, 92–93; revolution, 24, 144
Diegueño, 138
District Defense Committee (San Francisco), 202
Donnelly, John, 191
Dorame, Rosendo, 42, 110, 167
Douglas, Arizona, 129, 132

Downing, Mortimer, 84, 165, 195, 206, 207, 214, 217–18, 219, 223–24, 226
Duarte, California, 198
Durango, Mexico, 134, 148, 166

Eche, 50
Ecuador, 149
Edelman, John
Edendale, 172–73, 180, 182, 186
Edwards, Paul, 172
Eitel (socialist, met with Kōtoku), 103
El Centro, California, 111
El Grupo Anarquista "Obreros Libres", 45, 214
Elliott, James, 194
El Paso, Texas, 17, 44, 49, 76, 94, 129–31, 150, 166–67, 196
Emancipation Club, 83–84
Emancipator, 91
Emergency Program (E.P.), 206, 214, 219
Emerson, Laura Payne, 41, 115, 141–42, 154
Engleback (*El Rebelde* fundraiser), 53
Ensenada, Mexico, 141
L'Era Nuova, 58, 119, 134, 146–47, 149, 200
Escondido, California, 111
Esperanto, 45, 160
Espinosa, Albert, 68
Espinosa, José, 144
Espionage Act (1917), 184, 189–90, 194–95, 199
Esteve, Pedro, 109–10, 142–43, 161, 163
Ettor, Joe, 110, 155, 166, 223–24
Everett, Washington, 48, 190
Evolución Obrera, 57

Fabijanović, Stephanus, 44, 215–16, 218, 225–26
Fall, Albert, 136
Fasano, Michele, 200
Faure, Sébastien, 10–11
Federal Theater Project, 225
Feider, Charles M., 118
Fernandez, Alefo, 66, 74
Ferrer i Guardia, Francisco, 159
Ferris, Dick, 145
Figueroa, Anselmo, 85, 118, 140, 144, 155, 161–62, 172, 186
Fil di Fer, 85

Index

Filipinos, 24, 222
Finns, 26, 102
First African Methodist Episcopal Church, 88
Fitzgerald, Eleanor, 35
Fleischmann, Leopold, 103–4
Fletcher, Benjamin H., 166, 202
Flores, José, 144
Flores Magón, Enrique, anarchism, 5, 161, 218; arrest, 144, 182; arrival in Los Angeles, 82; deportation, 203–4; Edendale, 172; incarcerated, 162, 189, 202; organizing, 48, 132; in Mexico, 92–93, 215–16, 225; *Regeneración*, 55, 61; St. Louis, 94; *Les Temps Nouveaux*, 151; trial, 155, 186, 188
Flores Magón, Jesús, 92–93, 144
Flores Magón, Ricardo, anarchism, 135, 152; arrest, 94, 94, 98, 144; death, 203–4; Edendale, 172; Esteve, Pedro, 142–43; incarceration, 130, 132, 161, 172, 202–3; IWW, 110, 178, 182; Los Angeles, 82, 95, 162, 178, 188; Madero, Francisco, 134, 137; in Mexico, 92–93, 129; Peasants Syndicate, 216; PLM, 44; revolution, 94, 134, 140; Russian Revolution, 210; St. Louis, 93; *Les Temps Nouveaux*, 151; trial, 55, 155–56, 186, 188, 189
Flory, Ishmael, 222
Ford, Richard, 165–66, 191
Francisco Ferrer Association, 147, 212
Franck, Harry Alverson, 60
Free Harbor League, 22
free-speech fight, 41, 48, 58, 60, 110–11, 115, 126, 154, 169, 190
Freie Arbeiter Stimme, 63, 227
Fresno, California, 27, 30, 48, 49, 60, 108, 111, 115, 122, 126, 174, 190, 198
Fuertes, Antonio, 144
Fuerza Consciente, 51–52, 163
Fulton, Edward, 61
Furlong, Thomas, 98
Furlong Secret Service Company, 94
Furuseth, Andrew, 107–8, 116

Gaitán, Teodoro M., 162, 178
Galcotti, Guglielmo, 147
Gale, Linn, 201

Gale's Magazine, 201
Gallagher, Leo, 205
Gallagher, Mary, 202–5, 218, 225
Galleani, Luigi, 134, 144, 148–49, 200
Gallo, Firmino, 200
Gallo, William, 200
Gandolfo, Pietro, 217
García, Rafael, 215–16
García, Rosario, 144
Gartz, Kate Crane, 205
Gary, Indiana, 169
Garza, Catarino, 129
Garza, Manuel G., 150
Geary Act, 66
gender, 5, 26, 30, 34, 41
General Executive Board (GEB), 133, 176
Gentleman's Agreement (1907), 27, 88
George, Henry, 20
Germans: community, 26, 46, 88, 93, 137; migration, 138, 193; newspapers, 51, 60, 62; organizing, 5, 39–40, 63, 87, 100–102, 104, 115, 122, 141, 157, 168, 175, 179, 210, 215, 220, 227
German Socialist Menarche (Men's Choir), 104
Germinal, 196
Ghadar Party, 138, 203
Girardi, Egidio, 148
Giovannitti, Arturo, 155
Glendora, California, 198
Globe, Arizona, 43, 49, 57, 111, 132, 179, 193
Goethe, Johann Wolfgang von, 9
Goldman, Emma, 81, 86–87, 104, 141, 147–48, 154, 210, 226
Gomez, Eduardo, 85
Gompers, Samuel, 74, 78–79, 106–7, 108, 123
González, Jesus, 168
Goodwill Industries, 225
Goodyear Tire and Rubber Company, 23
Gran Liga Mexicana Empleados de los Ferrocarrileros, 42
Grave, Jean, 150
Gray, James, 66
Gray, Jim, 73, 77
Great Depression, 206, 212, 223
Great Migration, 28–29

Greeks, 26, 30, 112, 115, 122, 165
Grupe Frayhayt (Liberty Group), 147
Gruppo Autonomo (Boston), 148
Il Gruppo Diritto all'Esistenza (The Right to an Existence Group), 44, 134
Guabello, Spartaco, 200
Guadalajara, Mexico, 177
Guadalupe, Mexico, 137
Gue, Stanley, 168
Guernsey, W. D., 173
Guerra, José, 166–67
Guerrero, Práxedis, 48, 110, 132, 136
Guglielmo, Pasquini, 147
Gutiérrez de Lara, Lázaro, 38–39, 85–87, 97, 99, 102, 110, 118, 131–32, 152, 171, 179
Guzzardi, Raffaele, 149
Gyger, Theo, 51

Haberman, Roberto, 201
Haij, Alfred, 50
Hapgood, Hutchins, 104
Harding, Warren, 203, 205–6
Harlem Renaissance, 33
Harriman, Job, 15, 38, 40, 120–21, 158
Hartmann, Sadakichi, 104
Harvey, A. R., 194–95
Havana, Cuba, 159
Havel, Hippolyte, 104
Hawaii, 19, 24, 27, 165
Haymarket (Chicago), 47, 212
Haywood, William, 98–99, 110–11, 192, 194, 211
Hemet, California, 111
Heraldo de México, 51, 196
Hermanos Rojas, 219
Hernández, Miguel, 144
Herz, George, 71
Hill, Joe, 190
hobo. *See* tramps
Holston, A. R., 99–100
Holtville, California, 43, 49, 57, 111, 136, 138, 154, 221
Hombre, 58
Home Colony, 172, 186
Hoogendyke, William, 197
Horcasitas, Lisenciado Antonio, 93
Huelga General, 51–53, 163–64, 171, 176
Huerta, Victoriano, 162
Hughes, Langston, 222

Humbolt, Jean, 150
Hungarians, 5, 39–40, 100–102, 105
Huntington, Henry, 22, 74–76, 80
Husband, Patrick, 102

Idaho, 99–100
Imai, Uta, 92
Immigration Act (1917), 189, 193
Imperial Valley, California, 29, 43, 48, 56, 111, 114, 137, 221
Imperial Valley Press, 137
incarceration, 18, 55
India, 61, 92, 140, 163
indigenous, 19, 41, 48, 65, 96, 130, 133, 139, 144, 150–53, 219
Industrial Worker, 5, 41, 56, 60, 104–5, 113–15, 121, 124, 126, 133, 153–54, 225
Industrial Workers of the World (IWW), 41, 43, 46, 105, 137, 214; 217, 223, 224, 227; AFL, 14, 123–25; anarchism, 38, 119, 134; Baja raids, 137–41, 153; communism, 215, 222; Ettor and Giovannitti, 155; founding, 93, 225; free speech fights, 48, 58, 107, 127; growth in California, 109–15, 126, 132; multiracial, 5, 6, 42, 103; newspapers, 43, 51, 53, 56, 60, 61, 62, 105, 163–64, 176–78; organizing, 1, 6, 42, 43, 44, 48, 61, 83–84, 86, 100–101, 104, 117–18, 121, 153–54, 176–79, 204, 212–14, 216, 218–19, 221, 225–26; PLM, 2, 6, 48, 86, 100, 110, 133, 154, 181–82; Preamble, 4; principles, 41; railroads, 48; repression, 185, 190–99, 201–3, 204–6, 209; Russian Revolution, 201, 211; San Pedro, 204–5; songs, 44; street speaking, 47, 212; Wheatland, 163–73
Inose, Inosuke, 68
International, 41
International Anarchist Conference, 81
International Committee of the Mexican Liberal Party Junta, 101
internationalism: black, 3; friendship, 60; limits, 37–38, 73, 82–83, 88, 91, 121, 156; local forms, 5, 34, 36, 40, 82–83, 88, 101, 103, 105; PLM, 97; print-based, 60; socialist, 37, 39, 88–89, 92, 100
International Ladies' Garment Workers' Union (ILGWU), 199, 212, 217, 224, 226

International Socialist Review, 73
International Workers' Home, 45, 160–61, 172, 178
Ireland, 61, 160,
Ireland, William Francis, 175
Irish, 12–13, 26, 86, 93, 186
Italian Hall, 28, 44, 46, 82, 119, 171
Italians: anarchism, 44–45, 58, 60, 62, 90, 110, 131–32, 134, 140–41, 144, 146–49, 153, 155, 161–62, 187, 190, 200, 211, 215, 220, 224; community, 30–32, 45, 46, 50, 82, 85, 155, 221; laborers, 24, 30, 71, 75, 105, 115, 157, 165, 171, 175; migration, 28; newspapers, 50, 58, 60, 62–63, 84, 90, 131, 151; organizing 39, 113, 119, 122, 129, 138, 159–60, 179, 217, 220, 224
L'Italo Americano, 50
Italy, 8, 24, 36, 62, 104, 140, 200, 215

Janos, Chihuahua, Mexico, 137
Japanese: communism, 201; community, 2, 25, 31–33, 45, 98; exclusion, 88–90, 107, 141; Gentleman's Agreement (1907), 27, 88; JMLA, 14, 67–80, 90, 106; laborers, 27, 30, 109, 122, 165, 191; migration, 24, 27, 65, 90; newspapers, 61–62; organizing, 6, 13–14, 61, 66, 81–82, 91–92, 103–4, 112–13, 115, 122, 138, 179, 191, 197–98, 220; racism toward, 37, 98, 103, 108
Japanese internment, 65
Japanese Mexican Labor Association (JMLA), 14, 67–79, 90, 106
Jerome, Arizona, 48, 193
Jewish community, 26, 32, 44, 82, 220–21
Jiménez, Camilo J., 144
Jiménez, Chihuahua, 130
John Reed Club, 222
Johns, Cloudesley, 88–89
Johnson, Albert, 103
Johnson, Hiram, 165
Johnson-Reed Immigration Act (1924), 211
Joint Committee on Migratory Labor (JCML), 109, 115–17, 122–23,
Jozefoski, K., 141
jungle camps, 6, 36, 47
Justice Department (US), 190, 193–94, 198

Kakumei (*Revolution*), 91–92
Kaneko, Kiichi, 91

Katayama, Sen, 201, 212
Keiyaku-nin, 68
Kelly, Frank, 175–76
Kennett, California, 192
Khankhoje, Pandurang, 138
Kidder (atheist, met with Kōtoku), 103
Kiliwa, 138
King's River Canal & Irrigation Company, 20
Kitto, Byron, 218–19
Knights of Labor, 37
Koreans, 91, 220, 224
Kōtoku, Shusui, 103–4, 212
Kronstadt Rebellion, 210–11
Kropotkin, Peter, 9, 11, 60, 104, 148, 151, 153, 213, 221
Kropotkin Literary Society, 213, 216, 220, 224, 226–27
Ku Klux Klan, 205
Kushner, I., 223

labor contractors, 18, 26–27, 30, 67–69, 78, 80
Labor Temple, 37, 38, 44, 46
Lafayette, Colorado, 219
La Follette, Robert, 206
La Morticella, Andrea, 140
Lamson, Warren, 194, 198
Lance, Gaston, 186
Landauer, Gustav, 8, 60
Lara, Blas, 48, 162
Laredo, Texas, 93, 129, 200
Las Vacas, Coahuila, 167
Lauff (socialist, support of PLM), 99
La Verne, California, 198
Lazicki, W., 141
Leavenworth Penitentiary, 167, 189, 195, 202–4, 214, 219
lectores, 61
Leflin (imprisoned Anglo Wobblie), 154
Leiffert, P. H., 141
Leimert Park, California, 33
Lewis, Austin, 114, 117, 119, 124–25, 166, 202
Lewis, E. J., 153
Lewis, Ed, 154
Leyva, José María, 137
Libertad y Trabajo, 51, 110, 164
Libertarian Group, 45, 213–14, 216, 224

Index

Libertario Centro, 216
Liberty Group (Grupe Frayhayt), 147
Librería-Mexicana, 44, 46, 56
Lincoln, Abraham, 87
Lithuanians, 24, 39, 165, 220
Little, Frank, 42, 110, 115, 190, 193
Little Tokyo, 27, 30, 46
Live Oak, California, 92
Lizarras, J. M., 69, 70
Llano del Rio colony, 40–41, 158
Llewellyn Iron Works, 126
Lómas, Silvestre, 166–67
Long Beach, 120
Longo, John, 147, 149
Los Angeles Central Labor Council (CLC), 37, 40, 52, 85, 106, 120–21, 123–24, 168
Los Angeles City Water Company, 22
Los Angeles Hall of Records, 153, 155
Los Angeles Socialist, 51, 76
Los Angeles Times Bombing, 107, 127, 132, 153, 158, 169
Los Angeles Trades and Labor Council, 65
Los Angeles Unemployed Council, 222
Los Angeles-Pacific Railway, 114
Los Angeles's Council of Labor (COL), 66, 72–80, 108
Louisiana, 41, 180
Louisville, Kentucky, 215
Luchador, 45–46, 51, 225
Ludlow, Colorado, 49, 173
Lukács, Georg, 7
Lum, Dyer, 81
Luna, Odilón, 188
Luz (Light), 159

Madero, Francisco: Díaz opposition, 94; PLM, 90, 118, 129–30, 135–38, 140, 144–46, 152; president, 121, 148, 154, 159, 162; revolution, 150
Malatesta, Errico, 10, 153, 200, 215
Mammoth Hall, 61, 102, 170
Mapimí, 196
Maple, A. B., 153
Marburg, Cesar, 51
Marghetis, C., 50
Marine Transport Workers (MTW), 192
Martínez, León Cárdenas, 171
Martínez, Tomás, 191, 193, 196, 203

Marx, Karl, 7, 104, 117, 170
Marysville, California, 113, 166
Maya, 152
Mayo, 110
McCormick, A. I., 136
McEuen, William, 31
McKelvey, J. J., 166
McNamara, James B., 153, 158
McNamara, John, 153, 158
McWilliams, Carey, 2–3, 222
McWhirt, Charles, 194
Medina, Benigno, 191
Melcher Ocampo, Guautitlán, Mexico, 216
Mella, Julio Antonio, 201
Merchants and Manufacturers Association (M&M), 22, 37, 116
Mesabi Range, Minnesota, 190
Metal Trades strike (1910), 107, 117, 127
Metcalf, Arizona, 49, 57, 132, 193
Mexicali, Mexico, 49, 137–38, 144
Mexican Cigarmakers' Union, 38
Mexican Communist Party (PCM), 215
Mexican Defense Funds Committee, 100
Mexican Mutual Aid Association, 221
Mexico City, 28, 39, 49, 57, 93, 152, 159, 201, 204, 215
Miami, Arizona, 49, 132, 181, 193
Michoacán, Mexico, 1, 86
migratory workers, 3, 34, 48, 107–13, 115–17, 120, 122–25, 166
Military Intelligence Division (MID), 32, 57, 193, 198–99
Miller, John, 191
Miller, Loren, 222
Miller & Lux, 19–20, 28
Milwaukee, Wisconsin, 158, 162
Modern School, 45, 53, 179, 212, 227
Moffet, F., 205
Mojave Desert, 110
Moncaleano, Blanca, 44, 159–60, 162, 189
Moncaleano, Juan Francisco, 44, 159–63, 170–72, 177–78, 182
Monrovia, California, 198
Montebello, California, 33
Montenegro, 26
Monterrey, Mexico, 102, 200
Montevideo, Uruguay, 58
Montreal, Quebec, 94
Mooney, Thomas, 57

Index

Moore, Fred, 104, 154, 171
Morel, L., 150
Morelia, Michoacán, 1
Morenci, Arizona, 49, 57, 109–10, 132, 191, 193
Moreno, E. J., 191
Mosby, Jack, 140–41, 153–54
Mosquito, 31, 51, 84–85, 96
Moyer, Charles, 98–99, 110
multilingual, 5, 26, 35–36, 41–43, 58, 80, 81, 84–85, 130, 160, 195, 227
Municipal Employment Bureau, 173
Murphy, Joseph, 113
Murray Jr., John, 37, 66, 68–70, 72–74, 76–77, 79, 90, 100, 107, 131–32, 168
Murray, Sam, 140
mutualista, 92

National Guard, 180, 193
National Industrial Recovery Act (1933), 37
Nationalism and Culture, 227
National Students League, 222
Needles, California, 193
Negreira, B., 193
Negroes' National League, 102
Nerauchi, Teodocio, 61
Nettlau, Max, 60, 151
neutrality laws, 130, 132, 135–36, 144, 150, 167, 186
Newerf, (socialist, support of PLM), 99
Newllano colony, 41
New Orleans, Louisiana, 11, 28–29, 66
New Unionist, 43, 51, 219
New York City, 23, 56–58, 63, 101, 109, 141–42, 147, 163, 213
Nice, France, 226
Nichibei Shimbun (*Japanese American News*), 103
Nieto, A., 66, 74, 76
Noel, Frances Nacke, 38
Noels, P. D., 131
Norman, Lucía, 156
Norwood, E., 173
La Nueva Solidaridad, 196–97, 203, 214
Nuevo León, Mexico, 166
Nutti, Silvio, 171

Oaxaca, Mexico, 92
Obata, K., 69

Obregón Salido, Álvaro, 215, 219
Obreros Libres, 45, 214
O'Brien, T. J., 114
Odd Fellow's Cemetery, 170
Ogaz, Perfecto, 70
Ojeda, Armando M., 140, 170–71, 176–78
Olivares, Juan, 110
Ontario, California, 20
Open Forum, 214, 218, 223
Orizaba, Veracruz, Mexico, 59, 60
Ortega, Anastacia, 181
Ortega, Margarita, 141, 143
Osborne, J. B., 111
Otis, Harrison Gray, 21, 22, 75, 121
Owen, William C., 60–61, 154; anarchism, 10, 44, 152; Bakunin Institute, 203, 173; Christmas riot, 170–72; Emma Goldman, 81; escape through Canada, 186–88; plaza, 46; PLM, 141, 151–52; *Regeneración*, 55, 162–63; West Coast trip, 172–73
Oxnard, California, 14, 27, 30, 66–80, 90, 101, 106–8, 119
Oxnard, Henry, 67

Pachuca, Mexico, 196
Pacific Electric Railway Company, 199
Palacios, Rafael Romero, 162
Paladini, Aristide, 147
Palma, Raul, 188
Palomares, Fernando, 41, 48, 110–11, 114, 165
Panama Canal, 160–61, 197
Papai, 138
Parker, Carlton, 43, 165
Parsons, Albert, 47
Parsons, Lucy Eldine Gonzalez, 47, 173
Partido Liberal Mexicano (PLM), 1–7, 9, 39, 59, 90–91, 169–70, 173, 196, 204, 212–13, 215; anti-Chinese plank, 95–98; Baja raids, 127–46, 153–56; foundation of, 92–95; in-fighting, 162–64, 176–83; international controversy, 146–53; IWW, 41, 86, 114–15, 176–83, 195, 201; newspapers (see also *Regeneración*), 51–52, 55, 161; organizing by, 44, 48, 85–86, 102, 104, 110, 114–15, 158–59, 188, 219, 225; Rangel-Cline, 166–70; repression of, 98–100, 172, 185–86, 188–89,

Index

195, 206; revolution, 14, 60; United Laborers, 117–20, 122, 126
Pasadena, California, 111
Paterson, New Jersey, 44, 54, 58, 90, 119, 134, 147, 155, 200
Pelly, Bernard, 92
People's Paper, 51, 60, 72–73, 75, 77, 79, 91, 92, 102–3, 118, 135–36
People's Party, 37
Perales, Pedro, 168
Perrone, Filippo, 147
Peru, 149, 201
Pesotta, Rose, 224
Pesqueira, Jesús R., 144
Petit, Michel, 150
Pettibone, George, 98–100
Phelps Dodge Corporation, 19, 109
Philadelphia, Pennsylvania, 23, 53, 166
Philippines, 160
Phoenix, Arizona, 42, 48, 56, 102, 104, 110–11, 115, 133, 164, 167, 177–81, 213
Pico House, 32
Pima, 180
Plan of San Diego, 179, 181
Pluma Roja, 51–52, 162–63, 170
Polish, 24, 62, 93, 140
Pomona, California, 198
Portsmouth, West Virginia, 149
Portugal, 148
Portuguese, 27, 61–62, 227
Pouget, Émile, 8
Pouren, Jan Janoff, 101
Programa y Manifesta, 94–96
Proletarian, 103
Il Proletario, 166
Propaganda League of Mexicans, 176
La Protesta, 62
Pryce, Caryl Ap Rhys, 140–42
Public Ownership Party, 37, 85
Puebla, Mexico, 60
Puerto Ricans, 24, 165–66
Pyburn (American anarchist, met with Kōtoku), 103
Pujol, J., 196

Rahim, Hussein, 187–88
railroads, 17, 21, 26, 28, 30, 48, 74, 86, 114, 120, 145, 180, 204

Ramirez, Juan, 120–23
Ramirez, Manuel, 70
Ramos, Basilio, 179
Rangel, Jesús María, 164, 167–70, 178, 180
Ray, Arizona, 179, 181
Rebelde, 43, 46, 51, 53, 56, 176–78, 182, 191–95
Redding, California, 57, 113
Redlands, California, 42, 111, 190–91, 198
Redondo, California, 120
Reitman, Ben L., 104, 148, 154
Revolución, 51
Reyes, Bernardo, 102, 148
Rialto, California, 111
Rico, Louis, 188–89
Riddle, Claude, 83
Rincón, Juan, 162, 167
Ríos, Juan José, 225
Rising Youth, 221
Rivera, Librado: Arizona rebellion, 180–82; arrest, 98, 144, 181; incarcerated, 130, 132, 161–62, 172, 202–3; Mexico, 219; St. Louis, 93; trial, 155, 186, 189; United Laborers, 118
Riverside, California, 191, 198
Rizzo, Sam, 147
Road to Freedom, 62–63, 168, 182, 214, 217, 219–20
Roberts, Glen, 194
Robinson, Dudley, 136, 138, 155
Rocker, Rudolf, 60, 210, 220, 226
Rocker Publications Committee, 227
Rogat, Aaron, 216, 219
Rogers, A. G., 135
Roman Forum, 51
Roney, Frank, 168
Roosevelt, Franklin Delano, 225
Roosevelt Dam, 180–81
Rosario, Argentina, 58
Rose, Morris, 157, 170, 174–76
Rosen, James, 61
Rossi, Giovanni, 149
Rossoni, Edmondo, 166
Roy, Manabendra Nath, 201
Rubio, Pascual Ortiz, 225
Rudowitz, Christian Ansoff, 101
Russian Revolution, 5, 8, 128, 184, 209–10, 215, 219

Index

Russians: community, 32, 157, 175, 213, 220; organizing, 3, 5, 39–40, 60, 111, 115, 122, 140, 197–98, 217, 222–24; newspapers, 51, 56, 62–63, 100–101; and Japanese, 91
Russo-Japanese War, 91, 103

Sacaton, Arizona, 181
Sacco, Nicola, 200, 217–19, 222
Sacramento, California, 24, 27, 29, 92, 113, 164, 173, 190, 194–95, 197, 204
Sagitario, 219
Salinas, California, 27
Salt Lake City, Utah, 49, 212
San Antonio, Texas, 57, 93, 168, 196
San Bernardino, California, 17, 111, 120, 190
Sanchez, Juan, 170
San Diego, California, 49, 87, 125, 146; Baja raids, 141, 145; free speech fight, 41, 58, 127, 154–55, 171; IWW, 41–43, 111, 114–15, 133, 168; newspapers, 51, 56
San Dimas, California, 198
Sandino, Augusto César, 201
Sandoval, Francisco Ruíz, 129
San Fernando, California, 17
San Francisco, California, 18, 49, 50, 138, 145, 197, 206; District Defense Committee, 202; earthquake, 11; Japanese migration, 27; Labor Council, 108, 116; mayor, 74; newspapers, 35, 50, 56, 57, 58, 90, 186; organizing, 53, 102, 112, 172–73, 190, 198, 219; repression, 194–95
San Francisco earthquake (1906), 11, 27
San Francisco Labor Council, 108, 116
Sanftleben, Alfred, 44, 58, 59, 60, 62, 97, 99, 135, 209, 225–26
San Gabriel, California, 84, 120, 167, 197
San Joaquin Valley, 20
San Jose Labor Council, 108
San Juan del Rio, Mexico, 225
San Luis Obispo, California, 1
San Pedro, California, 43, 111, 120, 197, 204–5
San Quentin State Prison, 202, 204
Santa Ana, California, 111
Santa Ana Canyon, 205
Santa Fe Railroad, 17

Santa Maria, California, 102
Santa Monica, California, 22, 111, 199
Sarabia, Juan, 93–95, 97, 144
Sarabia, Manuel, 48, 93, 97, 110, 131–32
Sarabia, Tomás, 48, 132
Sastre, Manuel, 196–97, 199
Sawtelle, California, 111
Scandinavians, 62, 75, 157, 175
Seattle, Washington, 49, 92, 172–73, 226
Seattle Herald, 56
Seattle Star, 56
Seaward, Tom, 122
Sebastian, Charles, 171
Second Boer War, 140
second-class mail permit, 54, 94, 186, 194
Sedition Act (1918), 184, 186
Seidel, Emil, 158
Selective Service Act (1917), 199
Serbians, 220
Sernaker, Bernard, 147
Severance, Caroline M., 100
Shakai Kakumeito (Social Revolutionary Party), 103
Shasta County, California, 1, 192, 194
Shea, Hattie, 131
Sheridan, Walter, 56
Sikhs, 6, 24, 165
Silva, Prisciliano, 129–31, 137–38
Simpson Auditorium, 44, 46
Sinclair, Upton, 223
Sioris, P., 122
Slovenians, 26
Smith, J. C., 144
Socialism, 3–5, 39, 73–74, 87, 89, 91, 97, 102, 152, 222
Socialist Labor Party, 4, 39, 83, 100–101
Socialist Party, 37, 46; elections, 15, 66, 120, 158; ethnic locals, 46, 85, 100–104; Japanese exclusion, 73, 88; IWW, 83; PLM, 99–100; outlook, 3, 4, 38–39, 74, 86–87; organizing, 5, 14, 39–40, 80, 84, 121, 175, 223–34; structure, 6
Socialist Proletariat Club, 104
Socialist Women, 91
Social Science Club, 81, 89, 102
Sociedad Defensores de la Integridad Nacional (Society for the Defense of National Integrity), 146

Index

Soil, Lieu Sun, 163
soldaderas, 141
Solidaridad, 214
Solidarity (newspaper), 141, 166
Sonora, Mexico, 19, 32, 120,
Sorel, Georges, 8
Sosnovsky, Anna, 217–18
South Asians, 24, 61, 65, 82, 92, 113, 138, 187, 191, 202
Southern Pacific Railroad, 19, 21–22, 28, 30, 48
South Gate, California, 33
southwest United States, 19, 21, 28, 62, 84, 92, 95, 109–10, 115, 133–34, 164, 176, 178
Spain, 11, 17, 57, 62, 197, 203, 215
Spanish-American War, 128, 138, 140, 160
Spanish Civil War, 14, 128, 211
Spanish (immigrants), 17, 24, 93, 141, 147, 165, 192, 197, 203
Spayde, Fred C., 199
Speed, George, 112–13
Spencer, Herbert, 152
Spivak, Joseph, 44, 213–14, 216–17, 220
Spivak, Manya, 214
Spokane, Washington, 49, 110, 114, 127
Sprading, Charles, 104, 206, 217–18
Spreckels, Claus, 19
Spreckels, John, 145
Spreckels, Rudolph, 206
Steelink, Nicolaas, 202–3
Steimer, Mollie, 214
Stelton Modern School Group, 227
St. John, Vincent, 196
St. Louis, Missouri, 57, 93–94, 137
Stockton, California, 201
Sued Kalifornische Post, 60
Suito (JMLA member), 70
Sundstedt, May, 205
Superior, Arizona, 57, 181
Swedes, 24, 50, 88, 103
Sydney, Australia, 58
syndicalism, 3–5, 7, 41, 117–18, 215. *See also* Industrial Workers of the World (IWW)
Syrians, 98, 165

Tacoma, Washington, 172–73, 187
Taft, William Howard, 102, 105

Takahashi, T., 103
Tamaulipas, Mexico, 134, 166, 180, 219
Tampa, Florida, 57, 109, 161
Tampico, Mexico, 49, 57, 192–94, 196–97, 201, 219
Tapia de la Cruz, Primo, 21, 215
Tárrida del Marmol, Fernando, 151
Tellez, Alberto, 162
Les Temps Nouveaux, 150–51
Teodori, Ernesto, 147, 155
Texas Rangers, 167
Thompson, Edward, 109, 122, 125
Thousand Days' War (Panama), 140
¡Tierra!, 161
Tierra y Libertad, 9, 96
Tiger, Wanda, 218
Tillman, Benjamin, 87
Tokyo, Japan, 163
Tolstoy, Leo, 8, 104
Toluca, Mexico, 57
Tombstone, Arizona, 136, 186
Toronto, Canada, 94
Torreón, Mexico, 196
Tourmoux, A. L., 51
Trade Union Unity League (TUUL), 221–22
Trading with the Enemy Act (1917), 189
tramps (bums, hobos), 1, 29, 48, 60, 113, 116, 174
Trautman, William, 83, 225
Travaglio, Eugene, 187
Treaty of Versailles, 201
Treviño, Ricardo, 196
Tribuna Roja, 57
Trona, California, 193
Trowbridge, Elizabeth Darling, 38, 130–31
Tulare County, California, 27, 119
Turner, Ethyl Duffy, 38, 48, 130–32, 134–36
Turner, John Kenneth, 38, 90, 131–32
Turner Hall, 39, 199
Tveitmoe, Olaf A., 108, 116

unemployed army, 47, 157, 169–70, 173–76, 183
Unemployed Worker, 174
Unión de Fogoneros, 147
Unión Federal Mexicana (UFM), 14, 73–77, 79, 85

Unión Fraternal Mexicana, 84
Union Industrial, 110, 164
Union Labor Party, 158
Union Labor Political Club, 40
L'Union Nouvelle, 51
United Laborers, 14, 80, 106–9, 114–26
United Mine Workers (UMWA), 13, 125
United States Congress, 22, 27, 67, 184, 193
United States Postal Service, 54–55, 184, 186
unskilled workers, 14, 18, 29, 41, 73, 77, 80, 105, 108–9, 114, 116–17, 124–25, 175
Upland, California, 111, 198
Urrea, Teresa (La Santa de Cabora), 74
Utah Sugar Company, 71

Valades, José, 215
Valencia, Spain, 57
Vanzetti, Bartolomeo, 200, 217–19, 222
Vasquez, Leonardo, 168
Vasquez, Louis, 70–71
Velarde, Amelio, 119,
Velarde, Fernando, 41, 42, 104, 110, 111, 132, 140, 164, 177–79, 191, 191, 225
Velarde, Guillermo, 225
Velasco, P. Mares, 214
Velikij Okean (*Pacific Ocean*), 51
Ventura, California, 67, 71
Ventura Free Press, 69
Veracruz, Mexico, 59, 130, 173, 178
Vernon, California, 23, 84
Vidal, Jaime, 58, 147–48, 163
Villa, Francisco, 97
Villarreal, Antonio, 93–94, 97–98, 118–19, 130, 137, 152, 186
Vinette, Arthur, 37
Viramontes, Guadalupe, 119
Vitagliano, A. R., 159
Volcano Springs, California, 49, 76

Waldron, L. Milton, 102
Walker Hall, 198
Walton, Thomas "Ace", 222
Walt Whitman School, 212–13
Watts, California, 33
Weber, Max, 9, 11
Weinberger, Harry, 203
Weinstein, Harry, 121, 154
Welsh, 26, 140

Western Agricultural Contracting Company (WACC), 68–72, 78
Western Beet Sugar Company, 19
Western Comrade, 41, 51
Weyerhaeuser, 19
Wheatland, California, 15, 24, 43, 49, 164–66, 169, 171, 183, 190–91, 197
Wheeler, Fred, 37, 66–69, 74, 101, 158, 175
Whitley, George Washington, 121
Whitney, Charlotte Anita, 56
Widen (Swedish anarchist), 103
Wilkins, Bertha, 83
Williams, George, 103
Williams, Stanley, 138–39
Wilson, B. R., 200
Wilson, Jim, 136
Wilson, Woodrow, 193
Wirth, Rudolph, 141, 168
Wittling, Ben, 182
wobblies, *See* Industrial Workers of the World
Woman of the Twentieth Century, 92
women, 10, 216; anarchism, 45, 162, 173, 214; IWW, 41, 141; organizing, 74–75, 155–56, 165, 169, 199, 217, 222; Mexican Revolution, 141; socialism, 38, 91–92, 103; voting rights, 40; workers, 3, 198
Women's Trade Union League, 38
Wood, Jack, 61
Wood, T. L., 144
Woodbey, George Washington, 46, 47, 81, 87–88, 102, 154
Wooden Shoe, 51
Workers International Defense League, 188
Workmen's Circle 39, 213
Works Progress Administration (WPA), 224
World War I, 32, 40, 62, 140, 159, 176, 182, 201, 211, 226; American entry, 14–15, 113, 157, 190; draft, 199; Great Migration 28–29; repression, 43, 45, 54, 63, 95, 158, 185, 189, 206, 209
World War II, 32, 65
Wright, H. W., 154

Yamaguchi, Y., 69, 79
Yanovsky, Saul, 220

Index

Yaqui, 110, 179–80, 219
Ybor City, Florida, 54, 57, 61
Yiddish, 62, 101, 141, 211, 213, 219–20
Yoell, A. E., 108
Yolo County, California, 173
Yoshinari, K., 69
Young Men's Ferrer Club (Paterson), 200

Yucatán Peninsula, 134, 159
Yuma, Arizona, 48, 49, 76, 102

Zacatecas, Mexico, 225
Zionism, 221–22
Zurich, Switzerland, 226

David M. Struthers is an adjunct assistant professor
at the Copenhagen Business School.

THE WORKING CLASS IN AMERICAN HISTORY

Worker City, Company Town: Iron and Cotton-Worker Protest in Troy and Cohoes, New York, 1855–84 *Daniel J. Walkowitz*

Life, Work, and Rebellion in the Coal Fields: The Southern West Virginia Miners, 1880–1922 *David Alan Corbin*

Women and American Socialism, 1870–1920 *Mari Jo Buhle*

Lives of Their Own: Blacks, Italians, and Poles in Pittsburgh, 1900–1960 *John Bodnar, Roger Simon, and Michael P. Weber*

Working-Class America: Essays on Labor, Community, and American Society *Edited by Michael H. Frisch and Daniel J. Walkowitz*

Eugene V. Debs: Citizen and Socialist *Nick Salvatore*

American Labor and Immigration History, 1877–1920s: Recent European Research *Edited by Dirk Hoerder*

Workingmen's Democracy: The Knights of Labor and American Politics *Leon Fink*

The Electrical Workers: A History of Labor at General Electric and Westinghouse, 1923–60 *Ronald W. Schatz*

The Mechanics of Baltimore: Workers and Politics in the Age of Revolution, 1763–1812 *Charles G. Steffen*

The Practice of Solidarity: American Hat Finishers in the Nineteenth Century *David Bensman*

The Labor History Reader *Edited by Daniel J. Leab*

Solidarity and Fragmentation: Working People and Class Consciousness in Detroit, 1875–1900 *Richard Oestreicher*

Counter Cultures: Saleswomen, Managers, and Customers in American Department Stores, 1890–1940 *Susan Porter Benson*

The New England Working Class and the New Labor History *Edited by Herbert G. Gutman and Donald H. Bell*

Labor Leaders in America *Edited by Melvyn Dubofsky and Warren Van Tine*

Barons of Labor: The San Francisco Building Trades and Union Power in the Progressive Era *Michael Kazin*

Gender at Work: The Dynamics of Job Segregation by Sex during World War II *Ruth Milkman*

Once a Cigar Maker: Men, Women, and Work Culture in American Cigar Factories, 1900–1919 *Patricia A. Cooper*

A Generation of Boomers: The Pattern of Railroad Labor Conflict in Nineteenth-Century America *Shelton Stromquist*

Work and Community in the Jungle: Chicago's Packinghouse Workers, 1894–1922 *James R. Barrett*

Workers, Managers, and Welfare Capitalism: The Shoeworkers and Tanners of Endicott Johnson, 1890–1950 *Gerald Zahavi*

Men, Women, and Work: Class, Gender, and Protest in the New England Shoe Industry, 1780–1910 *Mary Blewett*

Workers on the Waterfront: Seamen, Longshoremen, and Unionism in the 1930s *Bruce Nelson*

German Workers in Chicago: A Documentary History of Working-Class Culture from 1850 to World War I   *Edited by Hartmut Keil and John B. Jentz*

On the Line: Essays in the History of Auto Work   *Edited by Nelson Lichtenstein and Stephen Meyer III*

Labor's Flaming Youth: Telephone Operators and Worker Militancy, 1878–1923   *Stephen H. Norwood*

Another Civil War: Labor, Capital, and the State in the Anthracite Regions of Pennsylvania, 1840–68   *Grace Palladino*

Coal, Class, and Color: Blacks in Southern West Virginia, 1915–32   *Joe William Trotter Jr.*

For Democracy, Workers, and God: Labor Song-Poems and Labor Protest, 1865–95   *Clark D. Halker*

Dishing It Out: Waitresses and Their Unions in the Twentieth Century   *Dorothy Sue Cobble*

The Spirit of 1848: German Immigrants, Labor Conflict, and the Coming of the Civil War   *Bruce Levine*

Working Women of Collar City: Gender, Class, and Community in Troy, New York, 1864–86   *Carole Turbin*

Southern Labor and Black Civil Rights: Organizing Memphis Workers   *Michael K. Honey*

Radicals of the Worst Sort: Laboring Women in Lawrence, Massachusetts, 1860–1912   *Ardis Cameron*

Producers, Proletarians, and Politicians: Workers and Party Politics in Evansville and New Albany, Indiana, 1850–87   *Lawrence M. Lipin*

The New Left and Labor in the 1960s   *Peter B. Levy*

The Making of Western Labor Radicalism: Denver's Organized Workers, 1878–1905   *David Brundage*

In Search of the Working Class: Essays in American Labor History and Political Culture   *Leon Fink*

Lawyers against Labor: From Individual Rights to Corporate Liberalism   *Daniel R. Ernst*

"We Are All Leaders": The Alternative Unionism of the Early 1930s   *Edited by Staughton Lynd*

The Female Economy: The Millinery and Dressmaking Trades, 1860–1930   *Wendy Gamber*

"Negro and White, Unite and Fight!": A Social History of Industrial Unionism in Meatpacking, 1930–90   *Roger Horowitz*

Power at Odds: The 1922 National Railroad Shopmen's Strike   *Colin J. Davis*

The Common Ground of Womanhood: Class, Gender, and Working Girls' Clubs, 1884–1928   *Priscilla Murolo*

Marching Together: Women of the Brotherhood of Sleeping Car Porters   *Melinda Chateauvert*

Down on the Killing Floor: Black and White Workers in Chicago's Packinghouses, 1904–54   *Rick Halpern*

Labor and Urban Politics: Class Conflict and the Origins of Modern Liberalism in Chicago, 1864–97   *Richard Schneirov .*

All That Glitters: Class, Conflict, and Community in Cripple Creek   *Elizabeth Jameson*

Waterfront Workers: New Perspectives on Race and Class   *Edited by Calvin Winslow*

Labor Histories: Class, Politics, and the Working-Class Experience   *Edited by Eric Arnesen, Julie Greene, and Bruce Laurie*

The Pullman Strike and the Crisis of the 1890s: Essays on Labor and Politics
Edited by Richard Schneirov, Shelton Stromquist, and Nick Salvatore

AlabamaNorth: African-American Migrants, Community, and Working-Class Activism
in Cleveland, 1914–45 *Kimberley L. Phillips*

Imagining Internationalism in American and British Labor, 1939–49 *Victor Silverman*

William Z. Foster and the Tragedy of American Radicalism *James R. Barrett*

Colliers across the Sea: A Comparative Study of Class Formation in Scotland and the
American Midwest, 1830–1924 *John H. M. Laslett*

"Rights, Not Roses": Unions and the Rise of Working-Class Feminism, 1945–80
Dennis A. Deslippe

Testing the New Deal: The General Textile Strike of 1934 in the American South *Janet Irons*

Hard Work: The Making of Labor History *Melvyn Dubofsky*

Southern Workers and the Search for Community: Spartanburg County, South Carolina
G. C. Waldrep III

We Shall Be All: A History of the Industrial Workers of the World (abridged edition)
Melvyn Dubofsky, ed. Joseph A. McCartin

Race, Class, and Power in the Alabama Coalfields, 1908–21 *Brian Kelly*

Duquesne and the Rise of Steel Unionism *James D. Rose*

Anaconda: Labor, Community, and Culture in Montana's Smelter City *Laurie Mercier*

Bridgeport's Socialist New Deal, 1915–36 *Cecelia Bucki*

Indispensable Outcasts: Hobo Workers and Community in the American Midwest,
1880–1930 *Frank Tobias Higbie*

After the Strike: A Century of Labor Struggle at Pullman *Susan Eleanor Hirsch*

Corruption and Reform in the Teamsters Union *David Witwer*

Waterfront Revolts: New York and London Dockworkers, 1946–61 *Colin J. Davis*

Black Workers' Struggle for Equality in Birmingham *Horace Huntley and David Montgomery*

The Tribe of Black Ulysses: African American Men in the Industrial South *William P. Jones*

City of Clerks: Office and Sales Workers in Philadelphia, 1870–1920 *Jerome P. Bjelopera*

Reinventing "The People": The Progressive Movement, the Class Problem, and the Origins
of Modern Liberalism *Shelton Stromquist*

Radical Unionism in the Midwest, 1900–1950 *Rosemary Feurer*

Gendering Labor History *Alice Kessler-Harris*

James P. Cannon and the Origins of the American Revolutionary Left, 1890–1928
Bryan D. Palmer

Glass Towns: Industry, Labor, and Political Economy in Appalachia, 1890–1930s
Ken Fones-Wolf

Workers and the Wild: Conservation, Consumerism, and Labor in Oregon, 1910–30
Lawrence M. Lipin

Wobblies on the Waterfront: Interracial Unionism in Progressive-Era Philadelphia *Peter Cole*

Red Chicago: American Communism at Its Grassroots, 1928–35 *Randi Storch*

Labor's Cold War: Local Politics in a Global Context *Edited by Shelton Stromquist*

Bessie Abramowitz Hillman and the Making of the Amalgamated Clothing Workers
of America *Karen Pastorello*

The Great Strikes of 1877 *Edited by David O. Stowell*

Union-Free America: Workers and Antiunion Culture *Lawrence Richards*

Race against Liberalism: Black Workers and the UAW in Detroit   *David M. Lewis-Colman*
Teachers and Reform: Chicago Public Education, 1929–70   *John F. Lyons*
Upheaval in the Quiet Zone: 1199/SEIU and the Politics of Healthcare Unionism
   Leon Fink and Brian Greenberg
Shadow of the Racketeer: Scandal in Organized Labor   *David Witwer*
Sweet Tyranny: Migrant Labor, Industrial Agriculture, and Imperial Politics   *Kathleen Mapes*
Staley: The Fight for a New American Labor Movement   *Steven K. Ashby and C. J. Hawking*
On the Ground: Labor Struggles in the American Airline Industry   *Liesl Miller Orenic*
NAFTA and Labor in North America   *Norman Caulfield*
Making Capitalism Safe: Work Safety and Health Regulation in America, 1880–1940
   Donald W. Rogers
Good, Reliable, White Men: Railroad Brotherhoods, 1877–1917   *Paul Michel Taillon*
Spirit of Rebellion: Labor and Religion in the New Cotton South   *Jarod Roll*
The Labor Question in America: Economic Democracy in the Gilded Age
   Rosanne Currarino
Banded Together: Economic Democratization in the Brass Valley   *Jeremy Brecher*
The Gospel of the Working Class: Labor's Southern Prophets in New Deal America
   Erik Gellman and Jarod Roll
Guest Workers and Resistance to U.S. Corporate Despotism   *Immanuel Ness*
Gleanings of Freedom: Free and Slave Labor along the Mason-Dixon Line, 1790–1860
   Max Grivno
Chicago in the Age of Capital: Class, Politics, and Democracy during the Civil War
   and Reconstruction   *John B. Jentz and Richard Schneirov*
Child Care in Black and White: Working Parents and the History of Orphanages
   Jessie B. Ramey
The Haymarket Conspiracy: Transatlantic Anarchist Networks   *Timothy Messer-Kruse*
Detroit's Cold War: The Origins of Postwar Conservatism   *Colleen Doody*
A Renegade Union: Interracial Organizing and Labor Radicalism   *Lisa Phillips*
Palomino: Clinton Jencks and Mexican-American Unionism in the American Southwest
   James J. Lorence
Latin American Migrations to the U.S. Heartland: Changing Cultural Landscapes in
   Middle America   *Edited by Linda Allegro and Andrew Grant Wood*
Man of Fire: Selected Writings   *Ernesto Galarza, ed. Armando Ibarra and Rodolfo D. Torres*
A Contest of Ideas: Capital, Politics, and Labor   *Nelson Lichtenstein*
Making the World Safe for Workers: Labor, the Left, and Wilsonian Internationalism
   Elizabeth McKillen
The Rise of the Chicago Police Department: Class and Conflict, 1850–1894   *Sam Mitrani*
Workers in Hard Times: A Long View of Economic Crises   *Edited by Leon Fink, Joseph A.*
   McCartin, and Joan Sangster
Redeeming Time: Protestantism and Chicago's Eight-Hour Movement, 1866–1912
   William A. Mirola
Struggle for the Soul of the Postwar South: White Evangelical Protestants and
   Operation Dixie   *Elizabeth Fones-Wolf and Ken Fones-Wolf*
Free Labor: The Civil War and the Making of an American Working Class   *Mark A. Lause*
Death and Dying in the Working Class, 1865–1920   *Michael K. Rosenow*

Immigrants against the State: Yiddish and Italian Anarchism in America *Kenyon Zimmer*

Fighting for Total Person Unionism: Harold Gibbons, Ernest Calloway, and Working-Class Citizenship *Robert Bussel*

Smokestacks in the Hills: Rural-Industrial Workers in West Virginia *Louis Martin*

Disaster Citizenship: Survivors, Solidarity, and Power in the Progressive Era *Jacob A. C. Remes*

The Pew and the Picket Line: Christianity and the American Working Class *Edited by Christopher D. Cantwell, Heath W. Carter, and Janine Giordano Drake*

Conservative Counterrevolution: Challenging Liberalism in 1950s Milwaukee *Tula A. Connell*

Manhood on the Line: Working-Class Masculinities in the American Heartland *Steve Meyer*

On Gender, Labor, and Inequality *Ruth Milkman*

The Making of Working-Class Religion *Matthew Pehl*

Civic Labors: Scholar Activism and Working-Class Studies *Edited by Dennis Deslippe, Eric Fure-Slocum, and John W. McKerley*

Victor Arnautoff and the Politics of Art *Robert W. Cherny*

Against Labor: How U.S. Employers Organized to Defeat Union Activism *Edited by Rosemary Feurer and Chad Pearson*

Teacher Strike! Public Education and the Making of a New American Political Order *Jon Shelton*

Hillbilly Hellraisers: Federal Power and Populist Defiance in the Ozarks *J. Blake Perkins*

Sewing the Fabric of Statehood: Garment Unions, American Labor, and the Establishment of the State of Israel *Adam Howard*

Labor and Justice across the America *Edited by Leon Fink and Juan Manuel Palacio*

Frontiers of Labor: Comparative Histories of the United States and Australia *Edited by Greg Patmore and Shelton Stromquist*

Women Have Always Worked: A Concise History, Second Edition *Alice Kessler-Harris*

Remembering Lattimer: Labor, Migration, and Race in Pennsylvania Anthracite Country *Paul A. Shackel*

Disruption in Detroit: Autoworkers and the Elusive Postwar Boom *Daniel J. Clark*

To Live Here, You Have to Fight: How Women Led Appalachian Movements for Social Justice *Jessica Wilkerson*

Dockworker Power: Race and Activism in Durban and the San Francisco Bay Area *Peter Cole*

Labor's Mind: A History of Working-Class Intellectual Life *Tobias Higbie*

The World in a City: Multiethnic Radicalism in Early Twentieth-Century Los Angeles *David M. Struthers*

The University of Illinois Press
is a founding member of the
Association of University Presses.

———————————

Composed in 10.75/13 Arno Pro
with Folio display
by Jim Proefrock
at the University of Illinois Press

University of Illinois Press
1325 South Oak Street
Champaign, IL 61820-6903
www.press.uillinois.edu